Australian Wine Vintages
Thirty Fourth Edition
2017

Robert Geddes MW

First Edition	November 1979
Second Edition	November 1981
Third Edition	September 1983
Fourth Edition	August 1985
Revised	December 1986
Fifth Edition	September 1987
Sixth Edition	August 1988
Seventh Edition	August 1989
Eighth Edition	August 1990
Ninth Edition	August 1991
Tenth Edition	August 1992
Eleventh Edition	August 1993
Twelfth Edition	August 1994
Thirteenth Edition	August 1995
Fourteenth Edition	August 1996
Fifteenth Edition	August 1997
Sixteenth Edition	August 1998
Seventeenth Edition	August 1999
Eighteenth Edition	August 2000
Nineteenth Edition	August 2001
Twentieth Edition	August 2002
Twenty First Edition	August 2003
Twenty Second Edition	August 2004
Twenty Third Edition	August 2005
Twenty Fourth Edition	August 2006
Twenty Fifth Edition	August 2007
Twenty Sixth Edition	August 2008
Twenty Seventh Edition	August 2009
Twenty Eight Edition	August 2010
Twenty Ninth Edition	August 2011
Thirtieth Edition	August 2012
Thirty First Edition	August 2013
Thirty Second Edition	August 2014
Thirty Third Edition	August 2015
Thirty Fourth Edtion	November 2016

Copyright © Robert Geddes 2016

This book is copyright.
Apart from any fair dealings for the purpose of private study, research, criticism or review, as permitted under the copyright act, no part may be reproduced by any process without written permission from the publisher.

ISBN 978-0-9924936-4-6
Produced by Everbest Printing Co Ltd
Typeset by Kirby Jones
Published by Geddes A Drink Publications Pty Ltd
Telephone (61 2) 9966 0631

THIS YEAR

Each year, Australian Wine Vintages sets out to showcase the very best of Australian wines. Inevitably there will be winners and losers in this process but we recognise that there are many wines outside the top 10 per cent that are worthy of attention, particularly emerging winemakers whose products are improving with each year. Put simply, Australia has an abundance of good winemakers.

In 2017 we have sought to address this issue with regular update of the AWV app, free for every purchaser of our book. With double the number of tasting notes and commentary on more wineries, the app will enable you to tap into a wider range of wines.

Australian Wine Vintages includes:
- Tasting notes on 5,000 + wines
- 361 wineries, including 73 new wineries since last year
- 1200 wines
- 255 new individual wines
- Over 200 Gold Star wines
- A list of Certified Organic and/or Biodynamic wineries
- A "quick guide to varieties and regions" which sets out our advice on which varietals to look for in each region
- Guides on when to drink each wine
- Indicative retail prices
- Alcoholic strengths
- Tasting terms

Free monthly updates – subscribe to our newsletter
Our free monthly newsletter is informative, fun and provides readers with all the latest news on wine vintages and trends. Subscribing is easy. Simply visit our website www.robgeddesmw.com and enter your email address.

Cellar management program
A cellar management program for wines listed in the book is available from: WineBase for Windows: The cellar management software, WineBase includes the Gold Book data as standard. www.winebase.com.au

Have any feedback?
I welcome your feedback and ideas. If you've found a new winery, a great restaurant or a memorable place to stay that you'd like to share with other AWV readers, then please write to me at rob@thegoldbook.com.au

Rob Geddes MW

Australian Wine Vintages
is now an app!

17,000+ Tasting notes

The best of Australian wine at your finger tips.

Add wines to your virtual cellar then hunt them down.

Know when to drink a wine and what to pair it with.

Available at www.robgeddesmw.com

INTRODUCTION TO THE 34th EDITION

Writing tasting notes for a book like this is also a chance to reflect on the winemaking process from vineyard to final consumer before judgement. Certainly the most desirable wines are made in small quantities, however the taste of wine is not the only motivation for its final price. You are drinking an experience, not only flavours, but uniqueness; be it made from old vines, in small quantities or because the vineyard or maker is famous. However you sip it, your wine is more than just a glass of flavours. Judging blind will never evaluate that aspect of a wine.

We have evolved our own way of tasting for the book. It is time consuming; from the time it takes to enter data through to the final rating and drink by. I call on industry specialists for help and am very grateful to the winemakers and buyers across the spectrum for their time and advice. When Marilyn Monroe said, "You can't have too much of a good thing", I know she meant skilled tasters to keep company during the hours of tasting required to fill the book and app. The gold book uses a collegiate approach. Each judge scores each wine then the discussion starts. The fundamental test is to consider the wines length of flavour, balance of flavours and structure, over all flavour complexity and intensity.

Next is the style, the level of development, harmony, varietal tipcite and affordability. Varietal correctness is about ensuring no surprises, insurance if you like that the rating applies to a flavour profile that to a degree conforms to the affordability. High-end dining and inner city wine bars are much more accepting of varietal diversity, hence you will find wine notes that refer to very ripe wines as 'for lovers of full bodied reds' to the other extreme of more savoury and acidic as 'inner city wine bar' wines.

Affordability and price; here we use a lens of three variables, based on the judgement of its flavour for the price. Does it exceed our quality price expectation? Achieve quality price value? Or does it follow others at achieving quality for the price?

Australian wine appears to be in an exciting place. Leaving aside the slow erosion that drought and

www.robgeddesmw.com

climate change have on vineyards; the 2016 vintage seems to be highly and widely regarded as a quality year across the board. With the low exchange rate against our major trading partners and the free trade agreement with China a period of widespread growth appears likely. This growth should flow through to better prices for River Murray growers who have had over a decade of doing it tough.

There is much current discussion of the WET tax as a serious political football with politicians wanting to change and the older established wine industry with significant physical assets in a strong position to prevail. In private discussions, these owners largely dismiss owning brands as less important than owning the means of production. This view will have a damaging influence on regional communities and damage the hopes of the next generation of winemakers. The issues of fairness across the different ideas about asset ownership with a clear divide between those with physical or intellectual assets comes at a critical moment as it has become nearly impossible to establish a significant estate winery today without side backing.

This is important as mature wine businesses with consideration of scale and volume a major part of their marketing have little affinity or understanding of the virtual wine sectors most important customers. The virtual wineries are important in developing restaurant brands and the starting point for new entrants into the industry.

The positives are that the quality of wine has never been higher across the board with genuine regional styles appearing with more consistency and definition. Medium bodied wines, around 13.5% alcohol, are becoming more common which makes for better and easier food matching.

Our largest plantings have seen exciting evolution, shiraz and grenache with more freshness, red fruits, spice notes, food friendly balance and complexity.

I find cabernet is still in the doldrums with the most exciting wines often coming from unexpected places such as Tasmania. The gift that cabernet brings is length of black currant fruit length with leafy edges to the flavour, distinctive fine tannins creating the linear structure and a profile that is rarely full bodied and always even, fine and long across the tongue in world class wines. Between Margaret Rivers Cullen, Woodlands, Cape Mentelle and Vasse Felix we have serious challengers. Smith & Hooper offer one of the best mixes of affordability and varietal personality in Merlot. Cabernet franc is also moving along especially in Orange where there seems to be an excellent understanding of its ability to give width to cabernet where it needs it, in the middle palate. Ross Hill, Woodlands and Terre a Terre are right on the money.

Shiraz tannins are rounder, sweeter, full up front on the palate, more abundant and seem to shape the way many non Western Australians think about cabernet tannins.

In exciting ways and across many regions shiraz and grenache are losing weight as a new appraisal of the ideal flavour spectrum and tannin profile. The new wave grenache are brighter red fruited, subtle spice and more modest silky tannins – ideal for food.

Shiraz will always be the stomping ground of the big Barossa styles but even here; more fruit freshness, less American oak, less added acid and tannin and overall more balance as they continue to hold the full bodied red lover close to their hearts.

Shiraz cabernet or vice versa are an Australian speciality offering seamless length and style which we need more of at all price points to help consumers appreciate this unique asset.

Shiraz blends are coming into a new era. The Barossa Valley Estate 2014 GSM is one of many different regional styles with a refit making them more at home on the table. Cinsault which is relatively rare is revealing itself as a great partner with either shiraz or grenache in this role as well.

Mataro lead I think with the 2012 Hewitson Old Garden looming large as evidence of the change of thinking supported by D'Arenberg and Master of Wine Andrew Callaird.

Australian Wine Vintages 2017 – Introduction

Malbec has under gone a reappraisal. It is a love or hate variety, assertive but fickle across the spectrum. In the vineyard managers dislike its uneven cropping from year to year because it can easily dominate in blends. Increasingly, the floral red fruits with a sappy edge are looking attractive with Bleasdale showing inspired leadership and a powerful contrast to the meaty, earthy, thick textures of Argentinean wines.

Chardonnay is still in a Victorian fascination with lower alcohols, although, producers in Mornington who stuck to their guns are exciting. Especially notable is the level of oatmeal like characters from lees work in Mornington Peninsula chardonnay. Take in the Adelaide hills and Margaret River and the quality of Australian chardonnay is very high, with tops just as complex as anywhere else and better value.

Mornington, Yarra and Geelong are extending their confidence and excursions with pinot noir as well, where many wines can be found with the exceptional pinot silky and plush tannins wed to red fruit flavours. We also have many world class wineries with a deeper understanding of varieties such as pinot gris/grigio.

The rocking horse of riesling between dry being less than 5 grams residual and discernible sweetness is a fascinating evolution with the heartland dry styles of SA shining and Victoria showing some fascinating development. Worth a mention are Bests and Pressing Matters in Tasmania that are showing extraordinary complexity. Lower alcohol with sugar seems to work best in cooler regions where higher alcohol and residual sugar seems to work best for the heartland styles.

The fact that terroir in Australia is arguably less significant than long experience with a wide number of varieties plus our belief in climate as the arbiter of quality allows our wine companies a dichotomy not available in many other countries where we can be strong in both pinot noir and shiraz.

I have learnt to appreciate this lesson from writing for Chinese consumer wine publications as wine is also about ideas and perception and how ideas get submerged over time.

Australian Wine Vintages 2017 – Introduction

Our ideas about interregional blending and screw caps are in reality very big topics that we need to keep alive as discussion in the world of wine

The idea of interregional blending is often overlooked. Ultimately, all wines are blends, even if they are from estate vineyards they still have different picking dates, different tanks or selected post oak maturation. Australia has interesting and original solutions to fine wine outside the vertically integrated and French inspired model of estate grown, fermented, cellar bottled approach. The most significant is the South Australian model inspired by Penfolds and Hardys with their inter regional blending approach to offering the best varietal wine regardless of origin. This approach in the hands of winemakers like Torbreck creates sublime wines in a tradition that must be promoted globally.

The other is screw caps where Australia has some heavy lifting to do. We are the largest significant producer to invest heavily in this technology and we need to keep promoting the benefits amidst a snow storm of cork industry inspired PR. Comparative closure tastings of the same variety under both cork and screw cap is the only way forward to win over a generation of wine drinkers or else we run the risk of seeing the spin merchants of cork ruin a good technology.

The 34th edition of Australian Wine Vintages faces head winds unparalleled in the history of the book. The reduction in the number of physical booksellers is dramatically reducing the distribution base and the rise of online commentary is making producing a hard copy book more difficult. To that end we have lifted the quality by tasting more wines which meant publishing the book in time for Christmas. The 34th is the first not to be released in time for Father's day, and I apologise to that loyal cohort of readers who have given the book as Fathers Days gifts sometimes over two generations. There is always the app with its extensive travel and food advice.

ACKNOWLEDGEMENTS

The book is the result of a community of tasters drawn from across the industry including winemakers, wine buyers, consultants and sommeliers. This year, we have further enlarged the number of buyers and specialist winemakers involved.

I am extremely grateful to the following for their help during the preparation of the 2017 book: Lisa Johnston, Lisa Webber, Sharon Foulis, Amanda Yallop, Samantha Connew, Kate Day, Tamara Ellison, Charles Hargrave, Daniel Parrott, Ben Tolstoshev, Neil Hadley, Harshal Shah, Sandy McKenzie, Scott McWilliam, Philip Shaw, Nick Blair, Tony Cosgriff and Greg Fitzsimmons. Thanks also to Ann Prosser who created the data base and processes the book would not proceed without her good foundations. Thanks to Chelsea van Deventer who oversaw this edition as marketing communications trainee, gratitude for bringing so many new systems and ideas.

CONTENTS

New this year	3
Introduction	5
Acknowledgements	10
How to use this book	12
Top 100	16
Gold Star wines	19
Introducing the Sydney International Wine Competition	26
Top 100 Sydney International Wine Competition	27
Australia and New Zealand vintages	35
Tasting terms	497
A quick guide to varieties and regions	507
Wine zones and regions	511

HOW TO USE THIS BOOK

Wines are listed alphabetically by the producers 'short name'; that is, the name by which the wine is commonly known to the consumer. Wines are listed accompanied by reduced-scale versions of the current labels.

TASTING NOTE

Wines in the *Gold Book* are not 'one-hit wonders.' We look to find passionate high quality wine producers and follow them based on their continuing performance across different growing seasons.

Tasting note writing can deconstruct wine by taste into different flavour and texture elements, or as I try to do, appreciate the taste and structure of wine as a story with a front, middle and end and provide a summary that also takes past vintages into account. The reality is that wine writers deliberately ignore bad wines as there are so many good wines available. This technique of criticism by omission works to help everyone by advancing good wines and leaving reputation and image damaging lesser vintages out of the glare of publicity. Australian Wine Vintages is not in this position because to be accepted in the publication is a mark of quality. It is sensitive to the nuances of criticism and offers a three tier definition of quality:

- star rating
- points out of 100
- the tasting note.

A tasting note, more often than not, is a wine description but rather than castigating the producer for real or imagined failings, it will balance an accent on the positives and gently point out or down play the negatives leaving the star rating and the score out of a 100 to do the work of quality assessment.

Hence a note like this one can be read as descriptive:

2012 Padthaway Chardonnay $30.00 Cellar Door tasting in 2014.

Pineapple fruit and coconut ice oak deliver old fashioned value. Fresher on the palate, cool fresh cut pineapple acid detail, medium bodied, vibrant and generous middle palate with a clean finish.

And deconstructed to mean.

Coconut is a USA oak descriptor and implies low cost oak. The fact it is coconut in Chardonnay and not nutty Brule vanilla French oak is a key pointer.

Pineapple is another pointer as the flavour in the tropical or 'bottled sunshine' spectrum of 90's ripeness than more up to date chardonnays which exhibit fresh pear, nectarine, stone fruit and/ or white peach.

Generous middle palate with a clean finish … The wine is rich in the middle of the tongue but has no length of flavour or structure which is a key aspect in making wine enjoyable.

VINTAGE
Refers to the year the grapes were crushed and fermented.

100 POINT RANKING:
Each wine listed is ranked out of 100.

95–100 Classic, a great wine.
Possessing considerable flavour intensity, harmony and complexity of elements with a delicate body. Extraordinary in terms of balance and harmony of detailed flavour complexity showing finesse, depth and length of flavour in the mouth, silky fruit texture and structural or winemaking detail as well as being relatively long lived. Australian Wine Vintages view is that moderate alcohol; medium bodied, fresh wines with moderate to high acidity are the ideal. Food friendly and delicious.

90–94 Outstanding: a superior wine.
Outstanding fresh fruit intensity in an interesting style with winemaker details, generosity and/ or varietal or regional purity. Will show refinement possessing intensity, complexity and definition, however, may be very ripe and powerful. Some wines will be very richly fruity, high alcohol and intense and described as "for lovers of ripe, full bodied reds".

85–89 Very good.
Very good with typical varietal flavours and intensity or complex style. Pleasurable flavour, body and style with moderate to rich fruit freshness, structure and medium length.

Australian Wine Vintages 2017 – How to use this book

80–84 Good wine.
Good wine without fault offering simple short length flavours and low flavour strength. A pleasant drink with little regional or varietal detail and good value for money- often under $15.00 retail.

70–79 Drinkable wine.
Drinkable wine that may have minor flaws, lacks intensity, flavour, generally straight forward.

With the Australian Wine Show system moving to point out of 100 as well as Gold, Silver and Bronze I offer the following conversion for readers.

Wine shows
- $15.5 \times 4 + 22 = 84$ Bronze is 84–90
- $16.9 \times 4 + 22 = 89.6$ Silver is 90–96
- $18.5 \times 4 + 22 = 96$ Gold Note in AWV gold is 95 or above.

DRINK
This is really a best before date and by far the most useful entry in the book. The 'Best Year to Drink' recommendation is not an attempt to identify the extreme limit of the wine's longevity. It is intended to identify the particular time frame, in our opinion, that will lead you to derive the greatest pleasure from drinking the wine. The actual year will vary with your cellaring conditions and how the wine is sealed. There's a useful rule of thumb in considering wine development – that a wine improves for a third of its life, remains on a plateau for another third and spends the remaining third declining gracefully into eventual feebleness.

STAR RATING
The more stars a wine has received indicates how much better it is than other wines at the same price.

Fundamentally, stars are about quality, pleasure and value for money. The difference between a 3 star and a 5 star wine of the same price is that we don't think the 3 star has the gravitas that other wines have at the same price.

Equally, a high score with 4 stars shows that we think this wine is amongst the best in that quality/price ranking. It is important to note that we do not use stars to rank the winery. The continual increases in quality and detailed varietal and regional expression thanks to specialisation by wine producers means there are few

Australian Wine Vintages 2017 – How to use this book

genuine all-rounders any more although notable exceptions such as d'Arenberg, Penfolds, Yalumba, Taylors, Tahbilk and De Bortoli do exist.

We only include wines we find interesting and freely admit we do not capture every interesting quality wine. Our focus is narrower and attempts more precision than awarding the total production of a winery a star ranking and focuses on individual wines.

As a very broad and indeed over-simplified guide, something like this:

- ★ Not used
- ★★ Reliable, agreeable drinking
- ★★★ Captures your attention with its quality and price
- ★★★★ Outstanding quality, intensity and length of flavour
- ★★★★★ A great wine, very pleasurable drinking
- ★★★★★ Among the great wines of the world. A 'Gold Star' award highlight indicates they are worthy examples of, and fit to rank alongside the equivalent varieties from anywhere in the world. In their best years these wines exhibit greatness sufficient to include them as top wines on the world's stage.

DRINK
This is really a "best before" date and by far the most useful entry in the book. The 'Best Year to Drink' recommendation is not an attempt to identify the extreme limit of the wine's longevity. It is intended to identify the particular timeframe, in our opinion, that will lead you to derive the greatest pleasure from drinking the wine.

The actual year will vary with your cellaring conditions and how the wine is sealed. There's a useful rule of thumb in considering wine development: that a wine improves for a third of its life, remains on a plateau for another third, and spends the remaining third declining gracefully into eventual feebleness.

CURRENT VALUE
The 34th edition uses the winery advised retail price.

TOP 100 WINES

1.	2006	Arras Blanc de Blancs Chardonnay
2.	2014	Audrey Wilkinson Vineyard The Ridge Semillon
3.	2014	Baileys of Glenrowan Petite Sirah
4.	2014	Baileys of Glenrowan Varley Shiraz
5.	2014	Barossa Valley Estate Grenache Shiraz Mourvedre
6.	2014	Best's Wines Bin 0 Shiraz
7.	2013	Black Jack Wines Block 6 Shiraz
8.	2012	Black Jack Wines Shiraz
9.	2014	Bleasdale The Petrel Shiraz Cabernet Sauvignon Malbec
10.	2014	Bleasdale Generations Malbec
11.	2014	Bleasdale Frank Potts Cabernet Sauvignon Malbec Merlot
12.	2013	By Farr Tout Pres Pinot Noir
13.	2013	Cape Mentelle Wines Cabernet Sauvignon
14.	2010	Casella Limited Release Cabernet Sauvignon
15.	2013	Cherubino Wines Margaret River Cabernet Sauvignon
16.	2015	Clonakilla Shiraz Viognier
17.	2014	Coldstream Hills Reserve Chardonnay
18.	2015	Crabtree Wines Watervale Riesling
19.	2015	Cupitt Alphonse Sauvignon Blanc
20.	2015	Dandelion Vineyards Wonderland of the Eden Valley Riesling
21.	2015	d'Arenberg The Noble Botryotinia Fuckeliania Sauvignon Blanc Semillon
22.	2013	De Bortoli Noble One Semillon
23.	2015	De Bortoli Yarra Valley Selection A5 Chardonnay
24.	2014	De Iuliis Talga Road Vineyard Shiraz
25.	2013	Domaine Naturaliste Morus Cabernet Sauvignon
26.	2015	Eldridge Estate Fume Blanc Sauvignon Blanc
27.	2015	Frankland Estate Smith Cullam Riesling
28.	2015	Frankland Estate Isolation Ridge Vineyard Riesling
29.	2013	Frankland Estate Isolation Ridge Vineyard Shiraz
30.	2015	Gaelic Cemetery Premium Riesling
31.	2014	Giaconda Estate Vineyard Chardonnay

Australian Wine Vintages 2017 – Top 100 Wines

32.	2014	Giant Steps Tarraford Vineyard Chardonnay
33.	2012	Grampians Estate Streeton Reserve Shiraz
34.	2013	Grampians Estate Rutherford Sparkling Shiraz
35.	2014	Granite Hills Riesling
36.	2014	Grant Burge Filsell Old Vine Shiraz
37.	2013	Grosset Gaia Cabernet Sauvignon Cabernet Franc
38.	2015	Gundog Estate The Chase Semillon
39.	2015	Heemskerk Southern Tasmanian Pinot Noir
40.	2015	Heemskerk Chardonnay
41.	2015	Helm Wines Classic Dry Riesling
42.	2014	Henschke Louis Semillon
43.	2015	Henschke Julius Riesling
44.	2012	Hewitson Old Garden Mourvedre
45.	2013	Hickinbotham The Peake Cabernet Sauvignon Shiraz
46.	2011	Howard Park Museum Release Riesling
47.	2012	Hugo Wines Reserve Grenache
48.	2012	Huntington Estate Estate Cabernet Sauvignon
49.	2012	Huntington Estate Block 3 Cabernet Sauvignon
50.	2015	Jacobs Creek Steingarten Riesling
51.	2015	Jaeschkes Hill River Estate Single vineyard Riesling
52.	2013	Jim Brand Wines Glenroy Vineyard Shiraz
53.	2014	Kalleske Old Vine Grenache
54.	2014	Karrawatta Christo's Paddock Cabernet Sauvignon
55.	2012	Katnook Odyssey Cabernet Sauvignon
56.	2014	Leconfield Shiraz
57.	2013	Lino Ramble Treadlie Grenache Shiraz Mataro
58.	2013	Longview Vineyard Devil's Elbow Cabernet Sauvignon
59.	2012	Lowe Mudgee Zinfandel
60.	2015	Mayer Dr Mayer Pinot Noir
61.	2015	Mayer Granite Pinot Noir
62.	2011	Meerea Park Alexander Munro Semillon
63.	2006	Mitchell Winery McNicol Shiraz
64.	2015	Moorilla Estate Praxis Series Musqué Chardonnay
65.	2014	Moorilla Estate Muse Riesling
66.	2014	Moorooduc Estate Robinson Chardonnay
67.	2014	Mount Langi Ghiran Langi Shiraz
68.	2014	Mount Langi Ghiran Cliff Edge Shiraz

Australian Wine Vintages 2017 – Top 100 Wines

69.	2013	Mount Mary Triolet Sauvignon Blanc Semillon Muscadelle
70.	2014	Mount Mary Quintet Cabernet Sauvignon Merlot Cabernet Franc
71.	2013	Mount Pleasant Rosehill Vineyard Shiraz
72.	2014	Mount Pleasant Old Paddock Vineyard 1921 Vines Shiraz
73.	2016	O'Leary Walker Polish Hill River Riesling
74.	2010	Paracombe Somerville Shiraz
75.	2012	Paracombe Shiraz Viognier
76.	2014	Paringa Estate Peninsula Shiraz
77.	2012	Penfolds St Henri Shiraz Cabernet Sauvignon
78.	2013	Penfolds Magill Estate Shiraz
79.	2013	Philip Shaw No 89 Shiraz
80.	2009	Pipers Brook Vineyard Tasmania Pinot Noir Chardonnay
81.	2014	Pooles Rock Single Vineyard Semillon
82.	2015	Ravensworth Riesling
83.	2012	Ringbolt 21 Barriques Cabernet Sauvignon
84.	2014	Ross Hill Pinnacle Series Cabernet Sauvignon
85.	2010	Rymill Maturation Release Cabernet Sauvignon
86.	2012	Schild Estate Ben Schild Reserve Shiraz
87.	2015	Seppelt Drumborg Vineyard Riesling
88.	2012	Seppelt Salinger Pinot Noir Chardonnay Pinot Meunier
89.	2016	Shaw and Smith Sauvignon Blanc
90.	2014	Shaw + Smith Shiraz
91.	2015	Soumah Single Vineyard Sauvignon Blanc
92.	2014	Stockman's Ridge Wines Rider Shiraz
93.	2015	Symphony Hill Reserve Verdelho
94.	2012	Tapanappa Whalebone Vineyard Merlot Cabernet Franc
95.	2014	Thorn-Clarke William Randell Shiraz
96.	2012	Tim Adams The Aberfeldy Shiraz
97.	2014	Tolpuddle Pinot Noir
98.	2013	Wynns Harold Cabernet Sauvignon
99.	2014	Wynns The Siding Cabernet Sauvignon
100.	2015	Yalumba Eden Valley Roussanne

GOLD STAR WINES

The Australian Wine Vintages gold stars recognises those vignerons and winemakers with the ability to achieve consistently high standards and is therefore a list of reliable wines any Australian could serve with pride.

Anderson Wines Cellar Block Rutherglen Durif
Anderson Wines Verrier Basket Press Durif Shiraz
Angove The Medhyck Shiraz
Annies Lane Copper Trail Shiraz
Arras Blanc De Blancs Chardonnay
Arras Brut Elite Cuvee 801 Pinot Noir Chardonnay
Arras Ej Carr Late Disgorged Pinot Noir Chardonnay
Arras Grand Vintage Pinot Noir Chardonnay
Audrey Wilkinson The Lake Shiraz
Audrey Wilkinson The Ridge Semillon
Baileys of Glenrowan 1920's Block Shiraz
Baileys of Glenrowan Durif
Baileys of Glenrowan Petite Sirah
Balgownie Estate Bendigo Shiraz
Balnaves of Coonawarra The Tally Reserve Cabernet Sauvignon
Bass Phillip Premium Pinot Noir
Bass Phillip Reserve Pinot Noir
Bekkers Syrah
Best's Great Western Bin 0 Shiraz
Best's Great Western Thomson Family Shiraz
Bethany Wines L&E Reserve Shiraz
Bindi 'Block 5' Pinot Noir
Bindi Quartz Chardonnay
Bird In Hand M.A.C. Shiraz
Bird In Hand Montepulciano
Bird In Hand Nest Egg Shiraz
Bird In Hand Riesling
Black Jack Wines Block 6 Shiraz
Bleasdale Frank Potts Cabernet Malbec
Bleasdale The Petrel Shiraz Cabernet Malbec
Bleasdale The Powder Monkey Shiraz
Bloodwood Wines Orange Riesling

Australian Wine Vintages 2017 – Gold star wines

Bowen Estate Coonawarra Cabernet Sauvignon
Bremerton Old Adam Shiraz
Brokenwood Wines Graveyard Vineyard Shiraz
Brokenwood Wines ILR Reserve Semillon
Brookland Valley Reserve Chardonnay
Brothers In Arms Shiraz
Brown Brothers Patricia Brut Pinot Noir Chardonnay
Brown Brothers Shiraz Mondeuse Cabernet
Burton McMahon D'Aloisio's Vineyard Chardonnay
Burton McMahon Pinot Noir Syme Vineyard
By Farr Farr Side Pinot Noir
By Farr Sangreal Pinot Noir
By Farr Tout Pres Pinot Noir
Calabria Family Wines Three Bridges Durif
Cape Mentelle Wines Shiraz
Cape Mentelle Wines Wallcliffe Sauvignon Blanc Semillon
Cape Mentelle Wines Wilyabrup Cabernet Sauvignon
    Merlot Cabernet Franc
Castagna Genesis Syrah Viognier
Castle Rock Estate A & W Reserve Riesling
Castle Rock Estate Porongurup Riesling
Charles Melton Voices of Angels
Cherubino Frankland River Cabernet Sauvignon
Cherubino Frankland River Shiraz
Clonakilla Ballinderry Cabernet Sauvignon Cabernet Franc
    Merlot
Clonakilla Canberra Viognier
Clonakilla Hilltops Shiraz
Clonakilla O'Riada Shiraz
Clonakilla Shiraz Viognier
Cloudburst Cabernet Sauvignon
Cloudburst Chardonnay
Cloudburst Malbec
Clyde Park Single Block B2 Pinot Noir
Coldstream Hills Reserve Chardonnay
Coolangatta Estate Woolstonecraft Semillon
Coppabella Sirius Chardonnay
Coppabella The Crest Pinot Noir
Coriole Lloyd Reserve Shiraz
Crabtree Wines Watervale Riesling

Australian Wine Vintages 2017 – Gold star wines

Craggy Range Wines Le Sol Syrah Gimblett Gravels
Craiglee Wines Shiraz
Crawford River Riesling
Cullen Diana Madeline Cabernet Sauvignon Merlot
Cullen Kevin John Chardonnay
Curly Flat Chardonnay
Curly Flat Pinot Noir
Dalwhinnie Eagle Series Shiraz
Dalwhinnie Moonambel Cabernet Sauvignon
Dalwhinnie Moonambel Shiraz
Dalwhinnie South West Rocks Shiraz
d'Arenberg Dead Arm Shiraz
d'Arenberg Ironstone Pressings Grenache Shiraz Mourvedre
d'Arenberg The Derelict Vineyard Grenache
d'Arenberg The Twenty Eight Road Mourvedre
Dawson & James Single Vineyard Chardonnay
De Bortoli Noble One
De Bortoli Reserve Release Selection A5 Chardonnay
Devil's Lair 9th Chamber Chardonnay
Domaine A Cabernet Sauvignon
Domaine A Lady A Fume Blanc Sauvignon Blanc
Domaine A Merlot
Dominique Portet Heathcote Shiraz
Dominique Portet Sauvignon Blanc
Elderton Wines Command Shiraz
Ferngrove The Stirlings Cabernet Sauvignon
Fletcher Wines The Minion Nebbiolo
Frankland Estate Isolation Ridge Riesling
Fraser Gallop Estate Parterre Semillon Sauvignon Blanc
Freycinet Chardonnay
Freycinet Pinot Noir
Freycinet Riesling
Genders McLaren Park Shiraz
Giaconda Estate Vineyard Chardonnay
Giaconda Estate Vineyard Nebbiolo
Giaconda Estate Vineyard Shiraz
Giaconda Yarra Valley & Beechworth Pinot Noir
Giant Steps Harry's Monster
Glaetzer Anaperenna Shiraz Cabernet Sauvignon

Australian Wine Vintages 2017 – Gold star wines

Grant Burge Meshach Shiraz
Grosset Gaia Cabernet Sauvignon Cabernet Franc
Grosset Polish Hill Riesling
Hardys Eileen Hardy Chardonnay
Hardys Eileen Hardy Shiraz
Hardys HRB D659 Riesling
Heemskerk Chardonnay
Heemskerk Pinot Noir
Henschke Cyril Henschke Cabernet Sauvignon Cabernet
    Franc Merlot
Henschke Hill Of Grace Shiraz
Henschke Julius Riesling
Henschke Mount Edelstone Shiraz
Hickinbotham The Peake Cabernet Sauvignon Shiraz
Houghton Jack Mann Cabernet Sauvignon
Howard Park Abercrombie Cabernet Sauvignon
Jacobs Creek Centenary Hill Barossa Shiraz
Jacobs Creek Johann Shiraz Cabernet
Jansz Late Disgorged Vintage Cuvee Chardonnay
Jasper Hill Emily's Paddock Shiraz Cabernet Franc
Jasper Hill Georgia's Paddock Shiraz
Jim Barry The Armagh Shiraz
Jim Barry The Benbourie Cabernet Sauvignon
Jim Barry The Florita Riesling
Kalleske Greenock Shiraz
Kalleske Old Vine Grenache
Karrawatta Christo's Paddock Cabernet Sauvignon
Keith Tulloch Hunter Valley Semillon
Keith Tulloch The 'Kester' Shiraz
Kilikanoon Morts Reserve Riesling
Kooyong Estate Pinot Noir
Leconfield Coonawarra Cabernet Sauvignon
Leeuwin Estate Art Series Chardonnay
Lillypilly Noble Blend
Lindemans Limestone Ridge Shiraz Cabernet
Lindemans Pyrus Coonawarra Cabernets
Longview The Piece Shiraz
Mayer Cabernet Sauvignon
Mayer Granite Pinot Noir
McGuigan The Philosophy Shiraz Cabernet Sauvignon

Australian Wine Vintages 2017 – Gold star wines

Meerea Park Alexander Munro Semillon
Montalto Vineyard The Eleven Single Vineyard Chardonnay
Montalto Vineyard Tuerong Block Single Vineyard
Moorilla Muse Extra Brut Rose
Moorooduc McIntyre Chardonnay
Moorooduc McIntyre Single Vineyard Pinot Noir
Moss Wood Cabernet Sauvignon
Mount Horrocks Clare Valley Semillon
Mount Horrocks Cordon Cut Riesling
Mount Mary Chardonnay
Mount Mary Pinot Noir
Mount Mary Quintet Cabernets
Mount Mary Triolet Sauvignon Blanc Semillon Muscadelle
Mount Pleasant Lovedale Semillon
Mount Pleasant Maurice O'Shea Shiraz
Mount Pleasant Rosehill Shiraz
Nick O'Leary Bolaro Single Vineyard Shiraz
Noon Eclipse Grenache Shiraz Graciano
O'Leary Walker Polish Hill River Riesling
Paringa Estate Shiraz
Paulette Polish Hill River Riesling
Penfolds 50 Year Old Rare Tawny Shiraz Grenache
Penfolds Bin 707 Cabernet Sauvignon
Penfolds Bin 95 Grange Shiraz
Penfolds Grandfather Mourvedre Shiraz
Penfolds Great Grand Father Rare Tawny
Penfolds RWT Shiraz
Penfolds St Henri Shiraz Cabernet Sauvignon
Penfolds Yattarna Chardonnay
Pepper Tree Coquun Single Vineyard Reserve Shiraz
Pepper Tree Elderslee Road Single Vineyard Cabernet Sauvignon
Petaluma Hanlin Hill Riesling
Peter Lehmann Margaret Semillon
Peter Lehmann Stonewell Shiraz
Peter Lehmann Wigan Riesling
Pewsey Vale Contours Museum Release Riesling
Pewsey Vale Single Vineyard Estate Riesling
Pfeiffer Christopher's VP

Australian Wine Vintages 2017 – Gold star wines

Philip Shaw No 11 Chardonnay
Philip Shaw No 89 Shiraz Viognier
Pierro Chardonnay
Pierro Reserve Cabernet Merlot
Pikes 'The Merle' Riesling
Pikes EWP Reserve Shiraz
Pressing Matters R139 Riesling
Pressing Matters R69 Riesling
Pressing Matters R9 Riesling
Richard Hamilton 'Centurion' Old Vine Shiraz
Sandalford Estate Reserve Shiraz
Seppelt Drumborg Chardonnay
Seppelt Drumborg Riesling
Seppelt Jaluka Chardonnay
Seppelt St Peters Shiraz
Seville Estate Old Vine Reserve Pinot Noir
Seville Estate Old Vine Reserve Shiraz
Seville Estate Reserve Chardonnay
Shaw & Smith M3 Chardonnay
Shaw & Smith Sauvignon Blanc
Shaw & Smith Shiraz
St Hugos Cabernet Sauvignon
St John's Road Block 8 Ebenezer Shiraz
Stonier KBS Chardonnay
Stonier KBS Pinot Noir
Stonier Reserve Pinot Noir
Symphony Hill Reserve Lagrien
Tahbilk 1927 Vines Marsanne
Tapanappa Foggy Hill Fleurieu Peninsula Pinot Noir
Tapanappa Piccadilly Valley Tiers Vineyard Chardonnay
Tapanappa Whalebone Vineyard
Taylors The Pioneer
Taylors The Visionary
Thomas Braemore Individual Vineyard Semillon
Thomas Braemore Semillon Cellar Reserve
Thomas Individual Vineyard Kiss Shiraz
Thomas Individual Vineyard Sweetwater Shiraz
Tim Adams Clare Valley Riesling
Tinklers U & I Shiraz
Torbreck Runrig Shiraz

Australian Wine Vintages 2017 – Gold star wines

Torbreck The Factor Shiraz
Vasse Felix Heytesbury Chardonnay
Voyager Project 95 Chardonnay
Voyager Project U12 North Block Cabernet Sauvignon
Wendouree Cabernet Malbec
Wendouree Shiraz Malbec
Wolf Blass Black Label Cabernet Sauvignon Shiraz
Wolf Blass Platinum Label Shiraz
Yalumba The Virgilius Viognier
Yarra Yering Dry Red No 1
Yarra Yering Dry Red No 2
Yarra Yering Pinot Noir
Yering Station Reserve Chardonnay
Yering Station Reserve Pinot Noir
Yering Station Reserve Shiraz Viognier
Yeringberg Shiraz

Introducing the Sydney International Wine Competition

For the first time Australian Wine Vintages is including the results from tastings organised by industry peers. Having judged the Sydney International Wine Competition (SIWC) I admire the professionalism and unique process used to select their award winners and see synergies for readers to find more good bottles of wine.

The SIWC is unique amongst the major international competitions as their primary objective is to help diners choose wines to complement the food on their table. The competitions award winners have won their place by being tasted alongside the appropriate food. The SIWC recipes are published on their website, offering useful advice and inspiration.

Australian Wine Vintages follows reliable Australian producers through the years, refining content to select the most consistent. The SIWC is a reliable source of advice for expanding consumers' choice by recommending quality wines and wine styles.

Judging wine with food at the competition selects current release wines with balance between fruit, acid, oak and tannin. Wines that are enjoyable to drink and taste better with food that you can buy now. This compliments Australian Wine Vintages as a source of advice on which wines to cellar, how long to cellar and when to drink the wines in your cellar.

Up to 15%, a maximum of 300 wines, from SIWC entries receive an award which is very low for wine competitions. Their selections of winners with Top 100, Blue-Gold or Gold are all judged with food.

The inclusion of the SIWC award winners offers readers another source of quality wines with diverse prices and origins and via their website recipes to pair with them. I hope this adds to your enjoyment when drinking or dining, tasting, travelling, cellaring or celebrating.

Top 100 Sydney International Wine Competition

Wine Maker	Wine Name	RegionName	Main Variety	Vintage
ALDI Stores	Tudor Central Victorian Shiraz	Central Victoria	Shiraz	2014
Angove Family Winemakers	Family Crest Grenache Shiraz Mourvedre	McLaren Vale	Grenache	2014
Atze's Corner Wines	The Bachelor	Barossa Valley	Shiraz	2014
Beresford Wines	Beresford Estate Shiraz	McLaren Vale	Shiraz	2013
Beresford Wines	Beresford Bell Tower	McLaren Vale	Shiraz	2013
Bird in Hand	Bird in Hand Nest Egg Shiraz	Mt Lofty Ranges	Shiraz	2012
Brash Vineyard	Brash Vineyard Cabernet Sauvignon	Margaret River	Cabernet Sauvignon	2013
CAPE BARREN WINES	Cape Barren Native Goose Shiraz	McLAREN VALE	Shiraz	2014
Casa Santos Lima, Companhia das Vinhas SA	LAB	Lisboa	Castelão	2014
Casella Family Brands	Limited Release Cabernet Sauvignon	Barossa Valley	Cabernet Sauvignon	2010
Casella Family Brands	Peter Lehmann Wines Botrytis Semillon	Barossa Valley	Semillon	2011
Casella Family Brands	Peter Lehmann Wines H & V Tempranillo	Barossa Valley	Tempranillo	2014
Castelli Estate	Il Liris Chardonnay	Great Southern	Chardonnay	2014
Castelli Estate	Riesling	Great Southern	Riesling	2015

Australian Wine Vintages 2017 – Top 100 SIWC

Wine Maker	Wine Name	RegionName	Main Variety	Vintage
Cellarmasters	Shark Block Mclaren Vale Cabernet Sauvignon	McLaren Vale	Cabernet Sauvignon	2013
Chalk Hill Wines	Alpha Crucis Cabernet Sauvignon	McLaren Vale	Cabernet Sauvignon	2012
Champagne Collet	Champagne Collet Blanc de blancs	Champagne	Chardonnay	NV
Champagne Collet	Champagne Collet Extra Brut	Champagne	Chardonnay	NV
Champagne Lanson	Lanson Gold Label Brut	Champagne	Pinot Noir	2005
Clairault	Clairault Margaret River Chardonnay	Margaret River	Chardonnay	2014
Coolangatta Estate	Coolangatta Estate Estate Grown Semillon	Shoalhaven Coast	Semillon	2006
De Bortoli Wines	Eight Year Old Fine Tawny	South Eastern Australia	Shiraz	NV
Deviation Road Winery	Deviation Road Loftia Vintage Brut	Adelaide Hills	Chardonnay	2013
DiGiorgio Family Wines	Coonawarra Chardonnay	Coonawarra	Chardonnay	2014
DiGiorgio Family Wines	Lucindale Botrytis Semillon	Limestone Coast	Semillon	2011
Domain Road Vineyard	Domain Road Vineyard Pinot Noir	Central Otago	Pinot Noir	2013
Domaine Naturaliste	Sauvage	Margaret River	Sauvignon Blanc	2014
Domaine Naturaliste	Discovery Sauvignon Blanc Semillon	Margaret River	Sauvignon Blanc	2015
Fermoy Estate	Fermoy Estate Reserve Cabernet Sauvignon	Margaret River	Cabernet Sauvignon	2013

Australian Wine Vintages 2017 – Top 100 SIWC

Wine Maker	Wine Name	RegionName	Main Variety	Vintage
Flying Fish Cove	Wildberry Reserve Cabernet Sauvignon	Margaret River	Cabernet Sauvignon	2013
Foley Family Wines	Vavasour Pinot Noir	Marlborough	Pinot Noir	2013
Framingham Wines Ltd	Ribbonwood Marlborough Pinot Noir	Marlborough	Pinot Noir	2014
Gatt Wines	Gatt High Eden Riesling	Eden Valley	Riesling	2010
George Wyndham	George Wyndham Founders Reserve Shiraz Grenache	Barossa	Shiraz	2013
Giesen Wines	Giesen Single Vineyard Clayvin Pinot Noir	Marlborough	Pinot Noir	2013
Gil Family Estates	Laya	Almansa	Garnacha Tintorera	2014
Glendon Vineyards/Landaire	Landaire Chardonnay-Handpicked Single Vineyard	Padthaway	Chardonnay	2014
Grampians Estate	Rutherford Sparkling Shiraz	Grampians	Shiraz	2013
Greystone Wines	Greystone Pinot Noir	North Canterbury	Pinot Noir	2014
Hemera Estate	Block 3A Limited Release Shiraz	Barossa Valley	Shiraz	2013
Jacob's Creek	Jacob's Creek Expedition Coonawarra Shiraz	Limestone Coast	Shiraz	2013
Jacob's Creek	Jacob's Creek Johann Shiraz Cabernet	Barossa	Shiraz	2010
Jacob's Creek	Jacob's Creek Reeves Point Chardonnay	Barossa	Chardonnay	2013

www.robgeddesmw.com

Australian Wine Vintages 2017 – Top 100 SIWC

Wine Maker	Wine Name	RegionName	Main Variety	Vintage
Jacob's Creek	Jacob's Creek Reserve Barossa Signature Shiraz	Barossa	Shiraz	2014
James Busby Fine Wines	Pensilva Estate McLaren Vale Shiraz	McLaren Vale	Shiraz	2014
Kalleske Wines	Moppa Shiraz	Barossa Valley	Shiraz	2014
Kim Crawford	Kim Crawford Small Parcels Spitfire Sauvignon Blanc	Marlborough	Sauvignon Blanc	2015
Kirrihill Wines	Kirrihill Wines, Regional Range, Clare Valley Shiraz	Clare Valley	Shiraz	2014
Langmeil Winery	Jackaman's Cabernet Sauvignon	Adelaide Hills	Cabernet Sauvignon	2011
Latitude 34 Wine Co.	The Blackwood Captain James	Blackwood Valley	Cabernet Sauvignon	2014
Leconfield Wines	Leconfield Coonawarra Cabernet Sauvignon	Coonawarra	Cabernet Sauvignon	2013
Longview Vineyard	Boat Shed Nebbiolo Rosato	Adelaide Hills	Nebbiolo	2015
Lowburn Ferry	Lowburn Ferry	Central Otago	Pinot Noir	2013
Lowburn Ferry	Lowburn Ferry Home Block Pinot Noir	Central Otago	Pinot Noir	2014
Matua Wines	Matua Single Vineyard Awatere Valley Sauvignon Blanc	Marlborough	Sauvignon Blanc	2015
Matua Wines	Matua Lands & Legends Marlborough Sauvignon Blanc	Marlborough	sauvignon blanc	2015

Australian Wine Vintages 2017 – Top 100 SIWC

Wine Maker	Wine Name	RegionName	Main Variety	Vintage
Matua Wines	Squealing Pig Central Otago Pinot Noir Rose	Central Otago	Pinot Noir	2015
McLeish Estate Wines	McLeish Estate Cellar Reserve Semillon	HUNTER VALLEY	SEMILLON	2007
Montalto	Montalto Estate Chardonnay	Mornington	Chardonnay	2014
Morris Wines	Morris Old Premium Rare Liqueur Topaque	Rutherglen	Muscadelle	NV
Mt Difficulty Wines Ltd	Mt Difficulty Bannockburn Pinot Gris	Central Otago	Pinot Gris	2014
Ngatarawa Wines Ltd	Ngatarawa Stables Reserve Hawkes Bay Syrah	Hawkes Bay	Syrah	2014
Palmer Wines	Palmer Cabernet Grandee Reserve	Margaret River	Cabernet Sauvignon	2013
Paracombe Premium Wines	Paracombe Shiraz	Adelaide Hills	Shiraz	2011
Paracombe Premium Wines	Paracombe Shiraz Viognier	Adelaide Hills	Shiraz	2011
Peccavi Wines	Peccavi Cabernet Sauvignon	Margaret River	Cabernet Sauvignon	2012
Peregrine Wines	Peregrine Rastasburn Riesling	Central Otago	Riesling	2010
Pernod Ricard Winemakers New Zealand	Church Road Grand Reserve Chardonnay	Hawke's Bay	Chardonnay	2013
Pernod Ricard Winemakers New Zealand	Stoneleigh Rapaura Series Sauvignon Blanc	Marlborough	Sauvignon Blanc	2015

www.robgeddesmw.com

Australian Wine Vintages 2017 – Top 100 SIWC

Wine Maker	Wine Name	RegionName	Main Variety	Vintage
Pernod Ricard Winemakers New Zealand	Stoneleigh Latitude Sauvignon Blanc	Marlborough	Sauvignon Blanc	2015
Pernod Ricard Winemakers New Zealand	Brancott Estate Terroir Series Fume Blanc	Marlborough	Sauvignon Blanc	2014
Pernod Ricard Winemakers New Zealand	Brancott Estate Terroir Series Sauvignon Blanc	Marlborough	Sauvignon Blanc	2014
Philip Shaw Wines	Philip Shaw No 89 Shiraz	Orange	Shiraz	2013
Pinnacle Drinks	Franklin Tate Reserve Margaret River Cabernet Sauv	Margaret River	Cabernet Sauvignon	2013
Pinnacle Drinks	Lobster Reef Hidden Marker Sauvignon Blanc	Marlborough	Sauvignon Blanc	2015
Pinnacle Drinks	Marlborough Sounds Sauvignon Blanc	Marlborough	Sauvignon Blanc	2015
Ringbolt Pty Ltd	Ringbolt Cabernet Sauvignon	Margaret River	Cabernet Sauvignon	2013
Robert Oatley Vineyards	Four in Hand Barossa Shiraz	Barossa	Shiraz	2014
Rockbare	Rockbare Tempranillo	McLaren Vale	Tempranillo	2014
Saint Clair Family Estate	Saint Clair Pioneer Block 9 Big John Riesling	Marlborough	Riesling	2013
Saint Clair Family Estate	Saint Clair Marlborough Premium Gruner Veltliner	Marlborough	Gruner Veltliner	2014

Australian Wine Vintages 2017 – Top 100 SIWC

Wine Maker	Wine Name	RegionName	Main Variety	Vintage
Seifried Estate	Old Coach Road Nelson Sauvignon Blanc	Nelson	Sauvignon Blanc	2015
Seville Estate	Seville Estate Chardonnay	Yarra Valley	Chardonnay	2014
Shingleback	Davey Estate Reserve Cabernet Sauvignon	McLaren Vale	Cabernet Sauvignon	2013
Shottesbrooke Vineyards	Shottesbrooke Estate Series GSM	McLaren Vale	Grenache	2014
Sileni Estates	Satyr 'Foothills' Pinot Noir	Hawke's Bay	Pinot Noir	2014
Spy Valley Wines	Spy Valley Gewurztraminer	Marlborough	Gewurztraminer	2014
Thorn-Clarke Wines	Thorn-Clarke Sandpiper Cabernet Sauvignon	Barossa	Cabernet Sauvignon	2014
Thorn-Clarke Wines	Thorn-Clarke Sandpiper Shiraz	Barossa	Shiraz	2014
Tinpot Hut Wines Ltd	Tinpot Hut Marlborough Sauvignon Blanc	Marlborough	Sauvignon Blanc	2015
Tohu Wines	Tohu Awatere Valley Pinot Gris	Marlborough	Pinot Gris	2015
Trentham Estate	Trentham Estate "The Family" Pinot Grigio	Murray Darling	Pinot Grigio	2015
Two Rivers Wines	Hidden Hive Verdelho	Hunter Valley	Verdelho	2015
Villa Maria Estate	Vidal Legacy Hawkes Bay Chardonnay	Hawkes Bay	Chardonnay	2014
Villa Maria Estate	Reserve Barrique Fermented Gisborne Chardonnay	Gisborne	Chardonnay	2013
Villa Maria Estate	Villa Maria Private Bin Hawkes Bay Syrah	Hawkes Bay	Syrah	2012

www.robgeddesmw.com

Australian Wine Vintages 2017 – Top 100 SIWC

Wine Maker	Wine Name	RegionName	Main Variety	Vintage
Villa Maria Estate	Villa Maria Private Bin Marlborough Sauvignon Blanc	Marlborough	Sauvignon Blanc	2015
Waimea Estates	Waimea Gewurztraminer	Nelson	Gewurztraminer	2014
Whitehaven Wine Co. Ltd	Whitehaven Awatere Single Vineyard 'Greg' Sauvignon Blanc	Marlborough	Sauvignon Blanc	2015
Yealands Wine Group	Yealands Estate Winemakers Reserve Sauvignon Blanc	Marlborough	Sauvignon Blanc	2014
Yealands Wine Group	Peter Yealands Pinot Gris	Marlborough	Pinot Gris	2015
Yealands Wine Group	Peter Yealands Reserve Pinot Noir	Marlborough	Pinot Noir	2014
Yealands Wine Group	Silverfern Pinot Noir	Marlborough	Pinot Noir	2014

| Vintage | Rank | Drink | RRP | Vol Alc |

ABEL'S TEMPEST BY HEEMSKERK
A part of the Treasury Wine Estates Group these are fresh, stylish and drink young wines made from Tasmanian fruit. They include Pinot Noir, Traminer, Sauvignon Blanc, Chardonnay and Sparkling Chardonnay Pinot Noir.
Winemaker: *Peter Munro*
Open: *No Cellar Door, 660 Blessington Road, White Hills*
www.heemskerk.com.au

ABEL'S TEMPEST BY HEEMSKERK
CHARDONNAY PINOT NOIR ★★★★★
Wow. Biscuity almost toffee and shortbread with the honey note of chardonnay. The palate is vibrant and well balanced with obvious yeasty depth and green apple acids to close. Rich, long and complete wine with the chardonnay finesse of Tasmania. Great for parties!

| 2010 | 94 | 2017 | $59.99 | 12.0% |
| 2011 | 93 | 2017 | $31.99 | 12.0% |

ABEL'S TEMPEST BY HEEMSKERK
CHARDONNAY ★★★★
Fruit comes from 75% white hills from Launceston and 25% from East coast fruit. The Heemskerk is all Coal River Valley bar a small block from Ouse in the middle of Tasmania. This is hard pressed, like Burgundy, all oak fermented and all gets malo, with 20% new oak barriques to retain the primary fruit and be upfront. The flavours are coiled in a ball of silky middle palate savoury and white pear fruit but no length.

2012	90	2016	$24.99	13.0%
2013	88	2017	$24.99	13.0%
2014	90	2019	$24.99	13.0%

ABEL'S TEMPEST BY HEEMSKERK
PINOT NOIR ★★★★
Tasmanian Pinot is all about freshness and pure delicate fruit. Vibrant purple hues with a focused nose of fresh cherry, raspberry fruit and lavender, with lush toasted vanilla oak. A polished and elegant Pinot that wins hearts.

Vintage	Rank	Drink	RRP	Vol Alc
2012	88	2020	$31.99	13.5%
2013	90	2018	$24.99	14.0%
2015	91	2020	$31.99	13.0%

ALL SAINTS
All Saints in Rutherglen is both a unique cellar door and home to one branch of the Brown family. The grand old castle styled winery evokes the history and significance of Australian wine while the Chinese dormitory shows how people lived. The winemaking approach is modern and innovative yet respecting of the distinctive regional varieties and styles. Their popular cellar door also has many interesting limited production table wines to taste as well as high quality liqueur muscat and topaque.
Winemaker: Dan Crane, Nicholas Brown
Open: Mon– Sat 9am–5.30pm, Sun 10am–5.30pm, All Saints Road, Wahgunyah
Ph: (18) 0002 1621 *www.allsaintswine.com.au*

ALL SAINTS
FAMILY CELLAR DURIF ★★★★
Ripe deep and fleshy cooler year notes with black berry black licorice white pepper. The well-made palate has soft fine tannins ripe fruits silky mouth full very ripe dark plum middle palate with fresh plum fruits and very soft fine grained to close.

Vintage	Rank	Drink	RRP	Vol Alc
2008	88	2017	$55.00	14.5%
2009	91	2020	$60.00	14.0%
2012	93	2019	$62.00	14.0%

ALL SAINTS
FAMILY CELLAR MARSANNE ★★★★
Varietal twangy yellow fruits, subtle marsanne white flower into oatmeal subtle oak spiced and minerality. The subtle palate is medium bodied full flavoured and long with good balance creamy textured cedar oregano oak spice, stables notes add to the yellow fruits. A pup with the fruit yet to take a lead role. Drink young for bright or hold for 3 and enjoy the honeysuckle. Made in the style of a chardonnay.

Vintage	Rank	Drink	RRP	Vol Alc
2009	87	2014	$30.00	12.6%
2010	90	2016	$30.00	13.2%
2013	89	2018	$35.00	13.5%

| Vintage | Rank | Drink | RRP | Vol Alc |

AMADIO
Caj Amadio had a successful career as a builder in Adelaide. As developer of a large vineyard near Kersbrook in the Adelaide Hills, he has allowed his son Danniel Amadio to develop a wide variety of brands and styles including some destined for China. Solid reliable wines appear under the Amadio label including exciting Italian varieties.
Winemaker: *Danniel Amadio*
Open: *No Cellar Door*
Lots 26–27 South Para Road, Kersbrook
Ph: (08) 8337 5144   www.amadiowines.com.au

AMADIO
HERITAGE SELECTION AGLIANICO ★★★★

Lavender and wormwood herbal aromas with a ripe, sweet, black fruited medium full body richness. Plenty of personality, power and balance. Black tea tannin flavours on the finish.

| 2011 | 88 | 2017 | $35.00 | 14.8% |
| 2012 | 89 | 2019 | $40.00 | 14.5% |

AMADIO
HERITAGE SELECTION MONTEPULCIANO ★★★★

Red cherry and herbal green leafy edges with a firm tannins and middle palate fruits. This is the most refined in body and style, with even length and structure, red fruit and leafy edges to the flavours.

| 2011 | 90 | 2017 | $35.00 | 14.5% |
| 2012 | 86 | 2018 | $40.00 | 14.5% |

AMADIO
HERITAGE SELECTION SAGRANTINO ★★★★

Herbal characters with hay/straw and red fruits on the nose. In the mouth very full bodied, mouth filling black fruit and dark licorice richness with tannin tenseness. Very warm on the finish.

| 2011 | 90 | 2018 | $35.00 | 14.8% |
| 2012 | 88 | 2018 | $40.00 | 14.5% |

Vintage	Rank	Drink	RRP	Vol Alc

ANDERSON WINES

Anderson Wines in Rutherglen is a blend of two generations of winemakers. Howard, with 40 years' experience in sparkling wine, and his daughter, Christobelle produce disciplined durif showing great understanding of the variety. Remarkably, they release the Cellar Block Durif with 5–6 years' maturation when it is, in their opinion, "ready to drink". Very small production and very high quality, including their remarkable sparkling shiraz which is aged on lees until sale.

Winemakers: *Howard and Christobelle Anderson*
Open: *Daily 10am–5pm, Chiltern Road, Rutherglen*
Ph: *(02) 6032 8111 www.andersonwinery.com.au*

ANDERSON WINES
CELLAR BLOCK RUTHERGLEN DURIF ★★★★★

Amazing colour in 2016 and a harbinger of a long life, brooding black hearted thick red-rimmed intensity. Typical of focused and concentrated Durif with a width of savoury cola graphite, into a red fruit core, gentle oak spices add a lift. The palate is layered waves of flavours; silky fine tannins create a density with tastes wed to red plum from the fruit basket across savoury and into cooked meats with the solid full bodied with fruit sweet and dark spicy tannins to finish.

Vintage	Rank	Drink	RRP	Vol Alc
2007	94	2020	$35.00	14.8%
2008	92	2018	$35.00	14.5%
2010	95	2022	$40.00	14.2%

ANDERSON WINES
VERRIER BASKET PRESS DURIF SHIRAZ ★★★★★

A wild bouquet garni, dried bay leaf oregano and rosemary on a Greek island going into a goat stew. Plenty of red and black fruits. The red fruit structure leads to a fleshy middle palate with the silky shiraz fine tannins holding the firmer durif to the back palate offers an easier take on the regional hero.

Vintage	Rank	Drink	RRP	Vol Alc
2007	93	2020	$34.00	14.8%
2008	95	2028	$32.50	14.0%
2010	91	2018	$32.50	14.0%

| Vintage | Rank | Drink | RRP | Vol Alc |

ANGOVE FAMILY WINEMAKERS
Angove Family Winemakers has been family run for 126 years. Thanks to talented viticulture and winemaking, they offer excellent quality and value table wines, sherry and brandy across a breadth of prices. A second cellar door in McLaren vale reveals their role as premium wine producers. Look out for "The Medhyk" McLaren Vale Shiraz.
Winemakers: *Tony Ingle, Paul Kernich, Ben Horley, Amelia Hildebrand*
Open: *Daily 9am–5pm*
Bookmark Avenue, Renmark
Ph: *(1300) 769 266 www.angove.com.au*

ANGOVE
THE MEDHYK SHIRAZ ★★★★★
Freshness of fruit in the polished nutty tight-grained oak aromas. Youthful, complex, balanced ripe fruit and oak in long and well-constructed fine grained tannins with a blackberry and black olive intrigue.

2010	95	2040	$65.00	14.0%
2011	Not made			
2012	94	2027	$65.00	14.5%
2014	94	2035	$65.00	14.5%

ANGOVE
NINE VINES GRENACHE SHIRAZ ROSE ★★★★★
Red fruits, crushed dried herbs, and tarragon like aromas herald the increasingly complex ongoing evolution of this wine. Drinks like a charm, fleshy fruits, and silky flavours of red fruits, raspberry, and red currant middle palate. Appealing texture gives weight to the fresh ripe fruits and the flicker of tannin gives a firm finish to the lingering red fruits.

2013	89	2015	$15.00	12.5%
2014	90	2016	$17.00	12.5%
2015	92	2016	$16.00	12.5%

ANGOVE
WARBOYS SHIRAZ ★★★★
Blackberry, verging on the very ripe jam, sweet vanilla and chocolate aromas. The fruit flavours are easy going ripe and concentrated, with good complexity from

the red cherry and black cherry medium length and well matched oak.

2011	91	2017	$35.00	14.0%
2013	93	2020	$35.00	14.5%
2014	88	2019	$42.00	14.0%

ANGOVE
WILD OLIVE SHIRAZ ★★★★
Black fruits with a savoury element of iodine and tapenade to the nose. The palate is delicious. Red fruits, and silky tannins with a generous middle and concentrated layers of fruit flavours and medium long.

| 2013 | 91 | 2016 | $20.00 | 14.0% |
| 2014 | 94 | 2019 | $20.00 | 14.0% |

ANGULLONG
The Angullong vineyards are located on the lower southern slopes of the Orange region at the foothills of Mt Canobolas, an ancient volcano. The Crossing family have farmed there for generations and are proving excellent grape growers and winemakers offering a diverse range of wines of uniform value and quality. They feature Italian varietals as well as French and have recently opened their cellar door at nearby Millthorpe.
Winemaker: *Jon Reynolds and Ben Crossing*
Open: *Weekends & Pub Hols 11am–5pm*
The Old Blue Stone Stables Cnr Park & Victoria Streets Millthorpe
Ph: *(02) 6366 4300 www.angullong.com.au*

ANGULLONG
FOSSIL HILL BARBERA ★★★★
Italian reds have a firmness that extends to the aromas, black cherry fruited, bramble, subtle oak leads to a long, taut, fresh red cherry, savoury middle palate. Excellent harmony and length of fruit, acids, fine grape tannins and oak that builds to a mouth-watering lingering fruit finish. Rich foods would find a great balance with this tannin acid freshness. Not a shiraz drinkers style.

2011	88	2015	$22.00	13.5%
2013	87	2017	$24.00	13.5%
2014	92	2019	$22.00	14.0%

ANGULLONG
FOSSIL HILL SANGIOVESE ★★★★★
Red cherry fruited, medium ripe, interest is from the subtle persistence of sandalwood oak. The palate has great finesse with lingering unsweetened cherry juice fruits. Very faithful winemaking to the traditions of Tuscany and the climate delivering in spades.

Vintage	Rank	Drink	RRP	Vol Alc
2013	88	2019	$22.00	13.5%
2013	90	2016	$24.00	13.5%
2014	94	2025	$22.00	14.0%

ANNIE'S LANE
This historic winery has been through several reinventions from the days when it was known as Quelltaler and Gran Fiesta sherry its most famous wine. The old vines are capable of serious quality which has been well handled by Alex McKenzie in recent years. Lovely cellar door.
Winemaker: *Alex MacKenzie*
Open: *Weekdays 9am–5pm, Weekends 10am–4pm*
Quelltaler Road, Watervale
Ph: (08) 8843 2320 www.annieslane.com.au

ANNIES LANE
COPPER TRAIL SHIRAZ ★★★★★
A big complex red in the cellaring style with concentrated balanced fruit and quality oak for the long haul. Aromas of black berry, black olive and oak with vanilla and coffee. The palate is full and intense, tannin, very long, firm even length, full bodied, savoury smoked meats with a long finish. Drink after 2020 or decant for half a day.

Vintage	Rank	Drink	RRP	Vol Alc
2012	92	2032	$79.99	14.5%
2013	94	2030	$79.99	14.5%

ANNIES LANE
QUELLTALER RIESLING ★★★★★
Lime and honey with the regional solid weight running into flavours that are ripe balanced, long round full flavoured, it has fruit weight with fine acidity and finishes with layers of flavour.

Vintage	Rank	Drink	RRP	Vol Alc
2014	95	2026	$26.99	12.5%
2015	92	2020	$26.99	13.0%

ANNIES LANE
THE LOCALS CABERNET SAUVIGNON ★★★★★
Classic cabernet sauvignon varietal whispers in the glass black currant blue berry, gum leaf, bay leaf, cardamom. The palate has excellent balance with well integrated fine grained tannins and an elegant temperament which creates a bundle of long middle palate black fruits. Ripper wine and ripper price.

| 2012 | 80 | 2015 | $22.99 | 14.0% |
| 2013 | 94 | 2018 | $22.99 | 14.0% |

ANNIES LANE
THE LOCALS SHIRAZ GRENACHE ★★★★★
Nice wine for dinner as it has a lot of subtle complexities with coffee oak, Indian spices, ginger wed to black plum fruit aromas. The palate has charm and grace with very fine tannins flowing even long and silky smooth with very good length supporting the dried brown spice flavours.

| 2012 | 93 | 2022 | $22.99 | 15.0% |
| 2013 | 92 | 2018 | $22.99 | 15.0% |

ANVERS WINES
Wayne and Myriam Keoghan established Anvers Wines in 1998, with the philosophy of producing only premium wines from low-yielding vineyards in McLaren Vale, Langhorne Creek and Kangarilla. Thanks to regional blending, their ripe style is fresh, complex and full bodied.
Winemaker: *Kym Milne MW*
Open: *By appointment only, 633 Razorback Road, Kangarilla*
Ph: *(08) 8323 9603* *www.anvers.com.au*

ANVERS
THE WARRIOR SHIRAZ ★★★★★
Lives up to its name. A dense, fruit sweet and elegantly oaked aroma, ripe, fresh and complex. Full bodied and even velvety tannins, flowing onto a generous bright-fruited middle palate, with ripe blackberry and blue fruits, and soft fine-grained tannins to finish, balanced with medium intensity oak.

| 2010 | 90 | 2019 | $55.00 | 14.5% |
| 2012 | 95 | 2022 | $55.00 | 14.5% |

| Vintage | Rank | Drink | RRP | Vol Alc |

APSLEY GORGE VINEYARD
Apsley Gorge produces distinctive, excellent quality Tasmanian chardonnay and pinot noir from a well-located vineyard on Tasmania's East coast. Brian Franklin has had more than ten years experience working vintage in Burgundy which has given his wine an articulate and individual style. The winery and shed like cellar door have a unique situation on the coast in Bicheno with views across Freycinet. Eat crays and drink Chardonnay!
Winemaker: *Brian Franklin*
The Gulch, Bicheno
Ph: *(03) 6375 1221* ***www.apsleygorgevineyard.com.au***

APSLEY GORGE VINEYARD
PINOT NOIR ★★★★★
Immediate complexity dark fruits, earthy stemmy spice aromas that an older generation will see as smelling of pythrum spice like mortein and fly tox sprays. The ripe fruits sweetness opens strongly up front black cherry soft into almost peppery spicy dry stemmy tannins that define the flavours and add a savoury edge to the middle palate and finish and slightly warm finish.

Vintage	Rank	Drink	RRP	Vol Alc
2008	86	2012	$52.00	14.0%
2011	94	2022	$60.00	14.5%
2012	90	2019	$60.00	14.5%

ARRAS
House of Arras is regularly our finest sparkling wine and certainly Australia's most consistent top-end performer, thanks to the availability of fruit from exceptional Tasmanian vineyards and a highly experienced and meticulous winemaker. Since 2011, this winery has been back in Australian hands.
Winemaker: *Ed Carr*
Open: *Tastings at Bay of Fires, 10am–5pm, 11am–4pm June/July/August, 40 Baxters Road, Pipers River*
Ph: *(1800) 263 254* ***www.houseofarras.com.au***

ARRAS
GRAND VINTAGE PINOT NOIR CHARDONNAY ★★★★★
The fruit has punch and complexity of spice toast, hot cross bun like subtle mustard pickles merging into poached apple submerged in yeasty oatmeal. The flavours are full in the middle palate, you really know you are tasting it, fleshy

width coupled with complex acid energy, giving breadth
silky drive guided by fine acidity, with
yeasty oatmeal lees farewelling the very
detailed finish.

2004	96	2015	$72.00	12.5%
2005	96	2020	$70.00	12.5%
2007	93	2018	$69.99	12.5%

ARRAS
BRUT ELITE CUVEE 801 PINOT NOIR CHARDONNAY ★★★★★

This is the wound-down version of the house vintage style. Fleshy and generous aromas, with flowers, white fruit and umami savoury yeast. The fruit sweetness rises to greet you, delivering a fleshy soft ripe front palate. The green apple acidity puts its foot on the pedal and runs long, with the subtle flavours of white fruit chardonnay-like flavours holding to the middle palate. Yeasty umami and a little dry tannin note to the finish.

| NV | 92 | 2017 | $49.99 | 12.5% |

ARRAS
EJ CARR LATE DISGORGED PINOT NOIR CHARDONNAY ★★★★★

Aromas are savoury or umami "master stock" deep, almost woodsy forest like mature fruit with aldehyde in a positive sense. In the mouth, creamy long texture with a mature complex lift of vibrant fruits and an amazing range of subtle flavours, seaside-like, mineral-aged chardonnay, lemon curd and short bread biscuit fruit sweetness, with yeast and lemon acids.

2000	94	2014	$190.00	12.5%
2001	94	2017	$190.00	12.5%
2002	95	2022	$149.99	12.5%

ARRAS
BLANC DE BLANC CHARDONNAY ★★★★★

White flowers, yeast oatmeal into yoghurt, poached white fruit into Quince and apricot notes start. The palate is like unrolling a mat in hurry starts a smooth unravelling runs into a click as the mat or in this case your tongue runs out of length, oatmeal, almond nougat, hint of honey. The palate is sophisticated and uber elegant, a special wine.

2004	94	2018	$79.99	12.5%	
2005	95	2020	$79.99	12.5%	
2006	94	2020	$79.99	12.5%	

AUDREY WILKINSON

Audrey Wilkinson is a famous, old Hunter Valley winery, now in the hands of the Agnew family. Consistent wine quality from wonderful old vineyards and a cellar door with expansive views of the Valley add to their charm. They recently became winemakers for Pooles Rock and Cockfighter's Ghost resulting in a rapid improvement in quality and variety.
Winemaker: *Jeff Byrne*
Open: *Daily 10am–5pm, Debeyers Road, Pokolbin*
Ph: *(02) 4998 7411   www.audreywilkinson.com.au*

AUDREY WILKINSON
THE LAKE SHIRAZ   ★★★★★

Dusty plums, dark chocolate and darker notes of oak. This is for the long haul dense, intense but shy on the nose it unfolds on the palate with soft balanced tannins supporting even long red fruit flavours.

2010	90	2022	$35.00	13.5%
2011	87	2019	$35.00	13.5%
2014	94	2029	$80.00	14.5%

AUDREY WILKINSON
THE RIDGE SEMILLON   ★★★★★

Held back two years prior to release, avoids the very lean acidic style so you can easily see the development into lemon with the developed bottle aged lanolin and waxy aromas. The palate is poised walks between teens and twenties the acidity is youthful racy and vibrant with the ripe fruits wears fashionable clothes showing orange peel, green apricot, waxy lemon flavours. Drinking this suits poetry reading.

2011	93	2020	$25.00	11.0%
2012	90	2030	$25.00	10.0%
2014	94	2020	$45.00	12.2%

| Vintage | Rank | Drink | RRP | Vol Alc |

AUSWAN
Auswan Estate was formed by experienced Chinese wine marketers through the merger of Inspire Vintage and Australia Swan Vintage in 2013. They have 10ha of shiraz planted in 1908 near Angaston with their cellar door in Tanunda and a winery near the Riverland. They purchase from growers across South Australia and export a number of brands to China, Singapore and Thailand.
Winemaker: Ben Riggs
Open: Daily 11am–5pm, 218–230 Murray Street, Tanunda
Ph: (02) 8203 2237   www.auswancreek.com.au

AUSWAN
1908 CENTENARIAN ★★★★★
This comes from a century old vineyard in the heart of the Barossa with only 160 cases produced each year. Youthful appearance with a very deep colour and powerful aromas of ripe fruit, fresh plum and vanilla with savoury elements, black plum fruits, cola, tar, liquorice aromas. In the mouth very ripe silky dark plum fruits wed to fine tannins with a long core of sweet fruits finishing vanilla, star anise and five-spice. A power house Shiraz.

| 2012 | 90 | 2018 | $240.00 | 15.0% |
| 2013 | 90 | 2020 | $240.00 | 15.0% |

BAILEYS OF GLENROWAN
Baileys have deep red soils ideal for bold red wines, old vines and a history of making a rich style of red wine that has improved in recent years, with vineyard expansion and a new winery. Most is dry grown. Their Petite Syrah is the variety durif, picked earlier and treated differently to be a medium-bodied wine with ripe, juicy fruit where as the durif is picked riper and receives American oak. Paul is proof good viticulturists also make good winemakers.
Winemaker: Paul Dahlenburg
Open: 10am–5pm daily, Old Block Cafe: 12pm–2.30pm, Sat and Sun, 779 Taminick Gap Road, Taminick
Ph: (03) 5766 1600   www.baileysofglenrowan.com.au

BAILEYS OF GLENROWAN
ORGANIC SHIRAZ ★★★★
The organic shiraz has ripe black fruits with salty chocolate and smoky spiced oak in proud support. Grainy tannins

Vintage	Rank	Drink	RRP	Vol Alc

and dense sweet, juicy fruit meld on the palate and continue through to finish softly. Enjoy with venison sausages and red currant sauce.

2012	92	2022	$27.00	13.5%
2013	92	2024	$27.00	14.0%
2014	91	2025	$27.99	14.0%

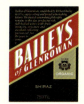

BAILEYS OF GLENROWAN
1920'S BLOCK SHIRAZ ★★★★★

The 1920s block shiraz is a stalwart performer in the cellar, thanks to the dry grown vineyard planted so long ago that provides the grapes. Small berries produce a deep yet brightly coloured wine that has a volume of soft round shaped tannins. The black plum fruit, chocolate-coated dates, liquorice and dried herb make for a smooth, complex finish.

2012	90	2028	$40.00	14.0%
2013	92	2033	$48.00	14.0%
2014	92	2024	$39.99	14.5%

BAILEYS OF GLENROWAN
DURIF ★★★★★

Mocha vanilla spice, and dark roasted oak notes with juicy dark plum and rich fruits to the perfumes. Ripe fruited and generous, the sweet oak builds a solid ripe back drop into this wine offering full bodied red grippy tannins, and the ability to age. Drink up to 20 years.

2010	90	2025	$25.00	15.5%
2012	90	2030	$27.00	13.5%
2013	92	2037	$27.00	15.0%

BAILEYS OF GLENROWAN
PETITE SIRAH ★★★★★

Cracking colour with purple fresh bright rim of a keeper. The aromas are bold graphite cola, tarry fresh fruit aromas. The palate is almost restrained after the nose, refined tension and balance of ripe fruit oak, real vineyard linear grainy grape tannins full bodied dark cherry and ripe black plum with a lingering plummy fruit finish. A very authentic made in the vineyard style with understated oak, very balanced.

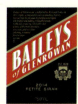

Vintage	Rank	Drink	RRP	Vol Alc
2012	91	2022	$27.00	13.0%
2013	94	2023	$27.00	15.0%
2014	96	2028	$27.00	15.0%

BAILLIEU VINEYARD
Baillieu Vineyard is located in Mornington at Merricks North. Planted in 1999, this ten-hectare, north-facing vineyard produces ripe reds in the regional idiom and appealing chardonnay.
Winemaker: Geraldine McFall
Open: Tastings at Merricks General Wine Store Daily 9am–5pm, 3458–3460 Frankston-Flinders Road, Merricks North
Ph: (03) 5989 7622 *www.baillieuvineyard.com.au*

BAILLIEU VINEYARD
PINOT NOIR ★★★★★

Strawberry, butterscotch oak and toasty fruits, with more masculine firm dry oak tannins framing the fruit, than many of this region. Fabulous flavour with confit of strawberry, fresh, cooked and patisserie styles.

2011	87	2016	$35.00	12.5%
2012	86	2016	$35.00	12.5%
2013	90	2020	$35.00	12.5%

BAILLIEU VINEYARD
SHIRAZ ★★★★

Raspberry, tomato bush, ripe to under-ripe character; liquorice black pepper aromas lead to an even palate, full up front with sweet raspberry fruit and a medium body elegant length, with a poised, fine tannins finish.

2008	87	2014	$25.00	12.5%
2009	89	2015	$25.00	13.5%
2012	89	2018	$35.00	12.5%

BAILLIEU VINEYARD
CHARDONNAY ★★★★

The soft generosity of Mornington is on display here with its ripeness. Aromas of nougat, and honey with cream, show that wine making plays a big part in the style, although a bit more restrained here than in 2010. The palate is initially silky and all that you can ask for from good

Vintage	Rank	Drink	RRP	Vol Alc

chardonnay, with middle fullness. The finish is subtle, layered and youthfully acidic in October 2012.

2009	90	2013	$20.00	13.0%
2010	92	2014	$20.00	13.5%
2011	88	2015	$25.00	12.5%

BALGOWNIE ESTATE
Established in 1972, Balgownie Estate has become one of Australia's great small vineyards, thanks to the firm style of its long-lived white label cabernet sauvignon and shiraz. Early releases of Yarra pinot are also exciting. The winery cellar door has spa in the Yarra Valley. Good value cellaring reds.
Winemaker: *Tony Winspear*
Open: *Daily 11am–5pm, 1309 Melba Highway, Yarra Glen*
Ph: *(03) 5449 6222* *www.balgownieestate.com.au*

BALGOWNIE ESTATE
BENDIGO CABERNET SAUVIGNON ★★★★★

Balgownie have captured cabernet characters of black currant, cherry and mint that are fresh and youthful. On the palate this wine becomes more nuanced, refined tannins and detailed thanks to the varietal structure that adds an extra dimension and powdery tannins. Give it a good decant if you are drinking it young.

2011	Not made			
2012	93	2026	$45.00	14.5%
2013	92	2025	$45.00	14.0%

BALGOWNIE ESTATE
BENDIGO SHIRAZ ★★★★★

Richly toasted oak with plenty of chocolate coated coffee beans, blackberry and a dose of black pepper. Fuller bodied and smoothly polished by a mocha oak regime. A baby, yet, give it a decade and it will reward you.

2011	89	2016	$45.00	13.5%
2012	95	2029	$45.00	14.5%
2013	91	2029	$45.00	14.08%

BALGOWNIE ESTATE
BENDIGO CHARDONNAY ★★★★★

Expressive stone fruit and citrus are crowned with nuts, cream, and an "Oh! So" polished palate. While 100% was barrel fermented and aged on lees, within the blend is a portion, which was fermented with wild yeast. The result is a gentle nougat refinement, a fine acid line and a chardonnay that glides through mid palate to finish long and fresh.

2011	88	2016	$45.00	13.0%
2012	92	2018	$45.00	13.5%
2013	94	2020	$45.00	14.5%

BALLYCROFT VINEYARD AND CELLARS

With Barossa shiraz and Langhorne Creek cabernet these wines play to regional hero strengths. Made with imagination and many subtle variations in the oak adding interest. The style is ripe and suits lovers of full-bodied reds. Tastings are by appointment, for 8 people maximum, with the winemaker, lasting 45 minutes.
Winemaker: Joseph Evans
Open: By appointment 11am–4pm
1 Adelaide Road, Greenock
Ph: (04) 8863 8488 *www.ballycroft.com*

BALLYCROFT VINEYARD AND CELLARS
SMALL BERRY CABERNET SAUVIGNON ★★★

For lovers of big reds. Dark chocolate fruit and oak, blackberry fruits, date and nutmeg clove spice. The palate is ripe rich structured and long with enormous drinkability. Candied cherry, red cherry and red plum, the flavours unfold long down the tongue with a soft finish of caramel and plum.

2009	91	2019	$44.00	14.5%
2010	91	2019	$88.00	14.5%

Vintage	Rank	Drink	RRP	Vol Alc

BALNAVES OF COONAWARRA

Family-owned and run, Balnaves of Coonawarra is on top of its game for wine quality, thanks to meticulously managed mature vineyards in the heart of Coonawarra and the long tenure of Peter Bissell in the winery. Good value here.
Winemaker: *Peter Bissell*
Open: *Weekdays 9am–5pm, Weekends 12pm–5pm, Pub Hols 10am–5pm, Main Road, Coonawarra*
Ph: *(08) 8737 2946 www.balnaves.com.au*

BALNAVES OF COONAWARRA
THE TALLY RESERVE CABERNET SAUVIGNON ★★★★★

A complex wine with both savoury and ripe fruits, in a web of dark berry fruits. Kirsch, ripe raspberry, paprika, celeriac, roasted acorn oak aromas with harmony. The palate flows, a luxury web of tannins and ripe berry flavours with subtle mint, hinting at things to come. Bridging tannins build chunky and gripping in youth.

2010	95	2025	$95.00	14.5%
2011	Not made			
2012	93	2027	$105.00	14.5%

BALNAVES OF COONAWARRA
CABERNET SAUVIGNON ★★★★★

Appealing tomato leaf, mint and roast meat aromas in a soft tannin, cola, tomato leaf, tobacco and roast meats flavoured wine. A good wine from a difficult year.

2009	90	2018	$39.00	14.5%
2010	92	2025	$39.00	14.5%
2011	85	2016	$35.00	14.5%

BALNAVES OF COONAWARRA
CABERNET SAUVIGNON MERLOT ★★★★

This is a lovely sweet fruited ripe wine with loads of appeal from its varietal bay leafy ripe black currant fruits, thyme and a lively ripe fruited palate with silky soft tannins and lots of noticeable sweet fruit flavours for short-term drinking.

Vintage	Rank	Drink	RRP	Vol Alc
2010	90	2016	$26.00	14.5%
2011	86	2014	$26.00	14.0%
2012	93	2018	$28.00	14.5%

BALNAVES OF COONAWARRA
CHARDONNAY ★★★

This has been created with complexity in mind and offers a lot. The oak personality is a classy vanilla and caramel barrel ferment with oatmeal crafted from lees stirring. Full bodied roaring flavours on release with lots of fruit intensity the wine maker has developed creamy lees and toasty dusty oak notes and full bodied massive fruit. A crossover from the old style power and simplicity into modern power and complexity.

2012	89	2016	$28.00	13.0%
2013	86	2016	$30.00	13.0%
2014	92	2017	$30.00	13.0%

BALNAVES OF COONAWARRA
SHIRAZ ★★★

This wine is distinctively shiraz; black berry and raspberry, dark spice with licorice from oak. The soft tannin medium bodied palate has a noticeable savoury edge with jammy ripe berry and violet fruit lingering on the finish.

2012	Not made			
2013	91	2020	$28.00	14.5%
2014	91	2020	$28.00	14.5%

BALTHAZAR OF THE BAROSSA

Balthazar is the brainchild of Anita Bowen who, with husband and wine industry legend, Randolph, created this richly evocative and flavoured label. Her career as a sex therapist adds spice to a story that can be told on wine quality alone.
Winemaker: *Anita Bowen*
Open: *Wine tastings on weekends at Small Winemakers' Centre, Chateau Tanunda, Stonewell Road, Nuriootpa*
Ph: *(08) 8562 2949* ***www.balthazarbarossa.com***

Vintage	Rank	Drink	RRP	Vol Alc

BALTHAZAR OF THE BAROSSA
SHIRAZ ★★★★

Aromas are dark berry fruits with strident tobacco oak notes. The palate starts ripe tannins plummy flavours soft middle palate ready to drink now flavours with a hot alcohol finish oak dries the finish.

2010	90	2022	$50.00	14.0%
2011	86	2017	$50.00	14.0%
2012	86	2018	$50.00	14.0%

BANKS THARGO

One of Coonawarra's smallest vineyards with 22ha planted in 1989 and most fruit sold to other wineries. These are rare releases only from the best vintages and in tiny quantities usually 600 to 800 cases. Regular trophy winners thanks to very low yields, they are excellent value for money.

Winemaker: *Emma Bowen & Shannon Sutherland*
Open: *By appointment. 217 Racecourse Road, Penola*
Ph: *(04) 0882 8124 www.banksthargo.com.au*

BANKS THARGO
CABERNET SAUVIGNON ★★★★★

This Bourneville cocoa St Estephe character cabernet with menthol dark olive dark fruited aromas. The palate is a deep dive in ripe red-fruited cassis and raspberry flavours framed by oak.

2012	95	2021	$23.00	14.5%
2013	88	2019	$23.00	14.5%
2014	90	2018	$23.00	14.6%

BANKS THARGO
MERLOT ★★★★★

Good intensity of merlot mulberry fruit with bay leaf and red capsicum aromas. Appealing density and length of flavour in the mouth with ripe fruit, big and butch with depth and power. Sweet fruited, cassis, and sweet cherry with more elements showing on the finish.

2010	93	2017	$19.00	14.0%
2012	92	2022	$19.00	14.5%
2013	89	2024	$19.00	14.5%

| Vintage | Rank | Drink | RRP | Vol Alc |

BAROSSA VALLEY ESTATE
Barossa Valley Estates Was formerly a cooperative of Barossa growers until purchased by the NZ based Delegats wine group in 2013 with positive results appearing almost immediately. The wines are fresher and more contemporary in style while maintaining the full bodied, soft, rich textured they have traditionally produced.
Winemaker: Michael Ivicevic
Open: Daily 10am–4.30pm
Seppeltsfield Road, Marananga
Ph: (08) 8568 6953 www.bve.com.au

BAROSSA VALLEY ESTATE
GRENACH SHIRAZ MATARO ★★★★★
This wine strikes a great balance, ripe while avoiding over-ripe. Aromas are liquorice, raspberry, thyme and savoury smoked meats, iodine seaside scents add a really classy complexity, resulting in reigned in ripeness rather than jam. Nicely chosen grenache, looking very fresh and modern. It is delicious in the mouth and the ripe grenache tannins are silky, sweetly round and generously mouth coating with fleshy middle palate flavour and equally proportioned tannin weight. A truly complex wine but really a definitive grenache despite the other varieties. The finish is cleaned by fine tannins with the grenache raspberry adding a final lingering perfume.

| 2012 | 88 | 2018 | $27.00 | 14.0% |
| 2014 | 96 | 2019 | $26.99 | 14.0% |

BAROSSA VALLEY ESTATE
SHIRAZ ★★★★★
This continues a theme of controlled ripeness; looking for the balance of freshness, purity and clean varietal expression with finesse that is distinctive to the 2014 reds from this label. The fruits flutter red into black with cranberry into raspberry and blackberry with the ripe fruits offset by the drying tannins. Rather jammy excess on middle palate flesh and fruit. It draws to a close with fruit and oak tannins and then the red fruits rear up and exert themselves on the finish. Tastes definitive Barossa and yet so drinkable.

| 2012 | 90 | 2018 | $27.00 | 14.0% |
| 2014 | 93 | 2018 | $26.99 | 14.0% |

Vintage	Rank	Drink	RRP	Vol Alc

BASS PHILLIP

Bass Phillip is among our leading producers. Genial, perfectionist owner, Philip Jones resolutely pursues low cropping via biodynamic viticultural practices to produce individualistic wines, including noteworthy rose, gamay, chardonnay and gewürztraminer. The pinot, in particular, is richly flavoured and textured on release and develops with aging.
Winemaker: *Philip Jones*
Open: *By appointment only, Tosch's Road, Leongatha*
Ph: *(03) 5664 3341* *www.bassphillip.com*

BASS PHILLIP
ESTATE GAMAY ★★★★

Solid fruit-driven wine, with complex aromas of red fruits, intriguing spices of bouquet garni and meat stock. This wine shows great personality, red berry primary fruit and subtle savoury, medium-bodied forthright mouth-filling flavour, with slick tannins and a smooth texture. The ingrained acidity makes for a food friendly finish. Not showy but a restaurateur's best friend for food matching.

2010	92	2016	$45.00	12.5%
2011	91	2017	$45.00	12.3%
2012	94	2018	$45.00	13.1%

BASS PHILLIP
ESTATE CHARDONNAY ★★★★

Bouyant style chardonnay for chardonnay hedonists. Bold colours. Honeyed, ripe fruited, oatmeal and yoghurt like lees creaminess, and old oak cedar aromas. The fruit is tropical, decisive ripeness, richly preserved pineapple, celebration cake, flavours with potential to grow more complete with two more years.

2011	90	2019	$65.00	12.4%
2012	93	2024	$65.00	12.9%
2014	92	2019	$65.00	13.3%

BASS PHILLIP
PREMIUM CHARDONNAY ★★★★

Intense generous aromas with a beautiful oak note rich and generous, oatmeal, Belgian white butter, spun sugar and caramel, honeyed, vanilla toffee almost confectionary. Lands in the mouth with silky richness, texture, balance and complexity, white nectarine and peach, seamless long and cleans up fine and mineral acids on the finish. For lovers of Meursault more than Puligny. Great balance.

2012	92	2019	$79.00	13.3%
2013	88	2016	$79.00	14.0%
2014	95	2022	$175.00	13.5%

BASS PHILLIP
ESTATE PINOT NOIR ★★★★★

Has delightful varietal aromas strawberry and red fruits with a fresh white mushroom. The palate has structure acid drive and energy carries the medium length of flavour, middle palate red fruits, appealing tension on the finish with white mushroom savoury.

2012	90	2018	$77.00	13.1%
2013	94	2034	$77.00	15.3%
2014	91	2019	$80.00	13.7%

BASS PHILLIP
PREMIUM PINOT NOIR ★★★★★

This has gravitas, refined perfume complexity, with dark fruits into earthy beetroot, savoury dried spice edge like harmonious oak. in the mouth knitted focus and complexity, sour cherry and violets floral top notes and a strong undercurrent of red fruits, taunt tannin acid balance that creates good even length. Needs time drink after 2018.

2012	93	2028	$165.00	13.5%
2013	96	2030	$145.00	14.9%
2014	93	2025	$175.00	13.6%

BASS PHILLIP
CROWN PRINCE PINOT NOIR ★★★★

Has a very deep colour which is not typical of the house style. Intense, with a rose floral edge to the strawberry fruit and a veal meat stock savoury edge. Medium body, even and good depth of fresh raspberry fruit on the middle palate and tannin weight with a good progression of tannins to the finish. A balanced style, with pinot tannins at their best.

2011	88	2018	$50.00	12.3%
2012	89	2020	$50.00	13.1%
2013	94	2023	$59.00	13.8%

| Vintage | Rank | Drink | RRP | Vol Alc |

BASS PHILLIP
RESERVE PINOT NOIR ★★★★★

A very complete wine with a layering of aromas; raspberry, red cherry into blue berry and more exotic fruits, new oak spices, incense, and finally showing bouquet garni dried oregano. The palate has silky tannins with weight, a savoury finish showing even drive and density of Grand Cru Burgundy with the added generosity of Australia. The cherry fruit is built on fine natural acidity, almost crunchy with silky three dimensional tannins weaving the fruit frame over your tongue and just needs time. Drink 2019.

Vintage	Rank	Drink	RRP	Vol Alc
2010	94	2025	$475.00	12.7%
2013	98	2045	$475.00	15.2%
2014	94	2026	$475.00	13.6%

BAY OF FIRES

Bay of Fires in Northern Tasmania produces a wide range of elegant Tasmanian wines, at affordable prices that can be easily found outside the island. The cellar door is worth a visit as you can also find the Arras sparkling wines.

Winemaker: *Penny Jones*
Open: *Daily 10am–5pm, 40 Baxter Road, Pipers River*
Ph: *(03) 6382 7622* *www.bayoffireswines.com.au*

BAY OF FIRES
PINOT NOIR ★★★★★

Deep colour for a Tasmanian pinot with a very complex aroma starting plum oak toast, reduction adds a savoury note. The palate is full on generous, deep flavours up front with a confectionary edge due to their brightness. Palate continues with red and black fruits with subtle whole bunch peppery top notes and oak support filling the luscious middle palate.

Vintage	Rank	Drink	RRP	Vol Alc
2012	87	2016	$49.99	13.5%
2013	90	2019	$42.99	13.5%
2014	92	2019	$42.99	13.5%

BAY OF FIRES
CHARDONNAY ★★★★★

Cool chardonnay white fruits gentle apple into nectarine with a gentle oak spice note like cinnamon lifting the interest a note. The honeyed leading edge to the palate is classy while oak spices and honey rushes along fruit weight holds the length, the "just there" oak flavours complicating flavour and supporting fruit length.

Vintage	Rank	Drink	RRP	Vol Alc
2012	91	2017	$49.00	13.0%
2013	94	2018	$42.99	13.0%
2014	93	2019	$42.99	13.5%

BAY OF FIRES
RIESLING ★★★★

Good, rich and floral more than citrus, rose and subtle musk with lemon citrus to the back of the bus in the aromas. The palate is bright fruited citrus and talc edged with good drive, lemon citrus intensity and mouth filling there is loads of fruit, clean balanced acidity and lemon sherbet that lingers.

Vintage	Rank	Drink	RRP	Vol Alc
2013	90	2019	$34.99	12.5%
2014	87	2019	$34.99	12.5%
2015	92	2022	$34.99	12.5%

BAY OF FIRES
SAUVIGNON BLANC ★★★★★

In the varietal zone tropical into passionfruit, with a cool edge of precise varietal herbs. The palate runs the race with a fresh start; even, silky texture, middle palate borders on creamy and stays racy pulling greener passion fruits tautness to tidy the finish.

Vintage	Rank	Drink	RRP	Vol Alc
2012	87	2015	$31.50	12.5%
2013	85	2015	$34.99	12.5%
2015	93	2018	$34.99	12.5%

BEKKERS WINE
McLaren Vale born and bred viticulturist Toby Bekkers produces exceptional shiraz and grenache from old vineyards in McLaren Vale. His wines are part of a new generation of winemaking moving towards fresher fruit flavours with more detail and softer texture.
Winemaker: *Emmanuelle and Toby Bekkers*
Open: *10am–4pm Thursday, Friday, Saturday (or by appointment)*
Aldinga Beach
Ph: *(04) 0880 7568* *www.bekkerswine.com*

BEKKERS
GRENACHE ★★★★★
Very vivid raspberry perfumed pink flowers floral scents that flow into oregano, dusty dark black berry fruit and orange peel. In the mouth a lean medium long fine tannin red fruits with oak tannins that dry chary and firm. A wine lovers' full bodied red for fire side drinking.

Vintage	Rank	Drink	RRP	Vol Alc
2014	90	2020	$80.00	15.0%
2013	88	2018	$80.00	15.0%

BEKKERS
SYRAH GRENACHE ★★★★★
A very modern style of big red with a lot of freshness; all the volume is turned up to create the house style. Showing red raspberry and mocha dark baked fruitcake, the palate is long silky grenache oaky and smooth with mature flavours cloaked in oak. Fine grained tannins star anise and charcuterie fennel seed on the finish with red grenache fruit richness.

Vintage	Rank	Drink	RRP	Vol Alc
2013	88	2019	$80.00	14.5%
2014	94	2018	$80.00	14.5%

BEKKERS
SYRAH ★★★★★
Very good colour, edge of cloudiness suggesting unfiltered. Black berry conserve and paste, liquorice and oregano aromas. The hallmark regional supple tannins frame ripe black berry flowing to the middle palate flavours, which are well crafted and regional while fine-grained shiraz tannins close the finish. Very sophisticated wine making style.

Vintage	Rank	Drink	RRP	Vol Alc
2011	85	2020	$110.00	14.0%
2012	85	2020	$110.00	14.5%
2013	90	2022	$110.00	14.5%

| Vintage | Rank | Drink | RRP | Vol Alc |

BEN'S RUN
Ben's Run is a low-yielding, Hunter shiraz vineyard. Owner, Norman Marran named the vineyard after his faithful kelpie, yet behind this rural façade lies an astute manager who is careful with his viticulture and winemaker selection. Quantity varies from 800 to 1000 cases of shiraz, sealed by Diam.
Winemaker: *Usher Tinkler*
Open: *No Cellar Door, PO Box 127, Broke*
Ph: *(02) 6579 1310   www.bensrun.com.au*

BEN'S RUN
HUNTER VALLEY SHIRAZ ★★★
Cinnamon oak and savoury plum fruit. Bright red fruit, with classic savoury plum and animale elements to the soft blackberry middle palate fruit.

2010	87	2016	$18.00	13.2%
2011	88	2017	$18.00	13.0%
2012	Not made			

BEST'S GREAT WESTERN
Best's Great Western in Victoria has a fascinating history and has recently enjoyed a run of very high quality releases. With vines planted from 1867 onwards, they reflect the best of Australian family-owned wineries. Respect for tradition with innovation to improve wine style. There are many elegant, medium-bodied supple red and white wines here. Their cellar door has a lovely atmosphere, thanks to its history and sense of place.
Winemakers: *Justin Purser and Viv Thompson*
Open: *Mon–Sat and Pub Hols from 10am–5pm, Sun 11am–4pm*
111 Best's Road, Great Western
Ph: *(03) 5356 2250   www.bestswines.com*

BEST'S GREAT WESTERN
RIESLING ★★★★
A florist shop in a glass with white and red flowers, a wet stone edge and very pretty. The palate is seamless, richly weighted it has integrated zest and white fruits very even long and complex with ripe fruit richness. Full middle palate, lemon myrtle like flavours, acid has finesse really well integrated, this will keep.

Vintage	Rank	Drink	RRP	Vol Alc
2014	93	2020	$22.00	11.5%
2015	94	2025	$35.00	12.0%
2016	94	2025	$35.00	11.5%

BEST'S GREAT WESTERN
BIN 1 SHIRAZ ★★★★★

Baby bro to bin 0 "this gas the house" style mid weight form with raspberry and raspberry leaf fruits sweet spices, walnut in the background. The fruit filled palate has the chimera herbal and raspberry flicker of the region, nicely weighted mid week drinking and fresh raspberry fruits in middle palate with a pretty spice into crushed road metal spice on the finish.

Vintage	Rank	Drink	RRP	Vol Alc
2012	90	2016	$25.00	14.5%
2013	91	2017	$25.00	14.0%
2014	89	2019	$25.00	14.0%

BEST'S GREAT WESTERN
CABERNET SAUVIGNON ★★★★

Fantastic value. Very pretty colour and very smart aromas, fruitful varietal cabernet blackcurrant blue berry leafy varietal aromas. The palate has excellent freshness length of fruit fine grained tannins, varietal purity, minerality, chalky tannins and even middle plate weight of dark fruit flavours. The winemaker stands in the vineyard not the cooperage here. Modernity is more fruit tannins and less oak tannins.

Vintage	Rank	Drink	RRP	Vol Alc
2012	90	2020	$25.00	14.0%
2013	89	2018	$25.00	13.5%
2014	94	2026	$25.00	14.0%

BEST'S GREAT WESTERN
BIN 0 SHIRAZ ★★★★★

Classic regional style, with reserve and focus black berry into raspberry and sweet spice. The palate is poised and muscular in the way of a marathon runner, not heavy textured with density of flavour, seamless tannins fresh balanced red fruits on the long palate of old vine shiraz in a network of perfume and spice, finishing unsweetened red fruit conserve understated now. Patience holds the key.

www.robgeddesmw.com

Vintage	Rank	Drink	RRP	Vol Alc
2012	95	2045	$75.00	14.0%
2013	96	2029	$75.00	14.0%
2014	95	2050	$85.00	13.5%

BEST'S GREAT WESTERN
PINOT MEUNIER ★★★★

Pinot family red cherry and floral berry fruit, with a mirepoix vegetal edge and overall subtle alluring complexities. The palate has lovely fruit weight and low key tannin balance to suit the vintage with berry fruit, a subtle vegetal edge to the mid palate and the finish is unformed and youthful, with red fruit flavours.

2008	88	2015	$60.00	12.5%
2010	92	2018	$60.00	12.5%
2011	87	2015	$60.00	12.5%

BEST'S GREAT WESTERN
OLD CLONE PINOT NOIR ★★★★★

This is a cracker! Justin Purser has made wine in Burgundy and this shows in the strawberry dried herbs, orange peel dried mushroom and oak spice aromas. The palate is ripe, rich texture from soft tannins, intense red fruit, very even and fine with a long thread of ripe raspberry fruits, the gentlest dried herb decorates and a youthful finish. This will age well.

2011	Not made			
2012	86	2018	$35.00	13.0%
2013	93	2028	$35.00	12.0%

BEST'S GREAT WESTERN
THOMSON FAMILY SHIRAZ ★★★★★

This is a dense rich wine, with complex vineyard-derived flavours of red cherry, preserved cherry and very fresh dark fruits with back notes of briar and earth. The medium full body is very long and even, with superfine tannins and mouth filling length of an even fruit and tannin structure with a fresh youthful finish. Fine Australian wine. Needs 12 hours decanting in its first decade and will easily age for 50 years.

2008	94	2028	$150.00	14.5%
2010	96	2035	$180.00	14.0%
2012	95	2050	$180.00	14.5%

| Vintage | Rank | Drink | RRP | Vol Alc |

BETHANY WINES
A friendly, small, family-run winery in a very historic section of the Barossa Valley. Their cellar door is popular with the locals and they offer a wide range of regional heroes.

Winemakers: *Geoff and Robert Schrapel*
Open: *Mon–Sat 10am–5pm and Sun 1pm–5pm, Bethany Road, Tanunda*
Ph: *(08) 8563 2086 www.bethany.com.au*

BETHANY WINES
EDEN VALLEY RIESLING ★★★★

Regional finesse, with a lemon into lime complexity and fragrance. The palate has well-balanced weight and length, fine with good fruit flavours balancing early drinking and mid capacity ageing. Flavours of lemon, gentle lime and talc, finishing long.

2013	86	2017	$18.00	12.0%
2014	88	2019	$18.00	11.5%
2015	90	2020	$24.00	12.0%

BETHANY WINES
SEMILLON ★★★★

Citrus peels, white fruited semillon notes with the usual youthful reserve, The palate is ripe, textural, balanced mouth filling youthful generous light bodied middle palate ripe flavours trails off on the long finish with lemon zest and white fruits. Value.

2012	88	2017	$18.00	14.0%
2013	83	2015	$18.00	13.0%
2015	88	2021	$20.00	12.6%

BETHANY WINES
GR SHIRAZ ★★★★★

Richly expressive of the vintage, plum conserve, dark dried spices into mocha oak, complex on release. The palate is rich black fruits, silky and plush tannins, generous fruit upfront and dark plum fruits with coffee and dark spice. Drink young.

2008	88	2018	$85.00	14.5%
2012	95	2034	$85.00	14.4%
2013	90	2022	$95.00	13.8%

| Vintage | Rank | Drink | RRP | Vol Alc |

BETHANY WINES
L&E RESERVE SHIRAZ ★★★★★
A serious shiraz, with plenty of oak showing plum, white pepper, fruit and cedar vanilla oak. In the mouth, youthful quality fruit and tannin balance with oak supporting the flavours. Fresh dark berry middle and sweeter oak notes that support the fruit with harmony and balance and a lingering red cherry.

2010	90	2025	$48.00	13.0%
2012	95	2022	$48.00	13.5%
2013	93	2020	$48.00	14.0%

BETHANY WINES
LATE HARVEST RIESLING ★★★
Fresh riesling aromas, floral, bath talc, rose, orange blossom and pineapple juice. The palate is intensely sweet in youth, tasting of unfermented grape juice with rich tropical riesling flavours of pineapple and mango, middle-palate intensity and drying acidity.

2008	85	2012	$22.00	8.5%
2009	86	2013	$22.00	9.0%
2014	90	2019	$22.00	12.0%

BINDI WINE GROWERS
By acclaim one of the greatest small producers in Australia. Bindi captures the flavours of their various individual vineyard sites through exacting grape growing, vine-by-vine decision making and winemaking that retains the essence of their sites. A very good vineyard with great winemaking.
Winemaker: *Michael Dhillon and Stuart Anderson*
Open: *No Cellar Door*
343 Melton Road, Gisborne
Ph: *(03) 54282564 www.bindiwines.com.au*

BINDI
QUARTZ CHARDONNAY ★★★★★
Spare and restrained with complexity on the edge. Minerality in the high quality, tight grained oak, lees and chardonnay citrus aromas. The palate has life. Drinks well young with elegance and refined flavours. Has enough white peach to justify drinking now and the pleasantly drying

Vintage	Rank	Drink	RRP	Vol Alc

phenolics both extend the food versatility and add quality and drive to make the palate long and interesting.

2012	94	2019	$75.00	13.5%
2013	95	2018	$75.00	13.5%
2014	93	2019	$85.00	13.5%

BINDI
'BLOCK 5' PINOT NOIR ★★★★★

This is a youthful complex wine. Red cherry, mineral with spices and subliminal toasty new oak notes. The palate is balanced, long and acidic in youth, and hints at its potential. The muscularity is in the length of flavours, the weave of fine acid structure and tannin. Time will unpack the lean line into a velvet glove.

2012	88	2018	$119.00	13.0%
2013	95	2020	$119.00	13.5%
2014	94	2022	$110.00	13.5%

BINDI
ORIGINAL VINEYARD PINOT NOIR ★★★★★

Solid greeting here of aromas like a firm handshake. The fruit is deep; full raspberry and red cherry. In the mouth, a firm line of youthful well-balanced and structured clean varietal red fruits with a lick of vanilla spice. The older oak helps fill the middle texture and weight, and acid adds length and impact on the finish where it adds freshness and length. Balanced broad and youthful.

2012	83	2016	$75.00	13.5%
2013	91	2019	$75.00	13.5%
2014	92	2021	$85.00	13.5%

BINDI
HEATHCOTE PYRETTE SHIRAZ ★★★★★

Very youthful perfumed red fruits and minerality, with a ripe sweep of very complete jammy fruit flavours. Closely controlled acid and soft youthful tannins, with a jammy red berry middle palate and firmness.

2012	94	2026	$40.00	13.0%
2013	93	2023	$40.00	13.5%
2014	90	2029	$40.00	13.5%

BIRD IN HAND WINERY

An Adelaide Hills-based winery, Bird in Hand takes local and Clare fruit, aiming high and delivering. The vineyard was planted in 1997 on 100 acres of ground set in a region known in the 1800s for its gold mines. Kym Milne MW is extremely experienced and has a gift for producing wine with depth and length of middle palate fruit that frequently see his wines in the winner's circle across many varieties.

Winemakers: *Andrew Nugent and Kim Milne MW*
Open: *Mon to Fri, 10am–5pm and Weekends and Pub Hols, 11am–5pm, Cnr of Bird in Hand & Pfeiffer Roads, Woodside*
Ph: *(08) 8389 9488   www.birdinhand.com.au*

BIRD IN HAND
M.A.C. SHIRAZ   ★★★★★

Wow. Fruit complexity starts with ripe red cherry into morello, black berry, various versions of Christmas cake and resin, toffee and spiced oak. In the mouth, a drink young well crafted, long palate with dark berry into fruit cakes with middle palate fullness. Fine tannins, mocha chocolate oak, yet the fruit never loosing flavour drive.

Vintage	Rank	Drink	RRP	Vol Alc
2010	95	2039	$300.00	14.5%
2012	96	2045	$300.00	14.5%
2013	94	2019	$350.00	14.5%

BIRD IN HAND
NEST EGG CABERNET SAUVIGNON   ★★★★

Very stylish with floral top notes into red currant, cranberry cabernet aromas that glide seamlessly onto your tongue with fresh red fruits, wild raspberry, bramble ripened and finesse with long flavours of cigar box and tobacco oak woven together. Classic and well made encompassing all of the positives and none of the negatives.

Vintage	Rank	Drink	RRP	Vol Alc
2010	90	2022	$95.00	14.5%
2012	93	2018	$99.00	14.5%
2013	94	2020	$99.00	14.5%

BIRD IN HAND
NEST EGG SHIRAZ ★★★★★
Red and black fruited raspberry brooding aromas, with a lower oak intensity that in previous vintages. The middle palate ripe fruits are succulent. Round, juicy and delicious, long, honest open fruits with plenty of layers of red and black fruit spices in oak. Classy young wine.

Vintage	Rank	Drink	RRP	Vol Alc
2011	Not made			
2012	95	2035	$99.00	14.5%
2013	95	2030	$99.00	14.5%

BIRD IN HAND
MT LOFTY RANGES MERLOT ★★★★
A bigger, well supported ripe red merlot style. Dark fruit and mineral spice with oak support to the ripe cherry fruit. The palate has a good line of dark ripe fruits, mulberry, fruit cake, mineral flavours and chalky tannins.

Vintage	Rank	Drink	RRP	Vol Alc
2011	88	2016	$40.00	14.5%
2012	92	2019	$42.00	14.5%
2013	89	2018	$42.00	14.5%

BIRD IN HAND
MT LOFTY RANGES SHIRAZ ★★★★
Lifted ripe red and dark cherry fruits; black olive and liquorice aromas of balanced oak, with youthful restraint. Lovely ripe fruited, dark cherry balanced tannins with mocha, choco oak layering vanilla into the ripe creamy berry flavour. Satisfying main course wine with enough tannin and oak sweetness to partner with any dark meat dish.

Vintage	Rank	Drink	RRP	Vol Alc
2010	89	2014	$35.00	14.5%
2012	91	2022	$42.00	14.5%
2013	94	2020	$42.00	14.5%

www.robgeddesmw.com

| Vintage | Rank | Drink | RRP | Vol Alc |

BIRD IN HAND
RIESLING ★★★★★

The aromas are subtle florals with a citrus lemon lime with spice. The palate is dry pineapple lime flavours with a musky lift, varietal vitality and good length and subtlety.

| 2015 | 96 | 2018 | $25.00 | 13.0% |
| 2016 | 90 | 2020 | $25.00 | 12.0% |

BIRD IN HAND
MONTEPULCIANO ★★★★★

A lot of perfume in the ripe black fruits with hand full of green herbs. Does not smell over ripe or stewed. In the mouth, silky tannins in a seamless length of berry fruits. Very rich, and a touch of herbs wed to quality tannins with long morish dark cherry flavours, and building in dryness with well managed grainy tannins. Another excellent wine from this winery.

2012	88	2018	$42.00	14.0%
2013	90	2018	$42.00	14.0%
2014	94	2019	$42.00	14.5%

BLACK WINES

Winemaker Robert Black was tempted by friend and now business partner James O'Neill to create and build a small range of wines under the BLACK label in 2014. With more than a decade winemaking between Orange and Mudgee his wines are driven by an appreciation of regional identity, tempered by friendliness and easy drinking approachability. Evident in all the BLACK Wines is Robert's individual winemaking style, softness and fullness, fresh clean flavours, elegant balance and supple mouth feel. Within the concept of a 'virtual' vineyard and winery Robert and James enjoy a freedom to produce and sell wines of their chosen style and region without being beholden to a particular variety or the vagaries of vintage.
Winemaker: *Robert Black*
No Cellar Door

Vintage	Rank	Drink	RRP	Vol Alc

BLACK WINES
SHIRAZ ★★★★
Ripe dark fruits and sweet oak notes flow into dark cherry and dark chocolate. The mid weight dark fruits have quite stern tannins plenty of middle palate complexity clad in vanilla oak and medium long dark fruits.

Vintage	Rank	Drink	RRP	Vol Alc
2014	90	2018	$24.00	14.5%
2015	86	2020	$24.00	14.5%

BLACK WINES
PINOT GRIS ★★★★★
Pear and chamomile fruit aromas with overall ripe fruit giving a good middle palate composed of fresh and cooked pears fruits, subtle spice and a slightly firm pear skin pith finish indicating it will age 2–3 years and partner food well.

Vintage	Rank	Drink	RRP	Vol Alc
2014	90	2017	$24.00	12.0%
2015	91	2019	$24.00	12.0%

BLACKJACK WINES
BlackJack Wines in Central Victoria's Harcourt area is a red wine specialist, producing small quantities of delicious supple wines, with energetic fresh fruit and subtle oak. The winery's Majors Line Bendigo Shiraz also offers substantial quality at a lower price point and is worth considering.
Winemakers: *Ian McKenzie and Ken Pollock*
Open: *By appointment only, LOT 2 Calder Highway, Harcourt*
Ph: *(03) 5474 2355 www.blackjackwines.net.au*

BLACK JACK WINES
BENDIGO SHIRAZ ★★★★★
The depth of expression is startling, elegant, bright raspberry shiraz berry fruits, olive and white pepper and well judged oak aromas. The wine is but a pup, and the vintage quality shines with effortless fruit flavours wrapped in excellent fine tannins showing length and fine balance. A slight sour raspberry edge to the fruit shows it was picked to perfection for aging.

Vintage	Rank	Drink	RRP	Vol Alc
2010	87	2015	$35.00	14.0%
2011	84	2016	$35.00	13.5%
2012	94	2024	$38.00	13.5%

BLACK JACK WINES
BLOCK 6 SHIRAZ   ★★★★★
Pretty spice, oregano like, leafy oily cool greenness to the nearly menthol wed to the red cherry notes in the aromas. A turnaround from the muscular and intense 2012 where the year suits the vineyard. The palate has the herbal edge of basil oil and oregano-like, with raspberry fruits and well-integrated oak with the tannins to hone a long stylish wine.

Vintage	Rank	Drink	RRP	Vol Alc
2011	Not made		$40.00	
2012	95	2029	$38.00	13.5%
2013	94	2026	$38.00	13.5%

BLEASDALE
Bleasdale is a superb old vineyard, with a number of great value wines across the full spectrum of Australian wine, including ripe-fruited soft tannin shiraz, blends and a local speciality, malbec, verdelho, as both a table wine and a superb 10-year-old liqueur style, with 18% alcohol. The National Trust listed cellar door is a gem, with a superbly preserved sense of the past, including a giant redgum grape press which will transport you back to the era of paddle steamers and full beards.
Winemaker: *Paul Hotker*
Open: *Every day, 10am–5pm. Closed Good Friday and Christmas Day 1640 Langhorne Creek Road, Langhorne Creek*
Ph: *(08) 8537 4022 www.bleasdale.com.au*

BLEASDALE
THE WISE ONE GRAND VERDELHO   ★★★★★
A pale mid-gold, 10-year-old; verdelho glace fruit, dried pineapple and serious cask aged. Refined sweet white style, with a rancio development and a decent rich middle palate with oak tannins to dry off. The finish is closer to white port and the older style white port to which the good old boys would add ice.

Vintage	Rank	Drink	RRP	Vol Alc
NV	92	2015	$16.00	18.0%

Vintage	Rank	Drink	RRP	Vol Alc

BLEASDALE
THE PETREL SHIRAZ CABERNET MALBEC ★★★★★

Looking good from the get go with a deep colour, fresh black berry, black currant and red fruit notes from the malbec fruits running seamlessly into cedar and oriental spiced oak notes. In the mouth, lovely weight, lively length and style showing plush tannins depth of flavour and even fullness, black fruited shiraz ripeness, red fruits, white pepper and piquant tannins to close the mouth feel on the finish.

| 2013 | 94 | 2020 | $30.00 | 14.5% |
| 2014 | 96 | 2019 | $30.00 | 14.0% |

BLEASDALE
FRANK POTTS CABERNET MALBEC ★★★★★

Based on cabernet (61%), yet the aroma is dominated by malbec's floral raspberry, rhubarb and red currant sappy lift and overall amazing complexity. In the mouth the silky tannins create an almost creamy texture to hold the intense, complex, jostling for position ripe fruit flavours, with excellent fruit length and flavour depth in a full bodied soft finishing red. The finish could be tighter, but with such complexity and texture it seems unfair to criticise.

2012	94	2019	$33.00	14.0%
2013	94	2025	$33.00	14.0%
2014	95	2024	$35.00	14.0%

BLEASDALE
GENERATIONS MALBEC ★★★★★

The challenge with this variety is to match the flavour to the perfume, a little goes a long way in a blend. Blue berry, raspberry, red currant and rose hip with a dark spice back drop. The palate has exceptional length, medium full bodied and balance with fragrant blue berry red fruits up front running long with a sappy juicy rhubarb edge to the finish.

2012	90	2018	$44.00	14.0%
2013	94	2017	$44.00	13.5%
2014	95	2023	$35.00	14.5%

Vintage	Rank	Drink	RRP	Vol Alc

BLEASDALE
THE POWDER MONKEY SHIRAZ ★★★★★
Simply put a lovely wine with drinkability flavours and complex harmony. Lovely colour and very regional lavish aromas deep dark fruit blue berry, crushed green herb looking like stems with mocha chocolate oak spice. The palate sings fresh ripe berry fruits beautifully wed to complex oak flavours a subtle stemmy pepper note holds the centre of the palate and the wine stays nimble thanks to fine tannins, fresh and delicate on the finish with lingering raspberry into savoury notes.

2012	96	2035	$70.00	14.0%
2013	93	2024	$70.00	14.5%
2014	95	2021	$65.00	14.0%

BLOODWOOD WINES
Rhonda and Stephen Doyle planted their pioneering Bloodwood Wines vineyard in Orange in 1983. They have a range of successful wines and styles, of which they are possibly best known for their delicious riesling. A must visit cellar door in the Orange region.
Winemaker: *Stephen Doyle*
Open: *By appointment only, 231 Griffin Road, Orange*
Ph: *(02) 6362 5631 www.bloodwood.biz*

BLOODWOOD WINES
SCHUBERT CHARDONNAY ★★★★
Oak spice complex fruits and focused, cashew and white butter. The sweeter oak notes join the fruit and bingo! The front palate bulges and then flies. The chardonnay presence is ripe white fruits, sweet brown spices and oak fleshiness in the middle palate.

2011	88	2016	$30.00	12.5%
2013	93	2017	$30.00	13.5%
2014	86	2018	$30.00	13.5%

BLOODWOOD WINES
CHARDONNAY ★★★★
Fresh and floral pears on brown sugar, gentle citrus, varietal purity with regional punch. In the mouth, good length stony acidity and gentle honey creamy lees play a supporting role in the mouth. As near to Australian Chablis as we go. Unadorned fruit with weight and length of the

Vintage	Rank	Drink	RRP	Vol Alc

vintage and Australian wine making style giving pears and white fruits and more silky generous mouth feel than the tightly drawn acid and fruits of Chablis.

2013	90	2014	$27.00	13.0%
2014	90	2018	$27.00	13.0%
2015	93	2019	$30.00	12.5%

BLOODWOOD WINES
ORANGE RIESLING ★★★★★

The light and tightness of an aromatic white in a cool climate. Talc, rose water, floral and subtle- an enchanting complexity of aromas. The palate has a drink now soft acidity wed to even long fruit with perfumed orange blossom, subtle pink grapefruit and then more floral top notes.

2011	88	2017	$26.00	11.5%
2013	93	2020	$29.00	11.5%
2014	92	2020	$29.00	11.5%

BLUE PYRENEES

Blue Pyrenees in the Avoca region of Victoria is now home to former Rosemount chief winemaker Andrew Koerner who has made his mark on wines from this large mature vineyard. Huge steps are being taken with red, white and sparkling wine styles and quality. The Richardson represents excellent semi matured value and quality.

Winemaker: *Andrew Koerner*
Open: *Mon–Fri 10am–4.30pm, Sat and Sun 10am–5pm*
Vinoca Road, Avoca
Ph: *(02) 9953 3690 www.bluepyrenees.com.au*

BLUE PYRENEES
CABERNET SAUVIGNON ★★★

Cola and menthol aromas lead to a soft, ripe easy drinking wine with interesting lemon citrus acid flavours in a dark berry generous middle palate. Appealing.

2011	88	2015	$20.00	13.5%
2012	83	2016	$22.00	14.0%
2013	87	2017	$20.00	14.0%

BLUE PYRENEES ESTATE
SHIRAZ ★★★★
Deep and complex spice notes in meaty shiraz, blackberry cola aromas. The palate is soft and ripe on entry, with deep middle palate flavours wrapped in appealing mocha chocolate oak. Blackberry fruit with a deep long structure and lingering red cherry.

2011	86	2014	$22.00	13.0%
2012	88	2016	$22.00	14.5%
2013	90	2018	$20.00	14.5%

BLUE PYRENEES
RESERVE SHIRAZ ★★★★
Concentrated aromas with blueberry, cola, maraschino cherry and granite mineral spice introduces a solid red wine. The palate is immediately generous, delivering ripe blackberry fruits with silky tannins and length of flavour. A cocktail of generous middle-palate berry flavours with appealing length and lingering maraschino cherry. Plump, powerful and medium bodied.

2008	90	2013	$35.00	14.5%
2009	89	2018	$50.00	14.5%
2012	91	2019	$40.00	14.0%

BLUE PYRENEES
ESTATE RED ★★★★★
Ripe fruited with primarily black and red-fruited edges of minty eucalypt and menthol central to the Victorian regional red styled aromas. The medium-bodied tight structure palate runs a gamut of red fruits, cranberry, raspberry and blackberry filling the middle palate with elegant tannins, medium length and even finesse.

2009	93	2026	$35.00	14.5%
2012	94	2020	$40.00	14.0%
2013	90	2020	$36.00	14.4%

| Vintage | Rank | Drink | RRP | Vol Alc |

BOREMBOLA WINES

Borambola Wines is located on a historic property, now host to this successful vineyard. The shiraz is particularly noteworthy, showing the Gundagai regional style; medium bodied, spicy and with significant tannins. The wine is named after a 1947 Melbourne cup winner that grazed the paddock later planted to vineyard in 1998.
Winemakers: *Chris Derrez & Lucy Maddox*
Open: *Daily 11am–4pm by appointment, 1734 Sturt Highway, Wagga Wagga*
Ph: *(02) 6928 4210 www.borambola.com*

BOREMBOLA WINES
HIRAJI'S SPELL SHIRAZ ★★★

Regional dried herbs, mineral brooding ripe red into darker fruits. Ripe fruit flavours with length and slightly tough tannins in youth wrapped around a solid middle palate with layers and depth of dark fruits and s firm tannins before the lingering raspberry fruit finish. For lovers of full bodied reds.

2011	86	2014	$22.00	13.0%
2012	89	2017	$24.00	13.5%
2013	89	2020	$24.00	13.8%

BOWEN ESTATE

Bowen Estate wines exhibit typical regional fragrance and tender "juicy fruit" flavours. At the southern, cooler end of Coonawarra, the Bowen family are one of the region's top producers, making wines faithful to their regional, varietal and vintage origins. Their vineyard is planted at nearly twice the average density with 4,000 vines per hectare which contributes to the style. Excellent value here.
Winemakers: *Doug and Emma Bowen*
Open: *Daily 10am–5pm, Riddoch Highway, Coonawarra*
Ph: *(08) 8737 2229 www.bowenestate.com.au*

BOWEN ESTATE
COONAWARRA CABERNET SAUVIGNON ★★★★★

A classic ripe year Coonawarra Cabernet. The essence of this wine is all about the fruit, lush black cherries and some tart redcurrants. However, there is some mint, dark chocolate and earth peeking through too. Velvety fine tannin, run long and coats the mouth, providing cabernet structure for the black fruit to hang off with oak richness filling in the gaps as a youngster. A fragrant wine that you can enjoy now or after a long rest in the cellar.

2012	94	2035	$32.00	14.5%
2013	88	2025	$32.00	15.5%
2014	93	2029	$33.00	14.5%

BOWEN ESTATE
COONAWARRA SHIRAZ ★★★★★

Very fragrant with toasty vanilla short bead oak underpinning the concentrated fruit. In the mouth, a juicy, beautiful drink young year with abundant ripeness, soft tannins, succulent, complex, more lo jubes, black berry and blue berry middle palate. Purity of flavour, balance, fruit sweetness and finely judged oak adding spices and subtle toast. This wine will benefit from a hearty roast with all the trimmings.

2012	90	2034	$32.00	15.0%
2013	91	2026	$32.00	15.5%
2014	93	2024	$33.00	14.5%

BOWEN ESTATE
COONAWARRA CHARDONNAY ★★★★

A richer style. Quality oak provides a spicy backdrop plus some flesh in the mouth for the ripe mandarin, peach and guava flavours topped with a dollop of rich cream. A light chill and some food would work well with this firm finish.

2012	85	2015	$23.00	14.0%
2014	87	2017	$23.00	13.0%
2015	87	2018	$24.00	13.5%

BOX GROVE
One of the first women graduates of Roseworthy in the 1970's and a Churchill Fellow, Sarah has been growing grapes in central Victoria since 1996 and making wine under her own label since 2008. Her speciality is Rhone varieties, Roussanne, Viognier, Shiraz, and the Italian varieties, Prosecco, Vermentino and Primitivo.
Winemaker: *Sarah Gough*
Open: *By appointment only, Box 86 Avenel*
Ph: *(04) 0921 0015 www.boxgrovevineyard.com.au*

Vintage	Rank	Drink	RRP	Vol Alc

BOX GROVE
ROUSSANNE ★★★★★

Fig and lime funky aromas with a savoury element make this an interesting food wine. This has a lively acid not often seen in roussanne. Subtle creamy and light bodied, with long, pear, fig and sweet lime flavours and lime tropical fruits to finish. Appealing texture.

2009	90	2016	$28.00	13.5%
2010	94	2019	$28.00	14.0%
2011	91	2017	$28.00	13.0%

BOX GROVE
VERMENTINO ★★★★

The savoury sesame seed elements add to the rock melon fruits with a palate full of summer laughter and an easy going quaffer style. Medium long, spiced apple fruits.

2011	90	2018	$22.00	12.0%
2012	88	2016	$22.00	12.7%
2014	88	2017	$22.00	12.7%

BOX GROVE
PRIMITIVO ★★★★

Licorice, and baked plum fruits aromas with an easy drinking soft round ripe palate of dark fruits and a savoury finish.

| 2012 | 91 | 2019 | $28.00 | 14.8% |
| 2013 | 90 | 2020 | $28.00 | 15.0% |

BRAND'S LAIRA
Purchased from McWilliam's by the Casella family who produce "Yellow Tail" in 2015 Brands is headed for change. The style is modern Coonawarra, uber-ripe fruit, very richly structured and powerful through to the finish.
Winemaker: *Peter Weinberg*
Open: *Weekdays 9am–4.30pm, Weekends 10am–4pm, Riddoch Highway, Coonawarra*
Ph: *(08) 8736 3260* ***www.brandslaira.com.au***

BRAND'S LAIRA
BLOCKERS CABERNET SAUVIGNON ★★★

The aromas are blue berry, sarsaparilla, wine gums and jubes. The palate is mouth filling, soft and round, where the middle palate is plump and full with dark fruits, rich flavour and soft tannins. A pleasant dry red in style.

Vintage	Rank	Drink	RRP	Vol Alc
2009	87	2018	$28.00	14.8%
2012	91	2017	$18.50	14.6%
2013	88	2019	$25.00	14.5%

BRANGAYNE OF ORANGE

Brangayne's vineyard ranges from 960 to 1,000 metres, making it one of the most elevated sites in the Orange region and helping to create intense varietally pure fruit flavours with delicacy. The district is at the forefront of Australian wines.
Winemaker: *Simon Gilbert*
Open: *Weekdays 11am–1pm & 2pm–4pm Saturday 11am–5pm, 837 Pinnacle Road, Orange*
Ph: *(02) 6365 3229   www.brangayne.com*

BRANGAYNE OF ORANGE
TRISTAN CABERNET SAUVIGNON SHIRAZ ★★★★

Very Bordeaux cabernet mineral and dark fruits with bandaid side notes. The palate is alive, more fruit full than the aroma suggests. The tannins are graceful, moving finely grained through the mouth while the red fruits have mulberry, blueberry and blackberry spectrum flavours. Pulls up fast.

Vintage	Rank	Drink	RRP	Vol Alc
2009	88	2015	$30.00	14.5%
2010	87	2013	$30.00	13.5%
2013	92	2019	$35.00	14.0%

BRASH HIGGINS

Former New York sommelier turned winemaker, Brad Hickey for Brash Higgins, is a producer of distinctive, ripe, full-bodied reds from Italian and French varieties.
Winemaker: *Brad Hickey*
Open: *By appointment only, 242 California Road, McLaren Vale*
Ph: *(08) 8556 4237   www.brashhiggins.com*

BRASH HIGGINS
NERO D'AVOLA AMPHORA PROJECT ★★★★★

Subtle youthful aromas white pepper white spice with red fruit. The palate has a dramatic soft tannin width, ripe cherry fruited, classic acid structure flavours into the spicy earthy complexity in the middle palate as the dark mat of tannins exert their gravity pulling the fruit into umami savoury broth territory without the bitterness.

Vintage	Rank	Drink	RRP	Vol Alc
2013	88	2018	$42.00	14.0%
2014	94	2019	$42.00	13.6%
2015	93	2019	$42.00	14.2%

BRASH HIGGINS
GR/M GRENACHE MATARO ★★★★

Subtle complexity fresh intensity of raspberry orange peel black licorice subtle spices. Grenache red fruit upfront into darker firmer tannins on the middle palate with the overall line of red fruits driving long in the mouth with medium tannins long flavours full bodied but not heavy finishes with savoury complexity.

Vintage	Rank	Drink	RRP	Vol Alc
2012	92	2022	$37.00	14.5%
2014	93	2018	$37.00	14.5%
2015	91	2020	$37.00	14.5%

BRASH HIGGINS
CBSV CABERNET SAUVIGNON ★★★★

The ripe fruit and oak is conventional in frame with black cherry, black currant fruits and vanilla oak. The palate works well, a grassy hay like herbal note that sits on the side with the smooth tannins gliding the black fruit effortlessly along in a generous ripe style. Long lived flavour with very even length and fresh acidity. The finish is ripe black currant, black berry, tobacco and currant juice and is firm and dry, and begs for a steak.

Vintage	Rank	Drink	RRP	Vol Alc
2010	90	2019	$37.00	14.5%
2012	90	2019	$37.00	14.5%
2014	90	2019	$37.00	14.5%

Vintage	Rank	Drink	RRP	Vol Alc

BREMERTON WINES

Bremerton have 290 acres at Langhorne Creek from which they select the best fruit each year and the balance is sold. A company on the move with a great cellar door and an increasing range of interesting varietals. Membership of the Bremerton Wine Society, entitles members to a discount of 20 per cent. Lunch 7 days a week and regional produce make this an important destination in the region.
Winemaker: *Rebecca Willson*
Open: *Daily 10am–5pm, Kent Town Road, Langhorne Creek*
Ph: *(08) 8537 3093* *www.bremerton.com.au*

BREMERTON
COULTHARD CABERNET SAUVIGNON ★★★★★

Intense aromas of black currant, dark olive, berry fruit with oak. In the mouth really good drinking. Open and juicy fleshy ripe black currants and fine tannins in fleshy fruit textures. 2,000 cases and sold only in independent retailers. The openness of the vintage and the winemaking style gives a special wine at a great price.

2008	86	2014	$22.00	14.5%
2012	85	2016	$22.00	14.5%
2013	93	2020	$22.00	14.5%

BREMERTON
SELKIRK SHIRAZ ★★★★★

This is a great drink off the blocks — not for keeping, just enjoying now. Plenty of toasty oak at the price with friendly mocha, chocolate, vanilla oak and ripe black fruits. In the mouth, a wealth of juicy fruits, silky, ripe plum and dark chocolate oak generosity. Not complex, but an ideal full bodied red lovers wine.

| 2012 | 92 | 2021 | $22.00 | 14.5% |
| 2013 | 90 | 2018 | $22.00 | 14.5% |

BREMERTON
OLD ADAM SHIRAZ ★★★★★

Aromas start ripe plums, cooler winter green herbs with a whisper of caramel oak and the biggest, darkest red wine colour. The palate is intense, fresh raspberry, red plum,

Vintage	Rank	Drink	RRP	Vol Alc

tangy cranberry like fruit elements add a sappy edge that keeps your mouth excited. Forgetting the fine, high quality silky, seamless tannins that, with the oak balance add a frame to the intense fruits and creates structure and length to this full-bodied wine.

2012	95	2022	$56.00	15.0%
2013	93	2026	$56.00	15.0%

BRIAR RIDGE

Briar Ridge is a boutique winery situated at Mount View in the Hunter Valley, drawing fruit from an extensive low-yielding quality company-owned vineyard. The arrival of former McWilliams winemaker Gwyn Olsen has lifted quality here. They typify traditional Hunter styles, especially the Karl Stockhausen signature wines.

Winemakers: *Gwyn Olsen and Karl Stockhausen*
Open: *Daily 10am–5pm, 593 Mount View Road, Cessnock*
Ph: *(02) 4990 3670   www.briarridge.com.au*

BRIAR RIDGE
STOCKHAUSEN SEMILLON ★★★★

A divergent style from the more correct Dairy Hill range. Appealing aromatics. Apple sorbet to the varietal lemon. The palate is a light bodied, classical semillon line of acidity, yet more round in the middle palate. Round and easy drinking with youthful generosity and flesh.

2013	90	2018	$26.00	11.0%
2014	91	2022	$28.00	12.0%
2015	93	2024	$28.00	11.0%

BRIAR RIDGE
DAIRY HILL SEMILLON ★★★★★

Classical Hunter semillon aromas in a lemon juice and mineral style. The palate is trim, taut, complex lemon citrus and lingering. A little forward compared to the 2014 at the same time. A faster maturing year on the face of it. Balances tradition and drinkability.

2013	92	2034	$35.00	11.0%
2014	96	2030	$35.00	12.0%
2015	94	2024	$35.00	11.0%

Vintage	Rank	Drink	RRP	Vol Alc

BRIAR RIDGE
DAIRY HILL SHIRAZ ★★★★

Deep dark berry fruits and tobacco oak in an expressive savoury shiraz, with cardamom and oregano spice in the regional manner. In the mouth, this is a winner; luxurious, soft round velvety tannins, ripe dark berry fruits with excellent length, middle palate depth and glider landing-like finish.

Vintage	Rank	Drink	RRP	Vol Alc
2011	94	2030	$60.00	13.1%
2012	Not made			
2013	96	2028	$60.00	13.5%

BROKENWOOD WINES

Brokenwood Wines remains true to its origins while having a flexible philosophy on expanding its range, based on the quality of differing East Coast regional varietals.

Winemaker: Stuart Hordern and Kate Sturgess
Open: Mon to Sat, 9.30am–5pm; Sunday 10am–5pm,
401–427 McDonalds Road, Pokolbin
Ph: (02) 4998 7559 *www.brokenwood.com.au*

BROKENWOOD WINES
SEMILLON ★★★★

Very shut down, a wet year Hunter nose with subtlety and a blank canvas with gentle juice and pulp notes. The palate offers pleasurable fruit weight length, soft acidity, a light body, middle palate length with lemon on the finish.

Vintage	Rank	Drink	RRP	Vol Alc
2013	90	2018	$25.00	11.0%
2014	94	2024	$25.00	11.0%
2015	87	2019	$25.00	10.5%

BROKENWOOD WINES
ILR RESERVE SEMILLON ★★★★★

An exceptional wine, as usual. Layers of aromas of fresh lemon, rain on asphalt on a summer's day and lemon butter. In the mouth, it is deeply flavoured, taut and long, with a blend of phenolics and acid, weaving a web of constrained beeswax, lemon and curd flavours.

Vintage	Rank	Drink	RRP	Vol Alc
2007	95	2015	$60.00	11.5%
2009	95	2019	$60.00	10.5%
2010	Not made			

| Vintage | Rank | Drink | RRP | Vol Alc |

BROKENWOOD WINES
CHARDONNAY ★★★★
Subtle understated white fruit delicacy and style with oak spice lifting the fruits into an appealing apple pie and crust. The palate is silky ripe smooth on entry fruits are ripe pear and nectarine mid palate then clipped acidity holds the fruit frame to the finish.

2012	88	2016	$28.00	13.0%
2013	89	2016	$28.00	13.0%
2015	90	2018	$28.00	12.5%

BROKENWOOD WINES
HUNTER VALLEY SHIRAZ ★★★★
A quality year and this wine has the style and character of the year. Red cherry, savoury miso umami and dried herbs lead the aromas. The medium-bodied palate is savoury fresh and the very fine grained tannins support the bramble, red plum, fruit long into the mouth, with a youthful acid clip in 2015. Good from 2017 onwards.

2010	90	2021	$40.00	13.5%
2011	90	2020	$40.00	13.5%
2013	93	2020	$40.00	13.0%

BROKENWOOD WINES
WADE BLOCK 2 SHIRAZ ★★★★
The style here is authentic less oaked and more reliant on fruit with the oak a careful and considered component. Red fruited and more vibrant than the usual suspects. The medium-bodied palate is long, bright red-fruited fine tannin acid balance making an elegant low oak fine tannin long age worthy wine.

2009	90	2019	$45.00	14.5%
2011	92	2020	$45.00	14.0%
2012	94	2024	$45.00	14.5%

BROKENWOOD WINES
GRAVEYARD VINEYARD SHIRAZ ★★★★★
This wine has the solidity of a classic, with seamless red fruit and fine oak and the balance tipping towards the fruit. The aromas start savoury with toasted whole grain bread, raspberry, red cherry, dried herbs and liquorice. The palate is a crescendo, starting with fresh berry, youthful slightly

grippy structure and medium-full bodied, mouth-filling red flavours to a deep finish, with firm caramel and dark chocolate dryness in youth. A subtle classic.

Vintage	Rank	Drink	RRP	Vol Alc
2009	94	2020	$150.00	13.5%
2010	Not made			
2011	93	2026	$150.00	13.0%
2012	Not made			

BROOKLAND VALLEY
Brookland Valley is situated in the heart of Margaret River in the Wilyabrup sub-region. The winery has a popular restaurant "Flutes" and a good record for quality wines.
Winemaker: *Ross Pamment*
Open: *Daily 10am–5pm, Caves Road, Wilyabrup*
Ph: *(08) 9755 6042 www.brooklandvalley.com.au*

BROOKLAND VALLEY
RESERVE CHARDONNAY ★★★★★
This has depth of nectarine, white fruit and high quality power from oak complexity leading to a full palate. In the mouth is starts with charm, really well integrated oak builds additional body into the silky texture with oatmeal led nectarine evenness showing excellent length and lingering oak toast.

Vintage	Rank	Drink	RRP	Vol Alc
2012	93	2017	$73.00	13.5%
2013	93	2020	$73.00	13.5%

BROTHERS IN ARMS
The Adams family have been grape growers since 1891 and built their winery in 2002. Langhorne Creek is home to the most velvety tannins in cabernet sauvignon in Australia. This label is often the most successful at capturing them within the Brothers in Arms wines. They also offer wines under Killibibin, No 6, 6th Generation and the Formby & Adams label.
Winemaker: *Jim Urlwin*
Open: *No Cellar Door P.O. Box 840 Langhorne Creek*
Ph: *(08) 8537 3070 www.brothersinarms.com.au*

Vintage	Rank	Drink	RRP	Vol Alc

BROTHERS IN ARMS
SHIRAZ ★★★★★
Deep brooding layered aromas with plum or Christmas cake coffee dark spice aromas. The fruits are plum, minty and dark fruits into dates flavours are wed to quality with fine tannins bridging the length of the palate to create a harmonious texture runs off reds fine tannins on the lingering fruit finish. Surprising elegance for such a big wine with great length of flavour.

2008	94	2018	$45.00	15.2%
2012	95	2025	$45.00	15.0%
2013	93	2020	$45.00	14.5%

BROTHERS IN ARMS
NO 6 SHIRAZ CABERNET SAUVIGNON ★★★★★
Hot year character puts this outside the usual deep richness. The aromas are rich fruit, Christmas pudding plums and dark brown spices touch of the rum and raisin chocolate. The palate is ripe fruited middle palate plums and dark spices, mouth filling flavours, sandy drying tannins finishes clove and nutmeg dark spices.

2006	90	2016	$24.00	14.5%
2012	91	2020	$24.00	14.5%
2013	87	2018	$24.00	14.8%

BROWN BROTHERS
Brown Brothers can entertain wine drinkers from novice to expert with ease, thanks to family ownership which has led the winery along the varietal path less trodden and through diverse vineyard holdings to the heights of wine quality.
Winemakers: Wendy Cameron, Geoff Alexander and Chloe Earl
Open: Daily 9am–5pm, 239 Milawa Bobinawarrah Road, Milawa
Ph: (03) 9817 0014 *www.brownbrothers.com.au*

BROWN BROTHERS
PATRICIA BRUT PINOT NOIR CHARDONNAY ★★★★★
The 2010 is their 13th release is whole bunch pressed and 100% malolactic fermentation and five years aging on yeast lees. This has a complex honeyed toast and brioche aromas, with an impressive harmonious palate with pinot noir strength and chardonnay finesse, soft textured, intensely flavoured the fine acid

Vintage	Rank	Drink	RRP	Vol Alc

carries the creamy rich oatmeal lees influenced flavours long in the mouth.

2006	91	2014	$45.00	12.0%
2008	92	2018	$47.00	13.0%
2010	94	2022	$47.15	12.5%

BROWN BROTHERS
PATRICIA SHIRAZ ★★★★★

Patricia can come from any region and is the best of the best; generally only 12,000–18,000 bottles are made with each vintage and not every year. The oak adds a lavish dimension against a blaze of red fruits with milk coffee, dried herb oregano and cedar into a flush of red fruit on the palate framed by high quality oak, ripe fruit flavours, silky tannins red berry plum fruits sitting amidst a sea of fine grained oak tannins.

2008	91	2022	$56.00	14.5%
2009	96	2019	$58.00	14.5%
2012	92	2024	$58.00	13.5%

BROWN BROTHERS
SHIRAZ MONDEUSE CABERNET ★★★★★

A unique to Brown Brothers blend and one of our great unsung heroes. With very appealing intensity of scented, ripe black fruit aromas, with a subtle tobacco edge. The palate's ripe and soft on entry, with a solid length of fruit; the tannins are firm, long and fine.

2005	90	2019	$40.00	15.0%
2006	90	2022	$40.00	15.5%
2008	92	2023	$40.00	15.0%

BROWN BROTHERS
PATRICIA CABERNET SAUVIGNON ★★★★★

Very powerful oak driven style, balanced like a dancer in her finest hour between black currant leafy youth and plum nutmeg cedar maturity in 2016. The plush silky tannins a weave of dark ripe dark fruits black currant fruit middle palate with nutmeg bay leaf earthy flavours with oak tannins drawing the ripe flavours out to a clean finish.

2008	92	2018	$65.00	14.5%
2009	93	2019	$65.00	14.0%
2010	90	2019	$65.00	13.5%

Vintage	Rank	Drink	RRP	Vol Alc

BROWN BROTHERS
NOBLE RIESLING ★★★★★

Only released in outstanding vintages this is delicious thanks to great fruit and bottle maturity. Big slightly acid and nutty aromas alongside the fresh lifted citrus riesling aromatics and classic botrytis orange marmalade, citrus and honey. The aromas follow through on the palate which is citrus marmalade, fresh apricot, concentrated and complex with a silky mouth feel and not over sweet thanks to acidity balances the sweetness to provide a subtle dry food friendly finish. It's not going to fall over anytime soon.

2007	Not made			
2008	90	2013	$28.00	8.5%
2009	93	2019	$28.00	9.5%

BUNNAMAGOO ESTATE
Bunnamagoo Estate is the NSW extension of the Broome pearl fisher Paspaley family. Comprising a 15-acre vineyard at 860 metres' altitude at Bathurst and a winery at Mudgee, with 300 acres of vineyard planted in 1995. Gradual refinement of the vineyard and winemaking styles has evolved, thanks to Robert Black's desire to produce friendly, approachable wines with a fine structure and layered flavours. Winery tours are available and a short film festival is held each March.
Winemaker: *Robert Black*
Open: *Daily 10am–4pm, Henry Lawson Drive, Mudgee*
Ph: *(02) 6373 3046 www.bunnamagoowines.com.au*

BUNNAMAGOO ESTATE
1827 HANDPICKED CHARDONNAY ★★★★★

Finely balanced with the white fruits fresh cut pear and apple subtle oatmeal wine making inputs and understated oak aromas. In the mouth very good wine making is evident honeyed silky chardonnay texture, very well balanced oak, subtle whisper of lees and middle plate fullness medium length with overriding refinement.

2012	88	2015	$39.95	12.0%
2013	93	2019	$39.95	12.5%
2014	90	2017	$39.95	12.5%

BUNNAMAGOO ESTATE
CHARDONNAY ★★★
Vineyards from Mudgee to Orange contribute unique fruit qualities very helpful for modern chardonnay styles such as this. The white fruits are in the caramel stone fruit with spice range while in the mouth drinkability roundness and middle palate fruit with a silky medium flavour length.

Vintage	Rank	Drink	RRP	Vol Alc
2013	90	2016	$21.95	13.5%
2014	84	2016	$21.95	13.5%
2015	86	2017	$21.95	13.0%

BURTON McMAHON
From two of Australia's most exciting young winemakers – Matt Burton at Gundog Estate and Dylan McMahon from Seville Estate comes Burton McMahon. It is the culmination of two winemaker friends and is focused on limited releases of small batch Chardonnay and Pinot Noir from Victoria. The wines can be tasted at Gundog Estate in the Hunter Valley.
Winemakers: *Dylan McMahon and Matt Burton*
Open: *Daily 10am–5pm, 101 McDonalds Road, Pokolbin*
Ph: *(02) 4998 6873*
www.gundogestate.com.au/burtonmcmahon

BURTON McMAHON
SYME VINEYARD PINOT NOIR ★★★★★
For 2015 they have added the source of the wine as the Syme vineyard. Without the handle of dominant aromas from oak or fruit it is easy to over look the deep harmony of strawberry fruit aromas in this wine. The red cherry fruited palate has stalk spicy tannins under a velvet coat of red fruits with length and gentle whole bunch spice notes to finish.

Vintage	Rank	Drink	RRP	Vol Alc
2014	93	2023	$36.00	13.0%
2015	90	2022	$36.00	13.6%

| Vintage | Rank | Drink | RRP | Vol Alc |

BURTON McMAHON
D'ALOISIO'S VINEYARD CHARDONNAY ★★★★★

Aromas are complex youthful white fruits, struck match and smokey bacon oak toast. The palate is full, balanced lovely fruit weight and freshness pears and white fruits chardonnay flavours with middle palate punch and youthful firm finish with lingering fruits and oak spice. Full bodied and burgundy like.

| 2014 | 92 | 2019 | $30.00 | 13.0% |
| 2015 | 90 | 2022 | $30.00 | 13.6% |

BY FARR

By Farr is produced by former Bannockburn winemaker, Gary Farr and his son, Nick. These are distinctive, small quantity, handcrafted Geelong wines made along Burgundian lines, from vines planted at a higher-than-average density for Australia.

Winemaker: *Nick Farr*
Open: *No Cellar Door, P.O. Box 72, Bannockburn*
Ph: *(03) 5281 1733 www.byfarr.com.au*

BY FARR
CHARDONNAY ★★★★★

This has great style and complexity, vanilla oatmeal malt with a fine weave of fruit with gentle herbal tea oak. The palate is youthfully fine with good line from acidity silky running long, fine even with a great-layered finish, barrel ferment at the end.

2013	95	2020	$76.00	13.0%
2014	95	2019	$76.00	13.0%
2015	93	2019	$76.00	13.0%

BY FARR
VIOGNIER ★★★★★

A mere pup in 2016 with savoury older oak spices and the early picked winemakers stamp all over it; understated power in youth with a delicate touch. Given 2 years from vintage and you will have a unique style, power and drive, concentration and balance with subtle peach, apricot with fine flavours and no oily heaviness.

2013	92	2019	$61.00	12.0%
2014	94	2019	$61.00	12.0%
2015	94	2022	$61.00	12.5%

Vintage	Rank	Drink	RRP	Vol Alc

BY FARR
FARR SIDE PINOT NOIR ★★★★★
Needs a decant to bring it into balance as on opening these are a bit confounding; fruit power with what at first seems green stemmy, the latter unfolds into a different and decisive style. The fruit length, balance shows restrained power on the palate and is full in the middle palate with long flavours with the stemmy spice adding to the fruit.

Vintage	Rank	Drink	RRP	Vol Alc
2012	94	2022	$68.00	13.5%
2013	95	2024	$80.00	14.0%
2014	93	2024	$80.00	14.0%

BY FARR
SHIRAZ ★★★★★
Medium bodied with spicy complexity, aromas ascend as if climbing a mountain; black berry blue fruits spices then smoked meats creates the peak. The palate is an understated and appealing weave of bright fruits and well judged quality oak with oregano savoury to finish. Well-balanced medium bodied savoury.

Vintage	Rank	Drink	RRP	Vol Alc
2012	92	2018	$55.00	13.5%
2013	92	2022	$61.00	13.5%
2014	92	2022	$61.00	13.5%

BY FARR
TOUT PRES PINOT NOIR ★★★★★
Amazing wine and an absolute joy to drink. Strawberry in as many ways as you can recall from fresh, wild some green ones and some confectionary with luscious oak notes in the back drop supporting the array of fruits. This is majestic, it is rich in flavour not heavy with mouth filling length tannin finesse flavour complexity, acid freshness balance and flavour complexity and very complete for a young wine. Simply magnificent — it was truly hard to put down the glass.

Vintage	Rank	Drink	RRP	Vol Alc
2011	96	2021	$110.00	13.5%
2012	95	2022	$110.00	13.0%
2013	97	2029	$110.00	13.5%

BY FARR
SANGREAL PINOT NOIR ★★★★★
Dive right in — ripe fruit notes from rose, raspberry and blueberry into earthy and chocolaty back drop. In the mouth this is ripe generous fruit, more dainty textured than the more expensive Tout Pres with elegant even

Vintage	Rank	Drink	RRP	Vol Alc

length of flavours, runs long, a racy but delicate acidity helps the finish into food friendly freshness.

2012	95	2028	$75.00	14.0%
2013	90	2019	$80.00	13.0%
2014	93	2025	$80.00	13.0%

Sangreal by Farr
PINOT NOIR 2013

CAILLARD WINE

Australia's man about wine, Andrew Caillard MW, applies his intelligence and experience to Caillard, to great effect, making an excellent version of Mataro that seems very well suited to the Barossa and modern red wine. It's a sensitively made example of a variety with tough tannins. Andrew has enlarged his offering recently to include a shiraz and a cabernet sauvignon.
Winemaker: Andrew Caillard MW
Open: No Cellar Door, 5 Annesley Street, Leichhardt
Ph: (02) 9560 5465 *www.caillardwine.com*

CAILLARD WINE
MATARO ★★★★★

Captures the pastille red fruits intensity of mataro, like a fresh raspberry with a mineral black tea oak. The palate has reigned in the tannins on previous years pumped up the fruit freshness so the palate starts ripe fruit, black cherry, raspberry rich red fruits, fine tannins and holds its line to cover the entire palate. Immediately engaging firm fine tannins run the length of the palate and gently dry the finish. The best of the line with the purest fruit flavours and finest tannins.

| 2013 | 90 | 2023 | $50.00 | 14.5% |
| 2014 | 95 | 2024 | $55.00 | 14.2% |

Caillard Mataro 2014

CAILLARD WINE
SHIRAZ ★★★★★

A pleasure to drink young, balances Barossa richness without over stepping the mark. Inviting complexity with red fruits, minerally edge of chocolate warm brown spice butterscotch oak. Lively ripe cherry fruits threaded together with supple long fine tannins that carry the ripeness into the middle mouth held to a focused length of very fine tannins with middle palate fullness and a clean finish.

| 2013 | 90 | 2020 | $50.00 | 14.8% |
| 2014 | 93 | 2022 | $55.00 | 14.1% |

2013 CAILLARD SHIRAZ

CALABRIA FAMILY WINES

Calabria Family Wines formerly known as West End is owned by Bill Calabria, one of the few wine industry owners who does not drink wine. Calabria is a brand within this successful company, which is a solid resource for value for money wines, excellent durif and botrytis semillon. During 2013–15 they expanded their ranges and increased quality very successfully.
Winemakers: Bill Calabria, Tony Steffania, Emma Norbiato and Jeremy Nascimben
Open: Weekdays 8.30am–5pm, Weekends 10am–4pm, 1283 Brayne Road, Griffith
Ph: 02 6969 0800   www.westendestate.com.au

CALABRIA FAMILY WINES
THREE BRIDGES DURIF ★★★★★

A mixture of quality oak, red plums and creamy vanilla oak. Starts very fine comprising of sweet fruit with silky length and a very refined blanket of tannins that cloaks the palate in a medium long finish.

Vintage	Rank	Drink	RRP	Vol Alc
2012	94	2024	$24.95	14.5%
2013	90	2022	$25.00	14.5%
2014	88	2020	$25.00	14.5%

CALABRIA FAMILY WINES
SAINT MACAIRE ★★★

A very rare variety that we will see more of as the planet warms as it is a late ripener. Was extensively planted in Bordeaux until 1850 and very popular in the 16th century onwards for the English market. Smells similar to petit verdot with a ripe sarsaparilla into tarry with a leafy note note and coconut butterscotch oak. The palate is sarsaparilla blue berry into fleshy purple and a floral top note with a vibrant fleshy purple fruit finish with the cabernet family tannins adding a grainy dryness.

Vintage	Rank	Drink	RRP	Vol Alc
2013	90	2017	$15.00	13.5%
2014	Not made			
2015	89	2019	$15.00	13.0%

| Vintage | Rank | Drink | RRP | Vol Alc |

CAMPBELLS
Campbells are Rutherglen producers who have moved with the times and make some fine red and white wines as well as superb traditional North East Victorian fortifieds.

Winemaker: Colin Campbell
Open: Mon to Sat 9am–5pm, Sun 10am–5pm, Murray Valley Hwy, Rutherglen
Ph: (02) 6032 9458 *www.campbellswines.com.au*

CAMPBELLS WINES
THE BARKLY DURIF ★★★★★

Ripe, big, bold and complete with soft tannin, ripe flavours and plenty of time to run. The dark plum fruit has dates and prune aromatic complexity. The palate is velvety soft tannins, raspberry jam tart fruits with a solid full body. Think cherry pie middle palate, and closes with dried dark spices and tarry fruits.

Vintage	Rank	Drink	RRP	Vol Alc
2011	Not made			
2012	90	2019	$60.00	14.0%
2013	95	2023	$60.00	14.0%

CAMPBELLS WINES
THE SIXTIES BLOCK CABERNET SAUVIGNON SHIRAZ TEMPRANILLO CARIGNAN ★★★★

A generous well priced wine with red cherry ripeness and enough tannin to be food friendly. Very fresh, polished, multilayered dark berries and black fruits, savoury oak spice, pepper and mocha oak. Floral influences, juicy ripe fruit middle with floral scents soft tannins create a long frame for the orchestra of fruits.

Vintage	Rank	Drink	RRP	Vol Alc
2011	93	2016	$30.00	12.5%
2012	92	2018	$30.00	13.0%
2013	94	2020	$32.00	14.5%

CAMPBELLS WINES
THE BROTHERS SHIRAZ ★★★★

Quality oak, cardamom, vanilla, fine grained and shy red berry fruit suggesting latent power, longevity and understatement. The palate has structure and depth with the flavours hinting at their capacity to age. Needs time to soften the crunchy, chalky tannins and weave the acid into what will become a long, plummy, serious firm-finishing red.

2011	Not made			
2012	Not made			
2013	93	2029	$60.00	14.5%

CAPE JAFFA

Planted in 1993 by the Hooper family and run by the next generation's team Anna making wine and Derek dealing with the world. Run on biodynamic and sustainable principles. With the maritime climate exerting a strong cooling effect on the limestone soils and vines the wines have ripe fruit and fine tannins.

Winemaker: Anna Hooper
Open: Daily 11am–4pm
459 Limestone Coast Road
Mount Benson
Ph: (08) 8768 5053 *www.capejaffawines.com.au*

CAPE JAFFA
EPIC DROP SHIRAZ ★★★★★

Epic by name and by nature. For lovers of full bodied reds with ripe raspberry, chocolate, and tobacco complexity. The palate has fruit drive with red cherry, cola, and modest tannins that are typical of the year, yet fleshy and full bodied in the middle palate. Well balanced and well handled given the growing season.

2010	90	2017	$28.00	14.5%
2012	90	2019	$29.00	14.5%
2013	91	2021	$29.00	15.0%

CAPE JAFFA
LA LUNE SHIRAZ ★★★★
For lovers of full bodied reds. Black cherry, blackberry and raspberry fruits that smells ripe, fresh and vibrant. The palate is soft, filled with generous ripe fruits and a full-bodied shapely and fresh touch of understated mocha vanilla with freshness.

Vintage	Rank	Drink	RRP	Vol Alc
2012	87	2017	$39.00	14.5%
2013	90	2018	$60.00	14.5%

CAPE MENTELLE
Cape Mentelle has mature, low-cropping vines producing stylish Margaret River wines. The recent wines are more sophisticated, well-balanced, concentrated and supple when young. The chardonnay, cabernet sauvignon and shiraz have the structure to age well. This winery regularly holds a "must attend" cabernet benchmark tasting.
Winemakers: *Robert Mann, Evan Thompson and Paul Callaghan*
Open: *Daily 10am–4.30pm, 331 Wallcliffe Road, Margaret River*
Ph: *(08) 9757 0888 www.capementelle.com.au*

CAPE MENTELLE WINES
WALLCLIFFE SAUVIGNON BLANC SEMILLON ★★★★★
Appealing richness with coconut macaroon with white fruits to the perfumes. The palate is alive with great drive of fruit and acidity. Very long, full and even, it has fleshy white peach flavours and lingers with subtle fresh green herbs.

Vintage	Rank	Drink	RRP	Vol Alc
2011	95	2022	$44.00	13.0%
2012	93	2023	$45.99	13.0%
2013	94	2018	$44.99	13.0%

CAPE MENTELLE WINES
CHARDONNAY ★★★★★
Yellow peach aromas with cantaloupe and the exquisite balance of quality honeyed oak. The full-bodied palate is rich, full, even and generous with quality oak and nougat flavours. A full-bodied intense and complex wine with balance that will see it fit in anywhere. Use the purity and freshness of Margaret River to build a complex wine.

Vintage	Rank	Drink	RRP	Vol Alc
2012	90	2017	$42.00	13.0%
2013	93	2019	$45.99	13.0%
2014	95	2019	$46.24	13.0%

CAPE MENTELLE WINES
SHIRAZ ★★★★★

The regional freshness meets ripe blackberry in complex subtle nuanced fruits, dark spices and oak with a mouthfilling middle palate. The tannins are refined and seamlessly wed to the ripe fruits.

2011	89	2018	$40.00	13.5%
2012	93	2029	$39.00	13.5%
2013	93	2020	$46.24	14.0%

CAPE MENTELLE WINES
ZINFANDEL ★★★★

Perfumes of berry fruits and black forest cake, and dark plum into black cherry. The tannins are very fine. The middle palate is black currant and black cherry rich, and the finish is firm and dry. Drink now with ribs or keep 6 years.

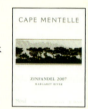

2011	93	2027	$55.00	14.5%
2012	94	2029	$59.00	14.5%
2013	92	2023	$50.00	14.5%

CAPE MENTELLE WINES
WILYABRUP CABERNET SAUVIGNON MERLOT CABERNET FRANC ★★★★★

A very solid wine with fresh just-ripe fruits showing a tobacco, red berry, sappy cranberry fruit and leafy, dark, dusty fruit aroma both savoury and dark berry fresh. The palate is restrained and complex, long and needs time. Fresh cranberry and dark berry fruit, freshening acids are firm and the fruit is elemental, long with Bordeaux-like length and structure. Very promising wine.

2010	89	2020	$49.00	13.0%
2011	90	2028	$49.00	13.5%
2012	95	2027	$52.00	13.5%

CAPE MENTELLE WINES
MARGARET RIVER CABERNET SAUVIGNON ★★★★★

Gentle and diffident, aloof but packing a wallop. Complex black currant and dark cherry roasted meats and fruit spices aromas lead to a palate with al dente finely wrought tannins and fine dark berry fruit. Structured long cabernet elegance, personified by the black currants trapped in a long web of fine tannins.

Vintage	Rank	Drink	RRP	Vol Alc
2011	94	2034	$90.00	13.5%
2012	93	2035	$91.99	14.0%
2013	96	2032	$94.79	13.5%

CAPEL VALE
Capel Vale has recently revisited its vineyard origins and has emerged with new labels reflecting a delicious selection based on its vineyards and the cool-climate regions of southwest Western Australia.
Winemakers: *Daniel Hetherington*
Open: *daily 10am–4pm, 118 Mallokup Road, Capel*
Ph: *(08) (08) 9727 1986 www.capelvale.com*

CAPEL VALE
WHISPERING HILL RIESLING ★★★★★
Shy spring flowers, bath bomb talc, lemony in youth, with a concentrated stone fruit densely structured palate. Lemony acids ring the dense fruit and hold the apple blossom and pithy stone fruits to task. Needs a couple of years.

Vintage	Rank	Drink	RRP	Vol Alc
2012	92	2022	$33.00	11.0%
2013	90	2023	$33.00	11.5%
2014	Not made			

CAPEL VALE
MARGARET RIVER CABERNET SAUVIGNON ★★★
This is one of Capel Vale's Regional Series. A generous handful of fresh garden herbs adds interest to the red currant fruit that also has an exotic spice blend. Some gentle grainy tannins and a juicy mid palate complete the picture.

Vintage	Rank	Drink	RRP	Vol Alc
2012	87	2018	$25.00	14.0%
2013	87	2017	$26.95	14.0%
2014	86	2018	$26.95	14.0%

CAPEL VALE
WHISPERING HILL SHIRAZ ★★★
Purple hued in the glass, Whispering Hill Shiraz opens to caramel, pepper, black olive, sage and gamey notes on the red cherry fruit nose. Not quite full bodied, it is an elegant mouthful with the alcohol giving a lift to that pepper prettiness and dark sweet chocolate finish. Drink it now or hold for the midterm.

2011	93	2018	$55.00	14.5%
2012	93	2019	$55.00	14.0%
2014	92	2020	$54.95	14.5%

CARILLION
The efforts of Geologist Dr John Davis have paid off; ideal wine growing localities along with the work of John's son Tim Davis, have resulted in fine cool climate wines. Available at the Ferment in Orange. Wines drawn from grapes grown on Boree Lane.
Winemaker: *Tim Davis*
Open: *Thursday–Monday 10am–5pm, 749 Mount View Road, Mount View NSW 2325*
Ph: *(02) 4990 7535 www.tallaveragrove.com.au*

CARILLION
THE CRYSTALS CHARDONNAY ★★★★★
Gold Medal at the 2015 Orange regional wine show. Nutty fresh oak evokes quality in the aromas. The palate is big without being heavy. The silky texture flows wide and long with the gentle complexity of good chardonnay, creamy vanilla with butter, nutty, and nougaut on the finish.

| 2013 | 90 | 2016 | $35.00 | 13.0% |
| 2014 | 92 | 2017 | $35.00 | 13.0% |

CARILLION
ESTATE GROWN CABERNET SAUVIGNON MERLOT ★★★★★
Blackcurrant and black olive briar seaweed like aromas with a black currant cabernet fruit, in a fresh medium long finish.

| 2010 | 93 | 2018 | $22.00 | 14.0% |
| 2012 | 89 | 2016 | $19.00 | 13.5% |

Vintage	Rank	Drink	RRP	Vol Alc

CASA FRESCHI
Casa Freschi thinks outside the square, making tiny quantities of intriguing, high-quality wines. Owner and trained winemaker, David Freschi draws from Langhorne Creek and the Adelaide Hills near Mt Lofty where his vineyard is planted at high density. Combined with high altitude, this brings intensity without heaviness to his white wines.
Winemaker: David Freschi
Open: No Cellar Door, PO Box 45 Ridge Road, Summertown
Ph: (08) 8390 3232 www.casafreschi.com.au

CASA FRESCHI
ALTEZZA ADELAIDE HILLS CHARDONNAY ★★★★
The aromas are complex with a mix of wine maker and fruit derived elements, baked apple, fresh apple, subtle pineapple and gentle honeyed aromas that suggest hazel nut will come in town. The palate has creamy texture, considerable concentration of fruit richness, delicate acids that sustain and refresh the flavour, and a long palate with hazelnut oatmeal flavours in the finish.

2007	92	2014	$45.00	14.0%
2011	89	2016	$45.00	12.5%
2012	94	2016	$45.00	12.5%

CASA FRESCHI
LA SIGNORA NEBBIOLO SHIRAZ MALBEC ★★★★★
An unlikely blend that works. The sappy malbec sits well with the redder fruits of Nebbiolo. In the mouth, sweet fruit, dark plum flavours and silky tannins drive the palate, sitting down hard on the delicacy of the nebbiolo, so this has generosity. The silky tannins make it delicate rather than austere.

2010	90	2017	$45.00	13.7%
2012	89	2019	$45.00	13.4%
2013	90	2019	$45.00	13.5%

CASA FRESCHI
LA SIGNORINA RIESLING PINOT GRIGIO CHARDONNAY ★★★★
Plenty of honey and a lightly burnt toffee wafts over the nose of red apple and grapefruit citrus in the La Signorina. The wild yeast and barrel ferment regime has softened and fleshed out the body while the bright acid retains a sense of

vibrancy. A wine that makes its presence known and will make a splash at your next dinner.

Vintage	Rank	Drink	RRP	Vol Alc
2012	94	2016	$30.00	12.5%
2014	84	2015	$30.00	13.0%
2015	91	2022	$30.00	13.0%

CASA FRESCHI
PROFONDO CABERNET SHIRAZ ★★★★★

This is a fruit slice pastry with fresh and dried plums. The palate has lovely tannin length and is silky and lush fruited with dark plums in a ripe rich round juicy mulberry dark berry compote. Adds a toss of tapenade savoury flavours on the finish.

Vintage	Rank	Drink	RRP	Vol Alc
2007	89	2015	$60.00	14.0%
2008–2012		Not made		
2013	92	2018	$55.00	13.8%

CASELLA WINES
While the company hops to the Yellow Tail tune there are hidden gems waiting to be discovered including the Reserve wines and the matured before release Casella 1919 reds.

Winemaker: John Casella
Open: By Appointment Only, 1471 Wakley Road, Yenda
Ph: (02) 6961 3000 *www.casellafamilybrands.com*

CASELLA WINES
LIMITED RELEASE CABERNET SAUVIGNON ★★★★★

Solid oak complexity but still allows the ripe varietal cabernet black currant black berry and a pinch of leafy herbs to show well. The full bodied palate is vanilla milk chocolate oak balanced to ripe black currant fruits with long even tannins laced with full bodied oak and fruit complexity.

Vintage	Rank	Drink	RRP	Vol Alc
2010	95	2022	$50.00	14.5%
2012	90	2022	$50.00	14.5%

CASELLA WINES
LIMITED RELEASE SHIRAZ ★★★★★

Regional Barossa shiraz spectrum dusty black olive and bay leaf with restrained oak aromas. The palate is ripe fruited milk chocolate oak ripe grape tannins and quality oak in balance that carries long with excellent dark fruit complexity length and regional flavour.
For lovers of full bodied reds and this delivers

2010	91	2018	$50.00	14.5%
2012	93	2022	$50.00	14.0%

CASTAGNA

For a glimpse inside the mind of Julian Castagna, check his web site and taste his wines to confirm he is an Australian original. Located in Beechworth, the local granite soils influence the style and the sunshine of different years affects the volume of flavour in his wines. Un Segreto sangiovese syrah may well be the red wine of the future, with its blend of savoury and fruit sweetness. This is in contrast with the more tensely tactile nebbiolo-driven Adams Rib and quite savoury sangiovese La Chiave, with its firm tannin and a finer fruit platform. Julian's diverse styles are united as food-friendly, medium-bodied wines.
Winemaker: Julian Castagna
Open: By appointment only, 88 Ressom Lane, Beechworth
Ph: (03) 5728 2888 *www.castagna.com.au*

CASTAGNA
ADAM'S RIB NEBBIOLO SYRAH ★★★★★

Appealing berry fruits, spicy and wild herb aroma with 70% Nebbiolo adding raspberry and rose. In the mouth, the earnest strength and length of the flavour of the property with the green herb element adding complexity to the fruit. A lovely soft tannin finish, with the refinement of Nebbiolo red fruit structure, fleshed out by shiraz dark berry fruit.

2011	Not made			
2012	90	2018	$35.00	13.0%
2013	92	2020	$35.00	13.5%

Vintage	Rank	Drink	RRP	Vol Alc

CASTAGNA
GENESIS SYRAH VIOGNIER ★★★★★
Quality shiraz with graphite floral, dark berry, dark chocolate panaforte and white pepper glossed by a smidgeon of viognier. The palate is ripe, fleshy fruit, silky and long fine tannins that glide smoothly with excellent length of blue and dark berry and fine white pepper savoury to finish. Very complete complex, fruit driven and savoury.

2011	Not made			
2012	95	2029	$75.00	13.5%
2013	95	2033	$75.00	13.5%

CASTAGNA
LA CHIAVE SANGIOVESE ★★★★★
Appealing complexity, violets, dark cherry fruits, briar, liquorice, minerality and sausage meat savoury. The palate has very good line and length with dark fruits and fine tannins, minerality, sausage savoury completes the fine tannin food friendly finish.

2010	96	2025	$75.00	14.0%
2011	Not made			
2012	Not made			
2013	94	2025	$75.00	13.0%

CASTAGNA
UN SEGRETO SANGIOVESE SYRAH ★★★★★
The aromas have a bright intensity, a dark red cherry complex with licorice savoury sausage meat with lift. The palate is berry fruited and finish with fine grained tannins and savoury.

2011	Not made			
2012	95	2034	$75.00	13.0%
2013	93	2022	$75.00	13.5%

CASTELLI ESTATE
A family owned company with 500 ton winery and restaurant in Denmark. Drawing on fruit from across southern WA and looking for the ideal location for each variety including Pemberton for sauvignon blanc, Frankland shiraz and cabernet, Denmark and Mt Barker for riesling.

Winemaker: *Mike Garland*
Open: *Daily 10am–10pm,*
380 Mt Shadforth Road, Denmark WA 6333
Ph: (08) 9848 3832 www.castelliestate.com.au

CASTELLI ESTATE
EMPIRICA FUME SAUVIGNON BLANC ★★★★

Expressive and modern savoury style with solids, wild yeast malt and wheat bix barrel ferment aromas adding an earthy base note. In the mouth fresh acidity, medium bodied and textural with a rounded middle palate that is shy in flavour at the moment, with a coconut brulee finish. Drink after 2017 if you like the honeysuckle exotica.

Vintage	Rank	Drink	RRP	Vol Alc
2013	88	2018	$28.00	13.5%
2014	92	2024	$28.00	13.3%

CASTLE ROCK ESTATE
Castle Rock Estate in Western Australia's cool Mount Barker region produces wines with characteristic delicacy, varietal character and freshness. The riesling is exceptional and older vintages can be purchased from the winery.
Winemaker: *Rob Diletti*
Open: *Weekdays 10am–4pm, Weekends 10am–5pm*
Porongurup Road, Albany
Ph: *(08) 9853 1035 www.castlerockestate.com.au*

CASTLE ROCK ESTATE
GREAT SOUTHERN CABERNET SAUVIGNON MERLOT ★★★★

Warmer and riper than the 2011. Aromas of ripe generous rich black plum and blackcurrant fruits with well judged oak. In the mouth, medium bodied and ripe Australian fruit, sweet length of black currant weight and richness with lingering flavours.

Vintage	Rank	Drink	RRP	Vol Alc
2010	91	2020	$20.00	13.0%
2011	90	2017	$22.00	13.5%
2012	92	2017	$22.00	13.5%

CASTLE ROCK ESTATE
GREAT SOUTHERN PINOT NOIR ★★★★

Fragrant varietally correct red fruits of raspberry, red currant and strawberry aromas. The palate is classy, good, plenty of tannins with fine acidity, and ripe red fruits. A creamy middle palate with subtle dried brown spices to finish. Needs food to bring out the best in this wine.

Vintage	Rank	Drink	RRP	Vol Alc
2012	88	2017	$35.00	13.5%
2013	91	2022	$35.00	13.5%
2014	90	2019	$38.00	13.8%

CASTLE ROCK ESTATE
GREAT SOUTHERN SHIRAZ ★★★★★

Fresh and interesting, as it is more medium bodied with oak and fruits of the forest and red berry aromas. Leading to an intense, sweet-fruited red berry palate. Long, fresh and quite unlike any other regional style in Australia, with raspberry and youthful chalky tannins.

Vintage	Rank	Drink	RRP	Vol Alc
2009	90	2021	$26.00	14.0%
2010	90	2019	$28.00	13.5%
2011	92	2019	$28.00	14.0%

CASTLE ROCK ESTATE
PORONGURUP RIESLING ★★★★★

Changed from Great Southern to Porongurup in 2015. Youthful taunt aging potential here with the elegance of a great wine. Aromas of gentle tropical fruit with a pure mouthful of laser etched acidity, fine length, fullness, a lovely line of delicate flavours and fine acidity.

Vintage	Rank	Drink	RRP	Vol Alc
2013	94	2030	$25.00	12.5%
2014	90	2020	$25.00	12.0%
2015	92	2025	$25.00	12.5%

CASTLE ROCK ESTATE
A & W RESERVE RIESLING ★★★★★

Showing its true colours on release, bath powder, musk, rose aromas. On the palate there are energetic lively flavours that fill the mouth with the flowery into tropical varietal personality with a youthful green apple into mineral acidity holding the finish to dry firmness. Will grow and glow with three years cellar time.

Vintage	Rank	Drink	RRP	Vol Alc
2011	95	2030	$35.00	12.0%
2013	94	2029	$35.00	12.0%
2015	94	2030	$35.00	12.0%

Vintage	Rank	Drink	RRP	Vol Alc

CASTLE ROCK ESTATE
GREAT SOUTHERN SAUVIGNON BLANC ★★★★

Passion fruit and pink grape fruit aromas with punchy pristine freshness. The palate has fresh summer drinking written all over it. Medium length, passion fruit and citrus flavours with freshness. The finish is clean and bright.

Vintage	Rank	Drink	RRP	Vol Alc
2013	86	2015	$18.00	13.0%
2014	92	2018	$20.00	13.0%
2015	90	2018	$20.00	13.0%

CENTENNIAL VINEYARDS

Centennial Vineyards, at Bowral in the NSW Southern Highlands, is the local quality leader in winemaking with pinot noir, tempranillo, chardonnay and sparkling wines showing great promise.

Winemaker: *Tony Cosgriff*
Open: *Daily 10am–5pm, 252 Centennial Road, Bowral*
Ph: *(02) 4861 8700   www.centennial.net.au*

CENTENNIAL VINEYARDS
RESERVE PINOT NOIR ★★★★

Appealing complexity and dimension to the aromas running flowery into red and blue fruits with seamless svelte style. The palate nails it sweet fruits tender tannins middle palate weight of red fruit flavours that linger entwined in enough tannin to offer cellaring short term.

Vintage	Rank	Drink	RRP	Vol Alc
2011	96	2020	$30.00	13.3%
2013	91	2017	$30.00	13.6%
2014	90	2017	$30.00	13.7%

CENTENNIAL VINEYARDS
SINGLE VINEYARD WOODSIDE TEMPRANILLO ★★★★

A good example of the elegant, perfumed style. In different years, swings from fragrant red berry ripe fruit and delicate structure with lower tannins to fruitcake and vibrant tannin acid.

Vintage	Rank	Drink	RRP	Vol Alc
2010	88	2014	$23.00	12.6%
2011	92	2022	$28.00	14.5%
2012	91	2022	$30.00	14.5%

CENTENNIAL VINEYARDS
METHODE CHAMPENOISE PINOT NOIR CHARDONNAY ★★★★
Easily amongst the best, if not the best, made from 100 per cent NSW fruit aperitif styled.

Vintage	Rank	Drink	RRP	Vol Alc
2004	85	2012	$28.00	11.5%
2005	87	2012	$28.00	11.5%
2006	89	2012	$28.00	11.5%

CENTENNIAL VINEYARDS
METHODE CHAMPENOISE BLANC DE BLANC ★★★★★
Takes a run through the orchard on its way to the bakery and kitchen while remaining true to the style with bottle maturity. Aromas of cool citrus lemon zest and nougat into chalky toast. The palate is light bodied yet creamy with expensive bottle aged lees adding to the length with a gentle vanilla honey croissant flavour.

Vintage	Rank	Drink	RRP	Vol Alc
NV	94	2020	$39.95	12.4%

CENTENNIAL VINEYARDS
RESERVE CHARDONNAY ★★★★
Really well made with balance. Perfumes leaning towards white butter, and cashew peanut brittle oak to match the ripe pineapple Orange regional fruits. The palate is pleasing, dense, full and balanced with fresh acidity holding it neatly. Full bodied Orange fruit has depth, tropical flavour richness, dense rich full bodied mouthful of wine with subtle oak to finish. Very generous with excellent balance.

Vintage	Rank	Drink	RRP	Vol Alc
2011	89	2018	$30.00	13.4%
2013	93	2017	$28.00	12.8%
2014	93	2018	$33.00	12.7%

CENTENNIAL VINEYARDS
RESERVE SINGLE VINEYARD SHIRAZ VIOGNIER ★★★★★
The aromas are muted. Possible cork influence with red fruits, savoury spice dried apricot and black berry. The palate is glossy ripe tannins, silky, even and flows well in the mouth. The finesse of the tannins and flavours are refined, medium bodied and long.

Vintage	Rank	Drink	RRP	Vol Alc
2011	96	2018	$30.00	14.5%
2013	91	2018	$30.00	14.6%
2014	93	2022	$33.00	14.5%

CENTENNIAL VINEYARDS
WINERY BLOCK CHARDONNAY ★★★★★

Cellar Door only. The complexities are here; nutty oak, a touch of brulee, yeasty, white stone fruits which glide effortlessly into the mouth balanced by richness to the layers of biscuit, white fruit, and creamy texture in silky malo white butter with honey and long. Very good wine for the price. Don't see good chardonnay at this price often.

2010	96	2015	$23.00	13.3%
2012	92	2018	$23.00	12.9%
2013	94	2018	$24.00	12.9%

CHALK HILL WINES

An interesting array of wines with both the regional heroes and some wine bar varieties. Admirable barbera and vermentino as well modern fresh styles of McLaren Vale's classic reds.

Winemaker: Renae Hirsch
Open: 58 Field Street, McLaren Vale, SA 5171
Ph: (08) 8323 6400 www.chalkhill.com.au

CHALK HILL
BARBERA ★★★★

A sea side whiff oyster dark fruits and bramble berry leads a toned palate appealing tannins and acidic keep the middle palate compact, a lick of kirsch middle palate, tangy tannins on the finish. Only medium long.

2012	90	2017	$28.00	14.0%
2013	93	2018	$28.00	15.0%
2014	91	2019	$29.00	14.0%

CHALKERS CROSSING

Chalkers Crossing at Young in NSW is in the Hilltops region. The vineyard has a terroir-based viticulture and wine focus that has seen it steadily refining its full flavoured wines. At Young, the lean poor soils are good for reds and the Snowy Mountains-influenced cool climate at Tumbarumba is ideal for whites. French trained, Celine Rousseau was awarded the 2002

Vintage	Rank	Drink	RRP	Vol Alc

QANTAS Young Winemaker of the Year and brings experience in Bordeaux, Champagne and the Languedoc to the winery. Add a maturing vineyard and this is a winery to watch.
Winemaker: Celine Rousseau
Open: Mon to Fri 9.30am–4.30pm
285 Henry Lawson Way, Young
Ph: (02) 6382 6900 *www.chalkerscrossing.com.au*

CHALKERS CROSSING
HILLTOPS CABERNET SAUVIGNON ★★★★★
Good intensity and personality showing the varietal range with black cherry and black currant, this is a mirrepoix cabernet. The structure is elegant medium bodied and supple tannins, black currant fruit is appropriately leafy in the back ground, which adds the mirrepoix notes with harmonious silky tannins generous black currant fruit length and refined tannins through the medium long finish.

Vintage	Rank	Drink	RRP	Vol Alc
2012	88	2016	$30.00	13.0%
2013	90	2017	$25.00	13.5%
2014	93	2024	$30.00	13.5%

CHALKERS CROSSING
HILLTOPS SHIRAZ ★★★★★
Savoury reds abound from this producer. The aromas are of raspberry, earthy beetroot and subtle spices. In the mouth, elegant and understated with very good length of ripe red fruit. An intense middle palate with fresh raspberry, even weight of flavour and spice to finish.

Vintage	Rank	Drink	RRP	Vol Alc
2010	91	2010	$30.00	14.5%
2012	92	2020	$35.00	12.5%
2013	93	2018	$30.00	13.0%

CHALKERS CROSSING
TUMBARUMBA CHARDONNAY ★★★★★
Fragrant French oak adds exotic notes of fresh leaf tobacco, white butter, caramel and banana to the subtle tropical fruit aromas. In the mouth, medium bodied and very harmonious controlled complexity with excellent length. Fruit strength with no flavour dominating and the wine covers the whole palate before the clean firm finish and whisper of oak toast.

Vintage	Rank	Drink	RRP	Vol Alc
2011	94	2016	$25.00	12.5%
2013	92	2016	$25.00	13.0%
2014	91	2019	$25.00	13.0%

CHANDON

Chandon (formerly Domaine Chandon) was established in the Yarra Valley in 1985, as part of Moët and Chandon's expansion into new-world sparkling wine production. The wide range of wines represents excellent quality and value, with finesse.
Winemakers: *Glenn Thompson and Adam Keath*
Open: *Daily 10.30am–4.30pm, 727 Maroondah Hwy, Coldstream*
Ph: *(03)97389200 www.domainechandon.com.au*

CHANDON
VINTAGE BLANC DE BLANC CHARDONNAY ★★★★★

Perfumes of lemon icing into chardonnay subtle honey. The palate is light, lithe and medium long with fresh vitality and crisp on the finish. Youthful and lively party starter or pick me up.

2009	94	2014	$40.00	12.5%
2010	93	2016	$41.00	12.5%
2012	89	2018	$40.99	12.5%

CHANDON
VINTAGE BRUT PINOT NOIR CHARDONNAY PINOT MEUNIER ★★★★★

The aroma whispers strawberry pinot ripeness. In the mouth this is expressed with strawberry sorbet-like cool precision and freshness filling the middle palate with the yeasty character at the back. The fruit balance gives wide appeal.

2010	94	2014	$41.00	12.5%
2011	90	2016	$41.00	12.5%
2012	90	2017	$40.00	12.5%

CHANDON
VINTAGE BRUT ROSE PINOT NOIR CHARDONNAY ★★★★

Rose petal, bruised rose petal, and mulberry aromas. In the mouth, the flavours jump straight to the middle palate with plenty of flavour, cooked strawberry and raspberry, pastry and firm enough on the finish to serve with picnics and chicken.

Vintage	Rank	Drink	RRP	Vol Alc
2006	90	2011	$40.00	12.5%
2008	94	2015	$40.00	12.5%
2011	90	2018	$40.00	12.5%

CHANDON
TASMANIAN CUVEE PINOT NOIR CHARDONNAY ★★★★★

Lanolin, chalky cool fruit with yeast in an aperitif style. Very dry, austere, chalky texture with bright apple fruit, a creamy texture and honey lees, with a fresh acid kick off the finish.

Vintage	Rank	Drink	RRP	Vol Alc
2006	91	2012	$40.00	12.5%
2008	92	2013	$40.00	12.5%
2009	90	2016	$40.00	12.5%

CHANDON
CHARDONNAY ★★★★

A very well styled and safe chardonnay, with lovely barrel ferment and ripe stone fruit complexity. The key is the flavour complexity, length and fine finish. A structured, ordered wine with quality flavours that won't disappoint. In the mouth, winemaker round creamy personality and subtle varietal, with quality structure and length of flavour.

Vintage	Rank	Drink	RRP	Vol Alc
2010	89	2014	$30.00	12.5%
2012	92	2018	$30.00	12.5%
2014	91	2018	$28.00	13.0%

CHANDON
PINOT NOIR ★★★★

Ripe strawberry and raspberry aromas with a woodsy mushroom oak element. The light bodied palate is fresh with natural acidity and long fruit flavours in a tender frame. Gentle tannins from fruit and oak with touch of cinnamon spice lead to a clean finish. A very modern style of just ripe fruits that will pair with food. A foxtrot rather a waltz.

Vintage	Rank	Drink	RRP	Vol Alc
2012	89	2019	$31.00	12.5%
2013	89	2018	$31.00	13.0%
2014	92	2024	$32.00	12.5%

CHANDON
SHIRAZ ★★★★
Very pretty weave of red fruits, with some spicy green peppercorn and whole bunch aromas. In the mouth, taut fresh fruited and just medium bodied, with a bright raspberry fruit length of middle palate flavour. Firming tannins, with a fine finish and layered flavours.

Vintage	Rank	Drink	RRP	Vol Alc
2012	94	2024	$34.00	14.0%
2013	95	2023	$34.00	13.5%
2014	93	2018	$64.00	13.5%

CHAPEL HILL
Chapel Hill's recent direction offers a full-flavoured, full-blooded approach to its wines, with plenty of structure. Promising cabernet sauvignon, mourvèdre and sangiovese as well.
Winemaker: *Michael Fragos and Bryn Richards*
Open: *Daily 11am–5pm, Cnr Chapel Hill and Chaffey's Road, McLaren Vale*
Ph: *(08) 8323 8429 www.chapelhillwine.com.au*

CHAPEL HILL
GORGE BLOCK CABERNET SAUVIGNON ★★★★
Formerly known as the Chosen Gorge Block. Varietal leafy edged blueberry and black currant aromas. The flavours land ripe, fruitful and varietal, with a black currant middle palate and a blonde tobacco leaf edge wrapped in fine boned tannins. A fresh acidity that makes it age worthy and part of the new generation more focused and varietally true McLaren Vale Cabernet Sauvignon.

Vintage	Rank	Drink	RRP	Vol Alc
2010	89	2028	$55.00	14.5%
2012	92	2028	$65.00	14.5%
2014	91	2026	$65.00	14.5%

CHAPEL HILL
SHIRAZ ★★★★
Appealing balanced black berry black berry fruit into ironstone dried blood aromas. The palate has medium long length fresh fruits brightness and even length mouth feel is excellent good tannin fruit balance without heaviness.

Vintage	Rank	Drink	RRP	Vol Alc
2012	88	2017	$30.00	14.5%
2013	90	2019	$30.00	14.5%
2014	90	2020	$30.00	14.5%

CHAPEL HILL
'THE VICAR' SHIRAZ ★★★★

Brooding fruits dark and sulking in the glass needs time to grow up in 2016. Starts out bright-fruited fresh with blackberry pip pulp; the palate is about fresh fruit, moderate intensity oak, lands well and stays around chat with animated fresh fruits and good tannin length. Notable freshness and brighter red fruits than previous vintages. Should hold its freshness for the midterm.

Vintage	Rank	Drink	RRP	Vol Alc
2012	91	2025	$75.00	14.5%
2013	94	2028	$75.00	14.7%
2014	92	2027	$75.00	14.5%

CHAPEL HILL
BUSH VINE GRENACHE ★★★★★

Seductive rose topped with strawberry, red cherry spice aromas. The palate has fine tannin length and intense middle palate fruit weighs in with layers and depth of ripe fresh raspberry fruits.

Vintage	Rank	Drink	RRP	Vol Alc
2012	89	2022	$30.00	14.5%
2013	92	2020	$30.00	14.5%
2014	94	2022	$30.00	14.5%

CHARLES MELTON WINES

Charles Melton Wines is one of the best representatives of the quality and individuality of the Barossa Valley, thanks to the high quality and rich fruit complexity of its wines. Winemaker, Charlie Melton is undoubtedly (although given to modesty), a leader in the refinement of Australian shiraz and Barossa shiraz in particular. All the wines here are an exciting new page in our national shiraz story, thanks to fruit selection and extended oak maturation to create wines with refinement.
Winemaker: *Charlie Melton*
Open: *Daily 11am–5pm, Krondorf Road, Tanunda*
Ph: *(08) 8563 3606 www.charlesmeltonwines.com.au*

CHARLES MELTON
NINE POPES SHIRAZ GRENACHE MATARO ★★★★★

A masterful, solid fruited, youthful wine. Fruits of the forest, summer pudding, spice, ripe with balanced oak, additions of oregano and dried herb backing the fruit. A long and age worthy balance of fruits, acidity and tannin

with plenty of tannin weight and
concentration to sustain the flavours which
run raspberry into black fruits plum and
smoked meat allied to firm tannins to close.
Very good lingering fruit.

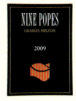

2010	93	2018	$65.00	14.5%
2011	Not made			
2013	94	2026	$70.00	14.5%

CHARLES MELTON
THE KIRCHE BAROSSA SHIRAZ CABERNET ★★★★★

A distinctive, superior aroma of aromatic cedar and
chocolate oak, ripe plum and dark cherry liquorice berry
fruits. In the mouth, this has silky, solid and
long, glossy smooth tannins in a food-friendly,
acid-sweeping tide of fresh cherry plum,
darker plum, prune fruits and chocolate
cedary oak length.

2010	90	2016	$32.00	14.5%
2011	Not made			
2012	93	2018	$32.00	14.5%

CHARLES MELTON
VOICES OF ANGELS SHIRAZ ★★★★★

Exotic spice, quite ripe fruits with a lot more interest and
dynamic aroma range. The palate has
great line and elegant fruits, is a touch
minty and has dark fruit cake spice lovely
delicacy to the tannins and fruit acidity
with good length.

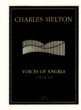

2011	Not made			
2012	90	2017	$65.00	14.5%
2013	94	2020	$65.00	14.5%

CHARLES MELTON
GRAINS OF PARADISE SHIRAZ ★★★★★

Savoury meat stock with a very good intensity and
complexity touch of green herbs. The
palate is a touch of vanilla patisserie oak
adds to the length of ripe berry fruits, with
harmony and balance with a dry tannin
dark chocolate finish.

2011	87	2019	$59.90	14.5%
2012	87	2018	$65.00	14.5%
2013	91	2019	$65.00	14.5%

www.robgeddesmw.com

| Vintage | Rank | Drink | RRP | Vol Alc |

CHATEAU TANUNDA
The Chateau Tanunda reinvigoration continues, with powerful wines including the 'Terroirs of the Barossa' releases. It is unique on many levels and is the only winery in the Southern Hemisphere that is entitled to use "chateau". This historic property is a 'must see' in the valley, complete with cricket pitch. The wines have never been better.
Winemaker: *Neville Rowe*
Open: *Daily 10am–5pm, 9 Basedow Road, Tanunda*
Ph: *(08) 8563 3888 www.chateautanunda.com*

CHATEAU TANUNDA
GRAND BAROSSA RIESLING ★★★★
Formerly The Chateau Eden Valley . This is restrained, lemon pulp and juice aromas peeking out of the early picked framework. In the mouth fresh ripe fruit builds complexity from lightness with moderate acidity into a very complete drink. Flavours emerge along the way with lemon, ripe lemon and lingering roses, then wet pebble mineral acidity on the finish. A well grown and made wine with breeding and class.

2012	88	2019	$23.00	10.5%
2013	94	2024	$23.00	10.5%
2014	96	2024	$23.00	10.5%

CHATEAU TANUNDA
TERROIRS OF THE BAROSSA GREENOCK SHIRAZ ★★★★
Individual vineyard wine grown on rocky ironstone soils. A big muscular powerful shiraz in the regional style, rich ripe long spicy oak, cinnamon nutmeg French oak aromas leading to blueberry, then blackberry fruit with good length. At around 14 to 15 alcohol you have it all. Using an apricot as the example; picked two weeks early leads to high acid and green crisp fruit, picked too late and you get fruit that is sweet and mushy, low in acid and flabby. The difference between brilliance and stupidity is about three days in the vineyard in 2013.

2011	Not made			
2012	90	2018	$48.00	14.0%
2013	90	2022	$49.50	15.0%

CHATEAU TANUNDA
TERROIRS OF THE BAROSSA LYNDOCH SHIRAZ ★★★★★

The cooler end of the Barossa is unyielding in youth and this is classic of the area. More woods like dried mushroom oak, dried herbs and spice, wet school pencil, and tomato concentrate aromas. A young coiled spring palate with silky tannins and the mouth feel is a compact, blackberry palate that is long and saturated in chocolaty oak. The regional spice expression sings on the finish with marjoram, black pepper, and thyme spices lingering on the finish. A great restaurant wine that will partner food. Drink after 2018.

Vintage	Rank	Drink	RRP	Vol Alc
2009	91	2019	$48.00	14.5%
2010	83	2016	$50.00	15.0%
2013	95	2022	$50.00	15.0%

CHATEAU TANUNDA
EVEREST SHIRAZ ★★★★★

Vanilla coconut into Indian ink, hard licorice, veal stock/ gravox and dark spice aromas. The intensity of the year is here with the balance of fruit and tannin, and needs time. The palate is firm and forceful ripe red and black cherry fruits and quality oak supporting the fruit. This will open into a fine tannin, sweet, fruit rich middle palate berry fruits wine. Drink after 2019.

Vintage	Rank	Drink	RRP	Vol Alc
2010	91	2020	$195.00	15.9%
2012	95	2020	$195.00	14.5%
2013	95	2025	$195.00	14.5%

CHATEAU TANUNDA
EVEREST GRENACHE ★★★★★

A big vibrant wine with finesse. The aromatic finesse is extraordinary; ginger, thyme, oregano, marjoram and rosemary, like a handful of Mediterranean herbs. The palate is gentle and very fine. Very long tannins initially with ginger nut snap biscuit flavours, gentle blueberry jam and building in complexity and weight into oak flavours and a sandalwood dusty finish.

Vintage	Rank	Drink	RRP	Vol Alc
2008	94	2019	$195.00	15.0%
2009	92	2020	$195.00	15.0%
2012	96	2024	$195.00	14.5%

| Vintage | Rank | Drink | RRP | Vol Alc |

CHERRY TREE HILL
Owners David Lorentz and family are passionate about their 35 acres of vines planted in 2000 near Sutton Forest. The vineyard is one of the highest in the region at 730 metres above sea level with riesling and chardonnay working well here. Additional plantings include cabernet sauvignon, merlot and pinot noir.
Winemaker: Anton Balog
Open: No Cellar Door
Hume Highway,
Sutton Forest
Ph: (02) 8217 1409 *www.cherrytreehill.com.au*

CHERRY TREE HILL
RIESLING ★★★★★
Fresh ripe limes and bath powder in varietal fresh aromas. In the mouth, the wine displays bright strong flavours and vibrant acidity; a flowery rose pot pourri that is fresh with the ripe fruit. A lovely evolution through talc, flowers and citrus, both in the palate of this wine, and for the next 5 years.

2006	92	2020	$35.00	12.8%
2008	90	2016	$35.00	12.8%
2014	92	2020	$35.00	12.3%

CHERRY TREE HILL
THE WEDDING RESERVE ★★★★
Earthy spice, black currant fruits lead to a bright fruited long raspberry, almost jammy raspberry and sweet rhubarb fruited wine with modest intensity and fine grained tannins to highlight the fresh red fruit length. Drink young. Has good acid for a Sunday roast and should be decanted for two hours to capture the fresh fruit.

| 2008 | 89 | 2019 | $35.00 | 14.0% |
| 2013 | 90 | 2016 | $32.00 | 14.0% |

Vintage	Rank	Drink	RRP	Vol Alc

CHERUBINO WINES
Young, widely experienced and talented Larry Cherubino is on top of his game for wine quality, thanks to meticulously selecting the best regions in Western Australia. Hallmarks are minimum interference winemaking creating wines with balance, excellent judgement, fruit concentration and natural acidity.
Winemaker: *Larry Cherubino*
Open: *No Cellar Door, 15 York Street, Subiaco*
Ph: *(08) 9382 2379 www.larrycherubino.com*

CHERUBINO
PORONGURUP RIESLING ★★★★★

A tightly closed youthful bud of a wine after an hour in the glass. Ripe lemon pith and gentle stone fruits with very fine delicate texture and a great length of rose and musk white flowers with persistence and length lasting 30 seconds after tasting in a rare display of delicacy with power.

2013	92	2019	$35.00	12.0%
2014	94	2027	$35.00	11.5%
2015	96	2025	$39.00	12.5%

CHERUBINO
PEMBERTON SAUVIGNON BLANC ★★★★★

Aromas with varietal push and fruit, subtle winemaker oak influence, with chicken stock, pink grapefruits, lavender, herbs and a wild ferment funk. Very complex wine and a meditation style rather than pure. The palate has authority and the oak adds creaminess. The weighty fruit texture is even and long and you know you're tasting serious wine with a flicker of oak adding to the finish and balanced oak complexity.

2012	90	2018	$35.00	11.5%
2013	90	2017	$35.00	12.5%
2014	93	2020	$35.00	13.0%

CHERUBINO
MARGARET RIVER CHARDONNAY ★★★★★

Quality oak and fruit balance with complexity with the hallmark Cherubino finesse and complexity. Vanilla pod, whiffs of "Bank" roll your own Dutch tobacco that all adds to the white peach aromas. The complex palate is fresh white peach upfront. Seamless, full bodied, and a touch of toasty oak adds to the stone fruits and the wine has an overall bbq white peach fruit complexity.

Vintage	Rank	Drink	RRP	Vol Alc
2012	95	2018	$49.00	13.0%
2013	93	2018	$49.00	12.5%
2014	92	2017	$49.00	12.5%

CHERUBINO
MARGARET RIVER CABERNET SAUVIGNON ★★★★★

Archetypical traditional cabernet aromas. Briar/ brick dust, dark berry perfection in the balance of savoury berry fruits. A very complete wine with the length and evenness of the brick dust, cut terra cotta flavours. A suggestion of dark chocolate, the tannins are refined and elegant with long bridging fruit. Displays structure with intensity and complexity.

Vintage	Rank	Drink	RRP	Vol Alc
2010	92	2020	$75.00	13.5%
2012	95	2026	$75.00	14.0%
2013	95	2019	$75.00	14.0%

CHERUBINO
FRANKLAND RIVER SHIRAZ ★★★★★

Has a magnificent lift in the flowery aromas of pure ripe fresh black and blueberry fruit. Intense powerful length and velvety, soft, ripe and silky even tannins, with so much vibrant fruit. There is a concentration and density in the fine French oak finishing the palate with a silky swath of vanilla.

Vintage	Rank	Drink	RRP	Vol Alc
2010	94	2022	$65.00	14.0%
2011	96	2023	$65.00	14.5%
2012	95	2027	$55.00	14.5%

CHERUBINO
FRANKLAND RIVER CABERNET SAUVIGNON ★★★★★

Intense super ripe red fruits aromas, with flirty notes from jam across to wine gum, cherry and into raspberry. Very full with ripe fruit on the opulent middle palate. Ripe tannins and fleshy mouth feel, that is full with red wine gum and fine grained chalky tannins that need food.

Vintage	Rank	Drink	RRP	Vol Alc
2011	96	2038	$110.00	14.5%
2012	96	2029	$110.00	14.5%
2013	93	2020	$110.00	14.5%

| Vintage | Rank | Drink | RRP | Vol Alc |

CLONAKILLA
Clonakilla in the Canberra district produces small quantities of very highly regarded wines from mature vines. The shiraz viognier is an Australian benchmark and recent releases of almost every wine have been amongst our best, including viognier, nouveau viognier and a complex Rhone red blend called Ceoltóiri.
Winemaker: *Tim Kirk*
Open: *Daily 11am–5pm, 3 Crisps Lane, Murrumbateman*
Ph: *(02) 6227 5877 www.clonakilla.com.au*

CLONAKILLA
SEMILLON SAUVIGNON BLANC ★★★★
Tropical and grassy together in the aromas, adding a subtle oak edge. The palate has a graceful, deep, ripe-fruited and flavour packed, mouth-filling palate. Really good summer drinking, with bounce and verve.

2012	87	2013	$25.00	12.0%
2013	88	2016	$25.00	12.5%
2014	91	2015	$25.00	12.0%

CLONAKILLA
RIESLING ★★★★★
Tight, bright and crisp, white pear and red apple fruits regional style. The palate comes alive with soft ripe fruits, creamy texture, plenty of drink young pleasure with middle palate concentrate, bright and starry in the mouth with flickers of flavour, acidity and a long structure.

2013	94	2029	$30.00	12.5%
2014	94	2028	$30.00	12.5%
2015	90	2023	$30.00	12.0%

CLONAKILLA
CANBERRA VIOGNIER ★★★★★
A successful 20 year search for the ideal style sees a nouveau wine made and released early and this a year later, quite restrained for the variety with shy aromas, which is really unusual in this variety, apricot, pith, and apple aromas with finesse. The palate is elegant it fills the mouth with a full even texture flavours run apricot and

rock melon with the finish nimble and
lithe with just a flick of spice and tannin.

2012	93	2017	$65.00	13.0%
2013	93	2017	$65.00	14.5%
2015	90	2020	$45.00	14.0%

CLONAKILLA
HILLTOPS SHIRAZ ★★★★★
Bright fruit, dark berry black berry mulberry with a
graphite mineral edge. In the mouth deceptive as the
texture is light but it is intense long flavour and very finish
very sophisticated tannins with a elegant layer of dark
spices on the mouth watering finish.
Excellent value.

2012	90	2018	$30.00	13.0%
2013	90	2019	$30.00	14.0%
2015	94	2022	$28.00	14.5%

CLONAKILLA
SHIRAZ VIOGNIER ★★★★★
A ripe fruit focus with seamless complexity into fruit
spices. The palate is a cosmos of subtlety, pulling your
mouth in different directions at the same time. The middle
palate glides violets, red fruits, savoury spice and sweeter
spices of cinnamon and cedar that flow evenly and full,
finishing long firming tannins wed to smoked meats and
savoury spiced charcuterie. A delicious
medium bodied savoury finishing style.

2013	96	2028	$105.00	14.0%
2014	91	2022	$105.00	13.5%
2015	95	2030	$90.00	14.0%

CLONAKILLA
BALLINDERRY CABERNET SAUVIGNON CABERNET FRANC MERLOT ★★★★★
This wine has a bounce in its step with positive fresh fruit
aromas in the red and black spectrum showing raspberry
and blackberry with an herbal back drop. It has well
defined ripeness, elegant overall supple middle palate
tannins and the acid runs the structure to
the finish. Quite shy in 2014 it has the
stamina to develop further.

2009	88	2015	$50.00	14.0%
2011	88	2016	$35.00	13.5%
2012	90	2025	$35.00	13.5%

| Vintage | Rank | Drink | RRP | Vol Alc |

CLONAKILLA
O'RIADA SHIRAZ ★★★★★

The black berry and raspberry fruit lift here, ripe, fresh yet fine, with a mineral peppery spice thread decorating the aromas. Delicious elegant medium bodied style slippery silky tannins fine threads of spice notes red fruits very complete and wholesome wine with a mouth watering draw in the tannins to close.

2012	93	2020	$36.00	13.0%
2013	89	2024	$36.00	14.0%
2015	95	2022	$36.00	14.5%

CLOUDBURST
This is a rare approach to Australian wine: a tiny dense planted vineyard at 10,000 vines per hectare between Wallcliffe, Wilyabrup and Ellen Brook in Margaret River. The approach to select the best vineyard cuttings, grown in the best environment possible with as little intervention as possible, hence Cloudburst as the vineyard is unirrigated. Wines are distinguished by a more austere style than your average Margaret River with a refined length of flavour.
Winemaker: *Will Berliner*
Open: *No Cellar Door*
Ph: *(08) 6323 2333 www.cloudburstwine.com*

CLOUDBURST
CABERNET SAUVIGNON ★★★★★

The fragrance is distinctive with violets, blackcurrant and bramble berry Bordeaux notes. A very polished palate with fine tannins, fruit sweetness and a smooth even fruit-tannin balance that bridges the front to back uniting fruit and tannins. The finish saves something until last with a concentrated black cherry fruit closing the flavours.

2012	95	2027	$250.00	13.5%
2013	97	2029	$250.00	13.2%
2014	96	2028	$250.00	13.4%

CLOUDBURST
CHARDONNAY ★★★★★

The colour is deeper than previous releases and the wine brings a forward fruit. This is a gentle but intense wine showing white fruits and matchstick winemaker complexity wedding pear fruits to oatmeal and gentle

Brulee herbal tea like subliminal oak to build refined and elegant aromas. The palate is generous, ripe and even with a satiny texture that builds from pear, white nectarine and white butter along the middle palate firming into a line of sweet oak spice.

Vintage	Rank	Drink	RRP	Vol Alc
2013	94	2023	$250.00	13.9%
2014	95	2020	$250.00	13.6%
2015	93	2020	$250.00	13.3%

CLOUDBURST
Wine with Life Force

CLOUDBURST
MALBEC ★★★★★
Bramble, mulberry, boysenberry fruits with moderate cedar spiced oak notes. The palate is bright fruited and youthful displaying cedar, Christmas cake, and fruit cake oak spices in the middle palate, continuing as soft tannins fruit bright with bramble pip and pulp fruits and the fruit cake oak spices brigade to follow.

Vintage	Rank	Drink	RRP	Vol Alc
2012	92	2022	$250.00	13.0%
2013	96	2027	$250.00	13.1%
2014	97	2021	$250.00	13.9%

CLOUDBURST
Wine with Life Force

CLOVELY ESTATE VINEYARD
Clovely Estate Vineyard in Queensland's South Burnett has 430 acres under vine, plus olives planted at 520 metres above sea label, where the altitude and sea breezes mitigate the prevailing climate. Additional Cellar Door at Moffatdale is open 10am–4pm Saturday, Sunday and Pub Hols.
Winemakers: Sarah Boyce and Stefano Radici
Open: Tues to Sat 11am–7pm, 210 Musgrave Road, Red Hill
Ph: (07) 3876 3100   www.clovely.com.au

CLOVELY ESTATE
RESERVE DOUBLE PRUNED
SHIRAZ ★★★★
Initially brooding asphalt black fruits and brown spices it kicks into black forest cake vanilla cherry juice, pip and pulp herbal, bitters herbs coconut all intense and competing for escape. The uber full-bodied palate is well balanced the cherry fruits start the procession the deep wide web of fine tannins sweep the fruit along, a flicker of darker fruits, dried herbs oregano like a chocolate edge to the finish.

Vintage	Rank	Drink	RRP	Vol Alc
2011	Not made			
2012	90	2018	$35.00	14.0%
2013	93	2023	$90.00	14.5%

CLYDE PARK

Clyde Park vineyard, planted in 1979, is situated 30 kilometres north of Geelong in a natural amphitheatre. The winery uses time proven, traditional techniques that impart the wines with density and strength from their firm tannins and fruit concentration.
Winemaker: Terry Jongebloed
Open: 11am–5pm Weekends and Pub Hols, 2490 Midland Highway, Bannockburn
Ph: (03) 5281 7274 www.clydepark.com.au

CLYDE PARK
SINGLE BLOCK D PINOT NOIR ★★★★★

Aromas are sweet oak notes, spices and vanilla; serve this in your biggest glass generous fresh focused and sweet fruit varietal notes. The palate is silky, smooth tannins, ripe red fruits run long and fine, very even, elegant and balanced long. Morish yet serious and age worthy.

Vintage	Rank	Drink	RRP	Vol Alc
2012	93	2026	$60.00	13.2%
2014	95	2025	$75.00	13.0%
2015	94	2025	$75.00	13.0%

CLYDE PARK
SINGLE BLOCK B2 PINOT NOIR ★★★★★

Lovely strawberry aromas, side notes of dried herbs, dried strawberry, svelte and high quality. In the mouth, this is deep and long, big, balanced and rich. Youthful with fresh and wild strawberry, great middle palate fullness with such richness the finish seems abrupt.

Vintage	Rank	Drink	RRP	Vol Alc
2012	95	2019	$60.00	12.4%
2013	91	2018	$75.00	12.5%
2015	93	2020	$75.00	13.0%

CLYDE PARK
CHARDONNAY ★★★

The aromas are complete, subtle creamy oatmeal and chardonnay white fruits. The palate has power and balance; viscous with a flick of white peach favours set in silky, generous oatmeal and honey to close. Delicious balance and complexity.

Vintage	Rank	Drink	RRP	Vol Alc
2009	89	2014	$35.00	13.0%
2012	95	2017	$35.00	12.5%
2015	94	2018	$40.00	13.0%

COBAW RIDGE
Cobaw Ridge is a special vineyard; a warm site in the cool Macedon Ranges region that is carefully managed with attention to detail and certified biodynamic in 2011. The vineyard is hand pruned, handpicked and hand tended. The savoury-edged chardonnay and peppery shiraz are excellent examples of the regional style and the Lagrein is a standout example of the structure, tannins and intensity of this little-seen variety.
Winemaker: *Alan Cooper*
Open: *Mon, Thurs, Fri 10–5pm, Weekends 12–5:30pm*
31 Peric Boyers lane, East Pastoria
Ph: *(03) 5429 5227 www.cobawridge.com.au*

COBAW RIDGE
LAGREIN ★★★★★
Really needs a decant for 5 hours. Dark fruits, blueberry, blackberry and liquorice with deft oak. The palate is tight blueberry fruited, with a long fruit texture in the middle, yet youthful and taut with long Italian dryness in the tannins and a peppery finish.

Vintage	Rank	Drink	RRP	Vol Alc
2008	91	2014	$40.00	13.0%
2010	94	2030	$60.00	13.5%
2011	Not made			
2012	Not made			

COBAW RIDGE
SYRAH ★★★★
A very intense wine, with a nod to Cote Rotie. The aromas are floral apricot and violets and juicy black fruits with white pepper spice lift. The palate has a silky glide to the tannins, with freshness in a medium-bodied and juicy-in-the-middle wine. It has a long, juicy, dark fruit layered finish, with chalky tannin and charcuterie-hung meat spice on the extended finish.

Vintage	Rank	Drink	RRP	Vol Alc
2006	93	2019	$45.00	14.0%
2010	95	2022	$50.00	13.6%
2011	Not made			

Vintage	Rank	Drink	RRP	Vol Alc

COLDSTREAM HILLS

The cellar door has a commanding view and the wines demonstrate great authority with their chardonnay and pinot noir amongst Australia's best. Part of Treasury Wine Estates they have enjoyed a long run demonstrating quality and stylistic evolution under Andrew Flemming. Their Reserve pinot noir label and from the Amphitheatre and Deer Farm sites are worth seeking out.

Winemaker: *Andrew Fleming, Greg Jarratt*
Open: *Daily 10am–5pm*
31 Maddens Lane
Coldstream
Ph: *(03) 5960 7000 www.coldstreamhills.com.au*

COLDSTREAM HILLS
RESERVE CHARDONNAY ★★★★★

The colour is pure with the pear and apple fruit aroma showing restrained and classic flinty oatmeal notes. Minerality in the precision of the aroma showing beautiful barrel ferment aromas. Delicious refined palate with varietal pear and apple flavours cloaked in complexity and running linear pulled to together by a slight phenolic edge. The acid shepherds the middle palate defining the structure refining the complex white fruits and barrel ferment to define the finish.

2013	95	2024	$59.99	13.0%
2014	96	2020	$59.99	13.0%
2015	95	2025	$59.99	13.0%

COLDSTREAM HILLS
YARRA VALLEY CHARDONNAY ★★★★★

Uses a complex pressing regime to create different wines. 550 litres press cut, (as versed to 650 l for other Australian producers) and the rest to other wines then 80% in old oak for 9 months and on lees and no malo. Barrels are immersion bend not fire bend oak. Seeks the modern Australian style, and the oak adds initial sweetness then the cool linear acidity guides the white nectarine fruits with middle palate strength of flavour.

2012	91	2016	$26.00	13.0%
2013	92	2018	$34.99	13.0%
2014	93	2022	$27.00	13.0%

| Vintage | Rank | Drink | RRP | Vol Alc |

COLDSTREAM HILLS
PINOT NOIR ★★★★★
Aromas are in the paddock and the orchard, earthy, strawberry and beetroot fruited which flow onto a solid seamless palate. Plenty of mouth feel and texture which will win people over. Silky soft tannins, fleshy even weight with fruit complexity, pretty strawberry and ripe raspberry. If you are learning about Pinot this is a great introduction.

2013	92	2025	$34.99	13.5%
2014	90	2019	$34.99	13.0%

COOLANGATTA ESTATE
Coolangatta Estate in the Shoalhaven area of NSW is a historic site with a resort featuring convict built accommodation. Small quantities of extraordinary semillon that ages well, with recent plantings of savagnin, tannat and tempranillo adding interest.
Winemaker: *Andrew Spinaze*
Open: *Daily 10am–5pm*
1335 Bolong Road, Shoalhaven Heads
Ph: *(02) 4448 7131 www.coolangattaestate.com.au*

COOLANGATTA ESTATE
WOOLSTONECRAFT SEMILLON ★★★★★
This wine is built to stay and the style has a great track record of well composed aromas with high acidity, light bodied, lemony spectrum flavours. The fresh apple fruit runs long and time is its friend.

2011	93	2025	$25.00	11.0%
2014	92	2025	$30.00	11.8%
2015	90	2033	$25.00	10.9%

COOLANGATTA ESTATE
ALEXANDER BERRY ★★★★★
Brings quality french oak caramel and white butter with ripe nectarine varietal fruit, there is an appealing maturity holding it together. Soft creamy mature fruits and well intergrated acidity combine with warm lemon butter and nectarine fruit with

Vintage	Rank	Drink	RRP	Vol Alc

generosity and a clean finish. Lovers of generous chardonnay will totally get this.

2012	87	2015	$25.00	12.0%
2013	86	2018	$25.00	12.7%
2014	94	2018	$25.00	13.5%

COPPABELLA
Part of the original cattle station of the same name, Alicia and Jason Brown took over Coppabella, the 175 acre vineyard (33% of the Tumbarumba region) in 2011. Results flowed in 2012 and the vineyard has not looked back with wine of increasing sophistication.
Winemaker: *Jason Brown*
Open: *By Appointment Only*
424 Tumbarumba Road
Tumbarumba
Ph: *(02) 6382 7997* *www.moppity.com.au*

COPPABELLA
SIRIUS CHARDONNAY ★★★★★
Think of watching the ballet with this wine; poised white, everything in synchronisation. Lovely balance with the gentlest lees influenced white fruit aroma notes. The palate has dry even tension and elegance, this is crafted with exquisite finesse, the fruit backed by a hidden oak orchestra with the flavours delivering length and a lovely shape. Long and even and the volume is turned down to sophisticated whisper.

2013	94	2022	$60.00	12.5%
2014	95	2020	$60.00	12.5%

COPPABELLA
THE CREST CHARDONNAY ★★★★★
Subtlety and nuance with the modern white fruit, with creamy lees notes, subtle oak, very polished style. The texture is silky, ripe fleshy generous 'sweet' note up front, middle palate with vanilla cream cake like layers and never losing its generous poise.

2012	92	2018	$30.00	12.5%
2014	91	2018	$30.00	13.0%

COPPABELLA
THE CREST PINOT NOIR ★★★★★
A step up from the 2014 with a delightful brown spice note as well as fresh raspberry and strawberry fruit. The fruit structure has ripe generosity, pure red fruits conserve and fresh flavours. Appealing tannin tautness and evolving red fruit flavours. Will take a few years.

| 2014 | 90 | 2019 | $30.00 | 13.5% |
| 2015 | 89 | 2022 | $30.00 | 13.5% |

CORIOLE
Coriole in McLaren Vale has been respected for over 40 years for its reds, especially the shiraz. The winery has recently introduced very intelligent renditions of selected Italian varieties, to add to the rising quality of their whites. Cellar door features a wealth of local produce.
Winemaker: Alex Sherrah
Open: Mon–Fri 10am–5pm, Weekends and Pub Hols 11am–5pm
Chaffeys Road, McLaren Vale
Ph: (08) 8323 8305 www.coriole.com

CORIOLE
ESTATE SHIRAZ ★★★★
Very good for the price. Dark berry, with a handful of green leaves showing sage-edged blackberry fruit aromas. Dark chocolate fruit flavours and elegant medium, full-bodied length, with freshness and soft fine tannins that have development potential.

2010	90	2020	$28.00	14.0%
2011	89	2017	$30.00	14.0%
2012	90	2020	$30.00	14.0%

CORIOLE
LLOYD RESERVE SHIRAZ ★★★★★
Ripeness with a warm regional embrace of brooding black cherry, blackberry and plum fruit richness of balanced oak setting the course for a long life. Liquid silk tannins, with surprising finesse and even length, wed to fresh blackberry and dark plum fruits with dimension, extension and interest. The ripe blackberry fruit explodes

Vintage	Rank	Drink	RRP	Vol Alc

on the finish which means most will be drunk before its prime.

2010	92	2028	$90.00	14.0%
2011	95	2016	$85.00	14.0%
2012	95	2032	$85.00	14.5%

CORIOLE
MARY KATHLEEN CABERNET MERLOT ★★★★★

Quality from the get go. Aromas are complex, with liquorice and minerality, rich black fruit, and raspberry confectionery notes adding detail. The full-bodied palate is black currant, raspberry and red currant. Generous flavours wrapped in delicious fine tannins, with fleshy black currant flavours. The tannins are silky, the oak balance is very good and the fruit medium long.

2010	90	2020	$90.00	13.5%
2011	94	2021	$50.00	14.0%
2012	95	2028	$50.00	14.0%

CORIOLE
McLAREN VALE FIANO ★★★★

There is such vibrancy and freshness to this McLaren Vale Fiano. Zesty lime and lemon citrus, pear and nuts lift this wine to be one of the Australian showcases of this varietal wine coming from low yield vines. The flavours explode in the mouth and finish with a ginger twist. Made to share, but you might find it hard to after that first glass. You'll want more.

2013	88	2016	$25.00	12.0%
2014	90	2017	$25.00	12.5%
2015	92	2018	$25.00	13.0%

CORIOLE
REDSTONE SHIRAZ ★★★

A good drinking wine that you will add to your standby list of sub $20 wines. Ripe fragrant red plum and cherry fruit with lashings of spice and pepper. The Redstone is fresh, soft and good to go now, but it could do with some mid-term cellaring to polish the powdery tannins more.

2010	86	2014	$18.00	14.0%
2012	88	2020	$20.00	14.5%
2014	89	2021	$20.00	14.5%

www.robgeddesmw.com

Vintage	Rank	Drink	RRP	Vol Alc

CORIOLE
CHENIN BLANC ★★★★
Honeyed, musk, gold delicious apples. The palate treads a line of medium long fruit weight with ripe yellow apples and rose water middle palate flavours underpinned by a steely acidity.

2013	90	2023	$16.00	12.5%
2014	90	2018	$16.00	12.5%
2015	87	2019	$16.00	12.5%

CORIOLE
SANGIOVESE ★★★★★
Developed colour. Aroma has weight and complexity with the presence of red currant raspberry into darker subtle oak. The palate has sweet fruits, appealing tannin, savoury liquorice middle palate weight with a lingering finish of red fruits.

2012	88	2018	$25.00	14.0%
2013	90	2019	$25.00	14.0%
2014	90	2019	$25.00	14.5%

CORIOLE
BARBERA ★★★★★
A gamut of aromas with blueberry fruits leading and then bayleaf and black tea. In the mouth a large volume of silky tannins and fresh acidity, rich middle palate flavours run through berry to darker elements. Medium long lingering blackberry jam. Good food wine.

2012	90	2016	$30.00	13.5%
2013	91	2017	$30.00	13.5%
2014	88	2018	$30.00	14.0%

CRABTREE WINES
Crabtree Wines in Watervale is a small Clare Valley estate respected for their careful, handcrafted production of reliable quality wines including the classic local riesling style, shiraz and tempranillo.
Winemaker: *Kerri Thompson*
Open: *Daily 10.30am–4.30pm, 1 North Terrace Watervale*
Ph: *(08) 8843 0069 www.crabtreewines.com.au*

| Vintage | Rank | Drink | RRP | Vol Alc |

CRABTREE WINES
WATERVALE SHIRAZ ★★★★★

Pretty, fresh, fragrant blue berry with subtle oak adding cedar to the aromas In the mouth a medium bodied, good length of black berry, prune, well made sensitive soft tannins that don't try too hard and as a consequence sits with fresh fruits wed to chocolate oak. The style is pretty, elegant and balanced with tannin finesse. Very good wine to take to a meal.

Vintage	Rank	Drink	RRP	Vol Alc
2012	89	2018	$25.00	14.5%
2013	90	2022	$25.00	14.0%
2014	93	2018	$30.00	14.0%

CRABTREE WINES
TEMPRANILLO ★★★★

The nose is very complex, varietal in the cola, earthy, meaty spectrum aromas reminding one taster of hunting in the paddocks, smells of offal and bloody meat and another of roast lamb with gravy. The palate has very fine tannins, fine acidity, with good dark berry varietal fruit length finishing low key cola and dried spice flavours. Best with a two hour decant.

Vintage	Rank	Drink	RRP	Vol Alc
2012	87	2016	$26.00	14.0%
2013	88	2018	$26.00	13.5%
2014	94	2022	$26.00	14.0%

CRABTREE WINES
WATERVALE RIESLING ★★★★★

The rich Watervale fruits in this wine have more orange blossom and hints of lime, feijoa, apple and custard apple. The fleshy palate is quite unique to this property with a wonderful weight of creamy fruit evenness and length of stone fruit flavour and a fine elegant acidity. The easy drinking qualities of this wine mean it will be drunk young but it has the weight and balance to age.

Vintage	Rank	Drink	RRP	Vol Alc
2013	92	2023	$26.00	12.5%
2014	95	2019	$26.00	12.5%
2015	95	2023	$26.00	13.0%

CRAGGY RANGE

Craggy Range's style of medium full-bodied reds is based on the Gimblett Gravels and its propensity for producing single-vineyard wines from quality sites in New Zealand ensures that this is one of New Zealand's most exciting wine producers.

Winemaker: Steve Smith
Open: Daily 10am–5pm
253 Waimarama Road, Havelock North, NZ
Ph: (64) 6873 7126 www.craggyrange.com

CRAGGY RANGE WINES
SOPHIA MERLOT CABERNET SAUVIGNON ★★★★★

Perfumes of blueberry and dried herbs, vanilla and oak spice. The palate is full, fruit rich and even, with boysenberry, blueberry top notes. A complex, fresh, bright drinking fruit with ripe tannins that are lovely and layered from fruit and oak to close. Drink 2018–2032.

Vintage	Rank	Drink	RRP	Vol Alc
2010	93	2024	$69.00	13.5%
2011	95	2035	$69.00	13.5%
2013	95	2032	$79.00	13.8%

CRAGGY RANGE WINES
LE SOL SYRAH GIMBLETT GRAVELS SYRAH ★★★★★

Tiered aromas with subtle oak, blueberry and dark berries, then dried herbs, and into sausage meat, and pepper smoked meats, and sandalwood. In the mouth, this has a firm even frame with youthful restraint and very good length of fruit. A touch of citrus and tannins with the spice flavours. Chinese green pepper through to white pepper and a fresh acid finish. No stems or viognier used. Start drinking in 2020.

Vintage	Rank	Drink	RRP	Vol Alc
2010	96	2029	$110.00	13.5%
2011	92	2022	$110.00	13.0%
2013	95	2035	$120.00	13.1%

Vintage	Rank	Drink	RRP	Vol Alc

CRAGGY RANGE WINES
BLOCK 14 GIMBLETT GRAVELS SYRAH ★★★

Black pepper, savoury, resinous and Rhone aromas, with varying degrees of raspberry/black olive in medium-bodied, elegant, moderate tannins and a spicy finish.

2006	90	2013	$39.00	13.5%
2007	88	2013	$39.00	13.5%
2008	89	2014	$39.00	13.5%

CRAGGY RANGE WINES
LES BEAUX CAILLOUX GIMBLETT GRAVELS CHARDONNAY ★★★★★

Developed colour, with seamless, fine, gentle lees, yoghurt and clotted cream aromas. There is an interesting gentle oak and stone fruit aromatic hand shake. The palate is classic chardonnay. Creamy, silky complexity of flavour and texture, lushly gliding with complex, fresh, yeasty, stone fruit and yoghurt middle palate flavours, in a very complete long wine. White burgundy style.

2009	90	2016	$79.00	13.0%
2010	95	2016	$79.00	13.5%
2011	93	2017	$79.00	13.5%

CRAIGLEE

Craiglee at Sunbury near Melbourne offers restrained shiraz, showing a great take on elegance and intensity, with peppery cool-climate flavours and the ability to grow more interesting as they age.

Winemaker: *Pat Carmody*
Open: *By appointment only, Sunbury Road, Sunbury*
Ph: *(03) 9744 4489* *www.craiglee.com.au*

| Vintage | Rank | Drink | RRP | Vol Alc |

CRAIGLEE WINES
CABERNET SAUVIGNON ★★★

Fresh red fruits showing raspberry sweet rhubarb cabernet notes. The palate is medium bodied soft tannins with oak defining the palate in youth, red fruits ripe tannins soft middle palate with peppery notes adding t the complexity.

2008	87	2015	$45.00	13.5%
2012	93	2023	$30.00	13.5%
2013	88	2022	$30.00	13.5%

CRAIGLEE WINES
SHIRAZ ★★★★★

Victorian spice box shiraz complexity with fresh red fruit brightness and life with white and black pepper aromas. The palate lines up the fruit and spice aromas wraps them in age worthy shiraz tannin that bridge front to back of tongue with acid fruit harmony on the finish. This will live a long time.

2012	95	2042	$57.00	14.0%
2013	89	2026	$50.00	13.5%
2014	96	2030	$50.00	13.5%

CRAIGLEE WINES
CHARDONNAY ★★★

Complex modern chardonnay subtlety with graceful intensity oatmeal, white fruits and gentle oak back ground. The fruits is ripe medium bodied finely textured silky with cedar and milk coffee oak on the medium long finish.

2009	89	2015	$30.00	13.0%
2013	93	2019	$32.00	13.5%
2014	89	2018	$32.00	13.5%

CRAWFORD RIVER

Crawford River in Victoria's vast Henty region focuses on riesling and cabernet. While revered for its sublime rieslings, the cabernet also captures the elegance of the regional climate.
Small quantities of a sweet riesling called 'nectar' are made.
Winemaker: *John Thomson*
Open: *By appointment only, 741 Upper Hotspur Road, Condah*
Ph: *(03) 5578 2267* *www.crawfordriverwines.com*

| Vintage | Rank | Drink | RRP | Vol Alc |

CRAWFORD RIVER
RIESLING ★★★★★
Small crop intensity, drought, ripe year. Whole bunch press and in press crush soaking for 6–8 years. This is a very precise wine with fine lime and white fruit aromas. In the mouth the rich even lime flavours cut fresh and long framed by chalky acidity, very good fruit intensity with texture, generous flavours and very good tension on the palate. Good drinking now, this will age long term. Generally 1,000 cases for the vintage. Regionality does not exist in Henty as the regional is so large. Solid variety.

2012	97	2040	$45.00	13.0%
2013	96	2020	$45.00	13.0%
2014	95	2028	$45.00	13.0%

CRAWFORD RIVER
CABERNET SAUVIGNON ★★★★
Sealed under cork. Bordeaux in Australia aromas, with oak and smoky medicinal tertiary dark berry fruit. The palate is complex, vinous developed flavours, slick tannins and plummy fruits. Read to drink today, with smoky savoury elements on the finish and firm oak tannins.

2005	88	2017	$40.00	14.0%
2006	88	2016	$40.00	14.0%
2008	90	2016	$50.00	13.0%

CROSER
Croser is the Petaluma-produced method champenoise based on pinot noir. Each year, variable amounts of chardonnay are used to assist the acidity and fruit balance. Big strides have been taken recently.
Winemaker: *Andrew Hardy*
Open: *Daily from 10am–5pm, Mount Barker Road, Bridgewater*
Ph: *(08) 8339 9300 www.croser.com.au*

CROSER
PINOT NOIR CHARDONNAY ★★★★
Aromas are complex, within the ripe edge of Australia. Strawberry apple nectarine and a marzipan seaside yeasty background. The palate is elegant, youthful and tight, with an even long focus of light-bodied flavours and a fine texture, zesty acids and a long dry palate.

2009	89	2014	$35.00	13.0%
2010	88	2015	$35.00	13.0%
2011	93	2020	$35.00	12.0%

Vintage	Rank	Drink	RRP	Vol Alc

CROSER
PROPRIETOR'S RESERVE PINOT NOIR ★★★★★
Receives an extra seven years on lees, giving toast and green apple flavours and a long finish, including brioche and panettone. This level of flavour allows for zero dosage compared to the 9–12gm of sugar in NV French.

Vintage	Rank	Drink	RRP	Vol Alc
1998	93	2012	$69.00	12.5%
1999	92	2012	$69.00	13.0%
2000	90	2012	$69.00	12.5%

CROSER
ADELAIDE HILLS NV ★★★★
Based on fruit richness in a bold style with nutty yeast, almost vegemite autolysis. Fresh, ripe, cool-climate red apples, pears and raspberry fruit aromas. Middle palate richness; lemon sherbet starts the plush length of lemon-edged citrus fruit to a yeasty finish.

Vintage	Rank	Drink	RRP	Vol Alc
NV	90	2017	$25.00	13.0%

CULLEN
Cullen Wines is a leader in achieving more finesse and fine details in its wines. Certified organic in 2003 and biodynamic in 2004. The biodynamic improvements are allied to an ideally located estate in Margaret River. These wines are highly individual and exciting each year.
Winemaker: Vanya Cullen
Open: Daily 10am–4.30pm, Caves Road, Cowaramup
Ph: 08 9755 5277 *www.cullenwines.com.au*

CULLEN
CULLEN VINEYARD SAUVIGNON BLANC SEMILLON ★★★★★
This wine is as much about finesse and texture as flavour. The aromas are complex, seamless subtle fruits, waxy, fresh, zesty kiwi fruit passion fruit herbs up front, oak spices and building honey suckle fruits just peaking through. The palate has energy, length, very finely structured fruit acid freshness and concentration with middle palate succulent ripe fruit pulled in on the complex finish by gentle oak allowing the lingering white fruits into honeysuckle to create complexity on the finish.

Vintage	Rank	Drink	RRP	Vol Alc
2012	90	2020	$35.00	11.0%
2013	94	2022	$35.00	12.5%
2014	93	2028	$35.00	13.5%

CULLEN
KEVIN JOHN CHARDONNAY ★★★★★

Focused regional fruit richness showing plush pears and figs, oatmeal, tight grained vanilla white butter french oak with a generous outgoing personality to the fruit aromas. The generous palate has length, white peach full bodied silky texture with finesse and very good length, balanced harmonious flavours, clean finishing and still a pup in 2016.

Vintage	Rank	Drink	RRP	Vol Alc
2012	95	2022	$105.00	13.0%
2013	95	2019	$105.00	14.0%
2014	95	2022	$105.00	13.5%

CULLEN
MANGAN PETITE VERDOT MALBEC ★★★★

Very unique wine with a big pitch of fruit and grape tannins. Great colour leads to a thick weave of dark fruits, minerality and meat stock with fresh thyme, black cherry aromas. In the mouth a long swathe of ripe black and blue fruit flavours underpinned by a long fine firm weave of tannin, fine acidity and layers in the middle. Serve with a cheese dish to unpick the sandy tannins from the fruit.

Vintage	Rank	Drink	RRP	Vol Alc
2012	90	2022	$45.00	12.5%
2013	90	2020	$45.00	13.0%
2014	90	2021	$45.00	14.0%

CULLEN
DIANA MADELINE CABERNET SAUVIGNON MERLOT ★★★★★

Cuts a fine and balanced line of elegant fresh red fruit leafy and umami aromas into a long fine even palate with classic flavoursome cabernet tannins powdery soft at first gaining strength wed to red fruits a cacao note overall building a plush frame in the middle mouth and sweeping to a very long conclusion with focus and finesse, with plenty of oak structure bedding the lingering red and black fruit for a long life. Drink 2019 onwards.

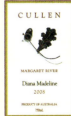

www.robgeddesmw.com

Vintage	Rank	Drink	RRP	Vol Alc
2012	95	2035	$115.00	13.5%
2013	96	2039	$115.00	13.0%
2014	95	2032	$125.00	13.5%

CUMULUS
Cumulus Wines is both the name of the wine and the company producing Climbing, Rolling, Rose and Cumulus wines. The vineyards straddle the divided between Orange at above 600m and Central Ranges when made from fruit grown below 600m. An experienced team and talented winemaking.
Winemaker: Debbie Lauritz and Matt Atallah
Open: No Cellar Door
Suite 6, Level 3, Building A, 20 Rodborough Road, Frenchs Forest
Ph: (02) 8977 2818 *www.cumuluswines.com.au*

CUMULUS
LUNA ROSA ROSADO MOURVEDRE SHIRAZ GRENACHE ★★★★★
Right in the zone with the gentle pomegranate, ripe tomato fruits backed by a flicker of dried orange zest aromas. The palate is well-woven, engaging texture and creamy seamless middle palate flowing pink and red flavours with cardamom before the fresh acids zips up the finish.

2012	88	2014	$15.00	11.5%
2015	92	2016	$15.99	12.2%
2014	88	2016	$17.00	12.0%

CUPITTS WINERY
NSW Rosie Cupitt is an innovative winemaker sourcing "hero varieties" from southern Australia including the Southern Highlands and Hilltops in NSW and the Yarra Valley. An evolving array of wines showing freshness, complexity and food friendly in style compliment the onsite restaurant.
Winemaker: Rosie Cupitt
Open: Wed to Sat 10am–5pm, 58 Washburton Road, Ulladulla
Ph: (02) 4455 7888 *www.cuppittwines.com.au*

CUPITTS
ALPHONSE SAUVIGNON BLANC ★★★★
This has bandwidth to the fruit seamlessly invoking the classic Pouilly Fume of France. Honeysuckle into herbal fruits with a faultless palate of tropical tones and more

lingering fresh white fruits and honey suckle picture perfect long, balanced intensity that lingers.

| 2014 | 89 | 2019 | $32.00 | 13.0% |
| 2015 | 94 | 2019 | $32.00 | 12.0% |

CUPITTS
DUSTY DOG SHIRAZ VIOGNIER ★★★★★

A bright delicious spectrum of red fruits, fresh liquorice, dusty chocolate and a touch of acid that adds lift to the aromas. The palate is tight, bright and firm tannins bridging the middle palate with red fruits adding length and keeping it mouth watering with a peppery finish.

| 2014 | 93 | 2019 | $52.00 | 13.5% |
| 2015 | 92 | 2018 | $52.00 | 14.0% |

CURLEWIS
The Curlewis Winery on the Bellarine Peninsula near Geelong specialises in complex pinot noir, with notable success, as well as a graceful and stately chardonnay. Annual yields are miniscule 1-1.5 tonnes per acre. Cold soaking, hot fermentation and post maceration techniques are used in Pinot Noir. All wines are made with wild yeast fermentation occurring naturally from the vineyard. Their wines spend up to 18 months in French oak barriques on lees. All wines are neither fined nor filtered at bottling.
***Winemaker:** Stefano Marasco*
***Open:** By appointment only, 55 Navarre Road, Curlewis*
***Ph:** (03) 5250 4567 www.curlewiswinery.com.au*

CURLEWIS WINERY
RESERVE PINOT NOIR ★★★★★

Stemmy peppery citrus notes, complex tangy stables that edge to the red fruits with an early picked character. In the mouth, a ripe red berry and nutmeg black pepper edge and fruits that are in touch with the barnyard. Drink up soon.

2010	92	2020	$60.00	13.0%
2011	Not made			
2012	85	2018	$43.00	13.0%
2013	91	2017	$65.00	13.0%

CURLEWIS WINERY
PINOT NOIR ★★★★★
Dried herbs, meaty and red berry fruits. In the mouth, layered red fruits, fine tannins and good lines of complexity with the fruit and tannins weaving together to build a tense chewy finish.

Vintage	Rank	Drink	RRP	Vol Alc
2010	90	2018	$40.00	13.0%
2011	90	2016	$40.00	12.0%
2013	92	2022	$45.00	13.0%

CURLY FLAT VINEYARD
Curly Flat in the Macedon Ranges is an extremely high-quality producer of Burgundian varieties. They seek "to express the footprint of the vineyard, rather than the thumbprint of the winemaker". An admirable sentiment.
Winemaker: *Phillip Moraghan and Matt Regan*
Open: *Weekdays by appointment, Weekends 12pm–5pm, 263 Collivers Road, Lancefield*
Ph: *(03) 5429 1956 www.curlyflat.com*

CURLY FLAT
PINOT GRIGIO ★★★★★
Vivid and poignant complex, fresh pear, red apple ripe fruit aromas, The palate is on the border line of oily and has fleshy middle palate pears and pomme fruits structure and the finish is brought about by tannins probably oak and skins. Has personality and real depth on the palate and is very in the winemakers style.

Vintage	Rank	Drink	RRP	Vol Alc
2010	92	2014	$26.00	13.6%
2011	91	2015	$29.00	13.0%
2015	91	2017	$34.00	13.6%

CURLY FLAT
CHARDONNAY ★★★★★
A fit toned athlete of a wine with rippling muscles showing the buttered caramel, toasted coconut, poached ripe fruits in classy oak. Winemaker input of caramel with the charming palate loaded with a youthful rich creamy even mouth feel and flavours that mirror the aromas.

Vintage	Rank	Drink	RRP	Vol Alc
2011	94	2020	$42.00	13.6%
2012	95	2020	$44.00	14.0%
2013	95	2023	$44.00	13.0%

| Vintage | Rank | Drink | RRP | Vol Alc |

CURLY FLAT
PINOT NOIR ★★★★★

Aromas are bound tight showing balance and potential with harmonious strawberry fruit and a touch of oak spice. In the mouth flavours of mushroom and tight grained oak all speak of quality and complexity. The wine delivers a journey of tastes and layers with grace and well scaled intensity. The texture shows rich even length, pinot-sity, sweet strawberry fruits and velvety tannins with the cherry fruit coming into more savoury flavours and layered finish.

Vintage	Rank	Drink	RRP	Vol Alc
2011	94	2022	$48.00	12.7%
2012	95	2026	$48.00	14.2%
2013	94	2026	$50.00	13.7%

CUTTAWAY HILL

Cuttaway Hill is in the cool Southern Highlands south of Sydney, producing medium bodied wines with freshness and flavour. Manager Mark Bourne has high standards and the wines are a good representation of the region.
Winemaker: *Mark Bourne*
Open: *Daily 10am–4pm, 12587 Hume Hwy, Sutton Forest*
Ph: *(02) 4858 1788* ***www.cuttawayhillwines.com.au***

CUTTAWAY HILL
SOUTHERN HIGHLANDS PINOT GRIS ★★★★

Plenty of rich varietal pear, yellow wine gums and stone fruits with a hoppy savoury edge in the aroma. The palate is generous and lively, fresh, rich, round and very gris in style with flavours rolling through pear, yellow wine gums, poached peach and a middle palate that balances fruitiness and acidity. The sort of wine that becomes a house pour in an inner city restaurant.

Vintage	Rank	Drink	RRP	Vol Alc
2013	88	2016	$28.00	13.5%
2014	85	2017	$28.00	13.5%
2015	89	2018	$28.00	13.5%

| Vintage | Rank | Drink | RRP | Vol Alc |

D'ARENBERG

d'Arenberg is a shiraz and grenache specialist which has moved with the times and the tannins and flavours have become more refined, brighter, fresher, finer and more harmonious in recent years. Whites are better than you would expect from this splendid red specialist and sweet whites can be exceptional at the top end. Gotta love a company like this: reliable, reasonable prices and widely available.

Winemaker: Chester Osborn
Open: Daily 10am–5pm, Osborn Road, McLaren Vale
Ph: (08) 8329 4888 www.darenberg.com.au

D'ARENBERG
DEAD ARM SHIRAZ ★★★★★

Aromas are blackberry, dark chocolate fruit complex, clove and dried spice aromas. In the mouth, fleshy wine with more generosity than the 2012 carraway, Indian spices, more meaty savoury with a jammy plummy drive and a chalky, sandy finish of youth.

2010	95	2043	$60.00	14.4%
2011	94	2035	$60.00	14.3%
2013	91	2028	$65.00	14.5%

D'ARENBERG
IRONSTONE PRESSINGS GRENACHE SHIRAZ MOURVEDRE ★★★★★

Good quality grenache notes lead the aroma. The well-judged oak introduces appealing dried herbs and the dark bramble and black berry fruits have complexity. Silky chocolate alongside the middle palate of raspberry puree, fresh fruits- rich and ripe- that linger through to the finish. Generous and uncomplicated this is easy to drink now.

2011	94	2019	$65.00	14.1%
2012	94	2025	$65.00	14.4%
2013	90	2020	$65.00	14.3%

D'ARENBERG
THE COPPERMINE ROAD CABERNET SAUVIGNON ★★★★★

A very appealing weave of ripe black currant, tapenade and currant fruits, leafy edged with classy oak adding to the complexity but not dominating. The fruit-tannin

Vintage	Rank	Drink	RRP	Vol Alc

balance is exceptional; a long red carpet of ripeness carries through the mouth, silky, concentrated and wed to black currant fruit, oregano oak spices and enough substance to take 15 years in the cellar.

2011	93	2040	$65.00	14.0%
2012	90	2030	$65.00	14.1%
2013	94	2032	$65.00	14.0%

D'ARENBERG
THE CUSTODIAN GRENACHE ★★★★★

Preserved cherry, sun-dried berry and mineral aromas in a compact edition. Soft, very sweet ripe fruit, raspberry and mineral flavours in a juicy style with a spicy peppery grip to the finish. Compact and classy.

2011	90	2017	$18.00	14.0%
2012	88	2018	$18.00	14.6%
2013	94	2020	$18.00	14.3%

D'ARENBERG
THE DERELICT VINEYARD GRENACHE ★★★★★

This wine seems very advanced and mature. Curious subtle aromas, nothing distinctive, smoked meats and earthy roast meats. The palate is lightweight, medium length, warm and short on the finish.

2009	86	2014	$30.00	14.5%
2010	95	2025	$30.00	13.5%
2011	83	2016	$29.00	14.4%

D'ARENBERG
THE FOOTBOLT SHIRAZ ★★★

Floral edged, sweet oak aromas with a fleshy front. A hearty handshake of tannins and well-made qualities for the price. Ideal for your next BBQ.

2010	90	2016	$20.00	14.1%
2011	89	2017	$18.00	14.2%
2012	86	2016	$18.00	14.6%

| Vintage | Rank | Drink | RRP | Vol Alc |

D'ARENBERG
THE TWENTY EIGHT ROAD MOURVEDRE ★★★★★

Very good varietal expose; fresh cut bloody meat, offal and more mineral savoury brine in a complex stony take on the variety. In the mouth, soft tannins and dark olive tapenade flavours, with salty brine minerals building towards the finish and dark olive dark fruit and vegemite minerality to close.

2009	86	2015	$35.00	14.3%
2010	94	2038	$40.00	14.0%
2011	93	2027	$40.00	14.0%

D'ARENBERG
THE GARDEN OF EXTRAORDINARY DELIGHTS SHIRAZ ★★★★★

A mouthful of black plum and berries have a sprinkle of thyme and sarsaparilla on the nose, becoming more blackberry pie on the palate. Those flavours last in the mouth, being extended by powdery fine tannins and a whip of fresh acid to complete.

| 2010 | 93 | 2024 | $99.00 | 14.0% |
| 2011 | 93 | 2021 | $99.00 | 14.8% |

D'ARENBERG
D'ARRY'S ORIGINAL SHIRAZ GRENACHE ★★★★

Ripe year wine with abundant dark licorice black plum, spicy fruits. The palate is juicy soft tannins ripe fruits deep mouthful, terrific flavour with freshness and generosity, lingers raspberry fruits with a chalky finish.

2011	86	2019	$18.00	14.2%
2012	90	2020	$18.00	14.5%
2013	94	2020	$20.00	14.5%

D'ARENBERG
NOBLE WRINKLED RIESLING ★★★★

Intense and complex, with exotic blonde toffee, caramelised palm sugar and citrus and tropical fruit. A zingy line of acidity and massive length.

2007	89	2012	$25.00	10.0%
2008	92	2013	$25.00	11.5%
2011	94	2021	$25.00	10.0%

DALWHINNIE

Dalwhinnie near Moonambel in Victoria has been managed by the Jones family since 1976. The wines are more about the Dalwhinnie vineyard and less about the variety – big full bodied, rich reds; soft and fleshy, with regional grippy tannins that turn silky textured around 10 years in the reds. Each variety is enshrined in an individual dance, full of seamless fruit and tannin.

Winemaker: David Jones
Open: Daily 10am–5pm, 448 Taltarni Road, Moonambel
Ph: (03) 5467 2388 *www.dalwhinnie.com.au*

DALWHINNIE
EAGLE SERIES SHIRAZ ★★★★★

Olive tarry black fruited and reserved, a serious closed style This is a superior, seductive wine with ripe berry fruits, soft tannins and a long, full middle palate. There are fine tannins and fruit in reserve. With impeccable balance now, it will evolve easily for many years.

2010	96	2039	$150.00	13.5%
2011	Not made			
2012	93	2030	$160.00	13.0%

DALWHINNIE
MOONAMBEL CABERNET SAUVIGNON ★★★★★

Lovely colour, with deep aromas of mineral, oyster shell, liquorice, earthy dark chocolate oak. Smells tannic and firm. Beautiful, soft and vibrant with great length. It just dances down the tongue with plenty of dark fruit, magnificent energy, the acidity to cellar, bridging tannins and a mouth-watering, fine grained tannin finish. Drink after 2018.

2011	Not made			
2012	86	2016	$55.00	13.5%
2013	95	2028	$55.00	14.0%

DALWHINNIE
MOONAMBEL CHARDONNAY ★★★★

Beeswax, charry, vanilla caramel oak complexity. The palate lacks definition yet offers youthful drinkability, with a soft, round friendly texture and smooth style for drinking young.

Vintage	Rank	Drink	RRP	Vol Alc
2011	92	2018	$42.00	13.0%
2012	90	2017	$42.00	14.0%
2013	87	2017	$45.00	14.0%

DALWHINNIE
MOONAMBEL SHIRAZ ★★★★★
Red fruit expression, blueberry and blackberry, fresh and complex and medium-bodied silky tannins with elegant proportions. A well balanced wine with tight dark fruits. Finishes with smoked meats and charcuterie flavours and chalky tannin textures. A lot to admire and patience is your friend here.

2011	Not made			
2012	90	2020	$65.00	13.0%
2013	92	2028	$60.00	13.8%

DALWHINNIE
SOUTH WEST ROCKS SHIRAZ ★★★★★
A style that continues to balance power with restraint. Has the tightness in youth, vivacity of ripe fruits and mineral edges on the back, with a long acid thread of tense dark fruits cola and tar. Not yet knit, it is detailed, tight and youthful.

2008	92	2017	$80.00	14.0%
2009	Not made			
2012	92	2026	$80.00	14.5%

DANDELION VINEYARDS
Dandelion Vineyards is owned by wine marketing professional, Zar Brookes and wife Elena, a trained winemaker. They produce single vineyard wines from South Australian vineyards in the Adelaide Hills, Barossa and Eden Valleys and McLaren Vale. All receive a whimsical name, thanks to Zar's impish sense of wine. The wide variety of vineyard sources creates a diverse number of wines, including Shiraz Riesling and Barossa Grenache Rose, which offer value and interest and many of which could be included.
Winemaker: *Elena Brooks*
Open: *No Cellar Door, 17 De-Caux Ave, Port Willunga*
Ph: *(08) 8556 6099 www.dandelionvineyards.com.au*

Vintage	Rank	Drink	RRP	Vol Alc

DANDELION VINEYARDS
WONDERLAND OF THE EDEN VALLEY RIESLING ★★★★★

The old vineyard that supplies this fruit is coveted by local Barossa winemakers who know it and has, for many years, been a core element of big riesling brands. Zar's charm has won the day here. Overall, pretty and fresh with lime, lemon juice and showing concentration, length and finesse in the mouth. It honours the citrusy bright acidity of Eden Valley riesling with a long, deep palate and extreme length of flavour.

Vintage	Rank	Drink	RRP	Vol Alc
2010	90	2018	$30.00	11.5%
2012	92	2023	$27.00	12.0%
2015	96	2020	$60.00	11.5%

DANDELION VINEYARDS
RED QUEEN OF THE EDEN VALLEY ★★★★★

Full of charm and interest and fascinating to play spot the smell and taste game, with as you sip with friends. A very elegant, restrained and interesting wine. Pretty spices, white pepper, and smoked meats note decorate the dark berry and sage fruit aromas with fresh appealing interest. The palate is ripe, soft tannins smoothly textured with dark berry, smoked meats and white pepper spice notes. Restrained oak in the middle mouth and on the finish.

Vintage	Rank	Drink	RRP	Vol Alc
2010	90	2022	$85.00	14.0%
2012	95	2022	$100.00	14.5%

DAVID HOOK WINES

David Hook founded his winery in the Hunter in the 1980s. He draws on NSW regions and his flying winemaker experience in the 1990s in Iberia, the south of France and the USSR, to produce an intelligent, new-generation style of Hunter wines from his eight hectares of old shiraz, semillon and chardonnay. Aged re-releases and a range of Italian varietals from regional NSW are available from cellar door.

Winemaker: *David Hook*
Open: *Daily 10am–5pm, Cnr Ekerts & Broke Road, Pokolbin*
Ph: *(02) 4998 7121* ***www.davidhookwines.com.au***

Vintage	Rank	Drink	RRP	Vol Alc

DAVID HOOK WINES
OLD VINES SHIRAZ ★★★★★

Deep and complex dark fruits almost tarry dried herbs oak spice adding a layer in the mouth, fairly subtle ripe round medium bodied crunchy red fruits, more about elegance than depth long silky tannins bridge the red berry fruit with finesse.

2011	95	2035	$40.00	13.5%
2013	93	2018	$40.00	13.5%
2014	90	2019	$40.00	13.5%

DAVID HOOK WINES
OLD VINES SEMILLON ★★★★★

An easy wine to own as you can drink young or cellar this beauty. Exotic fruit notes with the usual lemon complexity plus background lime and white stone fruit aromas. The youthful palate is seamless round weighty ripe fruits with length, old school grape growing and modern winemaking combining to bring fruit with focus and length.

2013	90	2022	$25.00	10.6%
2014	94	2036	$25.00	10.5%
2015	92	2024	$25.00	10.5%

DAWSON & JAMES

Dawson & James are experienced senior winemakers and old mates from the Hardy Wine Company. By focusing on "the best of the best" and only making two wines from mature vines grown in the Meadowbank vineyard, approximately 60 kms north west of Hobart, they produce excellent wines.
Winemakers: *Tim James and Peter Dawson*
Open: *No Cellar Door, RSD1470 Brookman Road, Hope Forest*
Ph: *(04) 1884 7900* *www.dawsonjames.com.au*

DAWSON & JAMES
PINOT NOIR ★★★★★

Red cherry, stalk and lots of savoury iodine with a nori roll savoury to the red fruits. In the mouth, a sweep of ripe fruits reined in by fresh acidity and charry oak, with concentrated flavours that hold long to the chalky youthful finish.

| 2010 | 89 | 2020 | $48.00 | 13.5% |
| 2011 | 92 | 2024 | $58.00 | 13.2% |

Vintage	Rank	Drink	RRP	Vol Alc

DAWSON & JAMES
SINGLE VINEYARD CHARDONNAY ★★★★★

A very consistent style and value too. Complex with well judged fine French oak and subtle white fruits wed seamlessly into a round and dense wine. In the mouth, fruit power backed by savoury winemaker flint and low key, but high quality oak. Flavours of fresh cut white fruit running towards tropical and green pineapple, dense and rich, fine acidity and flowing fruit power. Running even and long, propelled by fine grained acids and oak tannins. A full-bodied wine the finish that has dignity, tidy fresh acidity, and savoury winemaker elements.

| 2011 | 95 | 2025 | $48.00 | 12.7% |
| 2013 | 95 | 2020 | $48.00 | 12.9% |

DE BORTOLI

The De Bortoli Yarra Valley winery has become the flagship for the family, whose long-term commitment to dealing with agricultural cycles and probing of new styles, varieties and approaches puts them among the new leaders of the table wine industry. The wine quality continues to improve across the board, especially in the Yarra Valley, where world-class wines are being made. The joint venture PHI wines are excellent and will feature in due course. Expect a bigger entry each year for this company, as it spreads its wings and flies.

Winemakers: *Darren De Bortoli, Stephen Webber, Rob Glastonbury, Julie Mortlock, John Coughlan, Andrew Bretherton and Sarah Fagan.*
Open: *Daily 10am–5pm, Pinnacle Lane, Dixon's Creek*
Ph: *(02) 6966 0100* *www.debortoli.com.au*

DE BORTOLI
LA BOHEME ACT TWO YARRA VALLEY PINOT NOIR ROSE ★★★★★

Touch of herbal and strawberry and a Provencal pitch of savoury fruit and style on the nose. The multi-stage palate has soft acids and fresh strawberry middle palate flavours. Wild herbs on the finish and a fresh buoyant length, thanks to the fine acid. Lots of intrigue, detail and nuance. Less sweet than previous vintages.

| 2012 | 90 | 2015 | $20.00 | 13.0% |
| 2014 | 91 | 2016 | $22.00 | 12.5% |

Vintage	Rank	Drink	RRP	Vol Alc

DE BORTOLI
ESTATE GROWN YARRA VALLEY CHARDONNAY ★★★★

The best sort of complexity comes to your attention slowly as in this wine with each sip comes another experience. The fruit has been given an over coat of quality oak that adds appeal to create oatmeal, lemon meringue grapefruit aromas. The savoury wine making notes lie in the distant aromas and flavours, settling after a few sips. Even served chilled, the palate has drive and energy with oak wrapping the pure stone fruits to create a gliding, medium bodied palate with fresh finesse.

2012	88	2015	$31.00	12.5%
2014	94	2019	$30.00	12.5%
2015	92	2019	$25.00	12.5%

DE BORTOLI
RESERVE RELEASE SELECTION A5 CHARDONNAY ★★★★★

This is a very good wine. Citrus fruits cloaked in balanced winemaking showing creamy barrel ferment, appealing wild ferment, creamy oatmeal and subtle oak. The palate has pristine fruit length, depth with balanced acidity, flowing deep and long in the mouth.

2011	94	2016	$48.00	12.0%
2012	93	2016	$48.00	12.5%
2015	95	2020	$48.00	12.7%

DE BORTOLI
ESTATE GROWN YARRA VALLEY PINOT NOIR ★★★★

The style is confident, complex with strawberry into raspberry fruit, low oak and a flicker of savoury stems influence with the whole unit smelling solid. The palate is strawberry, flickers rose creamy soft tannins with the palate is thinly veiled soft fleshy red fruit, medium long.

2012	91	2017	$30.00	13.0%
2014	92	2022	$30.00	13.0%
2015	90	2020	$25.00	13.5%

| Vintage | Rank | Drink | RRP | Vol Alc |

DE BORTOLI
YARRA VALLEY ESTATE GROWN CABERNET SAUVIGNON ★★★★

A medium weight wine with varietal aromas in the attractive spectrum with leafy violets and black currant. In the mouth, this has great tannins- layered and running centre stage down the middle of the mouth wed to long ripe black currant and puree flavours, balanced by the leafiness. An individual style with Bordeaux ripeness and tannins that need food.

2010	90	2016	$36.00	12.5%
2012	90	2019	$36.00	13.0%
2013	90	2020	$36.00	13.5%

DE BORTOLI
YARRA VALLEY SELECTION A8 SYRAH ★★★★

Aromas are complex fruit spectrum perfumed Bourneville cocoa powder, peppery stemmy, plum mulberry leaf liquorice dark fruits. The soft tannins swamp the front palate then the red fruit flavours pick up blueberry, plum in the middle palate and the firm sandy tannins add glamour to finish. Food wine young and will age. Midweight fruit and full grape and peppery stem tannins. Decant this medium-bodied medium long wine for best effect.

2012	93	2026	$52.00	13.0%
2013	94	2026	$50.00	14.0%
2014	92	2022	$50.00	14.0%

DE BORTOLI
RIORRET THE ABBEY VINEYARD ★★★★★

Very well polished ripe fruit with a cascade of violets, fruits of the forest, and a black tea stemmy edge at the back, aromas. Very soft integrated tannins and fleshy fruit that will age well but is very desirable right now. Red cherry dark plum and firming tannin length. Needs food in youth to sort out the tannins.

2010	91	2018	$40.00	13.0%
2012	88	2018	$45.00	13.0%
2013	92	2025	$45.00	13.0%

| Vintage | Rank | Drink | RRP | Vol Alc |

DE BORTOLI
RIORRET BALNARRING VINEYARD ★★★★★

Great colour varietal. The aromas are subtle with meaty, into cocoa powder and regional jubey feminine buoyancy, showing red cherry and well balanced stem adding nutmeg spice and oak. The palate is rich with firm tannins and full and long strawberry middle flavours, grainy tannin savoury dictates it's going to take a while to come round, firm finishing structured and very subtle it's a keeper.

2010	90	2024	$50.00	13.0%
2015	94	2020	$50.00	13.5%

DE BORTOLI
'NOBLE ONE' (375ML) ★★★★★

Finesse within the powerful pure botrytis spectrum. Intense tropical mango, paw paw and apricot aromas. The palate is very rich and sweet, with candied long lusciousness. Low acidity and peaks of tropical and poached citrus fruits, after about 30 seconds. It draws to a close on the correct side of cloying.

2010	90	2017	$69.00	10.0%
2011	90	2021	$64.00	11.0%
2013	92	2029	$65.00	10.5%

DE IULIIS

De Iuliis is a much loved Hunter company, with a personable owner, old vines, delicious wines and top-end, age-worthy quality. What else can be added? Consistency and value across the board and a swag of awards. Notable semillon chardonnay and shiraz.

Winemaker: *Mike De Iuliis*
Open: *Daily 10am–5pm, 1616 Broke Road, Pokolbin*
Ph: *(02) 4993 8000 www.dewine.com.au*

DE IULIIS
AGED RELEASE SEMILLON ★★★★★

Pale green gold colour in a young, subtle, caramel-like burnt brown sugar aroma and a palate that is round, mouth filling and quite neutral in flavour, with the slightest hint of brown lime. Could have waited another 10 years to release this wine.

2006	93	2020	$30.00	11.5%
2007	94	2030	$30.00	11.0%

Vintage	Rank	Drink	RRP	Vol Alc

DE IULIIS
LIMITED RELEASE SHIRAZ ★★★★

Hunter savoury fruit aromas, dark spice and blackberry dark plum lead to a classic, smooth-textured, generous, silky tannin and sweet-fruited wine, with medium-bodied, polished old vine tannins. Spiced plum, savoury fruits on the palate and good length of ripe fruit sweetness. Elegant, lively, textured and nuanced; like a good book that keeps you wondering what's next. A cellaring style that is highly drinkable now.

2009	95	2029	$60.00	13.5%
2013	95	2035	$60.00	13.8%

DE IULIIS
STEVEN VINEYARD SHIRAZ ★★★★★

In this, Hunter edition berry fruits have a complex darker vanilla and chocolate oak notes. In the mouth a lovely balance and fluidity with fine tannins and black fruits wed to oak and the palate line is unbroken from front to back on the long finish.

2013	95	2030	$40.00	12.5%
2014	93	2015	$40.00	14.2%

DEEP WOODS ESTATE

Deep Woods Estate, part of the Fogarty Wine Group, is a Margaret River producer that consistently Impresses, with well grown and well made wines that exhibit freshness and length of bright regional fruit flavours.
Winemaker: *Julian Langworthy*
Open: *Wed to Sun 11am–5pm, Lot 889 Commonage Road, Yallingup*
Ph: *(08) 9756 6066* *www.deepwoods.com.au*

DEEP WOODS
HILLSIDE CHARDONNAY ★★★★★

Aromas of apricot and grapefruit with lively zesty intensity, low in oak and bright in fruit and confidence. The palate is full, rich not heavy, but complex with strands of oak, fruit and acidity weaving through the flavours and textures. Plenty of braided complexity with fruit doing the talking and grapefruit on the finish.

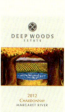

Vintage	Rank	Drink	RRP	Vol Alc
2012	91	2018	$20.00	13.0%
2013	90	2017	$20.00	13.0%
2014	96	2018	$24.99	13.0%

DELATITE
Delatite in Victoria's Mansfield region has recently implemented biodynamic management while evolving its wines and styles, mainly in delicate, fragrant white wines. All wines since 2009 have been made 'wild', without the addition of commercial yeast.
Winemaker: Andy Browning
Open: Daily 10am–6pm, 246 Stoneys Road, Mansfield
Ph: (03) 5775 2922 *www.delatitewinery.com.au*

DELATITE
DEADMANS HILL GEWURZTRAMINER ★★★★★
The style has changed with this wine and it is looking good and towards the next generation. Starts out as a 'tick the box' example of the variety with musk, rose petal, orange blossom, and lychee with an extra perfume and lift. Almost tropical, the palate has vibrant acidity wrapped in the same fresh fruits as the aroma. Lees has helped weave the finish of finely gripping acids, flavours and skin tannins, into a wine with a fresh moreishness. Very young and it will work hard for many years.

Vintage	Rank	Drink	RRP	Vol Alc
2012	92	2014	$25.00	13.5%
2014	94	2018	$25.00	13.5%
2015	94	2030	$25.00	13.0%

DELATITE
PINOT GRIS ★★★★★
Fruit and spice, a nod to Alsace, defined varietal personality, honest, with its bag of complexities, waxy, caramel pear the palate has length and line, freshness and finesse with a long line of pear and lemon zest flavours with a good finish and grip.

Vintage	Rank	Drink	RRP	Vol Alc
2012	88	2016	$23.00	13.5%
2014	92	2018	$25.00	13.0%
2015	93	2018	$25.00	13.0%

DEVIL'S LAIR

With 130 hectares under vine, Devil's Lair is a sizable producer across many prices and styles. Where it shines is with winemaker, Oliver Crawford and his strong affinity for chardonnay and other whites. He worked on the top Penfolds wines before joining Devils Lair and has great ability to produce complex chardonnay and fresh-balanced whites that are delicious to drink.
Winemakers: *Simon Robertson and Oliver Crawford*
Open: *No Cellar Door, Forest Grove, Margaret River*
Ph: *(1300) 651 650 www.devils-lair.com*

DEVIL'S LAIR
9TH CHAMBER CHARDONNAY ★★★★★

Nougat, praline almond toffee and balanced oak. The palate has control, with restful winemaker artifact making it silky, even creamy, with excellent acidity and vibrant stone fruit. It has fruit woven oak that is complex, lingering and layered on the finish, with vanilla and creamy yoghurt. Big style for a traditional chardonnay.

2009	94	2017	$99.00	13.0%
2011	95	2019	$99.00	12.8%
2012	Not made			

DEVIL'S LAIR
CABERNET SAUVIGNON ★★★★★

There is a fresh sprig of mint that sits well with the cedar, cassis and dark chocolate character of this wine. The muscular tannins hit mid palate and provide structure and finesse. Drink it or keep it – it has the ability for both.

2011	93	2020	$49.99	14.5%
2013	93	2025	$49.99	14.0%

DEXTER

Tod Dexter is an experienced winemaker, with a good track record for quality wine via Stonier and Yabby Lake. His vineyard at Merricks North in the Mornington was first planted in 1987 and is ideally located for the production of premium wine.
Winemaker: *Tod Dexter*
Open: *No Cellar Door, 210 Foxeys Road, Merricks*
Ph: *(03) 5989 7007 www.dexterwines.com.au*

| Vintage | Rank | Drink | RRP | Vol Alc |

DEXTER WINES
MORNINGTON PENINSULA CHARDONNAY ★★★★
Great style and understanding here with a riper edition in 2015. The sweet oak adds to the fruity intensity of the aromas and wild ferment notes add ginger to the stone fruit, subtle citrus complexity. The palate is ripe pears and white nectarine fruit filled, even in the middle palate. Overall; fuller and more up front than the 2014, with well judged balance to give the fruit a firing range proportional to its intensity.

2013	92	2018	$38.00	13.0%
2014	94	2019	$38.00	13.0%
2015	92	2019	$38.00	13.5%

DEXTER WINES
MORNINGTON PENINSULA PINOT NOIR ★★★★★
Opulent, complex and generous with ripe strawberry, red cherry pie and subtle vanilla that leads to a ripe evenly filled flavourful mouthful. Medium bodied, this juicy raspberry middle palate closes firm and fresh.

2013	90	2018	$49.00	13.5%
2014	87	2020	$49.00	13.0%
2015	94	2025	$49.00	13.3%

DOMAINE A
Domaine A, in the Coal River Valley of Southern Tasmania, is a precision-run vineyard that produces superb, medium-bodied wines that are surprisingly long lived.

Winemaker: *Peter Althaus*
Open: *Weekdays 10am–4pm, Tea Tree Road, Compania*
Ph: *(03) 6260 4174   www.domaine-a.com.au*

DOMAINE A
CABERNET SAUVIGNON ★★★★★
This is unusually 95% cabernet, from vines planted between 1979 and 1996 and first made in 1990. Matured for 2.5 to 3 years in oak prior to bottling and released 6 years after vintage, in a determined attempt to allow the wine to speak. Fine, gentle blackcurrant complexities with tapenade and savoury dark cabernet fruits. Cedar, sandalwood fragrance and back notes of subtle tomato bush. The palate is refined, with subtle ripe fruit and an open-fronted generous, medium-bodied wine of fine

Vintage	Rank	Drink	RRP	Vol Alc

grained tannins, building seamless in the middle and on the finish. It's a youthful, two-stage palate: fresh and vibrant up front, then running into more drying and complex savoury cedar characters and textures as it progresses.

2006	94	2019	$120.00	14.0%
2007	90	2016	$120.00	13.5%
2008	95	2035	$120.00	13.5%

DOMAINE A
PINOT NOIR ★★★

Good colour leads to the gentle spice of white pepper and strawberry fruits. In the mouth enjoyable, finesse, even and long, the red berry fruits have good length, the tannins are complete and contrast to the red cherry, white pepper flavours minty notes on the finish.

2008	90	2019	$90.00	15.0%
2009	92	2020	$90.00	13.5%
2010	89	2018	$90.00	13.7%

DOMAINE A
LADY A FUME BLANC SAUVIGNON BLANC ★★★★★

The nimble complexity of oak and aged Sauvignon Blanc showing quince, honeysuckle, lychee and vanilla coconut aromas. Starts out silky textured, yellow wine gums, medium-full body, then the long flavours get complex with plenty of new French oak tannins and low toast flavours. Oak dryness on the finish.

2012	95	2019	$60.00	13.0%
2013	93	2022	$65.00	13.5%
2014	94	2022	$65.00	15.0%

DOMAINE A
MERLOT ★★★★★

Rich ripe plummy fruits swing up to cassis and subtle mint with savoury oak spice and a touch of rancio aromas. Tender in the mouth, mid-weight, ripe berry with a lot of oak holding the flavour back but supporting texture and length with a high acidity on the finish. A wine to be judged at the table, not the bench. 86 on the bench 90 with food.

2005	91	2016	$90.00	13.5%
2007	95	2027	$90.00	13.5%
2010	90	2019	$85.00	14.0%

DOMAINE A
PETITE A CABERNET SAVIGNON MERLOT CABERNET FRANC ★★★

Understated at first, then detailed and rewarding requiring a meal to get completely acquainted. Aromas of pretty red and black fruits in the Bordeaux manner, with blueberry and black currant, leather, carbon, minerals and a leafy fresh tobacco note at the back. In the mouth this wine balances flavour and structure. Light medium bodied raspberry, red cherry then blueberry fruits with a cool grippy sandy tannin mouth feel that sits a while with plenty of flavour length.

| 2008 | 90 | 2018 | $55.00 | 14.0% |
| 2010 | 94 | 2020 | $45.00 | 14.0% |

DOMAINE NATURALISTE

Domaine Naturaliste is the result of Perth born California educated at UC Davis with a masters degree and 5 years winemaking in California with Francis Ford Coppola, 7 flexible years with Pierro until 2000. Many years consulting has given Bruce a roots up view of wine that shows in the style and flavour profile. Add in a custom crush facility and you have Domaine Naturaliste.
Winemaker: *Bruce Dukes*
Open: *No Cellar Door, 61 Hairpin Road, Carbunup*
Ph: *(08) 9755 1188 www.domainenaturaliste.com.au*

DOMAINE NATURALISTE
ARTUS CHARDONNAY ★★★★★

The full wild winemaking style creates a complex crème brulee hazelnut savoury edge to the citrus and stone fruit. The complex palate is silky, even and long, and compact. Nutty lees, subtle acidity and intense with a creamy gentle evenness on the complex honey pear and apple flavours that linger on the finish.

| 2013 | 94 | 2019 | $46.93 | 13.5% |
| 2014 | 95 | 2019 | $47.00 | 13.0% |

DOMAINE NATURALISTE
REBUS CABERNET SAUVIGNON ★★★★★

Truly excellent value for the price here with the complex leafy and red fruits wrapped in savoury smoked meats and oak. Soft tannins, very good middle palate, refined persistence, intensity and harmony with very good length.

Vintage	Rank	Drink	RRP	Vol Alc
2012	92	2025	$35.00	13.8%
2013	94	2021	$35.00	13.8%
2014	92	2018	$23.40	13.8%

DOMAINE NATURALISTE
FLORIS CHARDONNAY

Fresh white fruits in a subtle oak background. A gentle and savoury wine with a generous and full middle palate with white peach and oak spice. Pure even fresh fruit wrapped in fine French Belgian whole oak flavours.

Vintage	Rank	Drink	RRP	Vol Alc
2013	94	2020	$29.20	13.5%
2014	92	2017	$29.20	13.5%

DOMAINE NATURALISTE
SAUVAGE SAUVIGNON BLANC

Sauvage means wild ferment and in a ratio of 2 sauvignon to one semillon. It is fermented and matured in 500 litre puncheons for ten months. Complex development with ripe fruit, bees wax, lemon verbena, nettle and lychee with subtle oak toast aromas. Into the mouth with plenty of racy fruit power, pleasurable complexity from oak, youthful texture that will run long in the bottle. The flavours are complex; lychee, nettle fruit and oak milk chocolate, cedar oak with subtle oak tannins drawing through.

Vintage	Rank	Drink	RRP	Vol Alc
2013	94	2030	$29.20	13.0%
2014	95	2022	$29.20	13.0%

| Vintage | Rank | Drink | RRP | Vol Alc |

DOMANIQUE PORTET
The winemaker Dominique Portet, previously at Taltarni, has a Bordeaux background. Inspired by the Yarra Valley where he has established his new base, the wines show a delicious, delicate approach.

Winemaker: *Dominique Portet*
Open: *Daily 10am–5pm, 870 Maroondah Hwy, Coldstream*
Ph: *(03) 5962 5760* *www.dominiqueportet.com*

DOMINIQUE PORTET
CABERNET SAUVIGNON ★★★★

In the riper Yarra spectrum, with friendly black currant aromas in a juicy style, with ripe black currant berry fruits, subtle leafiness fine acids and balanced low tannins for drinking with or without food.

2009	Not made			
2010	92	2025	$42.00	13.0%
2012	92	2032	$48.00	13.5%

DOMINIQUE PORTET
FONTAINE ROSE ★★★★

Crunchy red fruits, mineral with toffee apple and a plump, up-front creamy rich palate. A well filled middle, with a lovely mouth feel and creamy ripe apricot and apple caramel fruit.

2010	90	2012	$26.00	13.6%
2011	89	2013	$26.00	13.0%
2013	91	2016	$26.00	13.5%

DOMINIQUE PORTET
HEATHCOTE SHIRAZ ★★★★★

Floral pepper spice with blueberry, blackberry and pretty vanilla caramel edged BBQ smoke oak. The sumptuous palate has very creamy, ripe, fine tannins that provide a silky rolling richness to the front and middle, with the liquorice, black fruit, spice and berry fruit unfolding into minerally tannins on the finish. Medium full bodied.

2007	Not made			
2008	92	2022	$45.00	14.5%
2009	Not made			
2010	94	2010	$48.00	13.5%

Vintage	Rank	Drink	RRP	Vol Alc

DOMINIQUE PORTET
ANDRE SHIRAZ CABERNET SAUVIGNON ★★★★★

Impressive intensity, yet restrained in its opulence with blackberry, fruits of the forest jam, mineral edged, liquorice, vanilla, caramel and coconut malt oak in balance. The quality is impressive with very stylish black fruit flavours, mouth-filling silky tannin, a medium full-bodied structure and silky tannins that roll down the tongue revealing the berry, liquorice, malt and long tannin structure. Food-friendly finish. Needs a decant; drink after 2015 and before 2022.

Vintage	Rank	Drink	RRP	Vol Alc
2006	92	2024	$120.00	14.0%
2008	91	2022	$150.00	14.5%

DOMINIQUE PORTET
SAUVIGNON BLANC ★★★★★

One of most sophisticated, oak fermented styles that needs to be served lightly chilled. Finesse and funky, exotic, subtle barrel-fermented aromas, with lychee and honey suckle. The light-bodied palate is understated, driven by delicate fresh acids and white nectarine middle palate fruits that will unfold with age into more honeysuckle exotica.

Vintage	Rank	Drink	RRP	Vol Alc
2011	91	2015	$26.00	13.0%
2012	92	2015	$28.00	13.5%
2014	92	2021	$28.00	13.5%

ELDERTON WINES

Elderton Wines in the Barossa Valley are consistently producing ripe, rich full-bodied reds based on family-owned, old vineyards and enjoying the rewards of quality production.

Winemaker: *Richard Langford*
Open: *Mon-Fri 8.30am–5pm, Sat Sun and Pub Hols 11am–4pm*
5 Tanunda Road, Nuriootpa
Ph: (08) 8568 7878 ***www.eldertonwines.com.au***

ELDERTON WINES
ASHMEAD SINGLE VINEYARD CABERNET SAUVIGNON ★★★★

The aromas are rock solid intense; violets and black olive as well as black currant fruit aromas and vanilla toast oak. The style is sophisticated maintaining Barossa softness, fruit sweetness with good length of fruit, touch of minerality very even and soft in the middle and the tannins build the finish. Restrained balance and thoughtful winemaking.

Vintage	Rank	Drink	RRP	Vol Alc
2010	96	2035	$100.00	14.5%
2012	92	2020	$100.00	14.5%
2013	92	2023	$100.00	13.5%

ELDERTON WINES
BAROSSA CABERNET SAUVIGNON ★★★★

The fruit has a raspberry intensity almost confectionary while the palate is soft easy drinking and pure red licorice flavour with fine soft tannins and lingering flavours.

Vintage	Rank	Drink	RRP	Vol Alc
2010	90	2024	$30.00	14.5%
2012	88	2018	$34.00	14.5%
2013	86	2018	$34.00	14.0%

ELDERTON WINES
ODE TO LORRAINE CABERNET SAUVIGNON SHIRAZ ★★★★

Bright Barossa berry fruits with freshness and life showing cassis, fresh raspberry and rhubarb red fruit aromas. The palate has bright ripe fruit up front and good length and the tannins join the fray adding drive and energy to the finish with a full bodied firm finish.

Vintage	Rank	Drink	RRP	Vol Alc
2010	93	2025	$55.00	14.7%
2012	91	2028	$45.00	14.5%
2013	91	2019	$55.00	14.5%

ELDERTON WINES
BAROSSA SHIRAZ ★★★★

Black berry chocolate pudding into mocha oak complexity. In the mouth, Barossa soft tannins, dark spices, black berry cola shiraz fruit flavours up front. Medium weight, good oak support with ripe length and a soft finish.

Vintage	Rank	Drink	RRP	Vol Alc
2009	87	2016	$27.00	14.5%
2012	89	2019	$30.00	14.5%
2013	86	2018	$34.00	14.0%

ELDERTON WINES
COMMAND SHIRAZ ★★★★★

Barossa big boldness with dense mocha chocolate dark plum fruit intensity. In the mouth the fruit is fresh, the flavours a melee of dark spiced, rich ripe and full flavours plums with fine soft tannins that plump up the mouth feel and length. The palate is very youthful and fresh and will age well into a chocolaty regional style.

Vintage	Rank	Drink	RRP	Vol Alc
2009	92	2018	$110.00	14.8%
2010	93	2030	$110.00	14.8%
2011	Not made			
2012	92	2027	$110.00	14.5%

ELDERTON WINES
WESTERN RIDGE GRENACHE CARIGNAN ★★★★

Blueberry and red fruits tempered by earthy tones. Perfumed, balanced mocha oak notes and savoury overall it is the picture of a modern Barossa red. The palate is gentle soft ripe tannins flowing red raspberry grenache fruit with complexity up front, fine tannins retaining freshness and finishes raspberry. An interesting variant on the GSM style.

Vintage	Rank	Drink	RRP	Vol Alc
2013	90	2018	$55.00	14.5%
2014	93	2020	$55.00	14.5%

Vintage	Rank	Drink	RRP	Vol Alc

ELDRIDGE ESTATE
Eldridge Estate of Red Hill, planted in 1984, is a small Mornington Peninsula vineyard with an outstanding range of wines, including the clonal blend which captures the essence of Mornington's very pretty pinot style with sweet fruit, yet retaining elegance.
Winemaker: *David Lloyd*
Open: *Mon to Fri, 12pm–4pm and Weekends, 11am–5pm*
120 Arthurs Seat Road, Red Hill
Ph: (+61) 414758960   www.eldridge-estate.com.au

ELDRIDGE ESTATE
CLONAL BLEND PINOT NOIR ★★★★
Red fruits seemingly traditional, less stalky, leather from old oak, aromas. The palate is an essay in generosity ripe strawberry-raspberry fruit, succulent soft tannins of pinot with good front and middle, oak to close.

2010	89	2015	$75.00	13.5%
2013	95	2023	$75.00	14.0%
2014	90	2019	$75.00	14.0%

ELDRIDGE ESTATE
NORTH PATCH CHARDONNAY ★★★★
Fresh pear, oatmeal, quite direct primary aromas after the complex honeyed 2012, with an upfront simple palate and a short finish.

2011	85	2015	$30.00	13.0%
2012	91	2017	$35.00	13.5%
2013	83	2018	$35.00	13.5%

ELDRIDGE ESTATE
SINGLE MV 6 CLONE PINOT NOIR ★★★★★
MV6 is among the latest ripening clones in the Mornington so some years are initially shy in aromas and flavour. Initially old oak mint and dried herbs citrus, with very youthful tight red fruits. The palate is refined almost lean, well balanced fine acids add length to the frame of the palate and the spices are from raspberry red cherry into clove. The clonal blend is more tannic and the MV6 more spare.

2012	85	2018	$55.00	13.5%
2013	88	2018	$55.00	14.0%
2014	94	2022	$68.00	14.0%

| Vintage | Rank | Drink | RRP | Vol Alc |

ELDRIDGE ESTATE
CHARDONNAY ★★★★★

Pleasant balance and drink soon style with a complex vanilla, peanut brittle French oak. The palate is generous old school style; up front ripe fruited, with a short, fat and wide texture.

2012	95	2022	$40.00	13.5%
2013	80	2016	$40.00	13.5%
2014	88	2018	$40.00	13.0%

ELDRIDGE ESTATE
PINOT NOIR ★★★★★

Strawberry almost luscious in the feminine style of the Mornington. A ripe round palate with easy drinking generosity and oak tannins to hold the frame and finish in the mouth.

2012	94	2026	$55.00	13.5%
2013	86	2017	$55.00	14.0%
2014	88	2018	$60.00	14.0%

ELGEE PARK

Elgee Park is a significant regional vineyard and produces a style of wine with cool varietal expressions that are medium bodied, refreshing and with moderate alcohol. Discernible acidity, meant for food.
Winemakers: *Geraldine McFaul and Kathleen Quealy*
Open: *Weekdays, 9am–5pm and Weekends, 8am–5pm, Wallace Road, Dromana*
Ph: (03) 5989 7338 www.elgeeparkwines.com.au

ELGEE PARK
FAMILY RESERVE CABERNET MERLOT ★★★★

Cool fruits and robust vanilla cedar oak overlay, with butterscotch ripe fresh black fruit aromas, but nothing vegetal. The flavours are refined, medium bodied, moderate alcohol, fresh acidity, with good soft tannins and pretty black and red fruits in the middle. This builds long flavours, with a gentle drying structure on the finish. Harmony, complexity and nimbleness. The reason this book exists is to recognise and celebrate such wines.

2009	88	2015	$30.00	13.0%
2010	85	2016	$35.00	13.5%
2012	94	2022	$35.00	13.0%

Vintage	Rank	Drink	RRP	Vol Alc

ELGEE PARK
FAMILY RESERVE PINOT NOIR ★★★★

Aromas are raspberry and red currant, with gentle oak. In the mouth, a fresh middle and lightweight strawberry, with subtle herb to finish and resinous oak.

2010	92	2018	$45.00	13.0%
2011	84	2015	$45.00	13.5%
2012	88	2017	$50.00	13.0%

ELGEE PARK
FAMILY RESERVE CHARDONNAY ★★★★★

Playing it safe here with fruit richness. Aromas are floral white flowers and white apple. In the mouth, a lot of fruit, with musk-like lifted aromatics and fresh, very low oak. Exotic flavours with a fruit-driven freshness in the middle palate.

2012	83	2016	$45.00	13.0%
2013	90	2017	$50.00	13.0%
2014	88	2018	$50.00	13.5%

ELGEE PARK
FAMILY RESERVE VIOGNIER ★★★★

A mix of old oak vanilla brulee, French oak and understated ripe apricot. A great drinker. The palate is vinous rich texture, low in flavour, fresh without capturing the generosity of the variety or the stone fruit flavours. Finishes medium long, with subtle oak tannins.

2009	88	2014	$35.00	13.5%
2011	84	2015	$35.00	13.5%
2013	86	2016	$30.00	14.0%

EPEROSA

Eperosa reflects a love of wine from Epernay and Barossa, which led to the name. Five hectares of shiraz planted in Eden Valley at the old Hamilton's Springton site between 1890 and 1960 mean these wines have depth and interest. Brett Grocke is a fifth-generation Barossan and a viticultural consultant caring for many small parcels across the valley. Their grenache is also worth seeking out.
Winemaker: *Brett Grocke*
Open: *By Appointment Only, 24 Maria Street, Tanunda*
Ph: *(0428) 111 121 www.eperosa.com.au*

Vintage	Rank	Drink	RRP	Vol Alc

EPEROSA
ELEVATION SHIRAZ ★★★★★
Fresh raspberry into blue berry, notes of sage and dried herbs adding to the fruit aromas. In the mouth medium full body with the very soft tannins wed to deep red cherry fruit flavours from tip of tongue across the middle palate, under pinned by fine tannins which run the length of the palate and will age well on the long finish.

2011	87	2016	$39.00	14.0%
2012	92	2022	$39.00	13.8%
2014	94	2023	$49.00	13.9%

EVANS AND TATE
Evans and Tate is a widely available West Australian winemaker, whose focus at the high end is now on its Redbrook vineyard at Margaret River. Since its purchase by McWilliams in 2007, this label has grown to be a highly visible WA brand.
Winemaker: Matthew Byrne
Open: Daily, 10.30am–5pm, Corner of Caves Road and Metricup Road, Metricup
Ph: (02) 9722 1200 www.evansandtate.com.au

EVANS AND TATE
REDBROOK CABERNET SAUVIGNON ★★★★
Complex, with dark chocolate, fine dusty cabernet fruit and a subtle tomato leaf edge to the aromas. Medium-bodied lush tannin fruited, elegant structure with fresh driving acidity and quality middle-palate red and black fruits. Touch of mushroom oak complexity and a clean, food-friendly acid finish.

2008	88	2018	$49.00	13.5%
2010	89	2019	$45.00	14.0%
2011	90	2019	$45.00	14.0%

EVANS AND TATE
METRICUP ROAD CHARDONNAY ★★★
Margaret River peach and subtle grapefruit, rich and ripe with balance and articulation. The palate treads the line between fashion and force, nicely crafted savoury up front mid-weight texture flavours. Wild ferment character, flinty then into

Vintage	Rank	Drink	RRP	Vol Alc

creamy lees, white fruit and finishing grape fruit tangy brightness.

2013	87	2016	$19.99	13.5%
2014	88	2018	$24.00	13.0%
2015	92	2019	$23.99	13.0%

EVANS AND TATE
REDBROOK CHARDONNAY ★★★★★
Complex and subtle funky flavours with wine maker skilled use of techniques with cashew, lees and wild ferment. The palate cranks up the Metricup road wine style and offers a creamy, rich, focused and harmonious palate, with the lees adding complexity. The overall effect is long, light footed and lithe with a clean, structured finish.

2011	89	2016	$33.00	13.5%
2012	84	2016	$45.00	13.0%
2013	94	2017	$49.00	13.5%

FAR AGO HILL WINES
Far Ago Hill Wines in the Canyonleigh sub-region of NSW's Southern Highlands is drier and further south than the majority of local Highlands vineyards. The region's climate seems ideal for pinot gris, where this vineyard offers faithful varietal examples with a refreshing acidity.
Open: *No Cellar Door, 1371 Tugalong Road, Canyonleigh*
Ph: *1300 769 217 or 0418 418 441* ***www.faragohill.com***

FAR AGO HILL WINES
CANYONLEIGH RESERVE PINOT GRIS ★★★★
Pale sunset pink coloured Pinot Gris is still the exception however, Far Ago has consistently lived on the pinker more floral scented side of the Gris spectrum. The fruit aromas are ripe in the garden flowers with musk and almond and good intensity of fresh pears. Plenty of up front flavour and succulent texture give this a welcoming personality, a full middle palate running close to oily, through pears and musk sticks but held in check by well balanced acidity.

2012	90	2015	$30.00	12.8%
2015	86	2017	$30.00	11.5%
2016	92	2020	$32.00	14.0%

Vintage	Rank	Drink	RRP	Vol Alc

FARR RISING

Farr Rising is the label created by Nick Farr, the son of winemaker Gary Farr, using an increased percentage of their own fruit. An excellent, early drinking version compared to the higher quality and more expensive By Farr Chardonnay. These wines all have a happy drinking spot around four years or better when it's all in balance.

Winemaker: Nick Farr
Open: No Cellar Door, 101 Kelly Lane, Bannockburn
Ph: (03) 5281 1733 *www.byfarr.com.au*

FARR RISING
SAIGNEE ROSE ★★★★

Barrel-fermented pinot noir rosé with a lovely salmon pink colour and oak-edged aromas with a lovely rounded and concentrated red berry flavour and texture. Classic refreshment of white, with the body of a red and a whisper of sweetness to keep it all juicy. Bargain.

Vintage	Rank	Drink	RRP	Vol Alc
2008	91	2012	$20.00	13.5%
2010	92	2014	$20.00	13.5%

FARR RISING
GEELONG CHARDONNAY ★★★★★

The family love of fine French style is here with the usual judicious balance. The "drink young" palate runs fresh fruit with lively and vibrant citrus, white fruits, pear and apple running from front to back. Full in the middle palate and holding on with white fruit oak for a food-friendly interest to the finish.

Vintage	Rank	Drink	RRP	Vol Alc
2009	90	2015	$35.00	13.5%
2010	88	2014	$35.00	13.0%
2014	90	2017	$35.00	13.0%

FARR RISING
GEELONG PINOT NOIR ★★★★★

Very good depth, red cherry, cherry pip and raspberry fruit aromas create interest, with freshness and lift. The palate has generosity and rich fleshy flavours. The acidity keeps the fruit tight and tidy. Good depth and intensity of red fruit, with a very good length of flavour. Finishes with stemmy dried herbs and spices. Just needs time to develop.

Vintage	Rank	Drink	RRP	Vol Alc
2009	91	2020	$39.00	13.5%
2010	88	2018	$39.00	13.5%
2013	92	2021	$39.00	13.5%

Vintage	Rank	Drink	RRP	Vol Alc

FERNGROVE

Ferngrove, on the Frankland River in the south west of Western Australia, has 225 hectares of favourably located vines, allowing the winery to supply both quality and quantity and a range of styles and price points. Overall, the wines are juicy fresh and elegant.
Winemaker: *Marco Pinares and Marelize Russouw*
Open: *Mon to Fri 10am–4pm, 276 Ferngrove Road, Frankland River*
Ph: *(08) 9855 2378 www.ferngrove.com.au*

FERNGROVE
COSSACK RIESLING ★★★★

Smoky, entering early maturity aromas with petroleum and lime. In the mouth, plenty of weight, pears, white flower and lime with the smoky thread running front to back and a hard finish.

2013	90	2018	$23.00	12.5%
2014	94	2018	$23.00	12.5%
2015	84	2017	$25.00	13.0%

FERNGROVE
DIAMOND CHARDONNAY ★★★★★

Ripe aromas of powerful ripe pears, mineral and very pure- quality oak purrs in the background. In the mouth, lavish ripe fruits and well-knit oak, a plush middle palate with initial generosity, clean clear flavours, medium long and well-judged oak.

2013	88	2018	$25.00	14.0%
2014	86	2017	$25.00	13.5%
2015	90	2017	$25.00	14.0%

FERNGROVE
DRAGON SHIRAZ ★★★★

Savoury oak and tidy raspberry aromas, with discrete dried herbs delivers medium weight intensity and moderate flavours.

2011	90	2016	$30.00	13.0%
2012	89	2019	$32.00	14.2%
2013	86	2017	$32.00	14.0%

| Vintage | Rank | Drink | RRP | Vol Alc |

FERNGROVE
KING MALBEC ★★★★

Sappy black currant and cranberry aromas with a light herbal sappy element to the medium length, followed by sweet rhubarb and black currant with firming hard tannins.

2011	88	2016	$30.00	13.0%
2012	90	2018	$32.00	13.6%
2013	85	2018	$32.00	14.4%

FERNGROVE
MAJESTIC CABERNET SAUVIGNON ★★★★

Pretty and stylish with very varietal cabernet leafy black currant aromas. In the mouth, lacks punch and intensity. Interesting fruit and good oak tannin finesse, with violets and black currant middle and a firm tannin finish.

2011	89	2025	$30.00	13.5%
2012	90	2017	$32.00	14.3%
2013	89	2018	$32.00	14.4%

FERNGROVE
THE STIRLINGS CABERNET SAUVIGNON ★★★★★

Plenty of richness here from oak and very ripe fruit with jam and fruit puree's appearing. In the mouth, a middle palate paradise of fruit ripeness with and a spectrum of fruit flavours. The oak balance is well handled and there is a savoury element to the flavours with its southern bright fruit freshness.

2009	92	2027	$60.00	14.0%
2010	93	2022	$60.00	13.5%
2012	92	2022	$70.00	14.0%

FIRST CREEK

First Creek is one of the Hunter Valley's better kept secrets. Liz Jackson has been making cracking wines across Hunter classics and also in Tasmania. Hers is the hand that rocks the cradle of many wines in the Valley in her role as a contract winemaker. Their "Winemakers Selection" represents exceptional value.

Winemakers: *Liz Jackson and Damien Stevens*
Open: *Daily from 10.30am, 600 McDonalds Road, Pokolbin*
Ph: *(02) 4998 7293 www.firstcreekwines.com.au*

FIRST CREEK
WINEMAKERS RESERVE SEMILLON ★★★★★

Excellent colour, classic aromas and brightness of fruit, with a touch of candle wax development. The palate is vibrant, long and intense, with superb texture and richness in the regional style. Good balance and a long life ahead. This is still young and needs time.

Vintage	Rank	Drink	RRP	Vol Alc
2009	95	2025	$35.00	11.0%
2010	90	2020	$35.00	11.0%
2011	94	2025	$35.00	10.0%
2012	88	2018	$35.00	11.0%

FIRST CREEK
WINEMAKERS RESERVE SHIRAZ ★★★★★

Minerally plum and very soft and round. For drinking early, with enough tannin for mid-term aging.

Vintage	Rank	Drink	RRP	Vol Alc
2009	88	2027	$45.00	13.0%
2010	90	2019	$45.00	13.5%
2011	91	2017	$45.00	13.0%

| Vintage | Rank | Drink | RRP | Vol Alc |

FLETCHER WINES
Fletcher Wines is a nebbiolo specialist, drawing fruit from the Pyrenees, Yarra and King Valley in Victoria and the Adelaide Hills. The Australian wines tasted are intense and savoury and a great introduction to the wonders of nebbiolo, with a beautiful balance of varietal tannin, fruit and acidity. They show excellent winemaking skills and a great understanding of the variety. Only 100 cases of each wine are made annually.
Winemaker: *Dave Fletcher*
Open: *No Cellar Door*
Ph: *(04) 1294 9791 www.fletcherwines.com*

FLETCHER WINES
THE MINION NEBBIOLO ★★★★★
A multi regional blend based on Victorian, not Mildura vineyards and the best performing vineyards and clones each year and Dave Fletchers deep understanding of the variety. Aromas are complex and balanced tarry dark fruits black tea subtle tomato leafy green herbs, leads in the mouth with raspberry on a long palate youthfully firm fine varietal dry tannins and gentle red raspberry fruits into savoury tannins on the finish.

2012	89	2015	$35.00	13.5%
2014	94	2019	$35.00	14.0%
2015	90	2024	$35.00	14.0%

FORBES & FORBES
Brothers Colin Forbes & Rob Forbes are Forbes & Forbes wines based on Eden Valley vineyards. They are both very experienced wine people with all the bases covered between them from planting to accounting and business leadership.
Winemaker: *Colin Forbes*
30 Williamstown Road, Springton
Ph: *(08) 8568 2709 www.forbeswine.com.au*

FORBES & FORBES
EDEN VALLEY RIESLING ★★★★
Aromas are gentle and interesting with a honeysuckle edge to the usual Eden Valley lemony riesling. The palate has roundness to the fleshy fruits in a range of lemons and the acidity is an undertow, not a current, shaping the flavour

length to linger. Tight structured and delicate with a sense of understatement and poise. Very good value.

Vintage	Rank	Drink	RRP	Vol Alc
2009	93	2019	$23.00	11.0%
2014	93	2022	$20.00	12.5%
2015	92	2022	$20.00	12.8%

FORBES & FORBES

FORESTER ESTATE WINES
Winemaker: Kevin McKay, Todd Payne
Open:
1064 Wildwood Road, Yallingup
Ph: (61) 8975 52788 www.foresterestate.com.au

FORESTER ESTATE
CABERNET SAUGIVNON ★★★★
Regional fruit aromas, in a broad cocoa, black currant to dense earthy clumsy breadth. The palate has the delicious Margaret River sweep of ripe fine black currant cabernet with pretty floral top notes and fine grained tannins to finish.

Vintage	Rank	Drink	RRP	Vol Alc
2008	85	2018	$32.30	13.5%
2009	86	2016	$32.30	13.5%
2012	91	2018	$37.99	14.0%

FORESTER Estate

FORESTER ESTATE
SEMILLON SAUVIGNON BLANC ★★★★★
This style carries a whisper of vanilla peanut brittle oak aromas with tropical sauvignon flavours. The oak adds creaminess to the middle palate. The fruit is flaring in a wide arc on the finish with tropical flavours and fresh acidity into lingering ripe lemon sherbet flavours.

Vintage	Rank	Drink	RRP	Vol Alc
2011	86	2013	$22.00	13.0%
2014	92	2018	$23.99	13.5%

FORESTER Estate

FOX CREEK WINES
Fox Creek Wines is a McLaren Vale winemaker known for producing rich, soft opulent reds with distinctive silky tannin from 60 hectares under vines around Willunga.

Winemaker: *Scott Zrna, Ben Tanzer*
Open: *Daily 10am–5pm*
Malpas Road
McLaren Vale
Ph: (08) 8557 0000 www.foxcreekwines.com.au

| Vintage | Rank | Drink | RRP | Vol Alc |

FOX CREEK
RESERVE SHIRAZ ★★★★

Ripe rich and full of dark berry, touch of spice and well judged oak. The flavours are ripe and even very lengthy only moderate tannin and will come into complete mature balance quite quickly drink over next 3 or 4 years.

Vintage	Rank	Drink	RRP	Vol Alc
2010	88	2020	$75.00	14.5%
2014	91	2020	$75.00	14.5%

FRANKLAND ESTATE

Frankland Estate in Western Australia's Frankland River region is a thoughtful producer, offering fine, fresh-fruit flavours wrapped in a ripe, but rarely heavy, style.

Winemakers: *Hunter Smith, Elizabeth Smith and Brian Kent*
Open: *Monday–Friday 10am–4pm, Weekends by appointment only, Frankland Estate, Frankland Road, Frankland*
Ph: *(08) 9855 1544* *www.franklandestate.com.au*

FRANKLAND ESTATE
OLMO'S REWARD ★★★★★

Detailed, complex and deep, a willing partner to a long lunch. Starts fresh with balanced complexity, brooding fruits of the forest, cabernet family aromas of violets, black currant, black olive and tapenade. Oak adding spice, savoury and roasted elements to the aromas. The palate has a plush mouth feel and silky tannins. The fruit runs over the top with mounting intensity through black currant into mulberry climbing the middle mouth restrained by subtle thyme and leafy notes that anchor it. Good balance, it is complete as a young wine and it will take years. Drink after late 2017. Needs a decant as a youngster.

Vintage	Rank	Drink	RRP	Vol Alc
2011	94	2029	$45.00	14.8%
2012	93	2022	$45.00	14.5%
2013	92	2026	$50.00	13.5%

Vintage	Rank	Drink	RRP	Vol Alc

FRANKLAND ESTATE
ISOLATION RIDGE CABERNET SAUVIGNON ★★★★
Restrained Cassis, deep wild and fresh raspberry with leafy edges. The palate is dark berry fruits into black olive, medium intense flavours, moderate tannins with a fine clean finish. Elegant claret like wine with food and lunch its friend.

Vintage	Rank	Drink	RRP	Vol Alc
2010	90	2022	$24.00	14.0%
2011	88	2016	$27.00	13.5%
2013	93	2020	$28.00	13.7%

FRANKLAND ESTATE
ISOLATION RIDGE SHIRAZ ★★★★
Simply put a very nice wine. Contemporary spicy style with very good range of expression. Red fruit cinnamon clove white pepper aromas with a palate showing the same set of flavours medium bodied medium plus length moderate tannins, oak spice with harmony and brightness.

Vintage	Rank	Drink	RRP	Vol Alc
2011	94	2024	$35.00	14.5%
2012	85	2015	$35.00	14.5%
2013	95	2021	$40.00	13.5%

FRANKLAND ESTATE
ISOLATION RIDGE RIESLING ★★★★★
Complexity and subtlety with floral nectar blossoms into a tighter edge fresh sage packaging herbal note. A full flavoured complex with appealing white fruits, again the sage herbal edge kept taut and tight with green pear fruit length, rose and musk that lingers with appealing interest. This is full flavoured, individual in its volume, interesting and long. If this wine was a person I would want to meet them.

Vintage	Rank	Drink	RRP	Vol Alc
2013	92	2030	$32.00	11.6%
2014	95	2035	$35.00	11.7%
2015	96	2026	$40.00	12.5%

FRANKLAND ESTATE
NETLEY ROAD VINEYARD RIESLING ★★★★★
Initially the aroma is stone fruit, apricot, then floral. It is misleading here as the racy palate is even better; a can of fruit salad citrus flavours with sweet orange blossom, apple, lime, nectarine, crisp acids and

Vintage	Rank	Drink	RRP	Vol Alc

musky fruits. A very good Netley Road and a lovely summer drink, with potential.

2012	91	2030	$27.00	11.0%
2013	92	2027	$27.00	12.3%
2014	95	2022	$30.00	13.0%

FRANKLAND ESTATE
POISON HILL VINEYARD RIESLING ★★★★★

Delicate citrus zest notes with a tight twangy citrus into white fruit touch of stone fruit supple subtle and building toward the finish with an appealing weave of citrus orange mandarin in white fruit salad fruit and fine acidity.

2013	93	2023	$32.00	10.8%
2014	91	2024	$30.00	12.5%
2015	89	2022	$40.00	12.5%

FRANKLAND ESTATE
ROCKY GULLY RIESLING ★★★★

This has a great green tinged colour which is always an indicator of well made wines. In the family style with more development, nectar blossom in spring into sweet green lime fruit with notes of riesling. The palate offers a powerful handshake of ripe fruits with full flavoured ripe lemon lime candy flavours in the middle that hold to the finish. Gets bonus points for affordability.

2013	92	2015	$18.00	11.5%
2014	88	2017	$18.00	11.5%
2015	90	2017	$20.00	12.7%

FRANKLAND ESTATE
SMITH CULLAM RIESLING ★★★★★

There are very restrained pure fruit aromas hinting at sage while offering subtle interwoven pineapple and lime aromas. A confident weave of elegant fruit, just hitting sweetness, and a delicate acidity gives this wine personality. In the mouth, classic "just-ripe" white pear fruit, sage, citrus zest, rose petal flavours with a supple interaction of mineral acid and "just-sweet" bright fruit in a long finish. A great mix of style and graceful balance with long lasting floral flavours.

2011	92	2028	$45.00	11.0%
2012	92	2018	$45.00	10.5%
2015	96	2023	$50.00	11.5%

FRASER GALLOP ESTATE

Fraser Gallop Estate in Margaret River seems to have a different vision for its wines than the rest of the region, with interesting styles that enhance the region's fruit purity. Quality winemaking is creating detailed, energetic flavours. Affordable quality.
Winemakers: Clive Otto and Kate Morgan
Open: By appointment only, 547 Metricup Road, Wilyabrup
Ph: (08) 9755 7553 *www.frasergallopestate.com.au*

FRASER GALLOP ESTATE
SEMILLON SAUVIGNON BLANC ★★★★★
You will love the complexity here, with its lychee gooseberry ginger barrel fermented sauvignon blanc, that makes this charming and gently exotic. The fresh fruits, nectarine and ripe fuji apple are mouth filling, long and very evenly balanced, contributing to a delicious wine with more than simple blended fruit complexity, thanks to the barrel ferment. Cutting-edge quality at the price, making it great value.

Vintage	Rank	Drink	RRP	Vol Alc
2012	87	2015	$23.00	13.0%
2013	90	2017	$23.00	13.0%
2014	94	2019	$23.00	12.0%

FRASER GALLOP ESTATE
PARTERRE SEMILLON SAUVIGNON BLANC ★★★★★
Ripe generous fleshy stone fruit wed to fine spicy oak in a seamless engaging and interesting set of aromas. Medium full bodied, tightly woven with energy and drive in the middle mouth. This is long and immediately likeable thanks to the fruit oak balance but will increase in complexity and weight in the medium term.

Vintage	Rank	Drink	RRP	Vol Alc
2012	96	2018	$36.00	13.0%
2013	92	2022	$36.00	13.0%
2014	95	2022	$36.00	12.5%

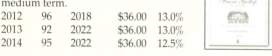

FRASER GALLOP ESTATE
PARTERRE CHARDONNAY ★★★★★
The house style of refined elegance is on display. Fine, tight-grained French oak, white butter and honey, with a creamy, wide and long fresh tide of discreet fruits. Subtle harmonious white fruit elegance and lemony citrus adds to the stone fruit flavours all on the finish.

Vintage	Rank	Drink	RRP	Vol Alc
2012	92	2017	$31.00	12.5%
2013	94	2023	$31.00	13.5%
2014	94	2023	$31.00	12.5%

FRASER GALLOP ESTATE
CABERNET SAUVIGNON MERLOT ★★★★

Youthful stalky cabernet aromas with stalk, chicory, black plum and cassis. In the mouth, firm fine tannins, medium body and a middle palate full of black fruit flavours, with a chalky finish. Drink after 2015.

2011	91	2015	$23.00	14.0%
2012	88	2016	$20.00	13.5%
2013	88	2018	$20.00	14.0%

FRASER GALLOP ESTATE
PARTERRE CABERNET SAUVIGNON ★★★★★

Very good value here. Dark, dense brooding aromas of cabernet fruits with berry, dark chocolate, herbs, mocha and quality oak. In the mouth, bright fruits, slightly chunky balance of tannin acids, overall slick butterscotch and dark berry, with soft tannins. Needs to bed itself down.

2011	91	2031	$36.00	14.5%
2012	94	2036	$40.00	14.0%
2013	89	2017	$40.00	13.5%

FREEMAN VINEYARDS

Brian Freeman thought outside the square when planting his 40-hectare Freeman Fortuna vineyard in the Hilltops region of NSW. Great soils, and a unique approach incorporating classic Italian varieties from the Veneto region, produce delicious and different wines.

Winemaker: *Brian Freeman, Xanthe Freeman*
Open: *By appointment only, 101 Prunevale Road, Prunevale*
Ph: *(02) 6384 4299* *www.freemanvineyards.com.au*

FREEMAN FORTUNA
PINOT GRIS PLUS ★★★★

An intriguing, funky, cheesy and almost butyric aroma make this a savoury white with tones of smoked meats. Changing in the mouth, beginning with stone fruits and apple, medium length with even and medium bodied fruit ripeness, followed by the blotting paper of the savoury sulphide like elements that descend on the finish adding phenolics to the white and yellow fruit. Needs decanting for 4 hours.

Vintage	Rank	Drink	RRP	Vol Alc
2010	89	2012	$25.00	14.0%
2011	88	2015	$25.00	13.5%
2012	75	2019	$25.00	13.0%

FREEMAN SECCO
RONDINELLA CORVINA ★★★★★

Earthy and savoury, you see the black fruits of Australia and the dried herbs like cedar, oregano and cardamom. The mouth feel from tannins is initially silky with a big bass cord of dark cherry fruits running the line from front to back, which later shifts into a gravely texture. A food friendly firmness that adds contrast and grip making this a great food wine.

Vintage	Rank	Drink	RRP	Vol Alc
2009	90	2018	$35.00	14.5%
2010	91	2020	$35.00	14.5%
2011	95	2022	$35.00	14.0%

FREEMAN
RONDO ROSÉ ★★★★

Classic, pale dry rosé in colour and style, orange salmon pink. Aromas of pomegranate, with a creamy, up-front round silkiness of texture and a little scratch of tannins to keep them tidy.

Vintage	Rank	Drink	RRP	Vol Alc
2012	87	2015	$20.00	13.5%
2013	88	2016	$20.00	13.5%
2014	Not made			

FREYCINET

Freycinet is a family-run, nine-hectare vineyard, an hour north of Hobart. Planted in 1980 on an amphitheatre-shaped, north-facing aspect that overlooks Great Oyster Bay and the Freycinet Peninsula, the site is exceptionally beautiful, as are the wines.
Winemakers: *Claudio Radenti and Lindy Bull*
Open: *May to Sept 10am–4pm, Oct to April 10am–5pm, 15919 Tasman Highway, Swansea*
Ph: *(03) 6257 8574 www.freycinetvineyard.com.au*

FREYCINET
PINOT NOIR ★★★★★

The opulent, hedonistic, exotic notes of ripe Pinot are here first rose petal, lychee, blue berry and cooked strawberry with fresh vitality, touch cedar spices in the back ground. The fruit depth is extraordinary ripe strawberry, red cherry fruit sweetness and flavour generosity in the middle with the cedar spices and young strawberry fruits and seeds lingering.

Vintage	Rank	Drink	RRP	Vol Alc
2012	96	2034	$65.00	13.5%
2013	94	2023	$65.00	14.0%
2014	94	2022	$65.00	14.5%

FREYCINET
CHARDONNAY ★★★★★

Ripe ample fruits like white nectarine and almost white peach fruit aromas, wed to oatmeal and subtle oak spice and cedar. The palate has lovely texture, there are long and silky and mouth covering fruit flavours wed to a subtle mineral acidity. Plenty of drink young pleasure with the balance to grow evenly in 2–3 years.

Vintage	Rank	Drink	RRP	Vol Alc
2013	95	2020	$41.00	13.5%
2014	91	2020	$41.00	13.5%
2015	92	2021	$41.00	13.5%

FREYCINET
RIESLING ★★★★★

Grapefruit tartness into thiol-like, smoky savoury aromas. The palate is white fruited, very good up front grape fruits in the middle citrus acidity and damped down on the slightly bitter finish.

Vintage	Rank	Drink	RRP	Vol Alc
2013	94	2020	$30.00	13.5%
2014	95	2025	$30.00	13.0%
2015	83	2018	$30.00	13.5%

Vintage	Rank	Drink	RRP	Vol Alc

FROGMORE CREEK

Frogmore Creek is an innovative organic Tasmanian producer with mature vineyards and interesting styles worth watching. Frogmore Creek is also the site of an innovative restaurant under Rueben Koopman opened for lunches and closed Tues and Weds with dinners by appointment. Cellar door features the largest varietal selection in Tasmania.

Winemaker: *Alain Rousseau and John Bown*
Open: *Daily 10am–5pm, 20 Denholms Road, Cambridge*
Ph: *(03) 6248 5844 www.frogmorecreek.com.au*

FROGMORE CREEK
RIESLING ★★★★★

Essence of lime white flower, with cool and fresh bright refined delicacy. Builds in the mouth, gaining flavour intensity and complexity with light-bodied fruit, subtle tangy acidity and freshening to the finish where the rose and talc bath powder shine with the ripe lemon acidity. Very well grown, lingering citrus flavours.

2010	89	2018	$24.00	13.0%
2013	92	2028	$24.00	12.5%
2014	95	2024	$26.00	12.8%

FROGMORE CREEK
FGR RIESLING ★★★★

Floral sweet lime iced rose water leads to a juicy sweet light framed delicate white wine style with rose, pineapple and a lime-fruited middle palate, before the lemony acidity finishes the flavours with presence and charm.
Aperitif or curry wine, not a dessert style.

2010	90	2016	$24.00	9.0%
2012	91	2020	$24.00	9.0%
2013	90	2018	$24.00	10.2%

FROGMORE CREEK
PINOT NOIR ★★★★★

One year in oak with 15% new oak. Juicy black cherry, dark spice and some whole berry, strawberry and a smooth, even full ripe and rich style. Cola black cherry and raspberry and firm tannins.

2009	90	2017	$36.00	14.0%
2010	92	2022	$36.00	14.0%
2013	93	2023	$36.00	13.5%

| Vintage | Rank | Drink | RRP | Vol Alc |

FROGMORE CREEK
42 DEGREES SOUTH PINOT NOIR ★★★★★
Very good bright colour leads to an intense nose of cherries in syrup fruit intensity, smoky vanilla toast oak notes. In the mouth varietal light long and appealing pinot red fruit spectrum flavours, raspberry length with an extra complexity of strawberry. Quite firm in the mouth that sits well with the intensity of the fruit.

| 2014 | 92 | 2020 | $26.00 | 13.5% |
| 2015 | 90 | 2018 | $28.00 | 13.8% |

FROGMORE CREEK
CABERNET SAUVIGNON ★★★★★
2012 was a great vintage in Tasmania. This is an exceptional wine with ripe blackcurrant fruits, smokey, saline oyster shell to the aromas. Fresh, fine black currant fruit flavours, an elegant long line of sweet fruited cassis in the middle and even length with subtle oak and acids, and a refined long fine grained tannin texture make this exceptional value.

| 2011 | 94 | 2037 | $34.00 | 13.2% |
| 2012 | 94 | 2028 | $34.00 | 13.5% |

GARTELMANN
Gartelmann in the Hunter Valley has a smart cafe and a range of wines drawn from selected growers within the valley, including Lovedale for semillon, shiraz and chardonnay, and Rylestone near Mudgee in NSW for petit verdot and cabernet sauvignon.
Winemaker: Liz Jackson & Jorg Gartelmann
Open: Mon–Sat 10am–5pm Sun 10am–4pm
Lovedale Road, Lovedale
Ph: (02) 4930 7113 *www.gartelmann.com.au*

GARTELMANN
BENJAMIN SEMILLON ★★★★
Lemon, earth and the full lemon grove effect with a flowery lift and youthful appeal. The palate is graceful, even, light bodied, and restrained. The citrus is vibrant, and long with nectarine on the finish. Made without piercing acidity to drink young with mid term cellaring.

2013	93	2023	$25.00	11.2%
2014	93	2024	$25.00	11.6%
2015	89	2020	$25.00	11.5%

GARTELMANN
DIEDRICH SHIRAZ ★★★★★

Varietal sweet dark berry fruits with appealing spice. The palate has soft ripe berry fruits with black berry bay leaf, eucalypt, mint, and plum backed to dark charry oak flavours with concentration and depth.

Vintage	Rank	Drink	RRP	Vol Alc
2010	90	2016	$45.00	14.0%
2012	Not made			
2013	92	2023	$45.00	13.7%

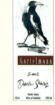

GARTELMANN
SARAH ELIZABETH CHARDONNAY ★★★★

Not lush buttery big this flinty savoury edged modern style has lemon citrus notes and relies on fruit and freshness, very low oak, medium bodied restrained delicate light fresh clean lemon flavours and medium long texture.

Vintage	Rank	Drink	RRP	Vol Alc
2010	86	2013	$30.00	13.5%
2012	89	2017	$30.00	13.0%
2014	89	2018	$30.00	13.5%

GARTELMANN
RYLESTONE CABERNET SAUVIGNON ★★★★

Cool cabernet aromas, cranberry, red currant fruit with elegance and fresh detail, low oak leading to youthful palate, needs three years. The fruit is sappy, red currant and blackberry and the tannins drying and chalky. Drink after 2016.

Vintage	Rank	Drink	RRP	Vol Alc
2010	90	2018	$35.00	14.5%
2011	89	2018	$35.00	13.5%
2012	88	2020	$35.00	13.8%

GEMBROOK

Gembrook Hill is the southernmost vineyard in the Yarra. Planted in 1983, it is owned by the Marks family. The wines are the flipside to most Australians and distinctive in their finesse, elegance, texture, natural acidity and cool climate attributes.
Winemaker: *Timo Mayer and Andrew Marks*
Open: *By Appointment Only*
2850 Launching Place Road, Gembrook Hill
Ph: *(03) 5968 1622 www.gembrookhill.com.au*

GEMBROOK HILL
YARRA VALLEY CHARDONNAY ★★★★★

Their first Gembrook Chardonnay since 2008, as sparkling took it all. Only 98 dozen made showing very fine subtle new oak, and refined white fruits, with strong middle palate white fruits and understated oak spice building citrus acids and fresh flavours that will grow into a creamy delicious wine in 8 years.

2008	90	2016	$50.00	13.0%
2009	Not made			
2014	96	2023	$50.00	13.5%

GEMBROOK HILL
YARRA VALLEY PINOT NOIR ★★★★

Diam Cork. The southernmost Yarra vineyard produces fine wines with high acidity. Strawberries with well judged toasty oak, with the usual pale colour and delicacy this winemaker brings to his wines. The palate is great pinosity very pure strawberry fruits ripe excellent fruit sweetness and generosity with a small savoury element anchoring the palate.

2011	88	2016	$55.00	13.5%
2012	95	2023	$55.00	13.0%
2013	94	2022	$55.00	13.5%

GEMBROOK HILL
YARRA VALLEY SAUVIGNON BLANC ★★★★

Lemon balm, pink grape fruits and quince aromas lead to a well-structured and textured modern style of creamy intensity. Well-filled middle palate with honey suckle complexity creeping in on the finish.

2013	88	2017	$33.00	13.0%
2014	91	2019	$33.00	12.5%
2015	91	2017	$33.00	13.5%

GEMBROOK HILL
THE WANDERER YARRA VALLEY SHIRAZ ★★★★

Lovely purity and elegance with savoury spicy regional fruit and stalk aromas, on the palate they have delicacy and nuance in a medium-bodied, juicy berry fruit, fleshy silky tannins. Artisanal style with quality, personality and consistent style.

2007	86	2010	$35.00	13.4%
2008	91	2011	$35.00	13.8%
2010	88	2012	$35.00	13.0%

| Vintage | Rank | Drink | RRP | Vol Alc |

GEMTREE
Gemtree Vineyards in McLaren Vale, has a massive 130 hectares under vine, uses 50% of the grapes for its own wines and sells the balance to premium boutique wine Companies, Australia wide. Family managed, the winery uses the most modern and environmentally gentle processes and selects the best fruit for their own label. Recent releases have included wines grown biodynamically.
Winemaker: *Mike Brown*
Open: *Daily 10am–5pm, 167 Elliott Road, McLaren Vale*
Ph: *(08) 83230802* *www.gemtreevineyards.com.au*

GEMTREE
PHANTOM RED BLEND IV ★★★★★
Ripe black currant with notes of hay, straw, liquorice and celery. In the mouth, taut and complex with a tight structure and savoury pecan pistachio pine nut on the liquorice fruit finish.

2010	89	2018	$25.00	14.50%
2011	90	2028	$25.00	14.50%
2012	90	2020	$40.00	14.50%

GEMTREE
OBSIDIAN LIMITED RELEASE SHIRAZ ★★★★★
Solid quality oak support for the ripe regional black cherry fruits with a commanding oak length and presence showing ripe fruits and dark spice that will come together in 4 + years.

2008	91	2025	$55.00	14.00%
2010	93	2035	$55.00	15.00%
2012	87	2019	$70.00	14.00%

GEMTREE
UNCUT SHIRAZ ★★★★★
Takes quality oak to ripe fruit building complexity. The palate is initially all oak overcoat with reasonable fruit fabric underneath that will soften in time and always have obvious oak flavours complicating the fruit.

2012	89	2019	$22.00	14.50%
2013	87	2018	$25.00	14.50%
2014	85	2017	$25.00	14.5%

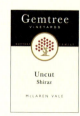

GEMTREE
WHITE LEES SHIRAZ ★★★★

Surprisingly fresh fruits with raspberry, blackberry date and oak aromas. In the mouth the fruit is formidable up front with silky rich oaky flavours, black olives and very long firm oak finish. Drink after 2018.

Vintage	Rank	Drink	RRP	Vol Alc
2008	90	2020	$45.00	14.50%
2009	88	2016	$45.00	14.50%
2011	93	2029	$45.00	15.00%

GENDERS

Genders in McLaren Vale was the first to plant Cabernet Sauvignon and the third to start cellar bottling in the 1960s. Today, it's a one-woman show, with Diana Genders running both the vineyard and the winery. Releases are cellared for 5 or 6 years prior to release in order to show the traditional regional cellaring style at its best. High quality and tradition all the way.
Winemaker: *Diana Genders*
Open: *No Cellar Door 22 Park Drive, McLaren Vale*
Ph: *(61) 4178 29985* **www.genderswines.com.au**

GENDERS
DUNCAN CABERNET SAUVIGNON ★★★★

Fruit power rather than varietalism. Ripe aromas rich Christmas pudding fruit complexity with chesterfield leather sweet oak. The palate is muscular McLaren Vale, an intense youthful middle palate rich with dark fruit and plenty of tannins adding a firm dry finish to the red cherry fruit. Needs a rare steak and a lover of full bodied red wine.

Vintage	Rank	Drink	RRP	Vol Alc
2002	92	2022	$55.00	14.5%
2006	90	2022	$55.00	14.5%
2009	89	2020	$55.00	14.3%

Vintage	Rank	Drink	RRP	Vol Alc

GENDERS
McLAREN PARK SHIRAZ ★★★★★

For lovers of full bodied reds. Traditional regional ripe style with long oak elevation showing blackberry, dark berry, cola fruits and oak on the sidelines with vanilla caramel elements. In the mouth, traditional dense dark fruit, firm grape tannins, ripe, rich and concentrated with the oak frames on the finish.

2001	92	2022	$55.00	14.5%
2005	94	2019	$55.00	14.8%
2012	91	2023	$55.00	14.5%

GEOFF MERRILL

Geoff Merrill is one of our larger-than-life characters. With vineyards in McLaren Vale and Coonawarra, his reds are given longer oak aging than many and offered with bottle age making them great value.
Winemaker: *Geoff Merrill and Scott Heidrich*
Open: *Mon to Fri 10am–4.30pm and Weekends 12pm–4.30pm*
291 Pimpala Road, Woodcroft
Ph: *(08) 8381 6877   www.geoffmerrillwines.com.au*

GEOFF MERRILL
BUSH VINE GRENACHE ROSE ★★★★★

A reliable rose that consistently delivers fresh strawberry, raspberry fruit and spice. Mid raspberry coloured, it is dry, medium bodied, silkily textured and long in length. Drink now and capture that youthfulness at play.

2013	92	2016	$21.00	13.5%
2014	89	2016	$21.00	14.0%
2015	89	2017	$21.50	13.5%

GEOFF WEAVER

Geoff Weaver's high-altitude Lenswood vineyard in the Adelaide Hills and his experience combine to produce wines with finesse and delicacy.
Winemaker: *Geoff Weaver*
Open: *No Cellar Door, 2 Gilpin Lane, Mitcham*
Ph: *(08) 8272 2105   www.geoffweaver.com.au*

| Vintage | Rank | Drink | RRP | Vol Alc |

GEOFF WEAVER
LENSWOOD SAUVIGNON BLANC ★★★★★

A taut toned wine of freshness and focus
with pineapple sage, leading to a long,
fresh riesling-esque lemon zest acidity and
tropical fruit in the middle palate and a
gentle long finish.

2011	92	2015	$25.00	11.5%
2013	93	2019	$25.00	13.0%
2014	88	2018	$25.00	12.0%

GEOFF WEAVER
FERUS SAUVIGNON BLANC ★★★★

Spicy, ginger snap biscuit, white butter oak and guava fruit
peeking around the oak door. Needs time for the
honeysuckle, lychee and guava to re-emerge. The fruit
richness is there and the oak is subservient
to the fruit, adding support to the palate
and transporting the fruit on a long ride of
rich, medium-bodied supple intensity.
Mind blowing after a year or two.

2005	86	2015	$38.00	13.0%
2009	88	2014	$39.00	13.0%
2013	93	2020	$40.00	13.0%

GEOFF WEAVER
LENSWOOD CHARDONNAY ★★★★

Oak gives honey and toast and the fruit is white apple and
shy. Heavy malo, less stirred, a rich,
creamy, ripe, round wine with a warm
yellow butter toasty popcorn palate. A
divisive style that old schoolers will
appreciate.

2008	90	2014	$25.00	13.5%
2012	90	2016	$40.00	12.0%
2013	94	2019	$40.00	13.0%

GIACONDA

Giaconda has carved an impressive niche in the Australian chardonnay firmament since planting in the 1980s. An intelligent and articulate ethos surrounds the wines and they are proof, if any was needed, that fine wine is grown more than it is made. The vineyard climate delivers fruit with finesse and the chardonnay needs time to show its funky best. The best way to purchase is via the mailing list, released Nov 1 each year.
Winemaker: *Rick Kinzbrunner*
Open: *By appointment only, 30 McClay Road, Everton Upper*
Ph: *(03) 5727 0246* *www.giaconda.com.au*

GIACONDA
ESTATE VINEYARD CHARDONNAY ★★★★★

The Burgundian savoury notes are all here savoury, very complete as a young wine with gentle oak, oatmeal with flint to balance wed to just ripe fruit with sophisticated elegance and the overriding minerality. The medium-bodied palate is very nuanced at first ripe fruits, seamless flickering to savoury minerality, struck flint notes wed to fruit ripeness with tension I the middle plate and the finish is creamy lees influenced with great length. Basically, the only way to record this wine experience is to drink it.

2012	96	2021	$110.00	13.0%
2013	95	2022	$129.00	13.5%
2014	95	2025	$120.00	13.8%

GIACONDA
ESTATE VINEYARD NEBBIOLO ★★★★★

Savoury, licorice, tamarind, hoisin, plum sauce, and oyster shell aromas. In the mouth classic light bodied fresh fruited raspberry with the varietal lightness at the front building tannins and acids on the finish.

2009	91	2017	$90.00	13.8%
2011	92	2018	$90.00	14.0%
2012	94	2022	$90.00	14.0%

Vintage	Rank	Drink	RRP	Vol Alc

GIACONDA
YARRA VALLEY & BEECHWORTH PINOT NOIR ★★★★★

On release, the oak covers the red cherries, berries and cinnamon, beetroot and root vegetable fruit, showing a lot of the precursors to forest floor funky aromas and no stems. It's medium to full-bodied with long, deep and generous red sweet red cherries and berries fruit. There is wonderful structure and length in this sublime wine. The finish is quite dry, lingering, savoury and spicy and seems set to become very complex over time.

Vintage	Rank	Drink	RRP	Vol Alc
2008	96	2026	$70.00	13.5%
2010	97	2030	$70.00	13.5%
2013	92	2022	$89.00	13.5%

GIACONDA
ESTATE VINEYARD SHIRAZ ★★★★★

An attractive, complex, spicy medium bodied "syrah" style of shiraz. Raspberry, black tea into red berry sandalwood spice aromas. The palate is medium-bodied ripe silky tannins with a determined length of flavour, complexity that builds through red fruits onto smoked meats and onto charcuterie and white pepper.

Vintage	Rank	Drink	RRP	Vol Alc
2011	90	2020	$80.00	13.0%
2013	94	2028	$89.00	13.5%
2014	92	2022	$89.00	13.8%

GIANT STEPS
Giant Steps must be the most cosmopolitan cellar door in the world, aided by a 34-hectare Yarra Valley vineyard and a stream of restrained, tightly structured wines with fine-tuned vineyard differences. Just lovely.
Winemaker: Steve Flamsteed
Open: Daily 10am–6pm, 336 Maroondah Highway, Healesville
Ph: (03) 5962 6111 *www.giant-steps.com.au*

GIANT STEPS
SEXTON VINEYARD CHARDONNAY ★★★★★
A wine made with discretion and judgement, rich yet elegant and very stylish aromas of creamy lees, oak and fresh pear. The palate is fleshy from the start, detailed and fine, with good acid drive that carries the fruit. The subtle complexities of apple acidity, peach, nougat, gentle butterscotch and subtle dark toast oak flavours create great length, structure and a long finish. Sexton is the cuddly brother and Tarraford the more racy.

2012	94	2026	$40.00	13.0%
2013	87	2016	$40.00	13.2%
2014	94	2019	$45.00	13.5%

GIANT STEPS
TARRAFORD VINEYARD CHARDONNAY ★★★★★
This wine reveals savoury, earthy, wild yeast, solids and less oak compared to the Sexton wine of the same year. In the mouth the acidity and the fruit is deep and long with a racy complexity. Generous apple and pear flavours that are lean and more highly strung due to the acidity. The finish has a tangy elegance with pith and minerals lingering.

2012	94	2020	$40.00	13.0%
2013	93	2018	$40.00	13.0%
2014	95	2022	$45.00	13.5%

GIANT STEPS
ARTHURS CREEK VINEYARD CHARDONNAY ★★★★★
Very savoury edged, with classic style chardonnay and flinty sulphide aromas making it taut and savoury. The palate is a surprising, plush, textured wine with cool white stone fruits that sweep in and run long with generosity and fresh appeal, while the savoury from the aroma is left behind.

2010	90	2015	$40.00	13.0%
2011	94	2018	$40.00	13.0%
2012	95	2019	$40.00	13.0%

GIANT STEPS
SEXTON VINEYARD PINOT NOIR ★★★★★
At first, pure flickers of fragrant strawberry, white pepper, pinot fruits into red cherry raspberry without excessive ripeness. Succulent generous mouth feel mirrors the

chardonnay from the same vineyard with balance, roundness and good varietal definition in the middle palate. A subtle stemminess closes the palate with grace.

Vintage	Rank	Drink	RRP	Vol Alc
2012	91	2020	$45.00	13.5%
2013	90	2019	$45.00	13.5%
2014	93	2020	$50.00	13.5%

GIANT STEPS
TARRAFORD VINEYARD PINOT NOIR ★★★★

Defined intense, floral and savoury with raspberry leaf; has more structure for aging than the Sexton.

Vintage	Rank	Drink	RRP	Vol Alc
2006	87	2010	$40.00	13.0%
2008	89	2012	$45.00	13.0%
2010	90	2016	$40.00	13.0%

GIANT STEPS
SEXTON VINEYARD MERLOT ★★★★★

Very pretty aromas of red fruits and well judged toasty oak adding charcuterie to help lift and season the raspberry fruits. In the mouth, juicy raspberry, silky tannins and a savoury note before the cedar oak builds and sustains the finish. Very good balance and fair complexity.

Vintage	Rank	Drink	RRP	Vol Alc
2012	89	2018	$40.00	14.0%
2013	91	2018	$40.00	14.0%
2014	92	2019	$45.00	14.0%

GIANT STEPS
HARRY'S MONSTER ★★★★★

This is as quirky as the name, beetroot and cranberry with smoked meats from oak. The palate is red fruits, cherry leafy spicy and full middle palate with lovely youthful tannins and fruit interplay and a savoury finish. Great length of flavour.

Vintage	Rank	Drink	RRP	Vol Alc
2012	92	2026	$55.00	13.6%
2013	92	2019	$55.00	14.0%
2014	92	2022	$55.00	14.0%

www.robgeddesmw.com

| Vintage | Rank | Drink | RRP | Vol Alc |

GLAETZER
There is much to admire in Barossa-based, Ben Glaetzer's mix of richness and freshness. Across the ranges, and within, consistency is a major part of the style. Astoundingly fresh, sweet fruit and ripe flavours, with exquisitely judged acidity and soft tannins. Worth every cent.
Winemaker: *Ben Glaetzer*
Open: *No Cellar Door, Lot 5, Gomersal Road, Tanunda*
Ph: *(08) 8563 0947 www.glaetzer.com*

GLAETZER
WALLACE SHIRAZ GRENACHE ★★★★
Red fruits, mainly raspberry and a nod to the Shiraz blackberry aromas while in the mouth you find soft upfront grenache driven raspberry flavours. Make this a go to wine for a BBQ as it has afternoon session ability but keep it cool.

Vintage	Rank	Drink	RRP	Vol Alc
2012	92	2019	$22.99	14.5%
2013	90	2017	$22.99	15.0%
2014	91	2018	$22.99	14.5%

GLAETZER
BISHOP SHIRAZ★★★★★
Lovely fresh vivid black plum and very ripe dark cherry aromas with oak in the back ground. The palate is soft, round and fresh subtle spice with the ripe red plum fruits leading and darker black berries on the finish. An essay in fresh flavoursome fruit and moderate oak.

Vintage	Rank	Drink	RRP	Vol Alc
2012	88	2019	$33.00	14.5%
2013	88	2018	$33.00	15.0%
2014	91	2018	$33.00	14.5%

GLAETZER
ANAPERENNA SHIRAZ CABERNET SAUVIGNON ★★★★★
Chocolaty, ripe blueberry, blackcurrant, violets with mineral cola edged background aromas. A huge mouthful of ripe fruit, very fleshy and yet constrained by youthful tannins and fresh acidity. The flavours are red cherry, black cherry, black

Vintage	Rank	Drink	RRP	Vol Alc

plum topping out with red cherry, raspberry and a super clean finish.

2012	92	2022	$52.00	15.0%
2013	92	2022	$52.00	15.5%
2014	92	2029	$52.00	15.0%

GLAETZER
AMON-RA SHIRAZ ★★★★★

Intense ripeness, red fruit into black berry into cooked plum with clove, prune and dark spices. The palate is rich full fresh fruit sweet uber full bodied, fresh, ripe, deep fleshy black fruits up front, fruit intensity plus acid holds the fruit length and structure with a long palate with lingering red fruit to finishes.

2012	90	2018	$100.00	15.0%
2013	94	2020	$100.00	15.5%
2014	93	2032	$100.00	15.0%

GLAETZER-DIXON

Winemaker, Nick Glaetzer has won awards as a Young winemaker of the Year and the Jimmy Watson award with a Tasmanian shiraz. Both are remarkable achievements. His wines are a darling of inner-city restaurant wine buyers. Their Germanic off dry riesling works well with food and the pinot offers value at diverse price points, while the shiraz is a peppery, cool climate, spice bomb style.

Winemaker: *Nick Glaetzer*
Open: *Wed to Mon 11am–5pm, 93 Brooker Ave, Hobart*
Ph: *(0417) 852 287 www.gdfwinemakers.com*

GLAETZER-DIXON
UBERBLANC ★★★★★

Wow -- musky rose water, lime leaf and ripe stone fruit aromas welcome you in a distinctive style. In the mouth, it lands silky plump ripe fruits on the front, masking the just off-dry sweetness until the flavour wave hits the middle mouth where the ripe apricot and rose water flavours sit amid a creamy silky textured length, to be cleaned up by the acidity on the finish.

2012	91	2019	$22.00	11.4%
2013	92	2017	$22.00	11.9%
2014	92	2018	$22.00	12.1%

Vintage	Rank	Drink	RRP	Vol Alc

GLENGUIN

Glenguin is a lower Hunter Valley vigneron and winemaker producing a reliable range of individual vineyard wines of consistent value and interest.

Winemaker: *Robin Tedder MW*
Open: *Weekdays 9 to 5pm, Weekends 10am–5pm, The Boutique Wine Centre, Broke Road, Pokolbin*
Ph: *02 6579 1009* *www.glenguinestate.com.au*

GLENGUIN
OLD BROKE BLOCK SEMILLON ★★★★

This has presence with appealing ripe lemon fruit notes. Glides across the tongue, softly balanced light bodied long moderate acidity soft flowing middle palate flavours.

2010	88	2016	$20.00	10.0%
2014	87	2017	$25.00	11.5%
2015	90	2021	$25.00	10.0%

GLENGUIN
SCHOOL HOUSE BLOCK SHIRAZ ★★★★

The lovely thing here is elegance, with raspberry fruits, subtle herbals into oak spices with a long mid weight palate red fruits, thyme middle palate fruit and moderate tannin profile with gentle lingering red fruit finish.

2011	93	2025	$30.00	13.0%
2013	88	2018	$30.00	13.5%
2014	91	2022	$30.00	13.5%

GLENGUIN
STONYBROKE SHIRAZ ★★★★

Bright colour fresh youthful red cherry and acid fruit notes leads to a bright tight red fruit chalky tannins and a medium long slightly drying raspberry fruited wine.

2009	88	2016	$23.00	13.0%
2011	90	2020	$25.00	13.5%
2014	86	2018	$25.00	13.5%

| Vintage | Rank | Drink | RRP | Vol Alc |

GLENGUIN
ARISTEA SHIRAZ ★★★★★

Dark plummy coal gassy fruits, acid lift with a balanced amount of mocha cola oak leading to a firm medium long palate with black fruits, oak tannins that linger to the medium long, steely acidity and a dry finish filled with sour red cherry flavours.

2008	Not made			
2009	90	2019	$55.00	13.5%
2014	90	2023	$55.00	13.5%

GOLDEN BALL

Golden Ball was initially planted in 1992 and is run within the organic and biodynamic ethos. This is a meticulously managed estate with minimal impact on the local environment and nearly 10 acres under vine, including recent small plantings of exotic varieties. Available in restaurants and via mailing list.

Winemaker: James McLaurin
Open: By appointment only,
1175 Beechworth Wangaratta Road, Beechworth
Ph: (03) 5727 0284 *www.goldenball.com.au*

GOLDEN BALL
GALICE CABERNET MERLOT MALBEC ★★★★

Crunchy red and black fruit, minty, bay leaf, beetroot, caramel black currant aromas. The medium bodied palate has a cabernet berry fruits and cool climate chalky tannin texture that will age and soften over the long haul. The youthful berry and beetroot fruit on the palate has line and length. Serve after 2018.

2011	Not made			
2012	93	2020	$55.00	13.5%
2013	89	2028	$60.00	13.8%

GOLDEN BALL
SHIRAZ ★★★★

Ripe dark berry, raspberry, dark bitter chocolate and a dash of bay leaf leading to a bountiful medium-bodied graceful palate of silky tannins. Full in the middle mouth, with unhurried fruit flavours, fine acidity and elegant, understated dark berry mineral spice offering a generous "drink now" or cellaring style.

Vintage	Rank	Drink	RRP	Vol Alc
2010	89	2017	$55.00	13.8%
2011	Not made			
2012	92	2023	$55.00	13.5%

GOLDEN BALL
LA BAS CHARDONNAY ★★★★★

Ready to drink complexity is one chardonnay's assets in the right hands. Here it is a complex nice mix of barrel ferment wild yeast and lees aromas which carry through to the palate. Plenty of weight and complexity toes the line between lush fruit ripeness and oak and tension from wild ferment and acidity to hold the frame long in the mouth. Well balanced wine making and well grown fruit.

Vintage	Rank	Drink	RRP	Vol Alc
2012	94	2019	$50.00	13.0%
2013	92	2017	$55.00	13.0%
2014	93	2019	$55.00	13.0%

GOLDEN BALL
CHERISH SHIRAZ ★★★★

Light and pretty aromas of raspberry, fruit tingles and fresh small berry juices. A full middle palate and the lemon edged raspberry berry fruits are generous and full, a satisfying yet chatty style.

Vintage	Rank	Drink	RRP	Vol Alc
2012	91	2016	$26.00	12.8%
2014	92	2016	$28.00	12.0%

GRAMPIANS ESTATE

Grampians Estate's Tom and Sarah Guthrie have some marvellous old vineyards and have shown enormous resourcefulness and dedication in dealing with the challenges of major fire damage to their beautiful property. Their wines are regular wine show winners.
Winemakers: *Hamish Seabrook, Don Rowe and Tom Guthrie*
Open: *Weekdays 12pm–5pm Weekends 10am–5pm 1477 Western Highway Great Western*
Ph: *(03) 5356 2400 www.grampiansestate.com.au*

| Vintage | Rank | Drink | RRP | Vol Alc |

GRAMPIANS ESTATE
RUTHERFORD SPARKLING SHIRAZ ★★★★★

Wonderful aromas, perfumed spice pepper into fresh berries and wedding charry oak into the aroma. In the mouth an excellent balance of sweetness, shiraz dark spices, raspberry fruits and very fine tannins- the flavours linger long and complex. A genuine style with very good flavour and tannin profile.

2008	90	2015	$35.00	14.0%
2011	96	2020	$35.00	14.0%
2013	93	2023	$35.00	14.0%

GRAMPIANS ESTATE
MAFEKING SHIRAZ ★★★★

Red fruits and menthol with a subtle cool climate spice and a touch of rising acidity. The red fruits are tidy, flavoursome and red cherry, with hot dry acidity prickling the finish. Drink soon.

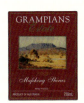

2010	88	2014	$25.00	13.5%
2011	87	2016	$25.00	13.5%
2013	84	2016	$25.00	13.5%

GRAMPIANS ESTATE ST
ETHEL'S GARDEN GULLY SHIRAZ ★★★★★

A rustic edge, with red plum blackberry dark spice fruits wed to waxy tobacco caramel and white butter like oak aromas. The fruit has drive and energy, ripe on the front with fresh red cherry and a touch of herb savouriness flows with a firm acidity. Bridging tannins and medium-bodied flavours of blackberry, butterscotch, maraschino cherry and cooked plums wrapped in fine grained tannins to finish.

2010	87	2018	$39.00	13.5%
2012	94	2029	$39.00	13.5%
2013	94	2033	$39.00	13.5%

GRAMPIANS ESTATE
STREETON RESERVE SHIRAZ ★★★★★

This is a big wine and a very pure shiraz. Varietal with Victorian spice box fruits, toasty oak in balance and ripe raspberry with appealing sage/oregano, black pepper back notes. The palate is ripe, tannins soft and the oak less overt than earlier years with deep morello red cherry fruit, peppery spices and meaty charcuterie flavours to finish, wrapped in oak on the end. Well balanced for the long haul with quality frame of tannins, fruit and oak.

Vintage	Rank	Drink	RRP	Vol Alc
2009	89	2018	$65.00	13.8%
2010	92	2025	$65.00	14.0%
2012	96	2035	$75.00	13.5%

GRAMPS

Gramps makes an excellent quality and value range of wines for everyday drinking. Selected from across South Australia's regions this label has reliably offered great value and good quality for many years. A safe name.

Winemaker: Bernard Hickin
Open: Jacob's Creek Visitor Centre Barossa Valley, Barossa Valley Way, Rowland Flat
Ph: (08) 8521 3111 www.gramps.com.au

GRAMPS
CABERNET SAUVIGNON MERLOT ★★★★

Dark chocolate oak notes and regional fruits with very soft tannins. Plump middle palate and medium length, there is a lot of refined tannins, silky texture wrapped in beetroot and rhubarb lingering ripe cranberry fruits. Steps up a notch on previous vintages.

Vintage	Rank	Drink	RRP	Vol Alc
2011	85	2015	$20.00	13.8%
2012	86	2015	$20.00	13.8%
2013	88	2018	$22.00	14.6%

Vintage	Rank	Drink	RRP	Vol Alc

GRAMPS
BAROSSA VALLEY GRENACHE ★★★★

This reliable producer offers a good "drink now" example of the variety's raspberry fruit and soft-tannin style.

2006	90	2010	$17.00	14.0%
2007	Not made			
2008	88	2012	$17.00	15.5%
2009	89	2013	$17.00	15.2%

GRAMPS
BAROSSA VALLEY SHIRAZ ★★★★

Aromas of jammy black fruit to raisin and oak to support the aromas. In 2011, lighter framed tannins and dark fruit with a blackberry jam finish.

2009	87	2014	$20.00	14.5%
2010	85	2013	$20.00	14.8%
2011	85	2014	$20.50	14.3%

GRAMPS
BOTRYTIS 375ML SEMILLON ★★★

Marmalade cointreau and wattle blossom aromas. In the mouth, liquorous, luscious sweet fruit with orange, lemon peel, candied Ditters cake and Cointreau. Bright lemon acids and medium long.

2006	90	2015	$18.00	11.4%
2008	90	2016	$19.00	9.0%
2011	90	2018	$19.00	11.4%

GRANITE HILLS
Granite Hills in Victoria's Baynton area is an estate, cool-climate, winemaker of intensely flavoured wines with more than 34 vintages' experience. One of the pioneers of peppery shiraz is still going strong.
Winemaker: *Llew Knight*
Open: *Daily 11am–6pm, 1481 Burke and Wills Track, Baynton*
Ph: *(03) 5423 7264 www.granitehills.com.au*

Vintage	Rank	Drink	RRP	Vol Alc

GRANITE HILLS
RIESLING ★★★

An individual regional style with complexity and different in a good way with aromas from granite soils that give roses, honeysuckle, and nectar blossom in spring riesling perfume with an edge that is gruner veltliner-like with white pepper. The texture is ripe round and long, yellow fruit and talc depth fruit complexity, peppery spices in the middle palate and overall exotic with yellow rind pith fruits just ripe orange that linger. Tasting this takes you a journey from soils to flower beds to orchards.

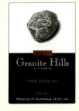

2010	86	2015	$24.00	12.5%
2013	92	2023	$25.00	12.5%
2014	95	2026	$25.00	12.5%

GRANITE HILLS
SHIRAZ ★★★★

A distinctive style with long oak age development adding a veneer of aroma and flavour. The plate is complete and mature with a round middle palate with silky tannins all very composed and harmonious in the middle mouth. Pepper, clove, plum and cedar complex qualities to finish. Love or hate style thanks to three years in oak.

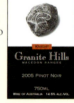

2004	90	2018	$32.00	15.0%
2005	90	2017	$35.00	14.5%
2009	91	2020	$35.00	14.5%

GRANT BURGE
Grant Burge is a family-owned and operated Barossa Valley-based producer whose substantial range of Barossa vineyards contributes reliable wines, including a very fine shiraz, 'Meshach'.
Winemakers: *Grant Burge and Craig Stansborough*
Open: *Daily 10am–5pm, Krondord Road, Tanunda*
Ph: *(08) 8563 3700 www.grantburgewines.com.au*

GRANT BURGE
SHADRACH CABERNET SAUVIGNON ★★★★★

Red and black currant fruits in the modern, fresh, early picked style, with balanced oak. The fruit is currany, with freshness and length and totally brighter, longer and fresher than most of 2009. The best fruit, the best oak and best winemaking gives long, fresh, bright fruit with moderate tannins.

Vintage	Rank	Drink	RRP	Vol Alc
2006	92	2017	$60.00	14.5%
2008	90	2020	$90.00	14.5%
2009	95	2023	$90.00	14.0%

GRANT BURGE
ABEDNEGO GRENACHE ★★★★

Red fruits, black berry, dried herbs and a savoury oak spice leads a big hearted cherry spice plum with silky textured Grenache tannins plump in the middle with dried herbs savoury spices on the finish. For lovers of full bodied reds.

Vintage	Rank	Drink	RRP	Vol Alc
2005	90	2016	$65.00	14.5%
2009	91	2018	$70.00	13.0%
2012	90	2019	$75.99	13.5%

GRANT BURGE
HOLY TRINITY GRENACHE SHIRAZ MOURVEDRE ★★★★

Great year complexity more than the individual components. Red fruit, liquorice allsorts, dark fruits with older oak notes and ready to drink. Silky ripe red fruits up front raspberry black berry middle palate drink up.

Vintage	Rank	Drink	RRP	Vol Alc
2010	91	2019	$45.95	14.5%
2011	88	2018	$45.95	14.0 %
2012	88	2018	$42.99	14.0%

GRANT BURGE
FILSELL OLD VINE SHIRAZ ★★★★★

The best ever under this label. Much better oak integration than previous years. In 2016, a sleeper that will go 15+ years, fresh fruits focused and a tightly held complexity of youth with red plum and black berry. The palate has balanced quality tannins and fruits, freshness of complex fruit allied to length and great winemaker judgement. The palate has excellent integration showing red and black fruit

length and a middle palate that flickers
raspberry, black berry and plum with fine oak
tannins and subtle oak spice on the finish.
While easy to drink young, you could cellar
this for 10+ years and have a very happy result.

Vintage	Rank	Drink	RRP	Vol Alc
2012	95	2028	$42.99	14.0%
2013	88	2020	$42.99	14.0%
2014	95	2030	$42.99	14.5%

GRANT BURGE
MESHACH SHIRAZ ★★★★★

Very fresh for a six year old and destined for a long, long life. The full suite of Barossa shiraz; blackberry, dark chocolate, plum with a clove spice edge in the aromas. The palate is saturated in dark fruits back berry turns redder and the tannins are finer allowing the fruit more room to show, more elegant finer structure red fruits flavours on the middle, savoury peppery, clove, dark earth, chocolate plum flavours.

Vintage	Rank	Drink	RRP	Vol Alc
2008	96	2035	$153.00	14.5%
2009	91	2028	$153.00	14.5%
2010	95	2047	$180.00	14.5%

GRANT BURGE
BALTHASAR SHIRAZ ★★★★

Very pretty and detailed peppery shiraz, dark plum, iodine and floral fragrant red fruits with very fine tannins. Chocolate fleshy oak makes this immediately drinkable, with its red fruit spiced and deep, juicy, lingering berry fruit flavours.

Vintage	Rank	Drink	RRP	Vol Alc
2009	94	2022	$45.95	14.5%
2010	94	2020	$45.95	14.5%
2012	94	2020	$45.95	14.5%

GRANT BURGE
THORN EDEN VALLEY RIESLING ★★★★★

Sweet lime and lemon aromas with punch and grace showing the varietal grapefruit sweet lime and rose spectrum flavours. Honest value and a touch of Eden Valley grace with a flair of fine acidity on the finish.

Vintage	Rank	Drink	RRP	Vol Alc
2012	88	2016	$23.00	12.5%
2013	88	2018	$23.00	11.5%
2014	90	2018	$25.00	12.5%

| Vintage | Rank | Drink | RRP | Vol Alc |

GREY SANDS

Grey Sands' owners waited 13 years for their first wines, proving theirs is a labour of love, with high ideals. The vineyard is planted at 8800 vines per hectare, which imparts fragrant flavours and rich structures. All bottled under Diam.

Winemakers: *Peter Dredge up to 2014 then Penny Jones in consultation with Bob Richter*
Open: *By appointment only, PO Box 518, Exeter*
Ph: *(03) 6396 1167* *www.greysands.com.au*

GREY SANDS
PINOT GRIS ★★★★★

Wow. Complex pear, apricot and marzipan aromas. In the mouth, a big ripe wine with intense dried apricot, pear and a very creamy rich -- verging on oily -- texture in the middle palate, with lingering fresh apricot, honey and fresh pear. If you love the Alsace style, this is for you.

2009	91	2015	$40.00	14.6%
2012	89	2018	$40.00	14.1%
2013	90	2018	$40.00	15.3%

GREY SANDS
PINOT NOIR ★★★

Minty stalky, wild savage and gamey. The palate is fresh strawberries with good depth and has layers of sweet spearmint and spice flavours and plenty of structured tannins on the finish, with old oak.

2008	90	2017	$39.00	14.6%
2009	94	2019	$40.00	13.0%
2010	88	2019	$40.00	13.8%

GREY SANDS
MERLOT ★★★★

Fragrant blueberry, plum, slightly minty, with violets, lovely tannins and depth; very exciting example of the variety, which needs decanting.

2006	88	2016	$35.00	13.7%
2007	91	2015	$40.00	14.0%
2008	89	2016	$40.00	14.0%

GROOM WINES

Groom Wines is the Barossa Valley side of Daryl Groom, a talented winemaker with extensive experience of high quality wines in the USA and Australia. Mature winemaker of sensible styles.

Winemaker: *Daryl Groom*
Open: *By appointment only, 28 Langmeil Road, Tanunda*
Ph: *(08) 8563 1101* *www.groomwines.com*

GROOM
ADELAIDE HILLS SAUVIGNON BLANC ★★★★

Ripe tropical fruit, with lemons, apple and pear. Ripe stonefruit and lemony edged sessionable, if you like the variety. Even length and a creamy texture.

2012	90	2015	$24.00	13.5%
2013	89	2015	$24.00	13.5%
2014	89	2016	$24.00	12.2%

GROOM
BAROSSA VALLEY SHIRAZ ★★★★

Plum, prune and clove Barossa shiraz spectrum aromas, with chocolaty oak adding to the overall complexity and poise. The soft Barossa tannins unroll like a carpet of silky quintessential big ripe Barossa shiraz with lots of punch. Oak and dark berry flavour with layers of plummy spiced fruit on the finish. Opulent and luxurious style of a big red lover's wine.

2010	92	2020	$49.00	14.0%
2011	90	2017	$49.00	14.5%
2012	94	2027	$49.00	14.9%

GROOM
BAROSSA VALLEY BUSH BLOCK ZINFANDEL ★★★★★

This is an elegant zinfandel style, with less ripeness and more freshness than most from the region. Spicy with berry fruits in the varietal manner, it has the usual tart acids and Christmas cake ripeness on the palate. Appealing cranberry length before the food-friendly tannins and acids in youth.

2011	86	2014	$32.00	14.5%
2012	94	2029	$32.00	14.9%
2013	92	2018	$30.00	13.8%

| Vintage | Rank | Drink | RRP | Vol Alc |

GROSSET WINES
Grosset Wines in the Clare Valley pays infinite attention to detail to produce wines from both Clare and the Adelaide Hills with remarkable finesse and elegance. Gaia is particularly magnificent.
Winemaker: *Jeffrey Grosset*
Open: *By appointment only, King Street, Auburn*
Ph: *(08) 8849 2175 www.grosset.com.au*

GROSSET
GAIA CABERNET SAUVIGNON CABERNET FRANC ★★★★★

Initially aromas are leafy black fruits, mulberry, violets, cranberry, cedar and tobacco oregano. The palate is refined and shows fine-grained tannin finesse with a classy-laced black currant and mulberry fruits and red currant cranberry flavours with very good length.

2011	89	2018	$74.00	13.7%
2012	95	2027	$74.00	13.7%
2013	95	2028	$79.00	13.7%

GROSSET
PICCADILLY CHARDONNAY ★★★★★

Masterful understatement and complexity with modernity. Intelligent oak, wild yeast and cloudy ferment notes add to the nectarine fruit aromas. The Adelaide Hills ripe fruits are fleshy and rich up front, full in the middle and all framed and driven by natural acidity. This is wine that allows the vineyard to speak for itself by judicious technique. Great food wine and must be up there amongst the best of new breed SA in Chardonnay. Ready to go now and over the next two years.

2012	93	2018	$59.00	13.5%
2013	90	2022	$62.00	13.5%
2014	95	2018	$62.00	13.0%

Vintage	Rank	Drink	RRP	Vol Alc

GROSSET
SEMILLON SAUVIGNON BLANC ★★★★★
Stylish and complex semillon perfume showing crunchy citrus backed by tropical fruits with an ascending interest. The palate is solid, fruit filled ripe citrus, tropical, even, long and round. The ascending scales of flavour and texture pulling long and finishing with just the right amount of grip to be a huge success.

Vintage	Rank	Drink	RRP	Vol Alc
2013	92	2017	$35.00	12.9%
2014	93	2020	$35.00	12.5%
2015	95	2019	$35.00	12.7%

GROSSET
POLISH HILL RIESLING ★★★★★
There is the generosity, refinement, balance and concentration that we have come to expect. The aromas are ripe, floral, and feminine with musk, white flowers, a touch of tropical fruit, talc, and lime. In the mouth there is an extremely subtle fine musk element along with citrus and lovely alignment of flavours and textures that fill your tongue.

Vintage	Rank	Drink	RRP	Vol Alc
2013	94	2028	$52.00	12.7%
2014	95	2033	$54.00	12.5%
2015	93	2029	$55.00	12.7%

GROSSET
SPRINGVALE WATERVALE RIESLING ★★★★★
A wine with balance and certain austerity to allow for time to weave its work. Balanced aromas of citrus, rose, white fruits and a whisper of dark spice lead the generous charge here. The palate is a crunchy haven for white flowery fruits with apple pear and rose flowing into a crisp finish. Will grow and is more youthful than the sister Polish Hill.

Vintage	Rank	Drink	RRP	Vol Alc
2013	92	2023	$36.00	12.5%
2014	92	2028	$40.00	12.5%
2015	93	2027	$40.00	12.7%

Vintage	Rank	Drink	RRP	Vol Alc

GROSSET
PINOT NOIR ★★★★

Very closed needs a decent decant for 2 hours. The aromas are strawberry fruits, hay, black tea stemmy notes and toasty oak. The palate runs from crystalline red fruits into strawberry, raspberry with very fine grained tannins that frame the flavours and build the palate.

2012	92	2022	$69.00	13.5%
2013	90	2019	$74.00	13.5%
2014	88	2020	$74.00	13.5%

GROVE ESTATE

Grove Estate is located near Young, in the Hilltops region of NSW with over 50 hectares of vines. The wines are the result of an extraordinary partnership of viticulturalist Brian Mullany with winemakers Richard Parker from Long Rail Gully and Tim Kirk from Clonakilla.
Winemakers: *Tim Kirk and Richard Parker*
Open: *Thurs to Sun 9.30am–4.30pm,*
4100 Murringo Road, Young
Ph: *(02) 6382 6999 www.groveestate.com.au*

GROVE ESTATE
HILLTOPS SOMMITA NEBBIOLO ★★★★★

Tight and youthful red licorice and plum, with a sandal wood spice. In the mouth this on the generous side with an almost fleshy, simple middle palate and dry grainy tannins to close.

2013	92	2020	$30.00	13.5%
2014	89	2019	$55.00	14.0%
2015	88	2019	$45.00	14.0%

GROVE ESTATE
THE CELLAR BLOCK SHIRAZ VIOGNIER ★★★★★

Such a pretty nose on this wine with a floral bouquet to the peppery, blue berry fruit. Fleshy, velvety and sits nicely in the medium bodied zone.

2013	93	2020	$35.00	13.5%
2014	90	2025	$35.00	13.5%
2015	89	2018	$35.00	13.0%

| Vintage | Rank | Drink | RRP | Vol Alc |

GUNDOG ESTATE
Several ranges of wine are available from Gundog Estate. Matt Burton is an experienced winemaker and has a distinct style aimed at freshness and medium-bodied wines from the Hunter, Canberra and, under the Burton McMahon label, a Yarra Valley chardonnay. Canberra Cellar Door near the historic village of Gundaroo is now open but please phone ahead (0412 371 666).
Winemaker: *Matt Burton*
Open: *Daily 10am–5pm, 101 McDonalds Road, Pokolbin*
Ph: *(02) 4998 6873* ***www.gundogestate.com.au***

GUNDOG ESTATE
WILD SEMILLON ★★★★

Aromas are fuller and more minerally decisive than the austere lemon of many Hunter semillon with wild bush blossom and touch of faint struck match. The palate is solid and very full for semillon with lemon and ripe apple mid mouth and the hallmark lemon citrus on the finish. Great wine with Thai food. A completely authentic style.

2013	90	2016	$30.00	10.8%
2014	93	2029	$30.00	10.5%
2015	88	2018	$30.00	10.0%

GUNDOG ESTATE
ESTATE SHIRAZ ★★★★★

Sweet berry fruits with a cool climate minty green herbs parsley edge to the aromas. The medium light bodied style is a complex, well balanced, easy drinking style. Soft up front and builds structure in the mouth with red fruit flavours and a medium long firm peppery finish. Charming spicy food friendly wine.

| 2012 | 92 | 2022 | $35.00 | 13.0% |
| 2013 | 92 | 2020 | $35.00 | 13.5% |

| Vintage | Rank | Drink | RRP | Vol Alc |

HAHNDORF HILL
GRU, as in Gruner Veltliner, leads the charge for Hahndorf Hill and its Austrian white wines. Larry has been in charge for 13 years and inherited an old planting of the Austrian reds, blaufränkisch and zweigelt. Taking the lead from these, he imported Gruner in 2006, quarantined till 2010 and planted that year. He has been generous with the cuttings and they are planted in 12 vineyards today.
Winemaker: Larry Jacobs
Open: Daily 10am–5pm, 38 Pain Road, Hahndorf
Ph: (08) 8388 7512 www.hahndorfhillwinery.com.au

HAHNDORF HILL
GRU GRUNER VELTLINER ★★★★★
Pear and pear drop aromas peach while in the mouth riesling like line of flavours, white fruits middle palate pineapple with a maze of complexity minerality, showing preserved, fresh and dried pineapple with a fresh acidity medium bodied orange pith grippy food firm tannin. 2015 seems riper in fruit profile.

2013	94	2017	$28.00	13.0%
2014	91	2018	$28.00	12.0%
2015	90	2018	$28.00	12.5%

HAMELIN BAY WINES
Winemaker: Julian Scott
Open: Daily 10am–5pm
199 McDonald Road, Karriedale
Ph: (08) 9758 6779 www.hbwines.com.au

HAMELIN BAY
FIVE ASHES VINEYARD CHARDONNAY ★★★★
Fresh and fruit rich with juicy directness. Pears and cucumber into struck flint. The palate has distinctive acidity, silky fruits and is full in the middle palate with fresh bright fruits and a grapefruit acidity to finish.

2011	87	2014	$30.00	13.0%
2012	88	2018	$30.00	13.0%
2013	94	2017	$30.00	13.5%

| Vintage | Rank | Drink | RRP | Vol Alc |

HANDPICKED WINES
An important exporter and pioneer of the Chinese market with a gung-ho approach to making wine accessible to the middle classes in China. Innovations such as tastings at duty free Sydney and have the order wine delivered in China are quite revolutionary.
Winemaker: *Gary Baldwin*
Open: *No Cellar Door, DMG FINE WINE, Level 18, 2 Park Street, Sydney*
Ph: *(29) 4757 888 www.handpickedwines.com.au*

HANDPICKED WINES
COLLECTION SHIRAZ ★★★★★
The dense fruits show strong regional personality with a liquorice, mineral, cordite core under the raspberry sarsaparilla aromas. In the mouth the linear qualities of great wine, long rimmed with acidity fine grained tannins that bridge the length of the palate with really complex dark fruits, citrus edged black berry fruits and fruit oak tannin.

| 2013 | 94 | 2020 | $69.99 | 13.6% |

HANGING ROCK WINERY
Hanging Rock Winery is a cool Macedon area vineyard and the winery of the redoubtable John Ellis. These appealing wines are made both from his own fruit and selected quality vineyards.
Winemaker: *John Ellis*
Open: *Daily 10am–5pm, 88 Jim Road, Newham*
Ph: *(03) 5427 0542 www.hangingrock.com.au*

HANGING ROCK
JIM JIM SAUVIGNON BLANC ★★★★
Guava and tropical fruits with a slight sweaty edge. Balanced, round, good intensity of pineapple lime flavours and a touch of firmness on the finish.

2012	83	2014	$30.00	13.2%
2013	88	2015	$28.00	13.0%
2014	90	2016	$28.00	13.5%

| Vintage | Rank | Drink | RRP | Vol Alc |

HARDY'S WINE COMPANY
Hardys offers cutting-edge quality from Australia's top vineyards and winemakers. For the first time wine under the Hardy Reserve Bin offering is included. Each wine receives a unique bin number to recognise the blend in a system that was started by Thomas Hardy and continues to be used.
Winemaker: *Paul Lapsley*
Open: *Daily 10am–4.30pm, Reynell Road, Reynella*
Ph: *(08 8329 4124) www.hardys.com.au*

HARDYS
HRB D659 RIESLING ★★★★★
Complex and elegant, this is special with a unique blend of lime, white fruits and mineral edges in the aromas. The palate has focus, line and length of velvet citrus lime in the middle palate good length, it rolls out the red carpet and stays for the photos. Excellent value and age-ability —it will be fascinating to see the effect of the years.

2013	95	2022	$29.99	12.5%
2014	94	2024	$29.99	12.5%
2015	95	2028	$29.99	12.5%

HARDYS
EILEEN HARDY CHARDONNAY ★★★★★
Very focused intensity, fruit spice, apple, almond, chamomile with harmony and complexity without heaviness. Spice elements from oak, the palate is seamless, full-bodied depth of fruit and white fruit flavour, fruit sweet ripeness with lingering ripe golden delicious apples with a honey oatmeal flick and very clean with finesse on the finish.

2012	93	2017	$95.00	13.0%
2013	96	2020	$95.00	13.0%
2014	94	2025	$95.00	13.5%

HARDYS
THOMAS HARDY CABERNET ★★★★★
Generous dark fruits, mulberry blackcurrant, cassis, iodine and leafy varietal notes. The fruit starts ripe berry fruit complex and runs along a glamorous weave of mulberry, blueberry, oyster shell and black currant fruit. With the tannins firing towards the finish to show a firm dry finish and oak tannins.

Vintage	Rank	Drink	RRP	Vol Alc
2010	95	2024	$129.99	13.5%
2012	94	2026	$129.99	14.0%
2013	93	2045	$129.99	14.0%

HARDYS
EILEEN HARDY SHIRAZ ★★★★★
Very complex subdued fruit with the earthy blackberry, meaty savoury, coffee cola oak spice. The palate is fruit sweet rich wed to quality oak the threads of fruit and oak tannins are full in the middle palate and the dark berry cherry fruits roll long on the finish.

Vintage	Rank	Drink	RRP	Vol Alc
2008	92	2030	$105.00	14.0%
2010	95	2029	$125.00	14.0%
2013	94	2022	$124.99	14.0%

HATHERLEIGH WINES
With a very experienced professional palate, wine industry consultant and scientist, Nick Bullied is a Master of Wine with 30 years' experience, high standards and an enormous passion for wine. This is reflected in the produce of his vineyard, Hatherleigh, located at 910 metres.
Winemaker: *Nick Bullied*
Open: *No Cellar Door, 5 Geebung Place, Rivett*
Ph: *(02) 6288 3505* *www.nickbulleid.com*

HATHERLEIGH
PINOT NOIR ★★★★
Maraschino cherry, subtle vanillin oak aromas lead to a medium-bodied silky tense palate with good front and middle raspberry fruit.

Vintage	Rank	Drink	RRP	Vol Alc
2006	92	2014	$39.00	13.5%
2007	90	2016	$39.00	13.5%
2008	88	2016	$39.00	13.8%
2010	Not made			
2011	Not made			

Vintage	Rank	Drink	RRP	Vol Alc

HEARTLAND

Heartland is a wine business collective of four experienced industry insiders, Barossa-based Ben Glaetzer, McLaren Vale Scott Collett, primarily Langhorne Creek sourced wines with a decadent mix of fleshy fruit richness, freshness and soft tannins. Very good value here.

Winemaker: Ben Glaetzer
Open: Daily 10am–5pm
The Wine House 1509 Wellington Road, Langhorne Creek
Ph: (08) 8537 3441   www.heartlandwines.com.au

HEARTLAND
DIRECTORS CUT SHIRAZ   ★★★★

Looking very mature and throwing a deposit in the glass. Bay leaf, herbal and the fruits are the classical ripe sweet fruited with soft tannin and flavours showing a mixture of overripe black current and tomato leaf, medium long.

Vintage	Rank	Drink	RRP	Vol Alc
2010	88	2016	$32.00	14.5%
2012	90	2022	$33.00	14.8%
2013	87	2018	$33.00	14.5%

HEATHCOTE ESTATE

Heathcote Estate is a prime location within Heathcote. Planted in 1999, specialising in shiraz with the vineyard divided into five individual blocks, with a small area of grenache. Aged in French oak they reveal the region's affinity with shiraz when made in a modern style.

Winemaker: Tom Carson
Open: Daily 10am–5pm, 98 High Street, Heathcote
Ph: (03) 5433 2488   www.yabbylake.com

HEATHCOTE ESTATE
HEATHCOTE SHIRAZ   ★★★★

Deep, earthy mineral oak, intense plum cake, Christmas spice and black berry fruit. The medium bodied palate has silky tannins, soft acids, building a sophisticated, even and very fine fruit tannin length. Classy, finishing silky with roasted dark spices.

Vintage	Rank	Drink	RRP	Vol Alc
2009	90	2022	$40.00	14.0%
2012	90	2022	$45.00	14.5%
2014	92	2026	$45.00	13.5%

Vintage	Rank	Drink	RRP	Vol Alc

HEEMSKERK
Charles Hargrave, formerly Chief Sparkling Winemaker for Treasury Wines Estates, has lifted Coal River based Heemskerk to become a producer of premium wines (chiefly sparkling) that showcase the island's best varieties, with classic Tasmanian delicacy and cool climate freshness. The second label, Abel Tempest, is sourced from the Tamar.
Winemaker: Peter Munro
Open: No Cellar Door, 131 Cascade Road, South Hobart
Ph: (1300) 651 650 www.heemskerk.com.au

HEEMSKERK
PINOT NOIR ★★★★★
This has wow factor, strawberry, Indian brown spices, cardamom, vanilla vibrant and complex. Pinot lovers could smell it all day such it has such allure and beauty. The palate is finely tannic with stemmy tension, strawberry and red currant fragrance. Delicate wrapping of berry red fruits and oak in a long tussle to the back of the mouth. Keep till 2018.

2011	94	2025	$60.00	13.5%
2012	93	2027	$60.00	14.0%
2015	94	2025	$60.00	13.5%

HEEMSKERK
CHARDONNAY ★★★★★
Historically one of our best Chardonnays, sourced from tiny vineyards across Tasmania. Balanced complexity and age ability led by fine French oak with a beautiful complexity notes of struck match, grape fruit, green apricot fruit complexity and oatmeal. In the mouth it is tightly structured, tangy acidity and the taut citrus flavours of good burgundy, long and refined now it will gain weight and expression drink after 2017. Time will offer you a great drink.

2013	94	2020	$49.99	13.0%
2014	95	2021	$49.99	12.5%
2015	95	2026	$49.99	13.0%

Vintage	Rank	Drink	RRP	Vol Alc

HEGGIES
Heggies is a good, mature vineyard at 480–520 metres up in the Eden Valley, owned by the Hill-Smith family of Yalumba fame.
Winemaker: Peter Gambetta
Open: Daily 10am–5pm, Eden Valley Road, Angaston
Ph: (08) 8561 3200 *www.heggiesvineyard.com*

HEGGIES VINEYARD
CHARDONNAY ★★★★

Subtle oak, vanilla, flinty, cool climate restrained pear and apple aromas. In the mouth, the texture is quite an achievement. Creamy and silky varietal texture, round with medium length fruits and a blue cheese element in the background but disjointed alcohol warming the finish.

Vintage	Rank	Drink	RRP	Vol Alc
2011	88	2015	$30.00	12.5%
2012	89	2016	$30.00	13.0%
2013	85	2016	$31.00	12.5%

HEGGIES VINEYARD
RIESLING ★★★★

The contrast to Pewsey Vale is marked with rose, talc bath powder aromas showing finesse, in an ethereal delicate waft. In the mouth plenty of length of flavour, detailed, pretty, and floral. Flavours with an acid drive helping the rose citrus flavours to a lingering fine long finish. A great Heggies; light bodied long and haunting floral finish. 2014 was a cooler year and picked over ten days and 2015 was picked in one night.

Vintage	Rank	Drink	RRP	Vol Alc
2013	89	2020	$24.00	12.0%
2014	92	2020	$26.00	12.0%
2015	94	2022	$23.95	12.0%

HEGGIES VINEYARD
VINEYARD BOTRYTIS RIESLING 375 ML ★★★★★

Pungent tropical botrytis riesling aromas, with candied peel, gingery spice and preserved pineapple leading to a rich and concentrated, sweet orange marmalade with a clean finish.

Vintage	Rank	Drink	RRP	Vol Alc
2010	91	2016	$27.00	10.0%
2011	90	2018	$29.00	10.0%
2012	90	2018	$29.00	11.0%

Vintage	Rank	Drink	RRP	Vol Alc

HELM WINES
Helm Wines is in Murrumbateman (ACT). Ken has been a tireless promoter of NSW wines and has helped create considerable interest in the rieslings of the region.

Winemakers: *Ken and Stephanie Helm*
Open: *Thurs to Mon 10am–5pm, Butts Road, Murrumbateman*
Ph: *(02) 6227 5953* ***www.helmwines.com.au***

HELM WINES
PREMIUM CABERNET SAUVIGNON ★★★★

Mature aromas with meaty, black currant, eucalypt and bay leaf. In the mouth mature soft tannins and ripe medium long black fruits. Some tomato elements and a pungent oak flavours lead to firm oak tannins on the medium long finish.

2008	86	2018	$53.00	14.8%
2009	83	2014	$53.00	14.0%
2010	86	2016	$53.00	13.5%

HELM WINES
CLASSIC DRY RIESLING ★★★★★

Plenty of alert and lively fruit here, twitching like a dogs ears at the park to go for a run. The palate lands full, ripe, and well balanced, with depth and length of taunt citrus running lemon lime flavours and gentle orange like acidity rather than searing lemony acid. The best of this line in recent times.

2013	88	2018	$28.00	12.0%
2014	88	2020	$35.00	11.5%
2015	95	2023	$35.00	11.8%

HELM WINES
HALF DRY RIESLING ★★★★

Aromas are ripe pineapple, with a green olive spiced clove backnote to the fruit. The palate is juicy full on the front of the tongue, with creamy ripeness and the sweetness buried in a mound of clove spice. Ripe apple middle palate fruits wrapped behind lemon and lemon oil acidity to give a chalky tense finish. Quite a performance for this wine.

2012	87	2017	$20.00	10.3%
2013	87	2017	$20.00	11.2%
2014	87	2017	$25.00	11.3%

Vintage	Rank	Drink	RRP	Vol Alc

HELM WINES
PREMIUM RIESLING ★★★★

Pretty, varietal pure aromas with perfume and poise. The palate strikes the line between crisp acidity and ripe fruit weight, the middle tongue flavour is lemon, citrus and rose. The acid firms the lingering citrus complexity. Very pure and focused.

2012	88	2016	$45.00	13.0%
2013	88	2033	$45.00	11.5%
2015	94	2023	$48.00	11.3%

HENSCHKE

Henschke, a family-owned winery established in 1868 in the Eden Valley within the Barossa ranges, patiently produces some of Australia's finest wines. The family is notable for its attention to detail and sustainable vineyard practices within the concepts of organic and biodynamic viticulture. Increased vineyard areas in the Adelaide Hills have added considerably to the diversity of the wines produced. Elevation and vine health are two reasons why this winery must be judged on its own terms, when compared to the region.

Winemaker: *Stephen Henschke*
Open: *Mon to Fri 9am–4.30pm, Sat 9am–12pm, 1428 Keyneton Road, Keyneton South Australia 5353*
Ph: *(08) 8564 8223 www.henschke.com.au*

HENSCHKE
CYRIL HENSCHKE CABERNET SAUVIGNON CABERNET FRANC MERLOT ★★★★★

With 4 years bottle age and coming from a great vintage, this is a great drink on release. Aromas are complex fresh fruits with a fine balanced weave of oak supporting the floral violets dark and red fruits cranberry, black currant, mulberry and plum framed by quality oak with tobacco dried herb spice. The fruit is the focus framed by quality tannins hence the palate is immediately engaging as a fine line of black currant fruits stride in sit regally in the middle plate with a fine weave of fresh ripe slightly chalky fruit tannins and high quality oak with low toast holding the black fruit cape of flavour long into the finish.

Vintage	Rank	Drink	RRP	Vol Alc
2010	94	2035	$140.00	14.0%
2011	Not made			
2012	96	2029	$140.00	14.0%

HENSCHKE
ABBOTTS PRAYER MERLOT CABERNET SAUVIGNON ★★★★★

Appealing mulberry into blueberry fruits and a trail of cabernet family aromas leafy cedar, dried oregano like oak notes add extra complexity. The palate has a great start with silky tannins and fleshy fruit full middle palate with the mulberry, blueberry and black currant flavours lingering. Very bright on release and will age gracefully.

Vintage	Rank	Drink	RRP	Vol Alc
2010	94	2034	$80.00	14.5%
2011	Not made			
2012	92	2025	$89.00	14.5%

HENSCHKE
HILL OF GRACE SHIRAZ ★★★★★

The Henschke "ballet slipper". Graceful, fruit and oak tannins as bones, acid for tendons and fruit for muscle moving to a classic tune and pirouetting gracefully across your tongue. Very complete, fine-muscled fruits of raspberry and blackberry, then beetroot, clove and five spice. In the mouth, creamy fine tannins support the fruit from the front to the long finish, wrapping ripe flavoured. A long, round middle palate that lingers with blackberry, prune to black plum and layered black spice and black fruit flavours. The acid tendons move seamlessly within the fruit and only show briefly on the finish.

Vintage	Rank	Drink	RRP	Vol Alc
2008	97	2042	$630.00	14.5%
2009	95	2035	$650.00	14.5%
2010	96	2039	$650.00	14.5%

HENSCHKE
MOUNT EDELSTONE SHIRAZ ★★★★★

An exceptional wine, with fresh red florals including rose hips, raspberry, sage, and black tea. Fruit complexity with vibrancy, elegant flavours of long fresh red fruit finesse with fine sandalwood and quality and fine grained oak, without a lot of toast flavours contributing. Black tea, raspberry, blackberry and black currant summer pudding flavours.

Vintage	Rank	Drink	RRP	Vol Alc
2009	95	2025	$125.00	14.5%
2010	95	2029	$118.00	14.5%
2012	96	2030	$140.00	14.5%

HENSCHKE
TAPPA PASS SHIRAZ ★★★★★

Recognises the efforts of growers with vines over 50 years old. Pretty, fruitful polished complexity further into intricate fresh fruit that starts out with aromas of blackberry graphite minerality and ends fresh sage. The palate is focused with a tight start, fine tannins silky in texture run the full length of the tongue with dark berry fruits flowing behind, filling the middle palate and the sage top note close behind until the finish. Refined and showing the small maker elegance that made Henschke virtually a household name.

Vintage	Rank	Drink	RRP	Vol Alc
2010	96	2029	$84.00	14.5%
2012	93	2028	$84.00	14.5%
2013	95	2035	$93.00	14.5%

HENSCHKE
KEYNETON EUPHONIUM SHIRAZ CABERNET SAUVIGNON MERLOT CABERNET FRANC ★★★★★

Quite tight in the Eden Valley way, with a leafy note at the back. In the mouth, the cabernet gives the shiraz savoury elements, with black fruits from plums. Rosemary and black fruit, with excellent length and even tannins and fruit structure that lingers long.

Vintage	Rank	Drink	RRP	Vol Alc
2009	90	2022	$45.00	14.5%
2010	92	2018	$50.00	14.5%
2012	91	2028	$50.00	14.0%

HENSCHKE
HENRY'S SEVEN SHIRAZ GRENACHE MATARO VIOGNIER ★★★★★

This wine is always a complex fruitful experience. Floral red fruit aromas with cherry raspberry and flowery diversity. The plush palate is ripe fruits and fleshy almost fruit preserve flavours, it's not sweet but is succulent with ripe fruits tannins have their say on the middle plate after the rapturous start and the then an appealing red fruit core lingers with intent on the finish leaving a solid red cherry berry fruit memory.

Vintage	Rank	Drink	RRP	Vol Alc
2012	96	2019	$32.00	14.5%
2013	88	2018	$32.00	14.5%
2014	91	2019	$33.50	14.0%

HENSCHKE
JULIUS RIESLING ★★★★★

Lovely green-gold colour leads to a nose with a breadth of lime spectrum aromas with subtle talc and wet stone minerality. The palate is brighter focused for the classic dry riesling lover this has lime pine, lemon zest flavours, fruit length and focus. The flavours are straight and true, rimmed by a fine ripe apple acidity, this is going to last a long time.

Vintage	Rank	Drink	RRP	Vol Alc
2013	93	2029	$35.00	11.5%
2014	92	2029	$32.50	11.5%
2015	95	2039	$36.00	11.5%

HENSCHKE
LOUIS SEMILLON ★★★★★

Good colour with a youthful shyness, thyme-like oak, lemon subtleties. The palate is true to the Barossa with a regional varietal generosity, flavour evenness and length, harmonious, round and long medium bodied with the dried herb oak spice briefly appearing. The shy fruit has the lead role here with the subtle oak spice of carbon-dried herbs.

Vintage	Rank	Drink	RRP	Vol Alc
2012	91	2020	$25.00	11.5%
2013	94	2028	$26.00	11.5%
2014	92	2025	$27.50	12.0%

HENSCHKE
PEGGY'S HILL RIESLING ★★★★

A smart little wine at a great price for the region and heritage. Classic riesling aromas of floral and spice; rose, pine lime and talc that lingers at the edge. The white fruit flavour extravaganza continues, artful winemaking cushions the tongue with plush silky round texture; white, lime and citrus flecks with the fine acid balancing the richness through the long finish. Great youthful drinking wine.

Vintage	Rank	Drink	RRP	Vol Alc
2013	92	2016	$21.00	11.5%
2014	90	2017	$20.00	12.0%
2015	92	2019	$20.00	12.0%

HENSCHKE
JOHANN'S GARDEN GRENACHE MATARO SHIRAZ ★★★★★

Fragrant with red fruits from grenache lifting into ripe more complex mineral dried sweet spice notes, red fruits sandalwood and cinnamon. The palate is soft tannin, medium bodied, gaining fullness in the middle with the initial ripe raspberry of grenache gaining momentum and tempered with more savoury red currant and mature dark spices, dried rosemary and ripe red cherry on the finish.

Vintage	Rank	Drink	RRP	Vol Alc
2012	92	2024	$46.00	14.5%
2013	92	2023	$45.00	14.5%
2014	94	2020	$51.00	14.5%

HENSCHKE
JOSEPHS HILL GEWÜRZTRAMINER ★★★★★

The technicolour dream coat aromatic bath powder mineral tightness with the intensity of floral lime, lychees and rose water. The palate is fragrant, dry, full flavoured fresh fruits, not oily but satiny texture, very middle palate generous with a lime citrus acidity and subtle lychee pith to close.

Vintage	Rank	Drink	RRP	Vol Alc
2013	90	2018	$28.00	12.5%
2014	88	2018	$30.00	12.5%
2015	93	2021	$31.00	12.5%

www.robgeddesmw.com

Vintage	Rank	Drink	RRP	Vol Alc

HENTLEY FARM

Hentley Farm has two vineyards. The old Hentley Farm vineyard covers 100 acres on the banks of Greenock Creek at Seppeltsfield and the Clos Otto vineyard is next door. The Beauty is sourced from a western-facing block of 1.2 hectares in front of the cellar door which exudes rustic charm, delicious full-bodied wines and a quality restaurant, open Thur-Sun for lunch and Sat for dinner.
Winemakers: *Andrew Quin*
Open: *Daily from 11am–5pm, ex Christmas Day, Gerald Roberts Road, Seppeltsfield*
Ph: *(08) 8562 8427 www.hentleyfarm.com.au*

HENTLEY FARM
THE BEAUTY SHIRAZ VIOGNER ★★★★★

Lifted apricot aromas in inky, tarry, earthy black liquorice, combined with underlying savoury meat stock. The palate is dark cherry and dark berry fruit, with a savoury edge of meat stock and earth, and full-bodied ripeness in the middle. For lovers of big red wines.

2010	90	2020	$55.00	14.4%
2011	89	2016	$55.00	14.0%
2013	88	2019	$55.00	14.0%

HENTLEY FARM
THE STRAY MONGREL GRENACHE SHIRAZ ZINFANDEL ★★★★★

Super ripe berry jam aromas of raspberry grenache, blue berry and toast. The soft palate is raspberry fruited and full in the middle palate, low tannin, easy drinking with black plum and a flicker of pepper mineral spice on the finish. Poker night wine with the boys.

2012	90	2020	$25.00	14.6%
2014	93	2018	$25.00	14.5%
2015	91	2019	$25.00	14.7%

Vintage	Rank	Drink	RRP	Vol Alc

HEWITSON

The wines of Dean Hewitson are a joy to taste. His style is at the elegant end of the Australian spectrum, creating wines with fruit appeal, well considered tannins, lower in oak and alcohol, balanced and faithful to their regions of origin, making them highly drinkable especially his "Baby Bush" and "Miss Harry". At the top end, "The Mad Hatter" and "Old Garden" are excellent examples of their regions and styles. They encompass freshness and regional/varietal integrity, making them both enjoyable and an education.

Winemaker: *Dean Hewitson*
Open: *No Cellar Door, 66 Seppeltsfield Road, Dorrien, Barossa Valley*
Ph: *(08) 8212 6233 www.hewitson.com.au*

HEWITSON
BABY BUSH MOURVEDRE ★★★★★

A great mouthful of wine to end the day. Optimistic and fresh. Flooding the mouth, initially with black fruits, notes of licorice, chicory into fennel and celery heart. The palate is full and soft in tannins in the middle, red jubey and round flooding the mouth with flavours. Firm chalky tannins cloak the full flavour potential with lingering ripe berry fruits.

2011	89	2017	$23.00	14.5%
2012	94	2025	$23.00	14.0%
2013	90	2017	$28.00	14.0%

HEWITSON
Baby Bush
2012
BAROSSA VALLEY
Mourvedre

HEWITSON
MISS HARRY GRENACHE SHIRAZ ★★★★★

Fresh floral raspberry, blackberry, rose geranium and wood smoke aromas lead to a taut rosehips, rare slightly jubey fruit fresh, moderate tannins which grows spicy and then firms on the finish. Cute compact and very fresh vibrant fruit flavours.

2011	91	2017	$23.00	14.0%
2012	92	2019	$23.00	14.0%
2013	93	2017	$28.00	14.0%

HEWITSON
Miss Harry
2012
BAROSSA VALLEY
Grenache Shiraz Mourvedre Cinsault Carignan

HEWITSON
OLD GARDEN MOURVEDRE ★★★★★
Youthful restraint with a prickle of acidity on the nose and date, prune and earthy black fruits. Has low slung berry fruits while classic, firm mataro tannins fill the mouth, linked with long firm oak structure and quite impenetrable in youth. Drink after 2016.

2010	94	2033	$120.00	14.5%
2011	90	2020	$120.00	14.5%
2012	93	2022	$120.00	14.0%

HEWITSON
THE MAD HATTER SHIRAZ ★★★★★
Black cherry fruit, with dried herbs, thyme and dark spices, makes this a great youthful drink. In the mouth, the tannin fruit structure is long and elegantly balanced, with flavours of red cherry building into a rich middle palate. As usual, the balance is classic age-worthy wine with youthful drinkability.

2009	92	2022	$70.00	14.0%
2010	92	2025	$70.00	14.5%
2012	93	2028	$70.00	14.0%

HEWITSON
GUN METAL RIESLING ★★★★★
Precise and pure regional style with restrained lemon pith and pear pulp riesling aromas. Well structured and well flavoured lemon into white pear with gentle middle palate weight.

| 2014 | 95 | 2030 | $28.00 | 11.5% |
| 2015 | 90 | 2019 | $23.00 | 12.0% |

Vintage	Rank	Drink	RRP	Vol Alc

HICKINBOTHAM CLARENDON VINEYARD

This vineyard has been given a new lease of life since February 2012 with the American Jackson Family Wines installing Charlie Seppelt as winemaker. Over 100 hectares of old vines and inspired winemaking make this the new winery launch of 2014. Some regard this as the best cabernet sauvignon in the McLaren Vale region and I see no reason to argue.

Winemaker: Charlie Seppelt, Chris Carpenter
Open: No Cellar Door 92 Brooks Road, Clarendon
Ph: (08) 8383 7504 *www.hickinbothamwines.com*

HICKINBOTHAM
BROOKES ROAD SHIRAZ ★★★★★

Appealing, complex, pretty floral lifted fruit, sarsaparilla, raspberry wed to oak spice aromas. The plate is long, fine and silky tannins up front appealing red fruited, elegant middle palate, slightly firm finishing as a young wine with fine oregano and vanilla oak spice to finish. Drink after 2017.

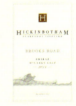

2012	92	2028	$75.00	14.5%
2013	94	2019	$75.00	14.5%
2014	92	2022	$75.00	14.0%

HICKINBOTHAM
THE PEAKE CABERNET SAUVIGNON SHIRAZ ★★★★★

The style is very consistent; across all the range, elegant as a result of considered decisions about just ripe fruit, subtle moderate oak. Fruit notes are red and black, minerals, dusty spice oak notes include cedar, oregano. On entry blue berry black berry with lovely complex cedar oregano oak spices which step into the fruits tannin and carry the flavours into deep red fruits blood plum entwined with oak spices creating a long layered complex wine.

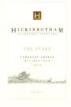

2012	96	2033	$150.00	14.5%
2013	96	2028	$150.00	14.0%
2014	95	2027	$150.00	14.0%

Vintage	Rank	Drink	RRP	Vol Alc

HICKINBOTHAM
TRUEMAN CABERNET SAUVIGNON ★★★★★
Understated elegance with fine red currant, beetroot, caramel and waxy notes from oak, subtle and harmonious. The palate has harmony with fresh ripe fruits and a touch of toasted coconut oak complexity. In the mouth very soft tannins with persistent length and excellent oak balance with red fruit length.

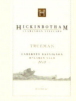

2012	96	2030	$75.00	14.0%
2013	92	2025	$75.00	13.5%
2014	94	2029	$75.00	14.0%

HIGHER PLANE
Higher Plane in Margaret River makes exciting wines, offering hints of the taste of the next generation of Margaret River wines. One to watch.
Winemakers: *Mark Messenger and Kym Eyres*
Open: *Daily 10am–5pm, 165 Warner Glen Road, Forest Grove*
Ph: *(08) 9258 9437* *www.higherplanewines.com.au*

HIGHER PLANE
MARGARET RIVER CABERNET SAUVIGNON ★★★★
Sweet oak leads the charge leafy briar varietal cabernet in the back ground adds form to the aromas .
In the mouth a wide and generous sweep of ripe tannins, dark fruits and chocolaty oak.

2010	90	2018	$45.00	14.0%
2011	90	2028	$50.00	14.5%
2012	88	2019	$50.00	14.0%

HIGHER PLANE
CHARDONNAY ★★★
Tight fruit oak lees complexity creating full and intense honey and pear aromas. The firm palate showing oak peanut brittle brulee oak intensity, a lot of lees creaminess provides some texture to offset the oak complexity finishes vanilla nougat spectrum.

2011	90	2017	$35.00	12.5%
2012	89	2018	$37.00	12.5%
2013	88	2018	$25.00	13.5%

| Vintage | Rank | Drink | RRP | Vol Alc |

HIGHER PLANE
THE MESSENGER MALBEC CABERNET SAUVIGNON MERLOT CABERNET FRANC PETIT VERDOT ★★★

This is complex, not definitively fruity it offers depth and complexity with mulberry black berry black currant and a swirling meat stock edge to the mix of aromas. Very good in the mouth, starts friendly and generous very easy to enjoy with good length of complex dark fruit, middle palate chocolate briar savoury flavours with fine firming tannins.

Vintage	Rank	Drink	RRP	Vol Alc
2011	88	2019	$65.00	14.5%
2012	92	2019	$65.00	14.0%

HILL SMITH ESTATE

The Hill Smith family referred to here are the owners of the Yalumba Wine company and 22 other vineyards with individual labels across Australia. Wines under this label come from the Adelaide Hills and Eden valley are often exceptional value.
Winemaker: *Teresa Heuzenroeder*
Open: *Flaxman's Valley Road, Eden Valley*
Ph: *(08) 8561 3200 www.hillsmithestate.com*

HILL-SMITH ESTATE
ADELAIDE HILLS CHARDONNAY ★★★★

Raunchy wild ferment struck match, subtle barrel ferment, funky notes and toasty oak, alongside wholesome varietal white nectarine chardonnay fruit. The palate is quite pure fruited with fine fresh acidity- a nod to chablis acidity with more traditional Australian fruit weight finishing smoked meat savoury notes, medium long.

Vintage	Rank	Drink	RRP	Vol Alc
2012	89	2015	$30.00	13.5%
2013	94	2017	$30.00	13.0%
2015	90	2018	$30.00	13.5%

Vintage	Rank	Drink	RRP	Vol Alc

HOLLICK

Coonawarra-based Hollick is one of a core of producers that have built a reputation for reliable wines. The style is on the move from more traditional to modern, becoming richer with rising oak levels.

Winemaker: *Joe Cory*
Open: *Weekdays 9am–5pm, Weekends and Public hols 10am–5pm*
Corner Riddoch Hwy & Ravenswood Ln, Coonawarra
Ph: *(08) 8737 2318* *www.hollick.com*

HOLLICK
BOND ROAD CHARDONNAY ★★★

Smoky ham and bacon savoury complexity and ripeness, it is all there and age will give it harmony. In the mouth medium bodied, rich, balanced and long, fresh and lively acidity holds the fruit flavour interesting to the finish.

Vintage	Rank	Drink	RRP	Vol Alc
2012	88	2016	$24.00	14.0%
2013	86	2016	$24.00	13.0%
2014	89	2019	$25.00	13.0%

HOLLICK
RAVENSWOOD CABERNET SAUVIGNON ★★★★

The aroma brings fine grained oak that compliments quality black fruits while side notes of pencil and smoked oyster add to the complexity. The palate offers cabernet line and fruit tension, good structure and a balance ideal for cellaring showing black currant fruit freshness- ideal for the long haul.

Vintage	Rank	Drink	RRP	Vol Alc
2010	90	2018	$80.00	14.5%
2012	95	2029	$80.00	14.5%
2013	94	2028	$77.00	14.0%

HOLLICK
WILGHA SHIRAZ ★★★★★

Ripe raspberry with an oak punch, perfumed red cherry fruits with good length, complex flavour, refined tannins and finesse. The palate runs long to the finish with red cherry, maraschino, raspberry and fine tannins.

Vintage	Rank	Drink	RRP	Vol Alc
2010	92	2020	$55.00	14.5%
2012	90	2026	$55.00	13.5%
2013	90	2029	$54.00	14.0%

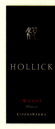

Vintage	Rank	Drink	RRP	Vol Alc

HOLM OAK VINEYARDS

Holm Oak has 12 hectares in the Tamar and the management style is meticulous, ensuring a pristine, fresh fruit style for riesling, sauvignon blanc, pinot gris and arneis. The chardonnay and pinot noir is full of interest and the cabernet is a star in ripe years. On the Tamar Wine route and well worth the time to visit.

Winemaker: Bec Duffy
Open: Daily from 11am–5pm Sept-May, 11am–4pm Jun-Aug, 11 West Bay Road, Rowella
Ph: (03) 6394 7577 *www.holmoakvineyards.com.au*

HOLM OAK
PINOT GRIS ★★★★

Well grown and well made. Slightly pink in hue with pinot gris floral to musk humanities and natural ferment funky waxy notes to the nose. The palate is gris-dom. Wide, soft, ripe, round textured, and long, dropping off on the finish with good clean fruit flavours and well made appeal.

Vintage	Rank	Drink	RRP	Vol Alc
2013	93	2018	$25.00	13.0%
2014	88	2019	$25.00	12.0%
2015	93	2017	$25.00	13.4%

HOLM OAK
PINOT NOIR ★★★★

Charming regional wine with bright fruit style. Pinot ripeness with fresh strawberry, touch spice. The palate has harmony and the delicacy of the Tamar, with freshness and bright fresh strawberry fruits. This is a light medium bodied easy to drink young style wine with the balanced prettiness of pinot.

Vintage	Rank	Drink	RRP	Vol Alc
2013	90	2017	$32.00	13.5%
2014	90	2018	$32.00	13.0%
2015	91	2019	$32.00	13.0%

HOLYMAN

Holyman and Stoney Rise Wine are from a vineyard planted in 1986 in Tasmania's Tamar Valley. Currently there are three hectares of pinot noir and one hectare of chardonnay. The resulting wines are in a cellaring style.

Winemaker: *Joe Holyman*
Open: *Thurs-Mon 11am–5pm Closed during Sept, 96 Hendersons Lane, Gravelley Beach*
Ph: *(03) 6394 3678 www.stoneyrise.com*

HOLYMAN
TASMANIA CHARDONNAY ★★★★

Outstanding young chardonnay with very good aging potential. Showing very subtle stone fruit at first, then minerality flinty aromas, (like well oiled steel), vanilla and honey oak notes in a fresh palate showing well balanced white nectarine fruit, long lively acidity and a tight hazelnut flinty youthful refined texture.

Vintage	Rank	Drink	RRP	Vol Alc
2009	90	2015	$45.00	12.5%
2012	93	2020	$45.00	12.5%
2014	95	2022	$45.00	13.5%

HOLYMAN
TASMANIA PINOT NOIR ★★★★

Fresh ripe aromas; raspberry, strawberry, stemmy whole bunch, and red cherry fruit aromas. In the mouth, it has an extra fruit dimension with plenty of ripe red cherry through to a stewed cherry middle palate with intense fruit and complex lingering red cherry flavours.

Vintage	Rank	Drink	RRP	Vol Alc
2011	94	2032	$45.00	14.0%
2012	94	2024	$50.00	13.0%
2013	93	2023	$50.00	13.5%

HOUGHTON

Houghton's top-level offerings under the Jack Mann label are the best wines from the company's extensive Frankland River vineyards and are always exceptional quality.

Winemaker: *Ross Pamment*
Open: *Daily 10am–5pm, 148 Dale Road, Middle Swan*
Ph: *(08) 9274 9540 www.houghton-wines.com.au*

Vintage	Rank	Drink	RRP	Vol Alc

HOUGHTON
JACK MANN CABERNET SAUVIGNON ★★★★★

Polished complexity with fresh ripe red and bramble into black currant fruit with oak spice aromas. The palate runs a long line of cabernet finesse black currant on tip of tongue the flavour runs unchanged long to the long finish, very fine tannins cloaked in black currant fruit flavours that turn chalky fine tannins.

2011	94	2040	$105.00	14.0%
2012	92	2022	$115.00	14.0%
2013	92	2020	$115.00	14.0%

HOUGHTON
MARGARET RIVER CABERNET SAUVIGNON ★★★

Surely not $16.00. Very varietal with black olive cabernet and a touch of spicy oak. The fruits are ripe and soft with plenty of upfront ripeness and middle palate sweet rhubarb, red currant into black currant cabernet spectrum medium long flavours.

| 2013 | 90 | 2017 | $16.00 | 13.5% |
| 2014 | 90 | 2016 | $16.00 | 13.5% |

HOWARD PARK

Howard Park is an ultra-premium West Australian producer with quality vineyards in the Margaret River and the Great Southern regions. The wines are meticulously made expressions of the best varieties within these regions.

Winemaker: Janice McDonald
Open: Daily 10am–5pm, Miamup Road, Cowaramup
Ph: (08) 9423 1200 www.howardparkwines.com.au

HOWARD PARK
ABERCROMBIE CABERNET SAUVIGNON ★★★★★

Fine cedar and dark fruits with sustained complexity that reveals itself as briar, cedar, mineral, dark fruit, pudding cabernet aromas with the mocha oak notes. The finely crafted palate has complexity with finesse, not at all heavy, medium bodied; long it can be drunk now to enjoy the initial softness of the pretty tight briar dark berry fruits which turn firm and dry on the finish. Age will increase the secondary savoury elements of this wine.

Vintage	Rank	Drink	RRP	Vol Alc
2011	95	2038	$110.00	14.0%
2012	93	2034	$113.00	14.0%
2013	92	2030	$125.00	14.0%

HOWARD PARK
GREAT SOUTHERN CHARDONNAY ★★★★★

The balance is seamlessly complex. The flagship chardonnay comes out swinging with a ripe elegance, rich, focused complexity with great mouth feel. Drinking pleasure is paramount here, with white fruits and ripe pear a hint of vanilla caramel all wrapped in chardonnay texture and so well judged.

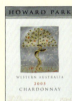

Vintage	Rank	Drink	RRP	Vol Alc
2013	92	2019	$54.00	13.0%
2014	93	2018	$54.00	13.0%
2015	93	2018	$54.00	13.0%

HOWARD PARK
GREAT SOUTHERN RIESLING ★★★★★

Spicy varietal vibrant citrus riesling with a full flavoured and rich depth of fruit and fullness in the mouth showing very much the house style of generous floral and citrus flavours with zippy acidity.

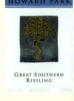

Vintage	Rank	Drink	RRP	Vol Alc
2012	94	2029	$32.00	12.0%
2014	93	2032	$33.00	12.0%
2015	92	2020	$33.00	12.0%

HOWARD PARK
PORONGURUP RIESLING ★★★★★

Fizzy citrus fruits with plenty of flesh and force. In the mouth a plush texture, fleshy with a core of citrus to stone fruit that runs long down the middle with fruit tingles like flavours without the sweetness. A completely different style of flavours with persistent length leaving the mouth with citrusy, almost tropical flavours within the length.

Vintage	Rank	Drink	RRP	Vol Alc
2012	88	2030	$33.00	12.0%
2014	95	2032	$34.00	12.0%
2015	92	2022	$34.00	12.0%

| Vintage | Rank | Drink | RRP | Vol Alc |

HUGO WINES
Hugo draws on 34 hectares of a family-planted old vineyard in the cooler foothills above McLaren Vale. A quiet achiever, making reliable wines since the mid 1980s that are excellent value.

Winemaker: *John Hugo*
Open: *Weekdays 9.30am–5pm, Sat 12pm–5pm, Sun 10.30am–5pm, Elliott Road, McLaren Flat*
Ph: *(08) 8383 0098* ***www.hugowines.com.au***

HUGO WINERY
CABERNET SAUVIGNON ★★★★

Deep blackberry, black plum and black currant fruits, with a vanilla oak edge. The wine has regional middle palate weight and slightly leafy varietal black fruits. The tannins are fine and the acids cleanse the finish.

2011	86	2016	$25.00	13.5%
2012	86	2018	$25.00	14.0%
2013	89	2019	$25.00	14.5%

HUGO WINERY
GRENACHE SHIRAZ ★★★★

Pale colour for this generally ripe house style with dark plum, minty dark fruits leading to a sweet raspberry fruit medium silky fleshy palate with a full body. Stylish fruit length with fine moderate intensity tannins. In the style of the ripe fruit and silky tannins of the region.

2011	89	2016	$21.00	14.5%
2012	89	2018	$29.00	14.5%
2013	87	2018	$29.00	14.5%

HUGO WINERY
RESERVE SHIRAZ ★★★★

Warm ripe blackberry, with fresh intensity and a traditional South Australian style for full-bodied red lovers. Sweet oak and deep liquorice-esque tarry fruits, with solid tannins, oak length and deep, minty, American-oak-flavoured deep fruit.

2010	90	2030	$45.00	14.5%
2011	Not made			
2012	91	2026	$45.00	14.5%

HUGO WINERY
SHIRAZ ★★★★
Well balanced vanilla cinnamon oak with ripe shiraz dark berry black olive side notes. The palate is a warm SA shiraz style. Silky tannins, a plush middle palate, dark cherry fruit and a generous, friendly old-school flavour and texture for the price.

2010	88	2019	$25.00	14.5%
2012	88	2018	$25.00	14.5%
2013	88	2018	$25.00	14.5%

HUNGERFORD HILL
Hungerford Hill and the associated Muse Restaurant are now owned by the Kirby family. With fruit from the Hunter Valley and other NSW areas, they have consistently improved in recent years.
Winemaker: Adrian Lockhart
Open: Sun-Thurs 10am–5pm, Fri-Sat 10am–6pm,
2450 Broke Road, Pokolbin
Ph: (02) 4998 7666 www.hungerfordhill.com.au

HUNGERFORD HILL
HUNTER VALLEY SEMILLON ★★★★
The aromas are classical Hunter semillon, early picked perfection with fresh lemon, lemon pie and a lime zesty back note. The palate is delicate fresh lemon and wax flavours, very pure even and long, with the freshest acid and the finest fruit flavours and length. This is an exceptional year.

2010	90	2015	$25.00	11.5%
2011	95	2027	$25.00	11.5%
2013	94	2023	$25.00	10.5%

HUNGERFORD HILL
TUMBARUMBA CHARDONNAY ★★★★
Gentle balanced aromas of apple and pear. A focus on purity, rather than winemaking complexity. The palate has a bright, mid-weight complexity and positive white fruits. Straight forward with refined balance.

Vintage	Rank	Drink	RRP	Vol Alc
2011	86	2016	$30.00	12.4%
2013	87	2020	$30.00	13.4%
2014	88	2018	$33.00	12.7%

HUNGERFORD HILL
TUMBARUMBA PINOT NOIR ★★★

Meaty, mildly peppery fruit and balanced oak aromas. In the mouth, appealing dry red flavours and style with a generous front palate and a stemmy frisky texture and acids to finish.

2009	89	2015	$35.00	13.5%
2010	80	2015	$25.00	12.5%
2013	85	2017	$25.00	14.8%

HUNGERFORD HILL
HUNTER VALLEY SHIRAZ ★★★★

In the Hunter regional style, finesse of savoury dried herbs and dark fruit aromas with well-judged vanilla oak leading a long firm light medium-bodied palate. Youthful, tight, firm length of raspberry fruit with good oak judgement that will unfold.

2010	88	2021	$35.00	13.5%
2011	90	2019	$35.00	14.0%
2013	89	2021	$35.00	13.7%

HUNGERFORD HILL
HILLTOPS CABERNET SAUVIGNON ★★★

Sweet dark oak notes of coffee, sweet chocolate, vanilla pod oak with ripe leafy spicy cabernet berry fruits. The palate is modern. Elegant soft tannins and elegant oak adds a vibrant exotic flavour to the firm black olive and dark berry cabernet flavours with fine grained tannins and oak spice flavours to finish.

2009	89	2019	$35.00	13.0%
2010	87	2016	$35.00	13.7%
2013	92	2020	$35.00	14.7%

| Vintage | Rank | Drink | RRP | Vol Alc |

HUNTINGTON ESTATE
Huntington Estate has old vines and a new owner. The wines are distinctively styled and capable of the long haul. Tim Steven's first wines show the "polished rusticity" that has brought the winery fame, but he's achieved better depth of flavour.
Winemaker: Tim Stevens
Open: Mon to Sat 10am–5pm, Sun and Pub Hols 10am–4pm, Cassilis Road, Mudgee
Ph: (02) 6373 3825 *www.huntingtonestate.com.au*

HUNTINGTON ESTATE
CABERNET SAUVIGNON
MERLOT ★★★★
An old-fashioned, attractive style which is undergoing a makeover, with fresher fruit flavours appearing from 2006.

2005	87	2015	$25.00	13.3%
2006	89	2012	$25.00	13.9%
2007	88	2014	$25.00	13.5%

HUNTINGTON ESTATE
SPECIAL RESERVE CABERNET SAUVIGNON ★★★★
This is a medium-bodied, well-balanced cabernet with considerable tannin for the long haul. Not for the faint hearted on release. The 04 was a wine with acidity giving length, while the 05 and 06 are more extracted wines in the modern style; different, fatter and thicker.

2005	88	2015	$33.00	13.2%
2006	91	2018	$33.00	13.2%
2007	87	2014	$33.00	12.4%

HUNTINGTON ESTATE
SPECIAL RESERVE SHIRAZ ★★★★
These wines have a decisive difference to South Australian fruit spectrum with their earthy red fruits, wintergreen, and dark spice savoury complexity. The palate has ripe tannins and smooth red fruit in a medium-bodied tight long wine with solid oak. The acids are youthfully firm.

2006	92	2025	$31.00	12.8%
2007	88	2014	$31.00	13.9%
2011	90	2029	$36.00	13.8%

HUNTINGTON ESTATE
BLOCK THREE CABERNET SAUVIGNON ★★★★★
Deep and dense cranberry, then savoury meaty chocolaty intensity weight and power. A concentrated voluptuous wine with cabernet rhubarb, very well balanced dark chocolate, nutmeg savoury and intensity wrapped in refined tannin bright tight complex structured evolving flavours and a firm finish.

Vintage	Rank	Drink	RRP	Vol Alc
2009	95	2030	$65.00	13.5%
2011	89	2023	$60.00	13.6%
2012	95	2035	$33.00	13.0%

IRVINE WINES
Irvine Wines is a small winemaker in the Eden Valley created by experienced winemaker Jim Irvine. He has been prepared to introduce lesser known grape varieties which add appeal to his offering. Recently his daughter has also taken a role in the winemaking.
Winemakers: *James Irvine and Joanne Irvine*
Open: *Daily 11am–4pm, Taste Eden Valley,*
6 Washington Street, Angaston
Ph: *(08) 8564 1110 www.irvinewines.com.au*

IRVINE WINES
BAROSSA MERLOT CABERNET FRANC ★★★★★
Very juicy and fragrant fruit aromas, with ripe berry and some herbs, raspberry, red currant and black currant, like a summer pudding. Very juicy, plump fine tannins, with depth and fleshy tannins on the middle palate holding a buoyant expression of sweet ripe fruits, with a savoury backdrop and fine tannins working the finish. Excellent, discreet style with the lushness.

Vintage	Rank	Drink	RRP	Vol Alc
2005	89	2014	$25.00	14.5%
2009	90	2016	$25.00	14.5%
2012	93	2016	$25.00	14.5%

IRVINE WINES
ZINFANDEL RESERVE ★★★★

Dried current prune fruits into the dark spices of ripe zinfandel. The fruitful palate has width and depth and the fruit cup cordial of zinfandel quickly asserts it's self with middle palate length of fruit cup cordial without the sugar, modest tannins and exotic clove spiced Christmas pudding flavours to close. Clever use of fruit flavours with modest tannins.

Vintage	Rank	Drink	RRP	Vol Alc
2010	89	2018	$45.00	15.5%
2012	95	2020	$45.00	15.0%
2013	93	2019	$55.00	15.0%

IRVINE WINES
EDEN VALLEY GRAND MERLOT ★★★★★

In the mouth, ripe silky dark plums with very good length and silky tannins. High intensity red fruits, with fresh acidity but musty, damp cork flavours.

Vintage	Rank	Drink	RRP	Vol Alc
2009	93	2019	$130.00	15.0%
2010	95	2022	$130.00	14.9%
2012	93	2025	$130.00	15.0%

JACOBS CREEK

Jacobs Creek has become synonymous with Australian wine but the company has not rested on its laurels and continues to refine its styles, offering a brilliant snapshot of the state of Australian-international value for money. The company aims for elegance in its wines and achieves this without the high-alcohol, fat formula-made wines of some of their peers. The move to regionality in the Jacobs Creek Reserve range is a significant move to elevate the brand and Australia's reputation.

Winemakers: *Ben Bryant, Rebekah Richardson*
Open: *Daily 10am–5pm, Jacobs Creek Visitor Centre, Barossa Valley Way, Rowland Flat*
Ph: *(08) 8521 3000 www.jacobscreek.com*

Vintage	Rank	Drink	RRP	Vol Alc

JACOBS CREEK
RESERVE ADELAIDE HILLS SAUVIGNON BLANC ★★★

The riper notes of passion fruit into fresh cut pineapple aromas. The palate is very sophisticated for the price; creamy, silky texture, middle palate with appealing fruity acidity and the same flavours on the finish.

Vintage	Rank	Drink	RRP	Vol Alc
2012	90	2014	$18.00	13.4%
2013	88	2016	$18.00	12.8%
2015	90	2017	$18.00	13.1%

JACOBS CREEK
RESERVE BAROSSA RIESLING ★★★

Pineapple lime fruits and punching far above its price. The palate is ripe, solid and well backed by acid, supporting a solid line of tropical fruits, with a lime zesty acid and rose petals lingering in the mouth.

Vintage	Rank	Drink	RRP	Vol Alc
2012	92	2020	$18.00	12.2%
2013	89	2016	$18.00	11.4%
2015	89	2018	$17.00	12.2%

JACOBS CREEK
STEINGARTEN RIESLING ★★★★★

Very scented white fruits; apple and pear, blossom, musk, bath powder and talc aromas. The palate is brightly nimble light bodied, very pure, long and fine balance. The complexity is elegance personified with fine acidity carrying long and subtle elements, floral on the finish. The best yet under this label.

Vintage	Rank	Drink	RRP	Vol Alc
2012	86	2022	$32.00	12.1%
2013	92	2025	$32.00	11.0%
2015	95	2027	$43.00	10.9%

JACOBS CREEK
REEVES POINT CHARDONNAY ★★★★

Bottle number 2,435 tasted. The oak is generous and the hearty style is bold and inclusively complex, with oak toast presence. The palate is complex: Oatmeal, lees, malt complexity and far more interesting than the nose, with bright fruit energy, delicious complexity and great length.

Vintage	Rank	Drink	RRP	Vol Alc
2007	90	2015	$30.00	13.8%
2012	90	2016	$35.00	13.0%
2013	95	2018	$32.00	13.4%

JACOBS CREEK
RESERVE COONAWARRA CABERNET SAUVIGNON ★★★

Black currant minty dark chocolate with a soft, long, medium bodied, varietal palate. Freshening acids on the finish ensure shelf life and the texture has tannins to dry the back with lingering black currant fruit.

2011	84	2013	$18.00	13.3%
2012	90	2016	$18.00	13.0%
2013	88	2018	$18.00	13.8%

JACOBS CREEK
RESERVE SHIRAZ ★★★

Punches above its weight, black berry and dark chocolate aromas with a blue berry top note. The palate is soft, the balanced use of mocha oak frames the soft tannins and juicy black berry and red plum middle palate flavours.

2011	88	2016	$18.00	14.1%
2013	89	2018	$18.00	14.5%
2015	88	2018	$18.00	14.7%

JACOBS CREEK
JOHANN SHIRAZ CABERNET ★★★★★

Incredible, ripe fresh fruit style, with svelte, bulging black currant and blackberry muscles. In the mouth, this floods with ripe bright fruit and delicacy in the black fruit. A touch of mint and leaf and tannin balance. Plush, silky soft tannin weds to the fruit depth and richness, with fleshy length unfolding darker berry fruits and powdery tannins.

2009	94	2030	$75.00	14.3%
2010	93	2032	$75.00	14.5%
2012	95	2037	$75.00	14.5%

Vintage	Rank	Drink	RRP	Vol Alc

JACOBS CREEK
CENTENARY HILL BAROSSA SHIRAZ ★★★★★

Spice, dark brooding fruits, fruit pudding supported by solid oak aromas. Ripe tannins, fresh and youthful red fruits, raspberry and blackberry which carries through to the finish lingering enticingly. Very good year and great balance.

2009	94	2034	$60.00	14.5%
2010	94	2020	$80.00	14.2%
2012	95	2027	$80.00	14.7%

JANSZ

Jansz is drawn from 22 hectares in Pipers River, planted in 1985. The winery uses a renowned Tasmanian method champenoise, a process we are obliged to call method traditionelle these days. It was initiated by champagne house, Louis Roederer and, under Natalie Fryar's care, has gone from strength to strength.
Winemaker: Natalie Fryar
Open: Daily 10am–4.30pm,
1216B Pipers Brook Road, Pipers Brook
Ph: *(03) 6382 7066 www.jansz.com.au*

JANSZ
VINTAGE ROSE PINOT NOIR ★★★★★

Aged for a minimum of 1090 days in the bottle pre-release, which fans of great sparkling will know adds quality. Musty-edged pink fruits, mushroom and ginger, adding woody character from the course grain corks. In the mouth, garden mushroom and compost spectrum; drying.

2008	93	2014	$47.95	12.5%
2010	92	2016	$47.95	12.0%
2011	90	2016	$52.95	12.0%

JANSZ
VINTAGE PREMIUM CUVEE CHARDONNAY PINOT NOIR ★★★★★

Very mature, rich yeast fresh bread, oatmeal aromas. The palate has a creamy texture, plenty of oatmeal lees into yoghurt, fresh acidity quality fruit weight and good line of sherbet lemony fruits run from fresh into apple and pear lingering cleanly.

2008	92	2017	$44.95	12.5%
2009	94	2017	$46.95	12.5%
2010	92	2018	$46.95	12.0%

JANSZ
LATE DISGORGED VINTAGE CUVEE CHARDONNAY ★★★★★

Aromas are from very long yeast age with oatmeal like yeast lees cloaking the white fruit. The palate is slippery in texture showing mature up front rich sparkling wine complexity, width and length with oatmeal lees richness, even and long the creamy yoghurt like texture wraps long flavours of subtle lemon citrus fruits with saline acidity lasting long in the mouth.

Vintage	Rank	Drink	RRP	Vol Alc
2005	94	2017	$50.00	12.5%
2006	92	2016	$55.95	12.0%
2007	94	2020	$55.95	12.0%

JASPER HILL
Jasper Hill is a cool-climate producer in Victoria's Heathcote area. The vineyard is run on biodynamic principles and the wines are convincing and impressive.
Winemakers: *Ron and Emily Laughton*
Open: *By appointment only, Drummond's Lane, Heathcote*
Ph: *(03) 5433 2528* *www.jasperhill.com*

JASPER HILL
EMILY'S PADDOCK SHIRAZ CABERNET FRANC ★★★★★

Very composed tight young red here with quality oak, red fruits, dried herbs, shiraz spices and mineral spice. The creamy quality oak notes support the fruit, very fine tannins, ripe fruits front palate, very drinkable now. This plump minerally ripe long wine has a fair dash of mocha and very fine tannins full of youthful vigour,"Penfolds-like" tannin, quite bright fruited. Freshest most balanced of the 2014's and very youthful in 2016.

Vintage	Rank	Drink	RRP	Vol Alc
2012	93	2022	$99.00	13.0%
2013	94	2029	$96.00	14.5%
2014	95	2027	$99.00	15.0%

JASPER HILL
GEORGIA'S PADDOCK SHIRAZ ★★★★★

Aromas are quite opposite to the 2012 with savoury notes of hoisin, soya, citrus peel, dark spices mineral and earth. The secondary notes reappear in the mouth, very full bodied more Heathcote minerals than Jasper Hill. Very full tannins showing the dark chocolate palate, gentle cherry mid palate and pepper to close. Very much drink soon vintage.

Vintage	Rank	Drink	RRP	Vol Alc
2012	95	2023	$76.00	13.5%
2013	92	2021	$73.00	14.5%
2014	88	2020	$76.00	15.0%

JASPER HILL
LA PLEIADE SHIRAZ ★★★★

Tempered by a European-styled elegance and in a totally different structure to most Australian shiraz, with a solid middle palate, less juicy up-front fruit, firmer tannins and lower oak. Uses two shiraz selections, one from France and one Australian. Aromas of star anise, gingerbread and liquorice. A full-bodied palate; red fruit / liquorice / black pepper and the tannins are assertive and silty in youth.

Vintage	Rank	Drink	RRP	Vol Alc
2008	90	2019	$70.00	15.0%
2009	90	2020	$78.00	14.5%
2010	91	2028	$68.00	15.0%

JASPER HILL
GEORGIA'S PADDOCK NEBBIOLO ★★★★★

The oak and tarry red fruit are balanced earthy dark notes with rancio and soya complexity. In the mouth, structure and subtle fruit presence, mineral length and harmony between wine maker and fruit handling, good tannins, ripe red licorice through oregano. The fruits are not over the top with well-judged tannins and very long in even flavour and texture.

Vintage	Rank	Drink	RRP	Vol Alc
2013	93	2019	$73.00	13.0%
2014	92	2022	$64.00	14.0%

JASPER HILL
OCCAM'S RAZOR HEATHCOTE SHIRAZ ★★★★

From the get go this has fruit presence; generous, ripe red cherry, maraschino and red plum fruit notes with vanilla oak in the back ground. This cuts a swathe through other wines with a very ripe long generous classic Heathcote red fruit flavours with exceptional flavour and tannin length, chalky finish thanks to the licorice tarry grape tannins.

Vintage	Rank	Drink	RRP	Vol Alc
2012	95	2022	$46.00	15.0%
2013	94	2019	$48.00	15.0%
2014	92	2022	$46.00	15.5%

Vintage	Rank	Drink	RRP	Vol Alc

JIM BARRY

Jim Barry Wines are Clare Valley winemakers with a sizeable range of reliable wines including exceptional shiraz and riesling. In recent years the wines have gained considerable freshness and intensity.

Winemaker: *Peter Barry*
Open: *Weekdays 9am–5pm, Weekends and Pub Hols 9am–4pm*
Craig Hill Road, Clare
Ph: *(08) 8842 2261* *www.jimbarry.com*

JIM BARRY
FIRST ELEVEN CABERNET SAUVIGNON ★★★★★

The style has stepped up with better fruit brightness, and regional and varietal personality. There is quality oak, choc-mint regional aromas as well lush blueberry and black currant. The palate has gained a little weight over prior years and the hall mark choc-mint is whispering in the dark berry back ground. The age worthy tannins remain the same with the fresh slightly spare style still in place. Great to see the sensible ripeness levels.

Vintage	Rank	Drink	RRP	Vol Alc
2010	93	2033	$60.00	13.5%
2012	91	2026	$60.00	13.5%
2013	92	2024	$60.00	14.0%

JIM BARRY
LODGE HILL RIESLING ★★★★★

The Barry's are blazing another path for Clare Riesling with wild yeast ferment driving the style. It is more complex than most and there is touch of green herb personality. The aromas smell delicious stone fruit, rose floral, spice ginger, green herbs and really interesting with great winemaking. Great line on the palate with fruit flavour evenness and lovely racy acidity tucked into the subtle lemon edged lime and rose flavours on the finish

Vintage	Rank	Drink	RRP	Vol Alc
2013	92	2023	$20.00	12.4%
2014	94	2020	$20.00	11.7%
2015	91	2020	$20.00	12.5%

Vintage	Rank	Drink	RRP	Vol Alc

JIM BARRY
THE ARMAGH SHIRAZ ★★★★★

Solid aromas, the fruit quality is immediate complex with depth black berry, raspberry plum, cooked plum, charcuterie, soya sauce adds complexity. The soft tannins are of the highest quality with bridging with seamless length from front to back palate and the youthful flavours are tucked away in the fruit and oak tannin length. The palate is concentrated without being gross or heavy, the finish keeps its sense of humour and leaves the mouth clean with gentle oak lingering. Keep a decade and drink for another.

2011	Not made			
2012	95	2040	$240.00	13.7%
2013	93	2034	$240.00	14.1%

JIM BARRY
THE FLORITA RIESLING ★★★★★

Water white colours and very pure, austere with the classic lime and lemon focused intensity. The palate has majesty, fresh citrus fruit driven. It is long and a very pure example of the variety with balanced acidity and lingering lime flavours. It is an understated wine, youthfully restrained, and based on the wines balance and vineyard reputation, has a great future.

2013	92	2033	$45.00	12.3%
2014	94	2030	$45.00	12.1%
2015	93	2013	$45.00	12.3%

JIM BARRY
WATERVALE RIESLING ★★★★

Almost tropical aromas with early season jasmine. The palate is rich, great early drinking style well balanced and long. Very full in the mouth with complex fruits mainly gentle fresh pineapple middle palate with a rose floral scented top note and medium long driven by the acidity.

2014	90	2018	$19.00	12.0%
2015	91	2018	$19.00	12.5%
2016	90	2019	$19.00	12.5%

| Vintage | Rank | Drink | RRP | Vol Alc |

JIM BARRY
PG SHIRAZ CABERNET ★★★★★

A serious sniff here of the superior fruit complexity yields fresh red berry; raspberry, blueberry and muscatel. The palate has concentrated fruit flavours raspberry, black berry, black tea with soft tannins sculpting the mouth feel and keeping the flavours moving to a firm finish where layers of berries, toast and charcuteries decorate the after taste.

2009	93	2028	$60.00	14.5%
2010	91	2025	$60.00	14.5%
2012	92	2027	$60.00	14.0%

JIM BARRY
THE BENBOURNIE CABERNET SAUVIGNON ★★★★★

What a nice wine. Flights of green cabernet. This is ripe, polished and balanced. Aromas are complex blackcurrant and blackberry with finesse and elegance. In the mouth it's liquid silk, running refined texture, not heavy but nimble lively layers of flavours with oak offering support and the overall wine showing finesse and elegance.

2010	94	2030	$70.00	14.0%
2011	Not made			
2012	95	2034	$70.00	13.55

JIM BARRY
THE COVER DRIVE CABERNET SAUVIGNON ★★★★

Exceptional value here the balance of Clare and Coonawarra makes a very complete wine at a great price. The fruit is varietal cabernet berry freshness with a savoury edge. The style is very consistent from year to year so the fruit has excellent line of flavour and length. Fresh and tight and sold to be drunk young, the fruit will soften with another year in bottle best 2017 -18

2012	87	2016	$22.00	14.0%
2013	92	2017	$22.00	14.0%
2014	90	2018	$22.00	14.0%

| Vintage | Rank | Drink | RRP | Vol Alc |

JIM BRAND

The Brand family have been in Coonawarra for decades and have hundreds of acres of vines to draw upon with their new company, established 2006. They are establishing a new generation of involvement based on a refined definition of regional quality. Several tiers of varietal wines are made and considerable amount is made as private label wines. They are more refined and elegant than many in Coonawarra.

Winemaker: *Sam Brand*
Open: *By appointment 9 Mary Street, Coonawarra*
Ph: *(04) 8877 1046* *www.jimbrandwines.com.au*

JIM BRAND
JIMS VINEYARD SHIRAZ ★★★★

The aroma is exceptional, complex and well integrated with blueberry and blackberry fruits. Mocha oak adds a backstop and the overall effect is inviting. The palate is very modern with fine tannins and ripe fruits. Blackberry flavours wed to fine tannins, charcuterie and blackberry linger on the finish and drinks extremely well young.

Vintage	Rank	Drink	RRP	Vol Alc
2010	93	2020	$35.99	14.0%
2012	91	2022	$35.99	14.5%
2013	93	2020	$35.99	14.0%

JIM BRAND
SILENT PARTNER CABERNET SAUVIGNON ★★★

Very good fruit quality polished ripeness without any artifice. Blackcurrant mint and the welcome savoury dark olive edge to frame the intensity. Lovely fresh and long black currant flavours too young in 2016 the tannins are silky and the oak beautifully judged to match the energy and flavour of the fruit. Drink 2018 onwards.

Vintage	Rank	Drink	RRP	Vol Alc
2010	90	2018	$35.99	14.5%
2012	89	2020	$35.99	14.5%
2013	95	2022	$35.99	14.0%

Vintage	Rank	Drink	RRP	Vol Alc

JOHN DUVAL
Based in the Barossa Valley, John Duval is one of our most talented and experienced red winemakers producing balanced, deeply flavoured wines with luxurious tannin richness and the highest level of quality.
Winemaker: John Duval
Open: Tastings available at Artisans of the Barossa Daily, 11am–6pm
Corner of Light Pass and Magnolia Roads, Vine Vale
Ph: (08) 8562 2266 *www.johnduvalwines.com*

JOHN DUVAL
PLEXUS SHIRAZ GRENACHE MOUVEDRE ★★★★★
Much tighter than the 2013, lifted, elegant brooding summer pudding freshness, finely spicy edges of clove and nutmeg. The palate is solid seamless taunt and controlled, ripe shiraz tip of tongue harmony builds into red fruit. Finely building tannins and plenty of complex sweet fruit from grenache and mataros. These create the deep middle palate with plenty of lingering black cherry fruits, and smoked meats in the firm tannins. A very complete mouthful of team players.

2012	93	2019	$40.00	14.5%
2013	91	2021	$40.00	13.5%
2014	94	2029	$40.00	14.5%

JOHN DUVAL
PLEXUS MARSANNE ROUSSANNE VIOGNIER ★★★★★
Restrained aroma, focused low oak and fruit complex, gentle oak spice and decisive complexity. The flavours get to the point quickly firm fruited with enough oak tannin to hold a long medium bodied textured palate with age worthiness. The palate is well put together, harmonious with marsanne minerality, orange peel, honeysuckle and a subtle floral lift of apricot in the finish. Better drink in 2017 onwards to enjoy the harmony of bottle maturity.

2013	91	2020	$30.00	13.5%
2014	92	2019	$30.00	13.0%
2015	90	2022	$30.00	12.5%

Vintage	Rank	Drink	RRP	Vol Alc

JOHN DUVAL
ENTITY SHIRAZ ★★★★★

Fruitful 2014's have a excellent fruit density over the ripe tannins, here lifted aromas into fresh fruit; plum, blue berry, black cherry with excellently judged oak spice on the trailing edge. The palate sweeps fresh fruits, unsweetened mixed berry flavours run long in the mouth, keeps its vibrancy with lovely accord of fruit tannins and acidity, harmonious with appealing oak balance showing dried herbs into smoked spice on the finish.

Vintage	Rank	Drink	RRP	Vol Alc
2012	92	2022	$50.00	14.5%
2013	91	2020	$50.00	14.5%
2014	93	2025	$50.00	14.5%

JOHN DUVAL
ELIGO SHIRAZ ★★★★★

Enjoyable fruit intensity with breadth and complexity, brooding fruits ripe black berry with a trail of savoury fruits and mineral earth, cooked dark plum, edge of hoisin, beef cubes for stock. The palate is complete, concentrated and complex running evenly with deep soft shiraz tannins rich red plum flavours, it is mouth filling with tannins to support the fruits never sinking into cloying or heavy, sandy tannins to close.

Vintage	Rank	Drink	RRP	Vol Alc
2011	Not made			
2012	94	2026	$120.00	14.5%
2013	91	2020	$120.00	14.5%

JOSEF CHROMY

One of the "go to" wineries of Northern Tasmania, with wines that are always in the zone for value and style. Their restaurant captures the Tasmanian buzz in delicious mouthfuls and is only 10 minutes from Launceston. The 61-hectare vineyard ensures that the wines reach the mainland in searchable quantities.

Winemaker: *Jeremy Dineen*
Open: *Daily, 10am-5pm. Larger groups are encouraged to phone ahead. 370 Relbia Road, Relbia*
Ph: *(03) 6335 8700 www.josefchromy.com.au*

Vintage	Rank	Drink	RRP	Vol Alc

JOSEF CHROMY
PINOT NOIR ★★★★★

This is an age worthy substantial wine that will reward cellaring. Aromas thread their way from red fruits to dark savoury, with strawberry, strawberry cane, red cherry, cherry pip and smoky stemmy aromas. The palate is taut, full flavoured, and firmly tannic with good acidity. The deep middle palate is firm and leads to a solid finish with red cherry fruits and oak.

2012	90	2019	$34.00	13.5%
2013	90	2017	$34.00	14.0%
2014	95	2032	$34.00	14.0%

JOURNEY WINES

When winemaking passion (as opposed to professional interest) drives a sommelier, the results can be spectacular. Damian North is one of a new breed of small-scale winemakers aimed exclusively at restaurants. His sensitivity to the interactions of food, guests and wine means that Journey Wines has manifest delicacy, nuance, length of unfolding flavour, complexity and sheer deliciousness. Damian's winemaking experience with Leeuwin Estate, Tarrawarra and in Oregon gives him the ability to think in many of wine's languages; including red and white, especially pinot noir and chardonnay.

Winemaker: *Damian North*
Open: *No Cellar Door, 1A / 29 Hunter Road, Healesville*
Ph: *(03) 5962 3149   www.journeywines.com.au*

JOURNEY WINES
CHARDONNAY ★★★★

This wine builds complexity, warm yellow butter and stone fruit, into a fresh complex seamless style with a round middle palate. The yellow wine gums, ripe stone fruit are finished by soft white fruits, fresh acidity and oak tannin giving a dry finish.

2011	88	2015	$30.00	12.5%
2012	92	2017	$32.00	13.0%
2013	90	2017	$34.00	13.5%

JOURNEY WINES
PINOT NOIR ★★★★
Very closed aromas in 2014, a red cherry core of fruit and very youthful. The palate is silky red cherry and red fruits in a light, fleshy and slightly chewy in texture. Delicacy and layers of fruits savouriness and minerals.

Vintage	Rank	Drink	RRP	Vol Alc
2012	94	2018	$34.00	13.0%
2013	91	2017	$34.00	13.0%

JOURNEY WINES
SHIRAZ ★★★★
Gentle and shy, with red fruits, mineral spice, quality oak support and dried herbs. The red fruits are up front and the middle palate has subtle, ripe cherry and raspberry, with a long, spicy firmness. Very youthful in 2015 and well made. Drink after 2017, with food.

Vintage	Rank	Drink	RRP	Vol Alc
2012	93	2020	$34.00	13.5%
2013	90	2023	$40.00	13.5%

JUNIPER ESTATE
One of the six original wineries in Margaret River (known then as Wrights) planted in 1973. Located within the Wilyabrup sub region, this is a large estate, producing wines with diversity and detail across the key regional wine styles. The vineyard's ranges are united by depth of flavour and elegance.
Winemaker: *Mark Messenger*
Open: *Daily 10am–5pm, 98 Tom Cullity Drive, Cowaramup*
Ph: *(08) 9755 9000 www.juniperestate.com.au*

JUNIPER ESTATE
AQUITAINE BLANC SEMILLON SAUVIGNON BLANC ★★★★
Gooseberry and honeysuckle, subtle oak aromas with balanced fruit intensity. The palate is heavy and rich with a fine weave of acidity and fruit oak weight, full and intense with solid fruit and oak weight building the length and density. Is at the fuller, oakier and more powerful end of the regional hero style.

Vintage	Rank	Drink	RRP	Vol Alc
2011	88	2015	$30.00	12.5%
2012	92	2023	$30.00	12.5%
2014	89	2022	$30.00	13.5%

JUNIPER ESTATE
AQUITAINE ROUGE CABERNET SAUVIGNON MALBEC MERLOT CABERNET FRANC ★★★★

The finesse of cabernet blends in Margaret River is world class; here with red and black fruits balanced by graphite toast oak intensity. The fruit medium body has appealing fruit complexity runs black currant malbec sweet beetroot and fresh red plum, cabernet tannins adding their chalky grip balancing the intense fruit complexity giving an overall balance says capable of aging. Youthful in 2016 drink 2018 onwards.

Vintage	Rank	Drink	RRP	Vol Alc
2012	89	2018	$37.00	14.0%
2013	86	2017	$37.00	14.0%
2014	93	2024	$37.50	14.0%

KALLESKE

The Kalleske family has been growing grapes at Greenock in the Barossa for six generations but only began winemaking this century. Pioneers of organic long before it was popular, this is a family with an innate knowledge of the vineyard's site. With a talented winemaker, the family is making huge strides to become one of the new stars of the Barossa. All the wines are certified organic by ACO.

Winemaker: *Troy Kalleske*
Open: *By appointment only, 6 Murray Street, Greenock*
Ph: *(08) 8563 4000 www.kalleske.com*

KALLESKE
CLARRY'S GRENACHE SHIRAZ MATARO ★★★★

Ripe blackberry and blueberry fruit, with subtle oak spices in the aromas. In the mouth ripe grenache rasperry and red cherry with moderate tannins firming and turning to brown peppery spices and on the finish.

Vintage	Rank	Drink	RRP	Vol Alc
2013	90	2016	$20.00	14.0%
2014	89	2017	$20.00	14.0%
2015	90	2018	$20.00	14.0%

KALLESKE
GREENOCK SHIRAZ ★★★★★

Ripe, deep fruits dark cherries and black berries, flinging off scents of tapenade dried herbs, gravy roast meat, caramel and minerals. In the mouth very pure regional fruits waltz in time with soft chocolaty tannins with fine length and notes of dark berry chocolate meat stock and spice before pulling up with a saliva inducing fine tannin dryness and a flicker of warmth. Full-bodied red lovers wine.

Vintage	Rank	Drink	RRP	Vol Alc
2012	94	2030	$38.00	14.5%
2013	90	2018	$40.00	14.5%
2014	95	2020	$40.00	14.5%

KALLESKE
JMK VP SHIRAZ ★★★★

Deep black fruit colour and brandy spirits aromas help add meat stock with subtle new oak. The palate is sweet more grunt than a ruby supported with oak which marks the finish with cinnamon oak spice adding the length.

Vintage	Rank	Drink	RRP	Vol Alc
2010	88	2017	$23.00	18.0%
2013	89	2018	$23.00	18.0%
2014	88	2020	$23.00	18.0%

KALLESKE
JOHANN GEORG SHIRAZ ★★★★★

Sourced from a single vineyard planted in 1875 that is dry grown and certified biodynamic. The result is a pretty, juicy bold red with lavender, raspberry, red cherry details. A wine that has real finesse and it is very intense along a palate that is long and smooth. A keeper.

Vintage	Rank	Drink	RRP	Vol Alc
2011	94	2029	$120.00	14.5%
2012	95	2020	$120.00	14.0%
2013	94	2025	$120.00	14.5%

KALLESKE
MOPPA SHIRAZ ★★★★

Distinctive aromas with a Mediterranean herb edge to the dark berry fruits showing rosemary and lavender dried pot pourri. In the mouth the fruits are medium bodied and the ripe berries lift the middle palate offering cherry to the savoury. Really well integrated wine with very good length.

Vintage	Rank	Drink	RRP	Vol Alc
2012	91	2018	$28.00	14.0%
2013	90	2019	$28.00	14.5%
2014	94	2019	$28.00	14.0%

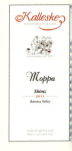

KALLESKE
OLD VINE GRENACHE ★★★★★

A fabulous wine. Varietal structure with old vine flavour complexity, floral red fruits, raspberry, appealing leathery old oak edges. The red fruits are flushed with savoury elements – smoked meats, fennel seeds and very up front. The flavours linger with raspberries and red pepper.

Vintage	Rank	Drink	RRP	Vol Alc
2012	94	2030	$45.00	15.5%
2013	90	2018	$45.00	15.0%
2014	94	2025	$50.00	14.5%

KALLESKE
PIRATHON SHIRAZ ★★★★

Pretty aromas, ready to drink young and to the point of Barossa with dark berry and cherry fruits edges show dried herbs minerality, meat stock, gravelly earthy tannins. The palate leads cherry fruits whereas the more senior wines show silky tannins and complex flavours. Here the fruit stands up on the tongue red and juicy with flavours freshness and great middle palate presence.

Vintage	Rank	Drink	RRP	Vol Alc
2012	89	2016	$23.00	14.5%
2013	89	2017	$23.00	14.5%
2014	92	2017	$23.00	14.5%

Vintage	Rank	Drink	RRP	Vol Alc

KALLESKE
ROSINA GRENACHE ★★★★★

Apricot puree and rose petal raspberry to the nose. The sweetness up front pleases the crowd and the tannins marry the fruit and finish. Would suit a hot outdoor bbq with a chill on the bottle.

2013	90	2016	$19.00	13.5%
2014	90	2015	$19.00	12.0%
2015	88	2017	$19.00	13.0%

KARRAWATTA
Located in Adelaide Hills, at Meadows planted 1996, and 1989 in Langhorne Creek to Sauvignon Blanc, Pinot Gris at Meadows and Shiraz, Cabernet Sauvignon at Langhorne Creek.
Winemaker: Mark Gilbert
Open: By Appointment Only, 818 Greenhills Road, Meadows
Ph: (08) 8537 0511 *www.karrawatta.com.au*

KARRAWATTA
CHRISTO'S PADDOCK CABERNET SAUVIGNON ★★★★★

Lush black currant, blackberry, oregano, cedar and tobacco aromas. The palate is fresh luscious tannins, same flavour complexities as the aromas, long black currant fruits and cedar with a savory bouquet of oregano. Mineral quality with a fleshy full middle palate, lovely seamless length.

| 2013 | 96 | 2025 | $54.00 | 14.7% |
| 2014 | 96 | 2033 | $54.00 | 14.5% |

KARRAWATTA
JOSEPH SHIRAZ ★★★★★

The price might seem steep but for the quality, it is not a lot. Juicy, vivid ripe aromatics of black berry, bay leaf and green garden herbs, an edge of pith and pulp of freshly squeezed berry juices. The palate is plush, ripe, smooth, even and long, alongside well-judged oak. The liqueured red fruits are persistent and wed to classy tannins. Going for beauty, not bulk this is a silky sheet of rippling fruit across the tongue.

| 2013 | 94 | 2022 | $54.00 | 14.6% |
| 2014 | 95 | 2035 | $54.00 | 14.5% |

KARRAWATTA
SOPHIE'S HILL PINOT GRIGIO ★★★

The Adelaide Hills does pinot grigio well and this is a good example. Fresh cut pear salad aromas and subtle cinnamon spice edges from old oak lead to a lively complex medium bodied palate. Ripe pear middle palate with additional pretty floral top notes and subtle pithy texture in an appealing dry finish.

| 2014 | 88 | 2016 | $26.00 | 12.0% |
| 2015 | 92 | 2017 | $26.00 | 12.0% |

KATNOOK
Katnook is a Coonawarra maker of wines with extensive vineyards at its disposal, producing a plush, signature-oak style of ripe wines, round and rich with soft tannins and quality oak.

Winemaker: *Wayne Stehbens*
Open: *Mon-Fri 10am–5pm, Sat & Sun 11am–5pm*
Riddoch Hwy, Coonawarra
Ph: *(08) 8737 0300 www.katnookestate.com.au*

KATNOOK ESTATE
CABERNET SAUVIGNON ★★★★

Aromas are closed and low-key blue berry menthol with reserved dark fruit aromas. In the mouth, dry firm and medium long, austere cabernet tannins backed by oak, medium-bodied medium long with tannins the centrepiece.

2011	90	2022	$40.00	13.5%
2012	88	2019	$40.00	13.5%
2013	84	2017	$40.00	13.5%

KATNOOK ESTATE
ODYSSEY CABERNET SAUVIGNON ★★★★

Cork finished. A lot of attention in the glass needed here. Spicy French oak notes with black currant, cassis and blue fruit; whilst these elements are lively in their own right, they need a lot longer to get it on. Teriyaki, tahini, cedar and dried herbs aromas. The fruits possess a classic and lovely presence with ripeness and evenness, fine tannins and flowing graceful length to close.

2009	90	2020	$100.00	14.5%
2010	92	2019	$100.00	14.5%
2012	94	2027	$100.00	14.5%

KATNOOK ESTATE
FOUNDERS BLOCK CABERNET SAUVIGNON ★★★

Coonawarra regional character with low oak showing choc mint and black currant regional aromas. The flavours are minty and the tannins furry, puckering, minty mid palate.

Vintage	Rank	Drink	RRP	Vol Alc
2011	88	2018	$23.00	13.5%
2013	87	2018	$20.00	13.5%
2014	83	2017	$20.00	13.5%

KATNOOK
ESTATE MERLOT ★★★

A complex oak and fruit weave that sits chocolate oak around cherry and plum pie fruit Milk chocolate the ripe fruit flavours make it easy to drink, the chocolaty tiramisu oak midpalate flavours help it along to be medium plus length.

Vintage	Rank	Drink	RRP	Vol Alc
2010	87	2014	$40.00	13.5%
2011	Not made			
2012	88	2018	$40.00	13.5%
2013	89	2019	$40.00	13.5%

KATNOOK
ESTATE SHIRAZ ★★★★

So ripe straight from the start ripe fruits sarsaparilla creamy ripe and super generous, oat meal edges of quality oak. Bold honest ripeness. In the mouth it is full and round ripe tannins and raspberry fresh fruits and wine gums towards the finish, round varietal shiraz tannins wed to oak voluptuous middle palate and gentle oak.

Vintage	Rank	Drink	RRP	Vol Alc
2011	Not made			
2012	92	2017	$40.00	13.5%
2013	92	2018	$40.00	13.5%

KATNOOK
PRODIGY SHIRAZ ★★★★

For lovers of full-bodied reds, I have got a treat for you. Liqueured cherry, coconut, blackberry, raisin fruits complexities in this powerhouse aroma. Super smooth and easy to enjoy, this is a velvet red carpet that rolls out across your tongue with high-quality oak adding to the sumptuous nature of the wine. Flavours are caramelised red plums and red currants, finishing clean and fresh. Drinking easily from release, it will hold for 15 years.

Vintage	Rank	Drink	RRP	Vol Alc
2009	90	2022	$100.00	14.5%
2010	92	2020	$100.00	14.5%
2012	94	2027	$100.00	14.5%

KAY BROTHERS
Kay Brothers' old vines in McLaren Vale provide excellent material for a range of ripe, rich red wines with shiraz the star.
Winemaker: *Duncan Kennedy*
Open: *Weekdays 9am–5pm, Weekends and Pub Hols 11am–5pm*
Kays Road, McLaren Vale
Ph: *(08) 8323 8201* *www.kaybrothersamerywines.com*

KAY BROTHERS
BASKET PRESSED GRENACHE ★★★★

Another ripper from this label. Shy red fruits and dried chicken spices are very focused here. In the mouth, very linear and lengthy, the soft tannins with medium intensity fruit possess a lovely minerality and gentle fruit power. Not the ripe powerhouse of 2012, but a charming fine boned savoury style to drink sooner. Finesse in grenache with a minerality.

Vintage	Rank	Drink	RRP	Vol Alc
2012	94	2028	$25.00	14.5%
2013	89	2018	$25.00	14.5%
2014	91	2022	$25.00	14.0%

KAY BROTHERS
AMERY BLOCK 6 SHIRAZ ★★★★★

Deep, dark colour with plum and black berry into earthy dark fruits. To taste the silky tannins are very regional and frame the dark fruit complexity with savoury meat stock and mineral initially until the carpet unfolds into a very long red berry finish. A wine for contemplation and drinking slowly on a thoughtful day such as Anzac day. Quality McLaren Vale reds have tannins that are part of the flavour as is the case here.

Vintage	Rank	Drink	RRP	Vol Alc
2010	94	2025	$80.00	14.5%
2012	95	2040	$80.00	14.5%
2013	93	2028	$75.00	14.5%

| Vintage | Rank | Drink | RRP | Vol Alc |

KEITH TULLOCH
Keith Tulloch is a fourth-generation Hunter Valley winemaker, with an enormous knowledge of the traditions of the region and who wants to see the area's wines enjoy the respect they deserve. The standards are high and the amounts are small.
Winemaker: *Keith Tulloch*
Open: *Daily 10am–5pm, Hermitage Road, Pokolbin*
Ph: *(02) 4998 7500 www.keithtullochwine.com.au*

KEITH TULLOCH
HUNTER VALLEY SEMILLON ★★★★★

The balance is lanolin edged citrus fruit, then talc and earthy minerality leading to a well balanced, delicate flavours with the typical big vein of fresh lemon citrus zing acidity driving the middle flavours and length with freshness. The essence of fresh lemon in the glass.

Vintage	Rank	Drink	RRP	Vol Alc
2013	95	2025	$28.00	11.0%
2014	92	2022	$28.00	11.5%
2015	89	2024	$28.00	11.0%

KEITH TULLOCH
THE 'KESTER' SHIRAZ ★★★★★

Solid ripe aromas dark spiced fruit cake hay oak spices. In the mouth this is superior, good length and fine tannins very even well centred long dark spiced plum cakes

Vintage	Rank	Drink	RRP	Vol Alc
2011	93	2026	$60.00	14.5%
2013	88	2024	$70.00	13.8%
2014	93	2028	$70.00	14.5%

KILIKANOON
Kilikanoon in the Clare Valley has been a modern success story, making some extremely fine wines from variously named blocks within the region. The quality is exceptional. The winery recently joined with other wine industry professionals to purchase the Barossa's Seppeltsfield, which has the southern hemisphere's most significant stocks of old fortified wines.
Winemakers: *Kevin Mitchell and Katie Turvey*
Open: *Thurs to Mon 11am–5pm, Penna Lane, Penwortham*
Ph: *(08) 8843 4206 www.kilikanoon.com.au*

Vintage	Rank	Drink	RRP	Vol Alc

KILIKANOON
MORTS BLOCK RIESLING ★★★★

House style here with width and depth of intensity. Ethereal lime potpourri, lemon, with lovely fruit sweetness fine grained acidity middle palate fullness and fleshy width.

2012	90	2017	$22.00	12.5%
2013	86	2018	$23.00	12.5%
2015	91	2020	$25.00	12.5%

KILIKANOON
MORTS RESERVE RIESLING ★★★★★

This is a stayer, gentle intensity, lime and fresh on nose. The palate is ample long very fine white fruit and a lingering white fruits woven into fresh fine acidity with very good length.

2012	90	2022	$35.00	12.5%
2013	93	2033	$35.00	12.5%
2014	93	2029	$35.00	12.0%

KILIKANOON
BLOCKS ROAD CABERNET SAUVIGNON ★★★★

Varietal nose pungent, rich and dense cassis/blue berry dominate slight leafy, black currant fruits with gentle menthol sedge. The palate runs long starts vibrant fresh blackcurrant fruits up front turning savoury earthy tapenade olive with length. Cabernet that tastes very varietal and ripe with soft tannins.

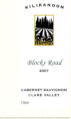

2009	91	2020	$33.00	14.0%
2010	88	2017	$33.00	14.0%
2013	92	2020	$33.00	14.0%

KILIKANOON
COVENANT CLARE VALLEY SHIRAZ ★★★★

Lots of appeal with this ripe blue berry, blackberry and liquorice scented aromas. It is mouth-filling full-bodied shiraz finishing layered with black fruits, spice and firm tannins.

2010	90	2020	$44.00	14.5%
2012	94	2022	$40.00	14.5%
2013	89	2021	$44.00	14.5%

Vintage	Rank	Drink	RRP	Vol Alc

KILIKANOON
THE DUKE CLARE VALLEY RESERVE GRENACHE ★★★★

Used to be the Duke with no reserve in the name. Layers in complexity with strawberry compote fruits and vanilla cedar, five spice mix oak spices adding to intensity and power. The palate via the oak is more tannic deeper wed to dark spice with soft tannins and red raspberry varietal flavours creating a dense core of flavour in the middle palate and lingering raspberry flavours.

Vintage	Rank	Drink	RRP	Vol Alc
2007	90	2014	$70.00	14.5%
2009	88	2016	$59.00	14.5%
2012	91	2020	$80.00	14.5%

KILIKANOON
ORACLE CLARE VALLEY SHIRAZ ★★★★★

Layered winemaker complexity myriad oak spices wrapped into a spectrum of red fruits. The palate has weight and density dark berry solidarity of oak and fruit, firm and strong in the middle palate lingering oak spices.

Vintage	Rank	Drink	RRP	Vol Alc
2008	89	2018	$80.00	14.5%
2010	92	2023	$80.00	14.5%
2012	90	2020	$80.00	14.5%

KINGSTON ESTATE

With an unusual variety as their lead, you could easily over look the shiraz and cabernets from this company. The $15 varietal range created by blending from South Australia's best regions is an easy drinking style, yet with enough balance and length of flavour and acids to suit a decent meal. The $25.00 range are great examples of modern Australian wine, sophisticated style with the punch of clean ripe fruit and fine tannins sufficient to hold 4–6 years.

Winemaker: Brett Duffin
Open: No Cellar Door, Peterson Road, Kingston on Murray
Ph: (08) 8583 0500 *www.kingstonestatewines.com*

| Vintage | Rank | Drink | RRP | Vol Alc |

KINGSTON ESTATE
ECHELON PETITE VERDOT ★★★★

From the top down this aroma has complexity with blueberry, raisins, fruits, dried herbs and gum leaf. The palate is massive, full bodied with silky tannins and even length. A raisins and plum pudding middle palate and dry dark licorice laced firm finish. A good introduction to the variety.

Vintage	Rank	Drink	RRP	Vol Alc
2009	90	2018	$25.99	14.5%
2010	92	2019	$25.99	14.5%
2012	92	2018	$24.99	14.5%

KINGSTON ESTATE
ECHELON SHIRAZ ★★★

For lovers of full bodied reds. Jammy black fruits with a fresh green herbs, thyme and sage in the background. Touch of rancio development with a solid plinth of ripe fruits and tannins built like the proverbial with cooked plum fruits.

Vintage	Rank	Drink	RRP	Vol Alc
2009	89	2017	$25.99	14.5%
2010	90	2020	$25.99	14.5%
2012	88	2018	$24.99	14.5%

KIRRIHILL

Kirrihill is a Clare Valley-based operation with vineyards across the premium regions of South Australia. This winery has offered very impressive quality for the price.

Winemakers: *Hamish Seabrook and Marnie Roberts*
Open: *Daily 10am–4pm, No 12 Main North Road, Clare*
Ph: *(08) 8842 4087* *www.kirrihillwines.com.au*

KIRRIHILL
VINEYARD SELECTION SERIES WATERVALE RIESLING ★★★★

Riper spectrum Riesling, with the Watervale generosity and lots of middle-palate fullness. Good "drink now" style, with seafood friendly balance.

Vintage	Rank	Drink	RRP	Vol Alc
2013	90	2018	$18.00	12.5%
2014	90	2018	$20.00	11.0%
2015	94	2019	$20.00	12.6%

| Vintage | Rank | Drink | RRP | Vol Alc |

KIRRIHILL SINGLE VINEYARD
VINEYARD SELECTION SERIES TULLYMORE CABERNET SAUVIGNON ★★★★

Floral rose like into black currant plum varietal and pencil shavings oak notes with harmony. The blackcurrant and dark plum fruit length is wed to firm even long tannins which create a dense full bodied firm finishing tannin with a layer of oak spices cedar oregano unfolding on the finish. For lovers of full bodied reds.

2010	87	2016	$20.00	14.5%
2012	88	2016	$25.00	14.5%
2013	92	2020	$25.00	14.8%

KIRRIHILL SINGLE VINEYARD
SINGLE VINEYARD TULLYMORE SHIRAZ ★★★★

For lovers of full-bodied reds this has a massive wine maker intensity. Oak spice richness and power with layers of vanilla caramel aromas. The palate has full-bodied firm finishing balance deep ripe luscious black cherry middle with the balance tipping the carpenters way, amazingly soft given the weight of fruit and oak with bourbon like oak dry finish.

2010	86	2016	$25.00	14.5%
2012	88	2016	$25.00	14.5%
2013	92	2020	$20.00	14.9%

KOONARA

Koonara, planted 1988 is run by Dru brother company to Reschke Wines run by Burke Reschke. Both are sons of Trevor Reschke, Peter Douglas, formerly Wynns chief winemaker is their consultant winemaker. Since 2013 Koonara have leased and managed the Kongorong Partnership Vineyard in Mount Gambier, which had previously sold its grapes to Koonara.
Winemaker: *Peter Douglas, (Dru Reschke Vigneron)*
Open: *Monday – Thursday 10am–5pm, Friday & Saturday 10am–6pm, Sunday & Pub Hols 10am–4pm*
44 Church Street, Penola
Ph: *(08) 8737 3222* *www.koonara.com*

KOONARA
AMBRIEL'S GIFT CABERNET SAUVIGNON ★★★★
The balance tilts towards subtle vanilla and toffee oak as a youngster, dark spices, grandmothers pantry, scents of old cinnamon, clove filled jars are often a note I find in these wines and here it is again. The palate delivers the house style silky tannins creating a satiny entry that flows long and even, faintest hint of mint on the black currant rich fruited palate flickers brown spices.

2010	90	2019	$40.00	14.2%
2012	90	2024	$40.00	13.9%
2013	92	2023	$40.00	13.9%

KOONARA
EZRA'S GIFT ★★★★
Aromas are classic Rhone syrah, more often seen in central Victoria, with black pepper, smoked meats, sausage meat cinnamon spices around a core of red fruits. The palate has soft tannins and nearly lives up to the incredible nose; spicy black pepper and cinnamon savoury around a core of red fruits. Very pretty and worth drinking to catch the freshness and spice.

2003	89	2017	$60.00	13.5%
2009	84	2015	$35.00	13.5%
2012	93	2017	$40.00	14.2%

KOOYONG
Kooyong is a 40-hectare vineyard founded in 1995 in the Mornington Peninsula, specialising in pinot noir and chardonnay. Kooyong uses 100 per cent natural fermentation in the processing. The property produces an exciting range of wines, including single vineyard editions when quality permits.
Winemaker: *Sandro Mosele*
Open: *Daily 11am–5pm, 263 Red Hill Road, Red Hill South*
Ph: *(03) 5989 2708* ***www.kooyong.com***

Vintage	Rank	Drink	RRP	Vol Alc

KOOYONG
CHARDONNAY ★★★★★

The classy sophistication of well-made chardonnay is on display, well-grown fruit, creamy oatmeal, flickering oak spice creamy citrus tangy fruit with length and well oak back ground complexity tight balanced good length and understated.

Vintage	Rank	Drink	RRP	Vol Alc
2012	95	2019	$43.00	13.5%
2013	91	2018	$43.00	13.5%
2015	92	2020	$42.00	13.0%

KOOYONG
ESTATE PINOT NOIR ★★★★★

This steps up intensity and complexity with a whole bunch spice and strawberry fruit concentration. The palate has fabulous fruit, ripe strawberry fruits, even long and fleshy generosity with very fine-grained tannins on the long finish.

Vintage	Rank	Drink	RRP	Vol Alc
2012	88	2017	$53.00	13.5%
2013	92	2021	$53.00	13.5%
2014	93	2019	$48.00	13.0%

KREGLINGER

Kreglinger Wine Estates produces the Pipers Brook and Ninth Island wines but only releases the Vintage Brut under its Kreglinger label.
Winemaker: *Rene Bezemer*
Open: Daily 10am–5pm, 1216 Pipers Brook Road, Pipers Brook
Ph: (03) 6234 2010 *www.kreglingerwineestates.com*

KREGLINGER
VINTAGE BRUT ★★★★★

Tasted twice within a month and the second bottle was even better than the first. Very fine and persistent mousse. Cool grown apple pear chardonnay and mushroom pinot fruit aromas, backed by a bready yeast aroma. The silky pear apple mid-palate flavours are framed by a green apple acidity. The finish is firm.

Vintage	Rank	Drink	RRP	Vol Alc
2004	88	2015	$50.00	12.5%
2005	91	2014	$50.00	12.5%
2006	88	2015	$46.00	12.5%

Vintage	Rank	Drink	RRP	Vol Alc

KRINKLEWOOD WINES
Krinklewood is a biodynamic vineyard in the Broke-Fordwich region of the Lower Hunter Valley. The scenic vineyard and cellar door are well worth a visit.

Winemaker: Rod and Peter Windrim
Open: Friday, Saturday, Sunday 10am–5pm, 712 Wollombi Road, Broke
Ph: (02) 6579 1322 www.krinklewood.com

KRINKLEWOOD
BIODYNAMIC HUNTER VALLEY SEMILLON ★★★
Appealing bright minerality, then lemons and talc into soapstone. The palate has weight and flavour; it is a zinger with lovely light-bodied texture with lemony fruit weight, fleshy body, evenness and fresh to the finish.

2010	87	2014	$22.00	9.8%
2011	Not made			
2015	92	2023	$24.00	10.0%

LA PROVA
La Prova the means "the trial", in Italian and refers to the Italian varieties Sam makes into small batches. If they are successful they continue to be produced. Restaurants love his high standards and wine styles. Draws on fruit from Adelaide Hills and the Barossa Valley. Sam trained at Lincoln University and has a degree in business. His "La Prova" label allows him to experiment and the company is moving ahead rapidly.

Winemaker: Sam Scott
Open: First weekend of each Month or By Appointment, 102 Main road, Hahndorf
Ph: (08) 8388 7330 www.scottwines.com.au

LA PROVA
NERO 'D AVOLA ★★★★★
Lovely colour, gentle ruby red should be. The red cherry is brightness with a fresh lift, touch of forest floor then white pepper garden compost adds contrast. The tight plate is food loving red and sarsaparilla fruits have line of middle palate focused with a juicy quality off set by fine grained tannins with the fruit lingering after the black tea tannin texture

Vintage	Rank	Drink	RRP	Vol Alc

has cleaned your mouth. Delicate detailed texture and focused flavours.

2013	89	2016	$25.00	14.0%
2014	93	2017	$25.00	13.4%
2015	93	2018	$25.00	13.7%

LA PROVA
MONTEPULCIANO ★★★★★

Technically a really good colour plenty of purple in the rim. Cool and fresh aromas not over ripe, mint on the side of the main course red cherry aromas. In the mouth flavours built on a good tannin basement wander through the orchard with raspberry and red plum into the kitchen garden with gentle parsley like green herbs, hint of mint and fine firm tannins to close the palate.

2014	92	2017	$25.00	12.5%
2015	90	2018	$25.00	13.2%

LAKE BREEZE

The Follett family have been grape growers in Langhorne Creek for over 120 years and winemakers for 25 years. They have rapidly built a reputation for consistently producing ripe silky tannin rich reds.

Winemaker: Greg Follett
Open: Daily 10am–5pm, Step Road, Langhorne Creek
Ph: (08) 8537 3017 www.lakebreeze.com.au

LAKE BREEZE
ARTHURS RESERVE CABERNET SAUVIGNON PETIT VERDOT MALBEC ★★★★★

The style is very defined cabernet with dark cabernet spectrum fruit aromas and tannins. This is a step up on 2013. Dark black currant, blue berry, black olive and bay leaf dark spice fruit. The palate is dark fruited smooth tannins black currant mid palate a floral sappy malbec note wed almost to mint fruits creates a complex middle palate while the tannins carry the fruit long.

2012	94	2028	$35.00	14.0%
2013	92	2026	$35.00	14.0%
2014	95	2025	$35.00	14.0%

Vintage	Rank	Drink	RRP	Vol Alc

LAKE'S FOLLY

Lake's Folly only produces three wines – two Chardonnays and a Cabernet blend similar to prestige Bordeaux from 50 year old vines. The Hill Block Chardonnay is the recent addition, based on a unique soil type, since Peter Fogarty purchased the winery and the experienced Rod Kempe took over winemaking.
Winemaker: *Rod Kempe*
Open: *Daily 10am–4pm, 2416 Broke Road, Pokolbin*
Ph: *024998 7507 www.lakesfolly.com.au*

LAKE'S FOLLY
CHARDONNAY ★★★★★

Wraps oatmeal, white nectarine fruits with subtle oak spice aromas. In the mouth, appealing silky, stylish white pear, almond, cashew- all the good things you like about chardonnay. Delicacy with a youthful finish, a touch chewy indicating time will help. Drink 2018 onwards.

2013	94	2026	$70.00	13.0%
2014	90	2019	$70.00	14.5%
2015	90	2023	$75.00	14.3%

LAKE'S FOLLY
HILL BLOCK CHARDONNAY ★★★★

A distinctive style savoury winemaking links citrus white fruit to cedar and barrel ferment aromas. In the mouth compact, complex and dense with seamless well-judged oak and fruits touch of barrel ferment liberal use of oak without it being over powering. Very concentrated fruit will age.

2013	94	2025	$80.00	13.5%
2014	92	2022	$80.00	14.0%
2015	94	2022	$85.00	14.1%

LAKE'S FOLLY
CABERNET ★★★★★

Medium intense looking well tempered and moderate in ripeness. The aromas are red fruits loose limbed and a of gangly cabernet sweet rhubarb and red currant fruit aromas, carefully judged oak adds to the weave and interest. Very good length, it sweeps into your mouth and runs long cabernet styled

Vintage	Rank	Drink	RRP	Vol Alc

silky red fruited raspberry ripe cranberry and black berry flavours blinding flavour depth and intensity along the way. The fine tannins to close are more fruit than oak and the finish is clean dry, balanced and stylish.

2012	90	2022	$65.00	12.0%
2013	95	2035	$65.00	12.6%
2014	94	2024	$75.00	12.5%

LANGMEIL

Langmeil offers drinkers a variety of well made and priced wines with excellent regional character, freshness, soft tannins and depth of flavour. Their offering reflects all that is good about the Barossa without excessive alcohol or oak. The cellar door site was established in 1842 and is a delight to visit. Their whole range of wines is worth investigation.

Winemaker: Paul Lindner
Open: Daily 10.30–4.30pm Cnr Langmeil & Para Roads Tanunda
Ph: (08) 8563 2595 *www.langmeilwinery.com.au*

LANGMEIL
JACKAMAN'S CABERNET SAUVIGNON ★★★★★

Superior fruit intensity here with top note aromas of ripe cherry fruits, black currant leaf and date. The silky slippery tannins glide into your mouth calling a chorus of black fruits dark plums and dates along for the ride. If you like big reds, this is your wine.

2009	90	2016	$50.00	14.5%
2010	93	2020	$50.00	14.5%
2012	90	2019	$50.00	14.5%

LANGMEIL
THE FREEDOM 1843 SHIRAZ ★★★★★

It punches powerfully even with a medium intense colour. Curious cola and coffee, complex at first then more dignified with violets, sarsaparilla, black tea and black berry aromas. In the mouth silky creamy tannins in the house style allied to elegant dark berry fruit length and complexity. Complex flavours, persistent fine tannins and firm oak on the long finish. Medium end of full bodied.

2010	92	2020	$100.00	15.0%
2012	94	2029	$125.00	14.5%
2013	93	2023	$125.00	15.0%

LANGMEIL
VALLEY FLOOR SHIRAZ ★★★★
This is very vibrant verging jammy perfumed with fresh raspberry and blackberry juice, black tea vanilla oak aromas hand full of crushed fine herbs destined for the roast chicken back it out. Smooth ripe round and generous red fruits red plum and modest tannins flow with generosity, finishing inky earthy.

Vintage	Rank	Drink	RRP	Vol Alc
2010	93	2022	$29.50	14.5%
2012	89	2028	$30.00	14.5%
2013	92	2018	$30.00	14.5%

LANGMEIL
BLACKSMITH CABERNET SAUVIGNON ★★★★
In the zone of fresh lively cabernet showing the state of thinking mid priced south Australian cabernet with the arrival red fruit raspberry and rhubarb aromas with a Barossa fruitcake spice element backing out the nose. Generous, minty even, fine tannins and fresh crunchy tactile tannin mouth feel with a big broad middle palate with a line of sucking red currant like dryness to the tannin finish.

Vintage	Rank	Drink	RRP	Vol Alc
2010	94	2024	$29.50	14.5%
2012	92	2019	$30.00	14.5%
2013	91	2018	$30.00	14.5%

LANGMEIL
ORPHAN BANK SHIRAZ ★★★★
For lovers of full bodied reds, a bouncing Barossa wine. Bright red plum fruit, bay leaf back stop; if this were a tennis ball it would bounce higher than any other. Nice oak touch, very thoughtful wine making with lovely balance overall. Ripe, fresh, fine tannin united by well judged oak firmness and lengthened with stewed plum.

Vintage	Rank	Drink	RRP	Vol Alc
2010	88	2026	$50.00	15.0%
2012	91	2020	$50.00	14.5%
2013	93	2020	$50.00	14.5%

Vintage	Rank	Drink	RRP	Vol Alc

LANGMEIL
FIFTH WAVE GRENACHE ★★★★

Intense, youthful, dense flavours of varietal red fruits; raspberry, sweet rhubarb, oregano, old oak and angostura savoury interest. The palate is generous, a big ballsy wine with fine tannins turns peppery spicy and the finish is laced with fine grained tannins.

Vintage	Rank	Drink	RRP	Vol Alc
2010	95	2020	$40.00	15.5%
2012	91	2025	$40.00	14.5%
2013	93	2020	$40.00	15.5%

LARK HILL
Lark Hill is a Canberra district winemaker of some of the area's best wines, a fact not unconnected with the vineyard's altitude – over 800 metres – and the owners' biodynamic practices. Museum releases available.
Winemaker: *David Carpenter*
Open: *Wed to Mon 10am–5pm,*
Cnr Bungendore Road & Joe Rocks Road, Bungendore
Ph: *(02) 6238 1393 www.larkhillwine.com.au*

LARK HILL
BIODYNAMIC SHIRAZ VIOGNIER ★★★★★

Viognier gives a muscatel raisins edge to the peppery spice, confit of dark berry fruits style shiraz. The palate is silky ripe and smoothly medium bodied with spice notes all over it of white and black pepper, lusciousness in the middle verging on sickly to some with firm bold tannins to tame the exotic middle palate. The components are singular in youth; a very interesting wine that will be over top to some and others will say it is an Australian Gimlett gravels.

Vintage	Rank	Drink	RRP	Vol Alc
2013	93	2023	$35.00	13.0%
2014	91	2020	$40.00	13.0%

LARK HILL
MR V BIODYNAMIC MARSANNE ROUSSANNE VIOGNIER ★★★★

Deep colour from being fermented on skins, which is a red technique rarely used in white wines. Aromas are very exotic, candied peel, ditters cake, ginger, glace fruits aromas. The plate is very dry but not drying or grippy the fruit balances the body and the red wine texture is offset by apricot, orange peel, camomile and chunky over texture. Yellow chartreuse like complexity. Fine dining style and a very authentic example of skins fermented whites.

Vintage	Rank	Drink	RRP	Vol Alc
2013	90	2016	$35.00	13.5%
2014	90	2017	$35.00	13.0%

LARK HILL
BIODYNAMIC RIESLING ★★★★

Deep in colour as a young wine. Complex, non Australian style is the byword of this wine. Pineapple fresh and zesty. In the mouth, a ripe fruit set of citrus and gentle varietal spice flavours in full bodied texture, a thick acidity that holds the fleshy fruits in place. In a restaurant will partner with a wide variety of foods.

Vintage	Rank	Drink	RRP	Vol Alc
2011	88	2016	$30.00	11.5%
2014	89	2022	$35.00	11.5%
2015	88	2019	$35.00	11.5%

LEASINGHAM

Leasingham is the oldest Clare Valley producer, with extensive historic vineyards and a great track record for quality. The less expensive reds, particularly Bin 56, are solid performers.

Winemaker: *Simon Osicka*
Open: *No Cellar Door, Dominic Street, Clare*
Ph: *(08) 8842 2785 www.leasingham-wines.com.au*

LEASINGHAM
CLASSIC CLARE RIESLING ★★★

Riesling florals overlaid with age contributing honey and lemon lime curd aromas and smelling youthful. The texture shows bottle mature roundness and the flavours are full and rich with a fine acidity, balancing the lushness on the palate. The finish is long and more-ish with lemon curd, lime zest, juice and acidity.

Vintage	Rank	Drink	RRP	Vol Alc
2005	90	2012	$39.00	12.0%
2006	90	2012	$39.00	12.0%
2008	89	2016	$34.99	12.0%

Vintage	Rank	Drink	RRP	Vol Alc

LEASINGHAM
CLASSIC CLARE CABERNET SAUVIGNON ★★★★
Full-bodied and tightly structured on release with great depth of oak and fruit flavours and a long tight finish. Requires patience to see everything marry.

Vintage	Rank	Drink	RRP	Vol Alc
2004	92	2024	$50.00	14.5%
2005	89	2024	$57.00	14.0%
2006	90	2019	$57.00	13.0%

LEASINGHAM
CLASSIC CLARE SHIRAZ ★★★★
Cooler edged South Australian fruit richness with interesting varietal minty blackberry fruit aromas leading to minty blackberry fresh fruited middle palate with moderate length.

Vintage	Rank	Drink	RRP	Vol Alc
2008	89	2020	$57.00	14.0%
2009	91	2025	$49.00	13.8%
2010	87	2016	$60.99	14.0%

LECONFIELD
Leconfield, founded in 1974, is a 43-hectare Coonawarra vineyard, proudly family owned and operated by Dr Richard and Jette Hamilton. The signature wine is cabernet sauvignon, supported by merlot, shiraz, riesling, chardonnay and SYN cuvée blanc. The quality overall has quietly and consistently increased in recent years.
Winemaker: *Paul Gordon and Tim Bailey*
Open: *Weekdays 10am–5pm, Weekends and Pub Hols 11am–5pm*
15454 Riddoch Hwy, Coonawarra
Ph: *(08) 8323 8830* *www.leconfieldwines.com*

LECONFIELD COONAWARRA
OLD VINES RIESLING ★★★★
Citrus notes fresh and youthful lemon pulp and pink grapefruit pith sherberty edge. The palate has drive fresh lemon candy round texture, pure fruited, and medium long with balanced freshness and integrated acidity in the lemon sherbet finish.

Vintage	Rank	Drink	RRP	Vol Alc
2013	88	2018	$20.00	12.0%
2014	90	2019	$24.95	12.0%
2015	90	2020	$26.00	12.0%

LECONFIELD COONAWARRA
CHARDONNAY ★★★★

Deep golden yellow as a young wine with a refined aroma showing positive French oak influence with vanilla and blonde toffee elements. It is really entering it secondary flavour stage. The palate has impressive complexity and full bodied richness with yellow peach and butter vanilla complexity, weight and fair length.

Vintage	Rank	Drink	RRP	Vol Alc
2012	90	2017	$22.00	13.0%
2013	90	2019	$24.95	13.0%

LECONFIELD COONAWARRA
CABERNET SAUVIGNON ★★★★★

Leafy, mint, cassis, black currant cabernet and oregano brooding together with dark chocolate and oak. In the mouth a lively, fresh and ripe black currant up front with very good fruit length, energy and drive. Varietal cassis, oak adding dark chocolate and Bournville cocoa to finish.

Vintage	Rank	Drink	RRP	Vol Alc
2012	93	2035	$31.00	14.0%
2013	92	2029	$33.50	14.5%
2014	93	2026	$35.00	14.5%

LECONFIELD
SHIRAZ ★★★★

Ripe, interesting fruit with warmly inviting black berry and mulberry fruit aromas that are rich without being overripe. Dense complexity of shiraz flavours. Red cherry into liqueur like sweet berry kirsch with well-balanced fine tannins and the subtle drying tapenade effect on the finish.

Vintage	Rank	Drink	RRP	Vol Alc
2012	90	2029	$31.00	14.0%
2013	91	2022	$24.95	14.0%
2014	95	2019	$26.00	14.5%

Vintage	Rank	Drink	RRP	Vol Alc

LECONFIELD
MERLOT ★★★★

Quite special for merlot to achieve this level of leafy mulberry complexity, with a fine balance of fruit, alcohol and oak. The palate has a terrific feel in the mouth. Soft tannins, bright berry fruits. Full and deep in the middle palate with the tannins drawing the fruit long and closing the palate with finesse.

Vintage	Rank	Drink	RRP	Vol Alc
2013	87	2018	$24.95	14.0%
2014	93	2018	$26.00	14.0%

LEEUWIN ESTATE

Leeuwin Estate is shorthand for excellence in Australian chardonnay, as well as being a 90-hectare Margaret River vineyard. The Horgans have ensured that the property makes a significant contribution to the culture of Australia via an extensive series of concerts and a restaurant.

Winemaker: *Paul Atwood*
Open: *Daily 10am–5pm Stevens Road, Margaret River*
Ph: *(08) 9430 4099 www.leeuwinestate.com.au*

LEEUWIN ESTATE
ART SERIES RIESLING ★★★★★

Who said Margaret River can't make Riesling. This old vine vineyard certainly leads the way. Very varietal fruit aromas showing talc and nectar filled blossom, sits on top of subtle green apple, lemon juice and zest in this very exact varietal nose. The dry palate is concentrated, dense, light bodied, long and lithe showing appealing drink young middle palate fullness and the chalky texture to the long finish with lingering floral talc, lime citrus and fresh flowers indicating it can age. Serve well chilled to focus the acidity.

Vintage	Rank	Drink	RRP	Vol Alc
2013	93	2019	$28.00	12.0%
2014	88	2019	$22.00	12.0%
2015	93	2022	$22.00	13.0%

Vintage	Rank	Drink	RRP	Vol Alc

LEEUWIN ESTATE
ART SERIES CHARDONNAY ★★★★★

Youthful balance that will age well currently fruit driven with citrus into tropical fruits and notes pith and peel and cinnamon oak. In the mouth balance is the key with a creamy even certainty of the fruit, excellent line of fine acidity running a subliminal and flavours with layers on the long finish and the oak drawing the palate to a defined conclusion. A very finely polished wine with concentration and substance for aging.

2011	96	2029	$85.00	13.5%
2012	95	2027	$94.00	14.0%
2013	94	2025	$94.00	13.5%

LEEUWIN ESTATE
ART SERIES CABERNET SAUVIGNON ★★★★★

This wine exhibits a rare delicacy with pure black currant cassis leafy varietal cabernet aromas. The medium bodied palate leads with soft tannins and appealing complexity of black fruit and wine gums finishing with fresh acids, fine grape tannins and lingering black fruits.

2009	94	2024	$61.00	14.0%
2011	92	2022	$65.00	13.5%
2012	84	2017	$65.00	13.5%

LEO BURING

A famous maker of white wine, whose name lives on in the private cellars of many, thanks to the longevity of the rieslings. Leo Buring's current releases of fine cellarable rieslings are from their traditional South Australian sources, along with some newer ones from Tasmania. Honouring a great tradition with high standards.
Winemaker: *Peter Munro*
Open: *No Cellar Door*

LEO BURING
CLARE VALLEY RIESLING ★★★★★

80% Watervale red dirt on limestone gives soft round wines with mineral and 20% from EV with linear structural acidity. Vintage looked good early as cool as 2002 and 4 below before a hot February. Winemaking likes to pick on lemon flavours before lime, rose or musk and this year has given generosity with deep fruits on the middle palate with pineapple lime juicy fruit flavours and lingering intensity. Has a deft level of balance with middle palate sweetness at the subliminal level so you don't perceive sweetness but texture. Watervale chalky acid verses seamless long acidity from Eden Valley. Drink this summer for a truly wonderful experience

2012	94	2025	$20.00	12.0%
2013	94	2030	$20.00	12.0%
2015	92	2021	$20.00	12.0%

LEO BURING
EDEN VALLEY RIESLING ★★★★★

Intense aromas and concentrated cellaring style of lemony, rose and talc intensity. The palate has subtle pineapple into lime juicy fruit flavours, with the linear acidity of the region and the varietal very long chalky finish. Cellaring style that needs time, drink after 2018.

2013	92	2017	$20.00	11.5%
2014	93	2020	$20.00	11.5%
2015	95	2045	$25.00	11.5%

LETHBRIDGE

Located 30 kms from Geelong, Lethbridge wines are most often seen on inner city wine lists where the high standards, delicacy and interest that their varietal wines exhibit are showcased to perfection. The top end wines, Allegra, Hugo George, Mietta and Indra are exceptional, rare and well priced for the quality. Their focus on regional expression, with high standards, makes them one of the most important wineries in the region.
Winemakers: *Ray Nadeson*
Open: *Daily, 11am–5pm, 74 Burrows Road, Lethbridge*
Ph: *(03) 5281 7279 www.lethbridgewines.com*

LETHBRIDGE
ALLEGRA CHARDONNAY ★★★★★

Very big savoury style with ripe fruits, a saffron-like spice thread and a wiry acidity with a determined almost quince fruit rich, oatmeal complex. Heavy and a grippy finish.

2011	90	2022	$75.00	13.5%
2012	95	2018	$75.00	13.5%
2013	90	2016	$75.00	13.5%

LETHBRIDGE
CHARDONNAY ★★★★★

Aromas are full and generous and made to show well in restaurants. Young, bold and complex so the balance is towards brulee honeyed, big, ripe, fleshy white peach fruits with depth and complexity. In the mouth, a ripe sweep of yellow spectrum fruit flavours builds a firmness towards the finish with citrus brown spices.

Vintage	Rank	Drink	RRP	Vol Alc
2010	94	2015	$40.00	13.0%
2015	92	2019	$45.00	14.2%

LETHBRIDGE
INDRA SHIRAZ ★★★★★

A solid aroma oak dried spice flows into dark berry fruits baked rhubarb red fruits into the smooth long palate with dark berry gravy roasted meats savoury flavours pepper and nutmeg with chalky tannins to close.

Vintage	Rank	Drink	RRP	Vol Alc
2011	90	2017	$95.00	12.5%
2012	95	2022	$95.00	14.0%
2013	92	2019	$95.00	14.0%

LETHBRIDGE
MIETTA PINOT NOIR ★★★★★

The aromas are sweet ripe fruits dried spices and strawberry fruit aromas. Line the mouth fleshy fruit cooked cherry fruit soft tannins appealing savoury, dried spice and mineral flavours and tannins that build gracefully through the middle and to the finish.

Vintage	Rank	Drink	RRP	Vol Alc
2011	88	2018	$95.00	12.0%
2012	95	2022	$95.00	13.0%
2013	93	2021	$85.00	13.0%

LILLYPILLY ESTATE WINES
Lillypilly has an enviable reputation as one of the leading exponents of botrytis wines in the world. The unique style and particular talent for blending different varieties in the Noble Blend creates wines of unparalleled complexity without the oily heaviness that can overtake these super sweet wines. They age extremely well. Noble Blend gets the accolade of "Family Reserve' when they are re-released as older wines. The Cellar Door

| Vintage | Rank | Drink | RRP | Vol Alc |

features some very original wines, including Fiumara 7, a liqueur fortified style of incredible complexity. The ripe, soft reds are similarly delicious drinking.
Winemaker: Robert Fiumara
Open: Mon to Sat 10am–5:00pm, 47 Lillypilly Road, Leeton
Ph: (02) 6953 4069 *www.lillypillywines.com.au*

LILLYPILLY
NOBLE BLEND 375ML ★★★★★
Pear nectar, fresh and clean, youthful and based on previous vintage will take its time. The palate is youthful balanced sweetness, pear into marzipan elegant brown spices creamed pears.

Vintage	Rank	Drink	RRP	Vol Alc
2011	90	2018	$23.50	11.0%
2012	93	2030	$27.50	11.0%
2015	94	2032	$32.00	12.0%

LILLYPILLY
VERMENTINO
Fresh cream on pears, fennel back notes, with a creamy texture, the round apple and pear lees influence the deep flavours on mid palate with crunchy acidity and long finishing green fig, green lime lifesaver like fruit to close. Won the best dry white varietal in Perth 2016.

Vintage	Rank	Drink	RRP	Vol Alc
2014	89	2016	$17.50	13.5%
2015	90	2018	$15.50	12.5%

LINDEMANS
Lindemans, at the top end, releases only 1,000 cases of each of these individual vineyard fine wines. Recent vintages are much better, having a medium-bodied structure with real elegance and finesse. 2007 was not up to the winemaker's standards and will not be released. The 2010s are the best yet, due to a more fleshy middle palate structure.
Winemaker: Brett Sharpe
Open: Daily 10am–5pm, McDonald's Road, Pokolbin
Ph: (03) 8626 2409 *www.lindemans.com*

Vintage	Rank	Drink	RRP	Vol Alc

LINDEMANS
LIMESTONE RIDGE SHIRAZ CABERNET ★★★★★

A bouquet of violets, pepper, nutmeg and earthy chocolate add to the complexity of the cherry berry fruit in this vintage of Limestone Ridge. A blend Coonawarra Shiraz and Cabernet that is consistently good drinking now or in the long term. Elegant fruit wrapped around soft regional tannins highlights the prettiness of the fruit and makes it a glassful to sit with.

2012	94	2036	$65.00	14.0%
2013	95	2029	$69.99	14.0%
2014	94	2030	$69.99	14.0%

LINDEMANS
PYRUS COONAWARRA CABERNETS ★★★★★

An elegant and fragrant nose of floral, black just-cracked pepper, vanilla, black currant and liquorice are just the beginning of the Pyrus story. Malbec adds interest by way of violets and berry fruit to the darker fruit and chocolate profile. The Coonawarra fruit is soft and powdery curvaceous tannins shape the mouth long into the finish. Give this wine at least half a decade to hit its stride.

2012	95	2030	$69.99	13.5%
2013	94	2026	$69.99	14.0%
2014	92	2035	$69.99	13.5%

LINDEMANS
ST GEORGE CABERNET SAUVIGNON ★★★★★

Fresh purple hues leap from the glass in this classic low yield Coonawarran. Mint, chocolate, violets and sandalwood adorn the varietal black currant and ripe berries. Oak adds richness and spice without obviousness. The balance in this wine is impeccable and it will continue to be one of the region's collectibles that will generously give its all to the patient cellarer.

2012	94	2028	$69.99	14.0%
2013	95	2033	$69.99	14.0%
2014	93	2029	$69.99	13.5%

| Vintage | Rank | Drink | RRP | Vol Alc |

LINO RAMBLE

Andy Coppard was raised in Margaret River, graduated in 2002 in oenology, then worked with McLaren Vale shiraz specialists, evolving the local style before establishing Lino Ramble in 2012. The label evokes the fun of childhood, and the wines speak of less intrusive winemaking, more respectful of vineyards and growers, avoiding jammy ripeness and fining to focus on fresh vineyard flavours and texture from fruit tannins and natural acid. Seeks to work with the varieties to style wines and buys his second use oak from mates in Margaret River making expensive wines to subtley enhance the style.

Winemaker: Andy Coppard
Open: By Appointment , 2 Hall Street, McLaren Vale
Ph: (04) 0955 3448 www.linoramble.com.au

LINO RAMBLE
TOM BOWLER NERO D'AVOLA ★★★★★

Varietal ripe dark cherry tarry fruits, a flicker of acid with the sarsaparilla edge of the variety and old oak. The dense palate starts full bodied solid with fine tannins to add structure with liquorice black fruits in the middle mouth a hint of raisin with a pleasant green herb edge that adds length. For lovers of full bodied reds wanting something different.

2014	92	2019	$30.00	13.8%
2015	90	2017	$30.00	13.8%

LOGAN

Logan is a family-owned winery with a vineyard in Orange and an excellent cellar door at Mudgee on the Lithgow Road. Good quality and value wines, made in a ripe and generous style.

Winemaker: Peter Logan
Open: Daily 10am–5pm,
Castlereagh Highway Appletree Flat, Mudgee
Ph: (02) 6373 1333 www.loganwines.com.au

Vintage	Rank	Drink	RRP	Vol Alc

LOGAN
ORANGE CHARDONNAY ★★★★

Peach nectarine fruit juice in wine gums leads to a developed upfront rich palate. Easy drinking wine bar style of chardonnay.

2011	86	2013	$25.00	12.5%
2012	91	2016	$25.00	13.0%
2013	85	2017	$25.00	13.5%

LOGAN
WEEMALA ORANGE RIESLING ★★★★

Rose and turkish delight aromas, a whisper of fruity sweetness, talc and lime flavours and in the Logan style of fruit interest with cute fun flavours.

2012	92	2022	$16.00	11.5%
2013	89	2017	$16.00	12.5%
2014	88	2018	$16.00	12.0%

LOGAN
WEEMALA ORANGE PINOT NOIR ★★★

Pretty red fruit, fine green herbs with a freshness and the fruit richness that is in the house style of supple sweet ripe fruit length and fine tannins to finish. They know what they are doing here and are a reliably styled wine.

2012	92	2019	$35.00	13.0%
2013	88	2019	$35.00	13.5%
2014	89	2016	$35.00	13.0%

LOGAN
ORANGE SHIRAZ ★★★

Aromatic sweet fruits with a weave of bramble, blackberry, cocoa powder and white pepper fruit aromas. The palate is tight, medium bodied, with fresh ripe blackberry flavours for drinking young. A medium bodied complex red, spice flavours with length and moderate alcohol, medium high acidity and a long firm finish.

2009	89	2016	$25.00	14.0%
2011	88	2017	$25.00	13.5%
2012	93	2020	$25.00	12.5%

LOGAN
ORANGE CABERNET MERLOT ★★★★
Good try in a tough year. Pretty cedar cranberry to black currant fruits with a leafy celery stalk edge. In the mouth medium light bodied, fresh easy drinking black currant middle and leafy finish.

Vintage	Rank	Drink	RRP	Vol Alc
2010	86	2014	$25.00	13.5%
2011	85	2014	$25.00	13.0%
2012	85	2016	$25.00	13.0%

LONGVIEW
Longview is a stunning family-owned vineyard just outside the historic township of Macclesfield in the Adelaide Hills. The area is a little warmer than other Hills' sites, which accounts for the style of their reds. The winery is a great Sunday destination, with great views from the cellar door, popular Sunday tapas and a function centre. The 4-star accommodation on Longview Vineyard has become one of the Adelaide Hills' primary B & B destinations.
Winemaker: *Ben Glaetzer*
Open: *Daily 11am–5pm, Pound Road, Macclesfield*
Ph: *08 8388 9694* ***www.longviewvineyard.com.au***

LONGVIEW
YAKKA SHIRAZ ★★★★★
Appealing layers, red fruits red cherry raspberry dried herb edge oak spice. Medium bodied age worthy short term red, firm oak tannins under pin the red and spicy fruits, flavours and tannins support each other and the finish as mineral element and some spice, mocha. A rich, full flavoured but not heavy soft finishing with pretty spices to finish.

Vintage	Rank	Drink	RRP	Vol Alc
2010	92	2016	$30.00	14.5%
2012	92	2019	$30.00	14.4%
2014	93	2018	$30.00	14.0%

LONGVIEW
THE PIECE SHIRAZ ★★★★★

This is a very easy to like wine. Great Sunday lunch style with all the cellaring done at the winery before release. Very ripe, fresh dark cherry into blackberry and dark plum aromas. Ripeness is the theme in the mouth; black fruit, velvet ripe slippery middle palate wed to fine round shiraz tannins. Flavours start shiraz berries with appealing fruit intensity, middle palate fullness, supple tannin and well-judged oak. Easy drinking with brown spices to garnish the finish. Great art, just like the label.

Vintage	Rank	Drink	RRP	Vol Alc
2010	96	2022	$70.00	13.5%
2012	92	2025	$70.00	14.5%
2013	94	2019	$70.00	14.0%

LONGVIEW
DEVILS ELBOW CABERNET SAUVIGNON ★★★★

Plenty of ripeness, black currant up front and leafy subtle mint fruits, soya sauce rancio note adds complexity. The palate is straighter than the devil's elbow long ripe fruits supple with the tip of tongue black currant fruits wed to fine tannin and living happily ever after for the length of the your tongue with black currant juice, pip and pulp flavours and tannin finesse, a sweet mint wrapper edge in a happy bond to the end. Morish.

Vintage	Rank	Drink	RRP	Vol Alc
2010	91	2022	$30.00	14.5%
2012	91	2023	$30.00	14.5%
2013	94	2020	$30.00	14.0%

LONGVIEW
BOATSHED NEBBIOLO ★★★★★

This has a positive focussed aroma and tropical allure, but the pomegranate dominates. The palate is juicy with blood orange and citrus. It has depth and layers of flavours that are unified with a sweaty edge. A rose for sauvignon blanc drinkers with enough tannin fruit and savoury to suit food.

Vintage	Rank	Drink	RRP	Vol Alc
2012	89	2015	$19.90	13.5%
2015	93	2017	$19.50	12.5%
2014	95	2017	$19.90	13.5%

Vintage	Rank	Drink	RRP	Vol Alc

LOWE FAMILY WINES

Lowe Family Wines is a Mudgee-based operation run by experienced winemaker, David Lowe. All the wines reviewed are organically certified. He recently acquired the Nullo Mountain Vineyard at 1180 metres, one of NSW's most interesting vineyards, which has increased the diversity of his offering. Also producing excellent preservative-free wines.
Winemakers: *David Lowe and Liam Heslop*
Open: *Daily 10am–5pm, Tinja Lane Mudgee*
Ph: *(02) 6372 0800 www.lowewine.com*

LOWE
RESERVE MERLOT ★★★
Scented plummy and soft with plenty of Mudgee fruitiness and flavour.

2005	87	2012	$25.00	13.0%
2006	86	2015	$25.00	13.5%
2007	87	2014	$30.00	12.7%

LOWE
BLOCK 8 SHIRAZ ★★★
Classic smoked meats in a spicy peppery shiraz with elegant brightness and fresh fruits up front. A dark berry middle palate spice and smoked meats ring in the finish. Very stylish.

2009	89	2018	$30.00	13.5%
2011	92	2022	$35.00	13.7%
2012	90	2020	$30.00	13.0%

LOWE
MUDGEE ZINFANDEL ★★★★
A very well made wine that is not ripe for a Zin with the savoury elements of Zinfandel smoked meats peppery dried herbs. The plate has ripe not over ripe flavours restrained medium bodied length and spices and dried herbs building in the middle with fine ripe tannins that keep a dry edge to the wine with soft lingering flavours.

2010	93	2024	$75.00	13.8%
2011	90	2020	$75.00	14.8%
2012	94	2019	$75.00	13.1%

| Vintage | Rank | Drink | RRP | Vol Alc |

MACFORBES
MacForbes is a one of the young Yarra winemakers doing interesting things. Like so many, he has had a stint overseas -- Austria in this case -- and has a passionate conviction for more sensitive winemaking, reflecting the subtlety of individual vineyards.

Winemaker: *Macgregor Forbes*
Open: *By appointment only*
770 Healesville Koo Wee Rup Road, Healesville
Ph: *(03) 9818 8099* *www.macforbes.com*

MACFORBES
YARRA VALLEY CHARDONNAY ★★★★
Well balanced modern style with winemaking part of the chorus with the fruits, flinty, fresh bread lees complexity. In the mouth pure long and balanced, the fruit is more citrus, winemaking serving to complex the fruit and acid line with weight in the mouth and on the finish.
Will age.

Vintage	Rank	Drink	RRP	Vol Alc
2013	92	2017	$30.00	12.5%
2014	91	2017	$30.00	12.5%
2015	93	2019	$30.00	13.0%

MAIN RIDGE
Main Ridge Estate, planted 1975, was the first of the Mornington Peninsula winemakers to achieve commercial production. Since then, the wines, through their beauty and reliability, have established an enviable reputation.

Winemaker: *Nat White*
Open: *Mon to Fri 12pm–4pm, Sat & Sun 12pm–5pm*
80 William Road, Red Hill South
Ph: *(03) 5989 2686* **www.mre.com.au**

MAIN RIDGE ESTATE
CHARDONNAY ★★★★★
Aromas of yellow peach, pineapple, quince and leatherwood honey. The palate is ready to drink with rich mature very silky texture, silky gliding length, pineapple yellow peach in the middle palate with subtle firmness. Generous ripe and ready style.

Vintage	Rank	Drink	RRP	Vol Alc
2012	95	2026	$55.00	13.0%
2013	95	2023	$55.00	13.0%
2014	90	2018	$65.00	13.0%

Vintage	Rank	Drink	RRP	Vol Alc

MAIN RIDGE ESTATE
HALF ACRE PINOT NOIR ★★★★★

Vibrant colour and aromas cascade out of the glass in a procession for red fruits from strawberry into cooked strawberry and puree and confectionary. In the mouth, a great tannin line with generous fruit complexity silky ripe fruited raspberry and red cherry up front with a spine of oak tannins drawing the wine long in the mouth. Well made wine.

2012	95	2026	$55.00	13.0%
2013	95	2023	$55.00	13.0%
2014	90	2018	$65.00	13.0%

MAJELLA
Majella is a 55-hectare vineyard in Coonawarra producing extremely high quality fruit, the best of which is kept for the winery's own wines, which are enjoying a growing reputation.

Winemaker: Bruce Gregory
Open: Daily 10am–4.30pm, Lynn Road, Coonawarra
Ph: (08) 8736 3055 *www.majellawines.com.au*

MAJELLA
THE MUSICIAN CABERNET SHIRAZ ★★★★

Lovely Coonawarra regionality black currant Arnott's mint slice biscuits is often used. The palate balances ripe fruits with low oak to give black currant black berry mint good length and the varieties march through your tongue supporting a long texture. A great casual glass of red with generosity and excellent price quality ration.

2012	89	2016	$18.00	14.5%
2013	88	2016	$18.00	14.5%
2014	89	2018	$19.00	14.5%

MAJELLA
CABERNET SAUVIGNON ★★★★★

Fruit freshness and appealing ripe red cherry regional mint into black currant aromas. The palate has long and lean reserve not over made here is even length of fine tannins and black currant with oregano leafy savoury decorating the black currant fruits. Drink after 2017. A sleeper

Vintage	Rank	Drink	RRP	Vol Alc
2012	91	2022	$33.00	14.5%
2013	91	2019	$35.00	14.5%
2014	92	2028	$35.00	14.5%

MAJELLA
SHIRAZ ★★★★★
Red cherry black berry Vanilla mocha choc chino oak aromas. The palate leads ripe red fruits, round slippery shiraz tannins and subtle graphite dried kitchen herbs spice oak sits in the passenger's seat giving directions as the fruits slips towards the finish with warmed butter caramel flavours.

Vintage	Rank	Drink	RRP	Vol Alc
2012	93	2018	$30.00	14.5%
2013	90	2018	$30.00	14.5%
2014	90	2020	$30.00	14.5%

MARSH ESTATE
Marsh Estate is 40 hectares planted in 1971, comprising "rain fed" (meaning unirrigated) semillon, chardonnay, shiraz, cabernet sauvignon and merlot. The quiet achieving winery regularly sells out at its cellar door, hence its low profile in restaurants. Now in its second generation of family ownership the company is getting a makeover in the areas of customer relations and packaging. Exports tiny amounts to Asia.
Winemaker: Andrew Marsh
Open: Weekdays 10am–4pm, Weekends 10am–5pm,
95 Deasy's Road, Pokolbin
Ph: 02 4998 7587 *www.marshestate.com.au*

MARSH ESTATE
POPPY'S MAVERICK ★★★★
Brown lime, dried herb and looking a touch Barossa. Developed in youth but still authentic lifted varietal aromas. The 2014 vintage fruit weight adds lustre to the vineyards always vibrant fruit rich style and the acids live among the tannins with a long firm flavoured fresh lime and lemon firm structure with a touch of white pepper on the finish. This is a very authentic wine with a unique personality and tannins to ensure age worthyness.

Vintage	Rank	Drink	RRP	Vol Alc
2011	92	2019	$29.50	12.0%
2013	90	2020	$29.50	12.0%
2014	95	2034	$29.50	12.0%

Vintage	Rank	Drink	RRP	Vol Alc

MAYER YARRA VALLEY

A small producer of hand crafted, single vineyard wines based on the belief that wines are made in the vineyard and therefore the result of careful selection of soil and site. The red wines use a variety of techniques that create exceptional flavour complexity with delicacy. They are unrefined and unfiltered and carry no back label. Very limited production and very high standards.

Winemaker: *Timo Mayer*
Open: *No Cellar Door Miller Road, Healesville*
Ph: *(03) 5967 3779* *www.timomayer.com.au*

MAYER
DR MAYER PINOT NOIR ★★★★★

A fan fare of fragrance; strawberry, raspberry, mineral, modern fresh, low oak food able aromas. The flavours are complex strawberry, floral raspberry full the mouth, fleshy and persistent with a lacy tannin texture, mineral stalky edge with delicate fine tannins to finish.

2013	95	2025	$55.00	13.5%
2014	96	2027	$55.00	13.0%
2015	93	2020	$55.00	13.5%

MAYER
GRANITE PINOT NOIR ★★★★★

Funky as one would expect from this label with a flinty edge decorating the white pear fruits and gentle oak contribution. The palate is full and generously textured and the acid balanced so while it is full flavoured it is balanced pear white nectarine white pear drop complex and clean on the medium long finish.

2013	92	2016	$55.00	13.5%
2014	Not made			
2015	95	2028	$55.00	13.5%

Vintage	Rank	Drink	RRP	Vol Alc

MAYER
CABERNET SAUVIGNON ★★★★★
A beautiful wine with handmade qualities, tannin finesse and fruit freshness and none of the thickness of more large volume wines. Aromas are blueberry, cedar, cassis fruits with a finely woven palate showing length, mouth filling flavours blue berry into cedar.

| 2014 | 90 | 2022 | $55.00 | 12.8% |
| 2015 | 94 | 2022 | $55.00 | 13.5% |

McGUIGAN WINES
Two brothers have been at the helm of this business for many years providing direction and character. Brian oversaw the float on the Australian stock exchange is now in retirement and Neil a career winemaker has seen the company presented with notable award wins and new wine style introductions in recent years.
Winemaker: *Peter Hall*
Open: *Daily 447 McDonalds Road, Pokolbin*
Ph: *(02) 4998 7402 www.mcguiganwines.com.au*

McGUIGAN
FARMS SHIRAZ ★★★★
Ripe, regional smelling of deep black plum, blackberry cooked dark plum and cloves fruit with subtle oak. In the mouth very soft tannins ripe fruits freshness and long taunt fresh red fruit favours excellent structure, middle palate fullness touch of sage spice and long fruits with long trailing gentle spice to finish. The texture is fine, the flavours elegant, very 2012 in personality with the finish lingering red fruits, tasting of the Rowlands Flat or Lyndoch end of the Barossa.

| 2009 | 89 | 2020 | $70.00 | 15.0% |
| 2012 | 95 | 2026 | $70.00 | 14.5% |

McGUIGAN WINES

McGUIGAN
THE PHILOSOPHY SHIRAZ CABERNET SAUVIGNON ★★★★★
Primarily Langhorne Creek with small parcels from multiple regions in South Australia and aged in French and American oak for two years prior to bottling and two years before. Complex aromas of blueberries, black currant warmed spices into mocha and cedar oak spice with early

Vintage	Rank	Drink	RRP	Vol Alc

maturity. In the mouth there are very refined tannins, sweet fruited and minty edged with very refined tannins, bright-restrained flavours remain elegant and good palate length with grainy tannins and lingering flavours.

2010	94	2034	$150.00	13.5%
2012	91	2020	$150.00	14.0%

McGUIGAN WINES

McLEISH ESTATE

Mature vines, well grown on good soils and a low profile with next generation Jessica just starting to take the reins. Made by Andrew Thomas the wines have elegance, freshness and work with food. A quiet achiever with consistent good quality and a rare example of Hunter Cabernet of note.
Winemaker: *Andrew Thomas*
Open: *No Cellar Door 462 DeBeyers Road, Pokolbin*
Ph: *(02) 4998 7754 www.mcleishhunterwines.com.au*

McLEISH ESTATE
SEMILLON ★★★★★

The aromas are classic strong year Hunter with surprising touch tropical lanolin baby blanket subtle, straw and lemon. The palate has weight and structure lemon curd and lemon confectionary with white fruit complexity and finishing fresh and clean. Drink now easy to enjoy style offering great pleasure at its core not the searing racy acidity.

2013	92	2023	$18.00	10.5%
2014	94	2021	$40.00	11.0%
2015	92	2022	$25.00	10.5%

McLEISH ESTATE
CHARDONNAY ★★★★

Has the zeitgeist of the times in the form of flinty struck match against the traditional white fruit and oak aromas. The palate is tight medium long with the faintest touch of red chilli herbals. The compact middle palate runs the creamy yoghurt, struck match in a core of activity like the illustration from Charles Schultsz of "pig pen" in Peanuts. The finish in 2016 is youthful, intense and gangly acidity, so wait until 2017 and keep for 2 years.

2009	90	2019	$18.00	12.8%
2014	90	2018	$45.00	13.5%
2015	89	2018	$45.00	13.0%

Vintage	Rank	Drink	RRP	Vol Alc

McWILLIAMS
One of the great names of Australian wine and owner of the Mount Pleasant winery with great old vineyards in the Hunter Valley. Additional wineries in West Australia with Evans and Tate and Brands Coonawarra in the premium sphere. A massive winery in Griffith is increasingly making great wines from Hilltops, Tumbarumba and Canberra at very good prices. Barwang is another of their labels.
Winemaker: Bryan Currie
Open: Wednesday–Saturday 10am–4pm, Jack McWilliam Road Hanwood NSW 2680
Ph: (02) 6963 3400   www.mcwilliams.com.au

McWILLIAMS
1877
The aromas are classic strong year Hunter with surprising touch tropical lanolin baby blanket subtle, straw and lemon. The palate has weight and structure lemon curd and lemon confectionary with white fruit complexity and finishing fresh and clean. Drink now easy to enjoy style offering great pleasure at its core not the searing racy acidity.

| 2008 | 96 | 2032 | $64.00 | 15.0% |
| 2014 | 93 | 2022 | $80.00 | 13.5% |

McWILLIAMS
ORANGE SAUVIGNON BLANC ★★★★
A little reduced but still aromatic with varietal passion fruit and grapefruit aromas with an herbaceous twist. Ripe, balanced fresh fruit helped by skill full wine making showing intensity, more passion fruit than pineapple flowing into tropical fruit flavours helped fine acidity to give length and freshness.

| 2014 | 90 | 2015 | $23.00 | 12.4% |
| 2015 | 90 | 2017 | $24.00 | 13.0% |

Vintage	Rank	Drink	RRP	Vol Alc

McWILLIAMS
CANBERRA SYRAH ★★★★★

Great colour leads to a modern aroma showing fresh raspberry fruit and white pepper into darker spices all build complexity. A delicious drink, balanced fresh fruits and fine tannins medium bodied starting with fresh red cherry fruit wed to fine tannins with a very good line and length, great middle palate with the sweeter spice notes building on the finish. Very easy drinking and great value.

| 2013 | 87 | 2017 | $24.00 | 13.5% |
| 2014 | 93 | 2020 | $25.00 | 13.5% |

MEEREA PARK

Meerea Park in the Hunter Valley's Pokolbin region is run by the Eather brothers, who are small producers making great wines, especially local shiraz and semillon. There is serious quality at the top end here.
Winemaker: Rhys Eather
Open: Weekdays 9am–5pm, 188 Pavilion B, 2144 Broke Road, (Cnr McDonalds Road,) Pokolbin
Ph: (02) 4998 7474 *www.meereapark.com.au*

MEEREA PARK
ALEXANDER MUNRO SEMILLON ★★★★★

Very, elegant, intense, classical lemon spectrum with fine lemon pith and pulp aromas, developing very slowly, hints of candle wax and typical of the high standards of this label and a five-year-old wine. The palate has silky voluptuous weight for the style and generous texture and length of ripe fleshy lemon fruits. Will develop if you can keep your hands off it.

2009	90	2019	$40.00	11.0%
2010	95	2020	$40.00	11.0%
2011	95	2019	$45.00	11.0%

MEEREA PARK
THE AUNTS SHIRAZ ★★★★

Pepper and spicy blueberry and plums are a fragrant mix in The Aunts, one of the single vineyard shiraz produced by Meerea Park. In true Hunter Shiraz style, it is medium bodied and some caramel oak provides some smoothness to the dusty tannins. Enjoy now or in the midterm.

Vintage	Rank	Drink	RRP	Vol Alc
2009	85	2013	$26.00	13.5%
2010	91	2010	$26.00	13.5%
2014	88	2024	$30.00	14.0%

MEEREA PARK
HELL HOLE SHIRAZ ★★★★★

The Hell Hole is another of the single vineyard wines from Meerea Park, this time from the Leonard Estate. This vintage has a charming nose of blue and black berry fruit, liquorice and toasted nutmeg spice. There is a real elegance to the finely tuned body here and some well judged coffee and dark chocolate oak adds flesh and extends the length.

Vintage	Rank	Drink	RRP	Vol Alc
2011	87	2017	$54.00	13.5%
2013	93	2033	$55.00	13.5%
2014	93	2025	$60.00	14.0%

MEEREA PARK
TERRACOTTA SHIRAZ VIOGNIER ★★★★★

A dollop of viognier (2%) co-fermented with the Hunter Valley Shiraz gives this wine a French accent, hence the 'syrah' on the label. It provides a peppery, floral veil adorning the vibrant, fleshy blueberry and cherry fruit and adds a polish to the tannins. A good wine for enjoying now but this is definitely worth cellaring for the future.

Vintage	Rank	Drink	RRP	Vol Alc
2011	87	2017	$55.00	13.5%
2012	Not made			
2014	94	2020	$70.00	14.0%

Vintage	Rank	Drink	RRP	Vol Alc

MEEREA PARK
ALEXANDER MUNRO SHIRAZ ★★★★★

Using their ripest fruit, this wine is a classic example of the regional style. The nose is emphatically hunter with leather and black fruit aromas aided with new oak to complex it. On the palate medium bodied with appealing sweet fruit.

2010	90	2020	$70.00	14.0%
2011	94	2035	$70.00	13.5%
2012	Not made			

MICHAEL HALL

Michael Hall was born overseas and had a successful career in jewellery before moving to Australia to follow his great passion for wine. His wines are the result of working closely with a limited number of grape growers who have exceptionally well located vineyards within the Adelaide Hills, Eden and Barossa Valley. Mainly sold in high-end restaurants.
Winemaker: *Michael Hall*
Open: *No Cellar Door 10 George Street, Tanunda*
Ph: *(04) 1912 6290 www.michaelhallwines.com*

MICHAEL HALL
ADELAIDE HILLS CHARDONNAY ★★★★★

Gentle, complex and refined stone fruit, flinty struck match, fine French oak vanilla bean and caramel, with a fresh line of fruits. Very low in tannins, this is a long, graceful, silky ball room gown of a wine with a long line of flavour. The finish offers a tang of tannin dryness to end the waltz.

2011	94	2017	$46.00	12.8%
2013	89	2017	$46.00	12.9%
2014	91	2018	$46.00	13.3%

MICHAEL HALL
GREENOCK ROUSSANNE ★★★★

A creamy and subtle food friendly wine. Early picked, wild yeast, barrel fermented with 22% new oak and 6 months on lees. Slightly herbal, sweet lime chamomile, and herbal and honeysuckle aromas. Gentle creamy white fruits in a silky light medium bodied wine. Gentle ripeness to the well balanced fresh ripe silky middle palate with a gentle drying finish.

Vintage	Rank	Drink	RRP	Vol Alc
2012	90	2016	$36.00	13.5%
2014	90	2017	$36.00	11.5%

MITCHELL WINES
Mitchell Wines are a well-established Clare Valley maker, with high quality vineyards and extensive experience in the area.
Winemaker: Andrew Mitchell
Open: *Daily 10am–4pm, Hughes Park Road, via Clare*
Ph: *(08) 8843 4258 www.mitchellwines.com*

MITCHELL
WATERVALE RIESLING ★★★★

Complex chamomile with subtle ginger and wild herbs to the wild yeast ferment. The mouth feel has width. Silky glossy slickness from lees age, which has merged the florals into fuller herbal tea flavours. A mouth coating 'new age' style of riesling and a significant divergence in style.

Vintage	Rank	Drink	RRP	Vol Alc
2012	94	2022	$24.00	13.0%
2013	90	2019	$24.00	13.0%
2014	90	2019	$22.00	13.5%

MITCHELL
McNICOL CLARE VALLEY RIESLING ★★★★

or aged rielsing here is a wonderful wine with a developed aroma. Exotic lime toffee and brulee aromas that are scaling the heights in 2014. It has fruit sweetness, white fruit flavours and the oiliness in the mouth of maturity but the flavours are stunning. On the money with a complexity beyond normal.

Vintage	Rank	Drink	RRP	Vol Alc
2007	91	2019	$45.00	13.5%
2008	91	2019	$45.00	13.5%
2009	95	2020	$45.00	13.5%

Vintage	Rank	Drink	RRP	Vol Alc

MITCHELL
SEMILLON ★★★★

This style works a treat. Inexpensive, cellarable, riper and more textural and fuller bodied than many, with a lick of oak, its ready to go on release.

2006	87	2015	$24.00	13.0%
2007	90	2016	$22.00	13.5%
2009	90	2017	$22.00	13.5%

MITCHELL
PEPPERTREE VINEYARD SHIRAZ ★★★★

Bay leaf eucalypt, dark spice, clove, nutmeg peppery pieces and earthy solidness. The eucalypt is a part of the wine that centres the palate and the tannin and acids run long like the palate is on rails. Long and even with smooth initial youthful tanning peppery fruits, dark plum with drive and energy that holds long. A new style for Clare Valley in my eyes.

2009	87	2017	$25.00	14.5%
2010	90	2022	$28.00	14.5%
2012	94	2028	$28.00	14.5%

MITCHELL
McNICOL CLARE VALLEY SHIRAZ ★★★★

Congratulations! This is a lively mature wine. The old new world style with beautiful colour revealing cardamom, sage and dark berry fruit aromas. The tannins have softened hence the flavours start silky and dark fruited; shiraz, cardamom middle palate followed by eucalypt and a touch of herb. There is lovely balance and mid-weight fine grained tannins and a lot of life in front of it.

2004	90	2015	$48.00	14.5%
2005	92	2019	$45.00	13.5%
2006	95	2026	$45.00	14.5%

| Vintage | Rank | Drink | RRP | Vol Alc |

MONTALTO

Montalto was founded in 1998 by international businessman, John Mitchell and his wife, Wendy, based on a deep love of wine. John's studies in viticulture led to the purchase of Red Hill South Vineyard and since then, the couple has added another 5 vineyards. Simon Black joined in time to build the winery in late 2009. Pinot and Chardonnay are focused across different sub regional sites. The Montalto restaurant has one hat from The Age.

Winemaker: *Simon Black*
Open: *Daily 11am–5pm 33 Shoreham Road, Red Hill South*
Ph: *(03) 5989 8412 www.montalto.com.au*

MONTALTO
ESTATE PINOT NOIR ★★★★★

Raspberry, pastry with a subtle herbal lick of celery balancing the fruit. In the mouth creamy textured, pale dry style with a good run of red fruits, confectionery, solid middle and layered finish. Made by a winemaker with good taste!

| 2012 | 94 | 2022 | $58.00 | 13.6% |
| 2015 | 92 | 2020 | $50.00 | 13.6% |

MONTALTO
ESTATE CHARDONNAY ★★★★★

Ripe fruits hints banana and musk with ripe white nectarine, integrated oak backs the fruits with subtlety and style. The palate has length, good flavour and brightness needs time for complete oak integration the fruit finishes with a nectarine skin quality. Drink 2017 onwards.

2011	92	2018	$39.00	13.0%
2012	94	2017	$39.00	12.8%
2015	92	2020	$42.00	13.3%

MONTALTO
MAIN RIDGE BLOCK SINGLE VINEYARD PINOT NOIR ★★★★★

Pretty positive pinot perfumed strawberry, strongly pinot and gentle oak showing brown spice aromas leads the a ripe sweet fruited silky strawberry flavours with fleshy texture up front

Vintage	Rank	Drink	RRP	Vol Alc

turns red cherry hints brown spice good length, vibrant crunchy raspberry.

2012	90	2018	$65.00	13.8%
2014	93	2022	$70.00	13.7%

MONTALTO
MERRICKS BLOCK SINGLE VINEYARD PINOT NOIR ★★★★★

Very pretty ripe raspberry aromas leads to a palate with a optimistic enthusiasm great depth and focused fleshy raspberry front and middle fruits with depth and drive. The palate has generosity here is a great contrast to the focus and complexity of the Tuerong Vineyard

2012	94	2019	$65.00	13.1%
2014	93	2022	$70.00	13.3%

MONTALTO
TUERONG BLOCK SINGLE VINEYARD ★★★★★

A super effort here with freshness and intensity with detail ripe strawberry varietal fruits and a lovely dried herbs, green herb complexity from gentle oak. The palate has drive and length, a more savoury style with oak tannins carry potential, a green herb edge and sinuous flavour with firmness. Not everybody's idea of great pinot but I am broadly accepting of the power with restraint, complexity and length.

2012	92	2019	$65.00	13.8%
2014	94	2020	$70.00	13.0%

MONTALTO
THE ELEVEN SINGLE VINEYARD CHARDONNAY ★★★★★

As they say in the game, this is "a pretty smart wine". The aromas here grow wings and fly, lifting the spring blossom fruit with bursts of high quality oak contributing white butter. Herbal tea spices and white fruits are subtle winemaker inputs in the background. The palate has very good framework, gentle nectarine apple and will grow into itself with enough subtle flavour to grow graceful the youthful acidity well framed fruits.

2011	95	2020	$55.00	13.0%
2012	91	2018	$55.00	12.7%
2014	94	2023	$60.00	12.9%

www.robgeddesmw.com

MOORILLA

Moorilla Estate is a small Hobart-based maker that painstakingly produces tiny quantities of very fine wines. Recent developments have seen stability in the winemaking and the extraordinary development of the site. Excellent accommodation and restaurant, as well as MONA, a world-class gallery that has catapulted this property to the fore of Australian wine.
Winemaker: *Conor van der Reest*
Open: *Wed to Mon 10am–6pm, 655 Main Road, Berriedale*
Ph: *(03) 6277 9900 www.moorilla.com.au*

MOORILLA
MUSE EXTRA BRUT METHODE TRADITIONELLE ★★★★★

Very closed and gentle rising bread aromas with lemon and saline mineral salts and oyster. The palate is balanced, medium long with very intense aperitif styled vital acidity. The fruit is very subtle, just ripe flavours of pristine green apple acidity and good length of lemon sherbet fruit.

2008	93	2017	$49.00	11.4%
2009	94	2019	$49.00	11.5%
2010	88	2020	$49.00	11.5%

MOORILLA
MUSE EXTRA BRUT ROSE ★★★★★

A rose petal, strawberry, fruit tingles note in an overall very fine fragrance. The palate starts fresh strawberry, creamy yoghurt elements up front, strawberry middle and backed by the lemony acidity driving the finish. Sommeliers style of the sparkling wine.

2008	93	2018	$49.00	11.5%
2009	94	2018	$49.00	12.0%
2010	92	2019	$49.00	11.9%

MOORILLA
MUSE MOORILLA VINEYARD RIESLING ★★★★

Floral complexity with rose, lemon, white fruits and refined in the mouth with the hall mark house style creamy subtle oak like influence. Gentle acidity combines adding a silky sheen to the feijoa, stone fruit flavours and a firming food friendly finish.

2011	88	2021	$30.00	12.7%
2013	90	2019	$39.00	13.7%
2014	92	2019	$39.00	12.5%

MOORILLA
MUSE ST MATTHIAS VINEYARD PINOT GRIS ★★★★★

The aromas have punch and complexity, woven from oak, white fruits plus honeysuckle, orange blossom, lychee with funky edges. The palate has powerful details with reserve in the texture, showing long and driven fine with a complexity of white fruits, citrus, blossom with white chocolate oak flavours.

Vintage	Rank	Drink	RRP	Vol Alc
2013	94	2016	$30.00	13.6%
2014	86	2018	$30.00	13.1%
2015	92	2021	$32.00	13.4%

MOORILLA
MUSE GEWURZTRAMINER ★★★

Rose, lychee, high sweet picked ginger and a liqueur like level of pure varietal intensity. Huge palate and very aromatic. Oily glycerol with rose water then a procession of sweet ripe stone fruits wrapped in lychee and lingering aromatics with warmth. Full bodied, full throttle flavours and a forceful personality that is not for the faint. A triumph of his style.

Vintage	Rank	Drink	RRP	Vol Alc
2011	94	2013	$35.00	14.2%
2012	92	2017	$35.00	13.5%
2013	94	2018	$35.00	14.6%

MOORILLA
PRAXIS SERIES MUSQUE CHARDONNAY ★★★

The best unoaked chardonnay of recent times. Musqué (Clone 76) is a recognised chardonnay variant with a muscat aroma and very helpful in unwooded chardonnay. Very pale colour leads to a sweet fruit aroma, lychee, white nectarine and muscat aromas. This is a fresh high quality early drinking chardonnay style with well-balanced subtle nectarine and elderflower flavour textural wine with lovely length. Drink well chilled and as young as possible.

Vintage	Rank	Drink	RRP	Vol Alc
2012	90	2015	$30.00	12.9%
2014	86	2016	$28.00	12.3%
2015	94	2018	$28.00	12.0%

MOORILLA
MUSE ST MATTHIAS VINEYARD CABERNET SAUVIGNON ★★★★

Cool climate stamp here and the warm Celtic smiles of blueberry violets and black currant with pleasantly herbal, cocoa and red capsicum aromas. Medium bodied with soft tannins and ripe black currant middle palate. Medium length and fresh finishing thanks to the light bright vanilla black currant tannins.

Vintage	Rank	Drink	RRP	Vol Alc
2010	94	2024	$30.00	14.2%
2011	92	2028	$35.00	13.5%
2012	90	2017	$35.00	14.2%

MOORILLA
CLOTH LABEL RED ★★★★★

This is a great experience in a delicate and understated style. The Cloth Labels take you on an unexpected and unpredictable journey. You will be coming back to the glass and finding new insights; trying to see round corners, finding blind alleys, dead ends and after another mouthful of food more is revealed. Raspberry, sour red cherry, cranberry, beetroot, nectarine and black pepper spice aromas. In the mouth, ripe fruited front and middle palate laced with root vegetables, then the red currant and strawberry take over with the finish showing black berry, beetroot, carboniferous and cardamom flavours in a ripe elegant poised fruit purity. Will age, but why wait?

Vintage	Rank	Drink	RRP	Vol Alc
2012	95	2028	$110.00	13.4%
2013	96	2026	$110.00	13.9%

MOOROODUC ESTATE

Moorooduc Estate is a high quality Mornington Peninsula maker specialising in Burgundian varieties. The winery has been continually improving since 1985 and the application in 1996 of traditional techniques, such as wild yeast ferments, has helped these complex, food-friendly styles. All the wines carry a rippling muscular fruit structure, making them easy to appreciate.

Winemaker: *Richard McIntyre*
Open: *Daily 11am–5pm, 501 Derril Road, Moorooduc*
Ph: *(03) 5971 8507* *www.moorooducestate.com.au*

Vintage	Rank	Drink	RRP	Vol Alc

MOOROODUC ESTATE
DEVIL BEND CREEK CHARDONNAY ★★★

Generous complexity open and friendly ripe fruits, cream and nougat, lead to a wild honey, nougat creamy medium long palate with winery style written all over its creamy almost butterscotch flavours.

Vintage	Rank	Drink	RRP	Vol Alc
2010	88	2013	$25.00	13.0%
2011	86	2014	$28.00	12.5%
2012	90	2015	$28.00	13.0%

MOOROODUC ESTATE
GARDEN VINEYARD PINOT NOIR ★★★

This vineyard is all MV6 hence it gets the extra help of stems. Needs a lot of air to draw the fruit into stemmy balance and intensity from complete whole bunch with its angostura like dark spice notes. Has ripe generous raspberry into strawberry fruit with the back ground stemmy notes and firm on the finish.

Vintage	Rank	Drink	RRP	Vol Alc
2012	86	2015	$35.00	14.0%
2013	93	2022	$55.00	14.0%
2014	93	2020	$55.00	13.0%

MOOROODUC ESTATE
CHARDONNAY ★★★★★

Articulate example of the divine right in modern Australian savoury chardonnay wild yeast and mineral flinty notes over stone fruits. If you think the nose is austere the palate course corrects elegant, full and round not heavy filled with poached white peach minerally long and morish on the finish where layers of nougat caramel flavours are building to add interest in the sunset years.

Vintage	Rank	Drink	RRP	Vol Alc
2012	90	2017	$37.00	13.0%
2013	93	2018	$38.00	13.0%
2014	91	2018	$38.00	12.5%

THE MOOROODUC
McINTYRE CHARDONNAY ★★★★★

Use your biggest glasses here and not too cold to capture the full expression of stone fruit, lemon honey stone Easter bun fruit floral spice. In the mouth, density complex white and cooked stone fruits with enormous middle palate flavour expression. Massive up front wine.

Vintage	Rank	Drink	RRP	Vol Alc
2011	93	2018	$65.00	12.5%
2013	94	2018	$65.00	13.5%
2014	92	2018	$65.00	12.5%

MOOROODUC ESTATE
DEVIL BEND CREEK PINOT NOIR ★★★

In the zone varietal sweet spices and red berry fruit aromas. The palate is a little gem, varietal texture sweet fruited middle, gentle and easy with plenty of detail on the finish.

Vintage	Rank	Drink	RRP	Vol Alc
2011	91	2015	$28.00	13.0%
2012	90	2017	$28.00	13.5%
2013	89	2016	$28.00	14.0%

MOOROODUC ESTATE
PINOT NOIR ★★★★★

Appealing dark spice fills in the sweet fruited elements of the aroma with a stern intensity. In the mouth ripe berry fruits raspberry, red currant with spice from the stems shading and adding nuance to the finish. Impressive ripe balance resulting in beguiling complexity.

Vintage	Rank	Drink	RRP	Vol Alc
2012	92	2018	$35.00	14.0%
2013	92	2019	$38.00	14.0%
2014	92	2018	$35.00	14.0%

THE MOOROODUC
SINGLE VINEYARD McINTYRE PINOT NOIR ★★★★★

Complex with the full winemaker arsenal used with discretion, stem and savoury red fruits both fresh and cooked. Aromas lead here with a savoury meatstock into strawberry and raspberry fruit complexity. Silky tannins flow into generous full bodied finely woven wine to create a nice acid balance. In the mouth extreme quality. The sort of wine no one will dislike.

Vintage	Rank	Drink	RRP	Vol Alc
2010	96	2023	$65.00	14.0%
2013	95	2021	$65.00	14.0%
2014	96	2018	$65.00	14.0%

| Vintage | Rank | Drink | RRP | Vol Alc |

MOPPITY VINEYARDS
Jason Brown has made a big impression in NSW wine circles, with his Hilltops red wines and a swag of recent awards for medium-bodied fresh elegant chardonnays and rieslings. Moppity is a rising star with a 100-hectare, Tumbarumba chardonnay vineyard and takes the opportunity seriously.
Winemaker: *Jason Brown*
Open: *No Cellar Door, Moppity Road, Young*
Ph: *(02) 6382 6222 www.moppity.com.au*

MOPPITY
ATTICUS CABERNET SAUVIGNON ★★★★
160 dozen for the planet and only made when the planets align. Low crop, increased canopy management and green harvest has created a complex fruit and savoury earthy minerality, dark chocolaty elements and subtle dark spices. The palate has a lick of spearmint and long flowing fruit with a middle palate and endless finish and very fine tannins with volume and grace. Will take a decade in the cellar plus.

| 2013 | 95 | 2033 | $45.00 | 14.0% |

MOPPITY
LOCK & KEY RESERVE SHIRAZ ★★★★★
Fabulous colour leads to blueberry and red cherry fruit aromas The palate has ripe dark fruits, soft tannin good middle palate depth of ripe fruit flavours red cherry, sarasprilla and well balanced use of oak spice to add a dark chocolate edge to the medium long finish.

2012	94	2019	$22.00	13.5%
2013	90	2017	$25.00	14.0%
2014	91	2018	$27.00	14.0%

MOSQUITO HILL
Southern Fleurieu extends from McLaren Vale almost to Victor Harbour in South Australia and is the scene for several small, high-quality operators, including Glyn Jamieson's Mosquito Hill. Plantings started with chardonnay in 1996 and include pinot noir, pinot blanc and savagnin.
Winemaker: *Glyn Jamieson*
Open: *No Cellar Door 18 Trinity Road, College Park*
Ph: *(0411) 661 149 www.mosquitohillwines.com.au*

MOSQUITO HILL
SINGLE VINEYARD CHARDONNAY ★★★★★

Very consistent style with subtle complexity, whispers oak, pear white fruits, yoghurt and lees edged creates an aroma of complexity and completeness. The palate is generous texture full bodied, medium long flavour, soft acidity with ripe white stone fruit and gentle oak. The oak has been really well judged to help the fruit but not dominate.

Vintage	Rank	Drink	RRP	Vol Alc
2012	90	2017	$22.00	13.0%
2013	90	2019	$24.00	13.2%
2015	91	2020	$24.00	12.9%

MOSQUITO HILL
SINGLE VINEYARD PINOT NOIR ★★★★★

The spice notes are more intense than the 2013. Red fruits, orange citrus, bergamot, cardamom and brown spices add to the ripe fruit creating complex ripe aromas. It has silky tannin length, edges into strawberry lusciousness. Balance harmony prevails with the seamless long palate gliding softly to a fine grained finish.

Vintage	Rank	Drink	RRP	Vol Alc
2011	92	2017	$24.00	13.2%
2013	90	2018	$33.00	13.8%
2014	92	2020	$33.00	13.0%

MOSS WOOD

Moss Wood is one of a handful of Australia's best wineries. Family owned and operated, with a long-term perspective to create pedigree from the vineyard site and lineage from the wines. The wines are deep, full of fruit freshness and complex, with superb fruit and balance.
Winemakers: *Keith and Clare Mugford*
Open: *By appointment only, 926 Metricup Road, Cowaramup*
Ph: *(08) 9755 6266* **www.mosswood.com.au**

MOSS WOOD
RIBBON VALE VINEYARD SEMILLON SAUVIGNON BLANC ★★★★

Delicious intense guava aromas with vitality, freshness and zip. Drink now style that will have you ordering a second bottle. This is ripe balanced and long with guava filling the mouth and lingering on afterwards.

Vintage	Rank	Drink	RRP	Vol Alc
2012	89	2015	$28.00	13.0%
2013	88	2017	$28.00	14.0%
2014	95	2017	$34.00	13.5%

MOSS WOOD
MOSS WOOD VINEYARD SEMILLON ★★★★

The fruit is latent, drink soon style, closed, a subtle smoky edge showing apple, pear white fruits. The palate has ripe texture and white fruits with fleshy ripe richness up front flavour and texture.

2013	89	2027	$30.00	13.5%
2014	94	2026	$35.00	13.5%
2015	88	2018	$38.00	14.0%

MOSS WOOD
MOSS WOOD VINEYARD CHARDONNAY ★★★★

Lemon pith and curd, young and jangly with background quality French oak leads to a full bodied palate with silky evenness of lemony flavour intensity, balanced fruit and winemaking textural elements. A youthful chewy edge on the finish says "age me". Full flavoured and balanced style with potential.

2011	93	2018	$65.00	14.0%
2012	90	2018	$54.00	13.5%
2013	93	2021	$65.00	14.0%

MOSS WOOD
MOSS WOOD VINEYARD PINOT NOIR ★★★★

A beautifully different expression here. Fresh exotic Asian spiced aromas with galangal lifting over plum varietal pinot. The mouth-filling big round intense palate has length, varietal personality and a lovely pinosity with an oak-edged finish that allows for aging.

2009	92	2017	$53.00	13.5%
2010	87	2017	$53.00	14.0%
2012	92	2017	$53.00	14.0%

MOSS WOOD
RIBBON VALE VINEYARD MERLOT ★★★★★

Fresh fruit and well judged oak here. Raspberry mulberry fruit, dark chocolate oak with a medium bodied sweet fruit.

Vintage	Rank	Drink	RRP	Vol Alc

Brightness and tender tannins with complex piquant fresh sappy raspberry and mulberry middle palate and a lick of dark chocolate oak to finish.

2010	87	2016	$50.00	13.5%
2011	85	2017	$50.00	14.0%
2012	89	2017	$50.00	14.0%

MOSS WOOD
RIBBON VALE VINEYARD CABERNET MERLOT ★★★★

Moody bramble fruits with black currant and red fruits, a lift of acidity, overall the aromas are deep quality berry fruit freshness. In the mouth fresh red and black fruits, medium bodied harmonious tannins and a firm drying finish.

2010	91	2022	$50.00	13.5%
2011	86	2015	$40.00	14.0%
2012	87	2019	$40.00	14.0%

MOSS WOOD
CABERNET SAUVIGNON ★★★★★

Latent, complex dark blackberry fruits with intensity and power well supported by integrated cedar tobacco oak. The fruit expression is ripe blueberry and black current, the tannins shift seamlessly into gear to support the fruit, and the oak adds a further supportive back drop to the fruit length and warm finish.

2010	89	2020	$90.00	14.0%
2011	91	2035	$115.00	13.5%
2012	90	2027	$125.00	14.0%

MOUNT HORROCKS

Mount Horrocks Wines is a Clare Valley producer of some remarkably good wines. There seems to be a real synergy with the vineyards, as the wines keep getting better each year.

Winemaker: *Stephanie Toole*
Open: *Weekends and Pub Hols 10am–5pm, The Old Railway Station, Curling Street, Auburn*
Ph: *(08) 8849 2202 www.mounthorrocks.com*

Vintage	Rank	Drink	RRP	Vol Alc

MOUNT HORROCKS
WATERVALE RIESLING ★★★★★

White flowers talc and lime. Possessing quite a subtle and complex elegance and grace. The plate is well known generous drink now pleasures with fleshy medium-bodied texture and good length, orchard blossom and citrus flavours and a firm finish.

Vintage	Rank	Drink	RRP	Vol Alc
2013	94	2022	$29.00	12.5%
2014	94	2024	$29.00	12.5%
2015	93	2020	$33.00	12.5%

MOUNT HORROCKS
CLARE VALLEY SEMILLON ★★★★★

Fabulous polished white gold colour sets up expectations and the oak as always makes this different with perfumed width deeper generosity in youth with of course citrus vanilla butter aromas. This semillon is a watercolour with a fresh timber frame. The acid is soft minerally, wet slate firm, you can tell it is from a rielsing maker. So much precision to the shape in the mouth; perfumed rounded rich texture, citrus cashew flavours youthful food friendly complexity and texture so it gets over the issue of making a semillon the can be drunk young.

Vintage	Rank	Drink	RRP	Vol Alc
2013	94	2037	$28.00	13.0%
2014	90	2025	$28.00	13.0%
2015	93	2021	$28.00	13.0%

MOUNT HORROCKS
WATERVALE SHIRAZ ★★★★★

Intensity and complexity with red fruits, morello cherry and black spices, smoked meats, bacon hock with gentle oak spice. The palate has fine tannins red fruits and a spike of morello rich fruits on the very good middle palate with a long line of oak framing the fruits and giving age worthiness to the wine. The finish is long and savoury, each way bet for the savoury peppery smoked meats now or let it fill out.

Vintage	Rank	Drink	RRP	Vol Alc
2012	94	2029	$35.00	14.0%
2013	92	2020	$35.00	14.0%
2014	94	2028	$45.00	14.0%

MOUNT HORROCKS
WATERVALE CABERNET SAUVIGNON ★★★★
Discretion here with a finely woven fruit oak complexity leading with varietal black currant, a hint of black currant leaf and fresh currant fruit aromas with balanced oak hinting at warmed butter, vanilla and toasted bread. In the mouth cabernet black currant up front, fine long fruit and tannin structure, the fruit is almost minty but swerves away and the fruit lingers ripe black currant flavours and fine tannins.

Vintage	Rank	Drink	RRP	Vol Alc
2012	92	2029	$38.00	14.0%
2013	93	2025	$38.00	14.0%
2014	94	2024	$45.00	14.0%

MOUNT HORROCKS
CORDON CUT RIESLING (375 ML) ★★★★★
Aromas of elderflower, white rose, apple and cinnamon pie fruits with an acid twang at the back. In the mouth, the palate is generously luscious with ripe apple and white nectarine fruit. Finesse and acid delicacy, lovely bright acids that leave a clean finish. Pair with fresh fruits.

Vintage	Rank	Drink	RRP	Vol Alc
2013	90	2017	$35.00	11.5%
2014	96	2022	$35.00	11.0%
2015	89	2020	$37.00	10.8%

MOUNT LANGI GHIRAN

Mount Langi Ghiran in the Grampians region of Victoria has been a long-term regional classic. Two cellar doors have seen some recent introductions, including a stylish off dry Riesling, that have extended the appeal of this company. It is now in very safe hands and the wines show it.

Winemakers: *Ben Haines*
Open: *Weekdays 9am–5pm, Weekends 10am–5pm, 80 Vine Road, Bayindeen*
Ph: (03) 5354 3207 www.langi.com.au

MOUNT LANGI GHIRAN
BILLI BILLI SHIRAZ ★★★

Love ripe fruit at a budget price then look here. The fruit is the thing not propped up by sugar varietal raspberry aromas with very good depth of flavour soft flavours easy drinking in a medium body with long red cherry into morello fruit flavours.

Billi Billi
2013 Shiraz

Vintage	Rank	Drink	RRP	Vol Alc
2011	89	2015	$18.00	13.5%
2012	84	2013	$18.00	14.0%
2013	92	2017	$18.00	14.4%

MOUNT LANGI GHIRAN
CLIFF EDGE SHIRAZ ★★★★★

Beautiful colour and fragrance of red fruits and spice, more accessible than the Langhi with ripe fruits pretty spiced oak notes. The anatomy of a medium bodied red, medium weight, elegant length of favour, even fine-grained tannins and spicy blue berry, to finish pepper. The tannins have a mouth watering quality that makes this a food or frolic style. Excellent quality and great value.

Vintage	Rank	Drink	RRP	Vol Alc
2012	84	2019	$30.00	14.0%
2013	90	2018	$30.00	14.3%
2014	95	2020	$30.00	13.8%

MOUNT LANGI GHIRAN
LANGI SHIRAZ ★★★★★

Balanced aromas showing complex high quality finesse and fresh fruits fine grained oak adding a cedar oak spice edge. The palate is not striving for grandeur, charming elegant length, fine grained tannins silky mouth feel a compote of red fruits dusted in black pepper with a pastry basket of flavours with a long a finish threading dark spices, licorice and black pepper. A great wine you can drink now or keep for decades.

Vintage	Rank	Drink	RRP	Vol Alc
2012	90	2020	$95.00	14.5%
2013	94	2027	$95.00	14.3%
2014	96	2042	$120.00	14.0%

MOUNT MAJURA VINEYARD

Mount Majura Vineyard is a small Canberra district vineyard which has recently undergone some modest expansion. There is a delicious, cool style from this vineyard, without excessive alcohol or ripeness that delivers wines with refreshment and mouth-watering appeal.
Winemaker: *Frank van der Loo*
Open: *Thurs to Mon 10am–5pm, RMB 314 Majura Road, Majura*
Ph: *(02) 6262 3070 www.mountmajura.com.au*

MOUNT MAJURA
PINOT GRIS ★★★★
Perfumed taut and refined with poached pears and lemon fruit aromas. The palate is creamy, the acids buoyant and the fruit long and firm, with the varietal lift of pears and cream–finish.

2011	92	2016	$25.00	12.0%
2012	87	2014	$25.00	10.5%
2013	89	2017	$25.00	13.5%

MOUNT MAJURA
PINOT NOIR ★★★★
Pleasantly funky with layers of aroma though fresh, rose, strawberry and truffle, spice, and earthy caramel in a drink young format. The mouth feel is silky and the build of tannins and flavours creeps up. It is complex and the finish has charcuteries, savoury stalks and acid. Food style and good value.

2011	88	2015	$25.00	13.5%
2012	89	2019	$27.00	13.0%
2013	90	2017	$27.00	13.5%

MOUNT MAJURA
DINNY'S BLOCK CABERNET FRANC MERLOT ★★★
Ripe raspberry and savoury with aniseed tapenade aromas. In the mouth medium bodied silky tannins with good length of sweet raspberry fruit showing liquorice and vegemite edges to the dark berries, showing a fine drying tannin acid finish with liquorice fruit to finish. Drink after 2015.

2008	87	2013	$23.00	14.0%
2009	89	2015	$25.00	14.0%
2010	91	2019	$27.00	14.0%

MOUNT MAJURA
SHIRAZ ★★★★★
Savoury complexity subtle dark chocolate and coffee oak welded to black pepper, black tea and blackberry fruits. In the mouth the lightest of medium body with fresh red fruits,

peppery spices, and dark stalky elements, dark chocolate and coffee on the finish. Wonderful, elegant style.

Vintage	Rank	Drink	RRP	Vol Alc
2010	89	2019	$30.00	14.5%
2011	90	2015	$30.00	13.5%
2012	94	2018	$32.00	13.5%

MOUNT MAJURA
TEMPRANILLO ★★★★★

Dusty dry fruits and brown spice with caramel in the varietal spectrum in the aromas. Displays medium bodied velvety tannins with bright acids now in a fine boned, medium bodied raspberry fruited structure with elegant fruit to the middle palate. It builds to a complex Christmas cake and plum fruit pudding flavour with subtle caramel oak in the finish.

Vintage	Rank	Drink	RRP	Vol Alc
2011	94	2018	$40.00	13.0%
2012	91	2020	$40.00	13.5%
2013	92	2022	$42.00	14.5%

MOUNT MAJURA
TSG ★★★★★

A mix of exotic coffee, hazelnut and blueberry spice. The palate starts sweet fruited, complex, meaty blueberry and spice. It's silky and evolves with the tannin balance showing lovely fine grained length and finesse and the spice possible from whole bunch on the finish. The fruit weight is medium and the overall style is delicious.

Vintage	Rank	Drink	RRP	Vol Alc
2011	95	2018	$30.00	13.0%
2012	89	2016	$30.00	13.0%
2013	94	2018	$32.00	14.5%

MOUNT MAJURA
TOURIGA ★★★★

Fruit richness with a pleasant mix of blueberry, blackberry and black cherry and dark spice. The medium bodied sweet ripe berry fruit, wed to quality tannins is juicy with good length of ripe fresh fruit. Turns peppery towards the finish with a chalky acid-tannin edge. The food choices are very wide with a wine of this style and quality.

Vintage	Rank	Drink	RRP	Vol Alc
2013	91	2018	$27.00	13.5%
2015	94	2019	$30.00	13.5%

Vintage	Rank	Drink	RRP	Vol Alc

MOUNT MARY

Mount Mary is an excellent quality small vineyard in the Yarra Valley. The wines are among Australia's best, demonstrating that a good vineyard and consistent management can deliver the goods each year. These are medium bodied wines, refined and with moderate alcohol and low oak, reflecting the vineyard and its seasons.

Winemaker: Sam Middleton
Open: No Cellar Door, 22–24 Coldstream West Road, Lilydale
Ph: (03) 9739 1761   www.mountmary.com.au

MOUNT MARY
TRIOLET SAUVIGNON BLANC SEMILLON MUSCADELLE ★★★★★

The style is always wound back and for the future, The fruit notes are fleshy, tropical notes over all citrus and fresh, subtle lees, less wild ferment, flint and minerality with great complexity. The palate is fleshy firmly structured with a plush ripe middle citrus into tropical, appealing wild ferment, minerality in the acidity middle palate plush, fruit pulls up a bit on the finish and drink younger compared to the tighter 2013.

2012	95	2028	$86.00	13.0%
2013	95	2026	$96.00	13.0%
2014	93	2021	$96.00	12.8%

MOUNT MARY
CHARDONNAY ★★★★★

This wine has a rare precision and great balance with a good future. Oatmeal, fruit and savoury complexity composed of fresh bright lively fruit, flint and oak-spiced aromas in tight focused frame. The palate is magnificent harmonious purring layers lie atop each other with the creamy drive of chardonnay under pinned by acidity with the wild yeast dryness holding the fruit in focus and the oak a whisper in the back ground and a layered flavourful yet youthful firm finish.

2012	90	2018	$86.00	13.5%
2013	94	2021	$103.00	13.6%
2014	95	2023	$103.00	13.3%

| Vintage | Rank | Drink | RRP | Vol Alc |

MOUNT MARY
QUINTET CABERNETS ★★★★★

Very complex, pure wine with fruit, mineral and dried spice seamless entwined curling out of the glass like smoke. The youthful vibrant palate balances ripe and dry tannins, offer red and blue fruits off set by dried herb from the oak, the grape tannins and oak march in step with the blue and red fruits with gentle energy and precision too the farthest reaches of your tongue where the red fruits lingers. Drink young or age. More left bank to the 2013 right bank. One of the wines of the year.

Vintage	Rank	Drink	RRP	Vol Alc
2012	92	2026	$130.00	12.9%
2013	95	2029	$150.00	12.9%
2014	96	2043	$150.00	13.0%

MOUNT MARY
PINOT NOIR ★★★★★

Exceptional perfumes rose into musk with the expressiveness of mature vines in a good season. Overall cherry fruits oak spices like a handful of dried cooking herbs. This lands very complete with graceful dignity, fruit driven in this vintage showing fresh ripe red cherry and raspberry fruits that centre the palate with layers of oak spices, fine dry tannin all supporting the flavours. The 2013 is all understated ease while the 2014 is more exuberant.

Vintage	Rank	Drink	RRP	Vol Alc
2012	94	2022	$130.00	13.1%
2013	94	2028	$136.00	13.0%
2014	95	2022	$136.00	12.8%

MOUNT PLEASANT

Mount Pleasant is one of the premier Hunter Valley vineyards and wines of McWilliams. The cellar door features a wide range of wines and back vintages and a restaurant of note. Living history, alive and interesting there has been a lift in quality across the range with many exciting releases . The cellar door is a must visit. Check the AWV app for the most recent news.

Winemaker: *Jim Chatto and Scott McWilliam*
Open: *Daily 10am–4.30pm, 401 Marrowbone Road, Pokolbin*
Ph: *(02) 4998 7505* ***www.mountpleasantwines.com.au***

| Vintage | Rank | Drink | RRP | Vol Alc |

MOUNT PLEASANT
ELIZABETH SEMILLON ★★★★★
Racy fresh youthful drinking style. Aromas are a fragrant estuary fresh crisp style with banana, and ripe lemon. The palate is detailed and regional. Varietal light and fresh and preserved lemon, lemon juice flavours and lingering lemon pith on the finish.

Vintage	Rank	Drink	RRP	Vol Alc
2005	90	2014	$23.00	11.5%
2012	85	2016	$20.50	11.0%
2014	90	2018	$19.00	11.0%

MOUNT PLEASANT
LOVEDALE SEMILLON ★★★★★
Very youthful as a 6 year old lemon butter into exotic fruit and mineral aromas just emerging while the palate has presence up front harmonious texture silky lemon shy fruit weight, medium length middle palate chalky acidity, mineral lemon into toasty flavours.

Vintage	Rank	Drink	RRP	Vol Alc
2005	90	2015	$60.00	11.5%
2007	92	2019	$60.00	11.5%
2010	92	2019	$70.00	10.0%

MOUNT PLEASANT
PHILIP SHIRAZ ★★★
Added points for being a graceful style. Very interesting wine, understated winemaking gives the fruit a chance to fly with a complex cherry fruit, oak spice, pepper, cardamom spice savoury notes. The palate is graceful, spare driven by fruit flavour not alcohol showing raspberry, plum and unsweetened red fruit puree flavours holding its line medium long till the curtain comes down with lingering oak spice.

Vintage	Rank	Drink	RRP	Vol Alc
2011	90	2018	$20.50	13.5%
2012	87	2017	$19.00	13.0%
2013	90	2018	$15.00	13.0%

MOUNT PLEASANT
ROSEHILL SHIRAZ ★★★★★

Fragrant blue and blackberry nori roll dark spice. In the mouth silky tannins sweet fruit and closed up flavours of a sleeper wine with firm tannin and fresh acidity and just needs time to soften. Drink 2020.

Vintage	Rank	Drink	RRP	Vol Alc
2007	90	2020	$32.00	13.5%
2010	85	2020	$37.00	14.5%
2011	94	2030	$39.00	13.5%

MOUNT PLEASANT
OLD PADDOCK AND OLD HILL SHIRAZ ★★★★★

A tumbling cascade of aromas, spice peppery herbs, minerals and taut black fruit. Silky tannins youthful medium bodied structure red fruit taut tannins with length and refinement and just such a good cellaring wine with long bridging fruit and tannins. Drink after 2018.

Vintage	Rank	Drink	RRP	Vol Alc
2009	89	2018	$35.00	14.5%
2010	90	2020	$35.00	14.5%
2011	94	2037	$49.50	13.5%

MOUNT PLEASANT
MAURICE O'SHEA SHIRAZ ★★★★★

A classic aroma, medium bodied colour and aromas with red cherry fruits and lifted pips, medium intense Hunter shiraz with oak. In the mouth very delicate balance of oak tannins and red berry salty plum fruit with closed youthful savoury oak and tannins. Needs time to mature.

Vintage	Rank	Drink	RRP	Vol Alc
2007	91	2020	$60.00	14.8%
2010	94	2018	$60.00	15.0%
2011	88	2020	$103.00	13.7%

MR RIGGS

Ben Riggs, a former winemaker with Wirra Wirra, is now behind the Galvanised Wine Group and the bold ripe style of South Australian wines.

Interesting experimental styles are made, as well as the more traditional. The Galvanised Wine Group includes the Penny's Hill and Mr Riggs labels, and joins together vineyards, wineries and brands such as Black Chook and Woop Woop, which can be found as far afield as Canada and China.

Winemaker: *Ben Riggs*
Open: *Daily 10am–5pm, 281 Main Road, McLaren Vale*
Ph: 08 8383 2050 *www.mrriggs.com.au*

| Vintage | Rank | Drink | RRP | Vol Alc |

MR RIGGS
McLAREN VALE SHIRAZ ★★★★★

For big red lovers. Full of brambleberry, dark chocolate, mocha and vanilla elements in a patrician style of bold authority. In the mouth, a ripe sweet fruited wash of silky tannins and sweet chocolaty fruit and oak flavours with darker berry flavours that is complete and compelling, mouth filling bold full bodied ripeness. It has a firm dry finish and will develop in the medium term.

| 2011 | 90 | 2020 | $50.00 | 14.5% |
| 2012 | 90 | 2019 | $50.00 | 14.5% |

NICK O'LEARY WINES
Nick O'Leary focuses his winemaking on small parcels of the highest quality Canberra District Riesling and Shiraz. One to watch.
Winemaker: *Nick O'Leary*

Open: *No Cellar Door Bungendore*
Ph: *(02) 6161 8739* ***www.nickolearywines.com.au***

NICK O'LEARY
BOLARO SINGLE VINEYARD SHIRAZ ★★★★★

Blackberry and the darker spices of carbon, clove and nutmeg mature in its depth and nuances of complexity with age worthy intensity. Ripe without being too warm; the fruits are smooth and long, red cherry and then turning savoury on the finish. Elegant, balanced and fresh, with a long late black pepper finish. NSW wine of the year in 2014 and several gold medals.

| 2011 | 94 | 2026 | $55.00 | 13.0% |
| 2013 | 95 | 2025 | $55.00 | 13.5% |

NOON
Drew Noon and wife Raegan run this small winery in McLaren Vale producing beautifully styled reds with character and grace.
Winemaker: *Andrew Noon MW*

Open: *Weekends in November 10am–5pm until Sold Out*
Rifle Range Road
McLaren Vale
Ph: *(08) 8323 8290* ***www.noonwinery.com.au***

Vintage	Rank	Drink	RRP	Vol Alc

NOON
ECLIPSE GRENACHE SHIRAZ GRACIANO ★★★★★

Dark fruits with a distinctive style, similar to 2012 in personality, with great focus and intent. Compote of red and black fruits, and white and brown spice with a mineral edge. Sea breeze saline-like acidity, raspberry, geranium and bay leaf with the hallmark tannin silky texture. The fruit shimmers with sage, thyme, and grapefruit and then the tannins are furry, as in youthful fuzz on a teenagers face. Time will shave the fur into a shapely tannin beard with dignity.

Vintage	Rank	Drink	RRP	Vol Alc
2012	95	2019	$90.00	15.9%
2013	96	2020	$90.00	16.0%
2014	96	2024	$29.00	15.0%

O'LEARY WALKER

O'Leary Walker is an under-marketed company with a talented team from a lovely region. A great understanding of the local vineyards and wonderful cellar door makes this a safe pair of hands when it comes to regional wines. Very good quality across the board. The crisp vineyard rieslings are masterpieces in the expression of local terroir.

Winemakers: *David O'Leary and Nick Walker*
Open: *Mon to Sat 10am–4pm, Sunday and Pub Hols 11am–4pm*
P.O. Box 49 Watervale
Ph: *(08) 8843 0022 www.olearywalkerwines.com*

O'LEARY WALKER
WATERVALE RIESLING ★★★★★

Not dominated by any particular aromas; lime and lemon with white flower, almost guava, in the background. In the mouth, teenager texture, with a refined acidity, making it clean and refreshing. The fruit structure is hiding behind a curtain of acidity and a few years will give this one a transcendent silky mature style.

Vintage	Rank	Drink	RRP	Vol Alc
2012	86	2016	$22.00	12.1%
2013	90	2020	$22.00	12.0%
2014	93	2024	$22.00	12.0%

O'LEARY WALKER
POLISH HILL RIVER RIESLING ★★★★★
Super fragrant lime zest and deep florals including musk leads to a bright lime flavour dry driven palate excellent acid line with a minerally wet slate in a winters day mouth-watering acidity and savoury umami finish.

Vintage	Rank	Drink	RRP	Vol Alc
2013	90	2022	$22.00	12.0%
2014	94	2029	$22.00	12.0%
2016	94	2028	$22.00	11.5%

ORLANDO
Orlando is a venerable producer of serious wines under its own name from the Barossa Valley, Coonawarra and Padthaway. The quality is always high and the wine style is determinedly elegant.
Winemaker: Bernard Hickin
Open: Daily 10am–5pm, Barossa Valley Way Rowland Flat
Ph: (08) 8131 2559 *www.jacobscreek.com*

ORLANDO
ST HELGA EDEN VALLEY RIESLING ★★★★
Regional finesse with white fruit freshness, apple, pear and musk. The palate is full, richly flavoured, drink young, with middle palate fullness and evenness. Really impressive in 2016; this is forward, fresh and mid-term.

Vintage	Rank	Drink	RRP	Vol Alc
2013	90	2023	$21.00	11.4%
2014	90	2026	$21.00	11.0%
2015	92	2020	$20.00	11.5%

ORLANDO
ST HILARY CHARDONNAY ★★★★
Finesse and lemony nearly grapefruit aromas very stylish back ground oak. In the mouth creamy lees texture this is silky and rich in the middle palate punching very strongly with medium full toned pear and white fruits and very good length and a clean finish. Value for money generous style with a nod to Australian chardonnay history.

Vintage	Rank	Drink	RRP	Vol Alc
2012	90	2021	$21.00	13.7%
2014	91	2017	$21.00	13.2%
2015	91	2018	$21.00	13.2%

ORLANDO
JACARANDA RIDGE COONAWARRA ★★★★

Quite robust aromas of mint, eucalypt, leather, forest and blackcurrant. Long firm and tannic. A good middle palate and tannin length, but a bit quiet in youth low in fruit and needs time to soften. Lovely silkiness with ripe tannins and long length.

Vintage	Rank	Drink	RRP	Vol Alc
2009	94	2025	$63.00	14.5%
2010	94	2031	$63.00	14.5%

PARACOMBE WINES

A wonderful vineyard on a site that was acclaimed in the 19th century. Today the Drogemuller's make a range of wines that are always ripe and high in quality at good value prices.

Winemaker: *Paul Drogemulle, James Barry*
Open: *By Appointment Only*
PO Box 82 Paracombe
Ph: *(08) 8380 5058* *www.paracombewines.com*

PARACOMBE
SAUVIGNON BLANC ★★★★

Catches the passion fruit wave of the Adelaide Hills with style and grace. Full flavoured and plenty of up front pineapple tropical richness.

Vintage	Rank	Drink	RRP	Vol Alc
2013	90	2016	$21.00	13.0%
2014	92	2016	$21.00	12.5%
2015	88	2017	$21.00	13.0%

PARACOMBE
CHARDONNAY ★★★★

Appealing ripe stone fruit, gentle oak spice chardonnay aromas. The long palate has subtle oak, bright stone fruit flavours, and just a hint of wine maker lees influence on the finish. Great drinkability

Vintage	Rank	Drink	RRP	Vol Alc
2014	91	2018	$21.00	12.5%
2015	90	2017	$21.00	13.0%
2016	91	2019	$21.00	13.0%

PARACOMBE
HOLLAND CREEK RIESLING ★★★★★
A classy wine that will please, showing the floral notes of riesling with the brown classic spice aromas. Tropical fruit leaps out of the glass; pineapple, banana and lime flavours. A lick of spirit lemonade in a ripe round full flavoured early drinking style, with a layer of subtle savoury on the clean finish.

Vintage	Rank	Drink	RRP	Vol Alc
2014	90	2020	$20.00	13.0%
2015	93	2020	$21.00	12.5%

PARACOMBE
SHIRAZ VIOGINER ★★★★★
Very ripe and rich with flowery, musk rose top notes over the solid dark cherry and black plum aromas with subtle mocha and oak spice notes. In the mouth this generous ripe and full complex dark fruits with a floral top notes and a lingering finish.

Vintage	Rank	Drink	RRP	Vol Alc
2010	90	2018	$23.00	16.0%
2011	95	2018	$23.00	14.8%
2012	90	2020	$23.00	16.0%

PARADIGM HILL
Paradigm Hill in the Mornington Peninsula is easily one of 'our most interesting' producers. The family-owned winery is fastidiously pursuing regional varietal expression in their wines with finesse and intensity.
Winemaker: *George Mihaly*
Open: *Weekends 12pm–5pm*
26 Merricks Road, Merricks
Ph: *(03) 5989 9000* *www.paradigmhill.com.au*

PARADIGM HILL
RIESLING ★★★★
Fresh lime aromas with a tight long focused palate. Fruit, mushy pear and acid with dry talcy taste. Capacity to evolve.

Vintage	Rank	Drink	RRP	Vol Alc
2013	88	2016	$33.00	13.1%
2014	90	2019	$38.00	12.7%
2015	88	2022	$35.00	12.9%

Vintage	Rank	Drink	RRP	Vol Alc

PARADIGM HILL
COL'S BLOCK SHIRAZ ★★★★★

Shiraz (due to nutrient efficiency) can be smelly like burnt rubber, this one has an aroma compound that smells of cold fried onions or more normally white pepper, it's not disruptive burnt rubber. Bright fruits and very pinot ruby. Mortein fly tox, onion pyrethrum aromas leads to a firm tannins smoky black fired onions, with firm length and no bitterness.

2012	90	2020	$49.00	13.1%
2013	88	2019	$49.00	12.8%
2014	88	2018	$48.00	12.4%

PARADIGM HILL
L'AMI SAGE PINOT NOIR ★★★★★

Interesting Burgundian approach, singular with depth and complexity and avoiding overt fruitiness. Fruits with fresh and cooked strawberry with vanilla biscuity older and new oak on the nose and palate.

2012	88	2019	$60.00	13.3%
2013	88	2022	$66.00	13.5%
2014	88	2018	$66.00	12.8%

PARADIGM HILL
LES CINQ PINOT NOIR ★★★★

Strawberry, older and new nutty toasty oak. The red fruited palate is fresh lithe long and quite firm on the finish. Has a few Burgundian notes and pleasingly delicate.

2012	93	2020	$80.00	13.8%
2013	93	2022	$80.00	13.5%
2014	90	2022	$85.00	12.8%

PARINGA ESTATE

Paringa Estate's, Lindsay McCall, is best known for his pinot noir but the winery has a decisive quality shiraz and chardonnay as well. The reserve wines are at another level and the winery offers half-bottles and magnums.
Winemaker: *Lindsay McCall*
Open: *Daily 11am–5pm*
44 Paringa Road, Red Hill South
Ph: *(03) 5989 2669 www.paringaestate.com.au*

PARINGA ESTATE
PINOT NOIR ★★★★★

Tough vintage has given this wine mint menthol aromas and a lean angular palate with firm dry tannins and charcuterie spices on the medium long finish.

Vintage	Rank	Drink	RRP	Vol Alc
2009	89	2015	$60.00	14.5%
2010	90	2018	$60.00	14.5%
2011	85	2016	$60.00	13.5%

PARINGA ESTATE
SHIRAZ ★★★★★

Beautiful aromatics sweet and savoury blackberry with black and bush pepper smoked meats resin and a smooth fully ripe palate almost luscious with blackberry and pepper on the finish.

Vintage	Rank	Drink	RRP	Vol Alc
2008	90	2015	$50.00	14.5%
2009	89	2014	$50.00	14.5%
2010	91	2017	$50.00	14.0%

PARINGA ESTATE
THE PARINGA SINGLE VINEYARD SHIRAZ ★★★★★

Extra oak is a positive in this wine lending structure and age worthiness lovely savoury plum and cracked black pepper with lavish intensity showing the same flavours as the aromas. Great potential needs time to find its feet

Vintage	Rank	Drink	RRP	Vol Alc
2010	94	2025	$80.00	14.0%

PARINGA ESTATE
THE PARINGA SINGLE VINEYARD CHARDONNAY ★★★★★

A full and rich style with complexity from popcorn oak adding a sweet note to the vanilla nutty rich and savoury aromas. The palate has excellent integration, fruit weight as well great oak integration. Full bodied style with weight and substance and well crafted savoury and buttery elements off setting the oak and fruit sweetness.

Vintage	Rank	Drink	RRP	Vol Alc
2009	93	2017	$50.00	14.5%
2010	92	2016	$50.00	14.0%
2011	94	2019	$50.00	13.5%

Vintage	Rank	Drink	RRP	Vol Alc

PARINGA ESTATE
CHARDONNAY ★★★★★

Released with an extra two years maturity helping weld the fruit and oak. Orange zest, ginger and exotic chardonnay aromas with smoky toasty oak richness and a full bodied fruit rich middle palate with richness from smoky creamy nutty oak complexity and excellent integrated complexity.

2009	90	2013	$35.00	14.5%
2010	92	2014	$35.00	14.5%
2011	90	2017	$35.00	13.5%

PARKER ESTATE

Parker Estate is a Coonawarra vineyard producing Bordeaux-style reds of remarkable quality. The flagship wine, Terra Rossa First Growth, is an extraordinary achievement.

Winemaker: *Pete Bissell*
Open: *Daily 10am–4pm Riddoch Highway Coonawarra*
Ph: *(08) 8737 3525* *www.parkercoonawarraestate.com.au*

PARKER COONAWARRA ESTATE
TERRA ROSSA MERLOT ★★★★

Strong oak taste, plums and vanilla. Silky tannins up front and middle palate oak complexity. The acid attenuates the fruit and oak flavours and the finish is firm, dry and hot.

2012	84	2016	$34.00	14.0%
2013	88	2018	$34.00	14.0%
2014	84	2018	$34.00	14.5%

PARKER COONAWARRA ESTATE
TERRA ROSSA CABERNET SAUVIGNON ★★★★

Very Coonawarra with black olive, mint, blackcurrant and savoury cabernet elements in the nose. In the mouth, good interest with blueberry into black fruits with very soft tannins. Medium long flavours.

2012	91	2022	$34.00	14.0%
2013	88	2020	$34.00	14.5%
2014	88	2019	$34.00	14.5%

PARKER COONAWARRA ESTATE
TERRA ROSSA FIRST GROWTH ★★★★★

The regional minty chocolate is here as well as meaty, mirrepoix, cedar oak and black fruit. In the mouth its youthful primary dry tannins, firm and low key fruit flavours', and medium long date and prune with an emphatic dry finish. Keep for a decade before trying again.

2007	Not made			
2008	89	2020	$110.00	14.5%
2009	84	2017	$110.00	14.0%

PASSING CLOUDS

Passing Clouds is a Bendigo district maker with very individual wines of grace and power and the region's blackcurrant berry and mint flavours.

Winemaker: *Graeme and Cameron Leith*
Open: *Daily 11am–5pm 30 Roddas Lane Musk*
Ph: *(03) 5348 5550 www.passingclouds.com.au*

PASSING CLOUDS
MUSK CHARDONNAY ★★★

Initial oak aromas give way to musk/peach/pear chardonnay fruit with Freshness. For early drinking the fruits medium weight and appley.

2007	85	2012	$23.00	13.0%
2009	85	2012	$24.00	13.0%
2011	85	2013	$24.00	11.5%

PASSING CLOUDS
GRAEME'S BLEND SHIRAZ CABERNET ★★★★

Very good colour in 2013. Aromas are intense red fruit, savoury edged with anise fennel, bay leaf, and lemon myrtle. The plush palate is from a warm year with rich fruit and soft tannins creating a very even rich flowing red. Fruit spectrum with youthful understatement and very long flavours.

2011	85	2016	$30.00	13.5%
2012	93	2026	$31.00	13.9%
2013	95	2026	$31.00	14.0%

Vintage	Rank	Drink	RRP	Vol Alc

PASSING CLOUDS
THE ANGEL CABERNETS ★★★★★

Black currant, cardamom, dark chocolate, catmint and fine French oak. The palate is medium full bodied, good ripe fresh flavours with fresh acidity and intensity of black fruit flavours in the long middle palate. A little longer, fresher and leaner than the regional shiraz.

Vintage	Rank	Drink	RRP	Vol Alc
2005	89	2012	$30.00	13.0%
2008	92	2022	$36.00	13.4%
2013	92	2023	$47.00	14.0%

PASSING CLOUDS
RESERVE SHIRAZ ★★★★

This is a very good looking glass of wine with a medium intensity fresh ruby rim. Aromas are fresh and tightly held offering raspberry, white pepper and then into red cherry, Dr Pepper fruit aromas with exotic spices. The medium bodied intense palate has time on its side. Pure shiraz dark berry fruits and brooding flavours sit within a volume of silky tannins and ripe blackberry, finishing pepper, juniper, clove and herbal tea to finish. Drink 2020 onwards.

Vintage	Rank	Drink	RRP	Vol Alc
2006	86	2013	$35.00	14.9%
2010	86	2017	$40.00	14.5%
2012	95	2035	$47.00	13.5%

PAULETT POLISH HILL RIVER WINES

Paulett Polish Hill River Wines is a Clare area producer of finely crafted wines. Their shiraz vines are over 70 years old.
Winemaker: *Neil Paulett*

Open: *Daily 10am–5pm, Sevenhill Mintaro Road, SA*
Ph: *(08) 8843 4328* **www.paulettwines.com.au**

Vintage	Rank	Drink	RRP	Vol Alc

PAULETT POLISH HILL RIVER
ANTONIA RIESLING ★★★★★

The great wines here are gentle in youth, with slatey lime lemon and grape fruit pith wrapped in mineral aromas. The palate's open textured yet restrained and fine in flavour with a silky entry and lime juicy subtle nectarine like concentration in the middle and the finish is velvety soft and long with layers of finely wrought acid and the flavour lingers.

Vintage	Rank	Drink	RRP	Vol Alc
2012	94	2023	$50.00	12.0%
2015	94	2033	$50.00	12.5%

PAXTON WINES

Paxton Wines in McLaren Vale has a viticulturally exemplary 80-hectare vineyard growing fruit which they sell to others and producing small amounts of showcase wines under their own Paxton label. Since 2005, Paxton vineyards have been farmed using biodynamic principles and became fully certified in 2011.
Winemaker: *Richard Freebairn*
Open: *Daily 10am–5pm*
68 Wheaton Road, McLaren Vale
Ph: (08) 8323 9131   www.paxtonvineyards.com

PAXTON
THOMAS BLOCK CHARDONNAY ★★★★

Pretty oak spice notes lead to white nectarine fruited middle palate with generous weight and a soft finish. Mid-week, easy drinking style.

Vintage	Rank	Drink	RRP	Vol Alc
2011	89	2015	$29.00	13.0%
2012	82	2015	$29.00	13.0%
2015	89	2018	$25.00	13.0%

PAXTON
AAA SHIRAZ GRENACHE ★★★★

Floral top notes into graphite saline minerality. The fruits are the thing- ripe raspberry, cooked strawberry, soft tannins and a middle palate complex with a peppery spice, oregano note adding to the top and firming finish.

Vintage	Rank	Drink	RRP	Vol Alc
2011	89	2016	$23.00	14.0%
2012	90	2020	$23.00	14.0%
2014	89	2018	$20.00	14.0%

PAXTON
JONES BLOCK SHIRAZ ★★★★★

Fresh dark cherry, balanced, built to age and oak spice complexity with dried herby oregano, and fresh sage. Dark cherry fruits with fruit sweetness up front and oak quality to hold the fruit intensity, there is medium plus length and lingering oak spices. Midterm cellaring, belongs to the South Australian full bodied red soft finishing style with balance.

Vintage	Rank	Drink	RRP	Vol Alc
2009	88	2017	$40.00	14.0%
2010	88	2017	$40.00	14.5%
2013	90	2020	$40.00	14.5%

PECCAVI
Peccavi Estate is a small family vineyard located in Yallingup, one of the "sweet spot" sub-regions in the north of Margaret River. He has a very experienced team including Bruce Dukes (Domain naturalist) and regional hero Brian Fletcher helping drive a vision for great wines.

Winemakers: *Brian Fletcher, Amanda Kramer, Bruce Dukes*
Open: *No Cellar Door 1121 Wildwood Road, Yallingup Siding*
Ph: *(04) 0954 4630 www.peccavi-wines.com*

PECCAVI
CHARDONNAY ★★★★★

Full and rich with bright fruit, intense edges, a flinty complexity and detailed with tropical fruits. The bold palate has yellow fruit with depth and length. Oak plays a subtle role against such deep ripe fruits. The house style is rich, full flavoured and has a freshening acidity to the finish.

Vintage	Rank	Drink	RRP	Vol Alc
2011	92	2017	$58.00	14.0%
2012	88	2016	$58.00	13.5%
2013	93	2019	$58.00	12.5%

Vintage	Rank	Drink	RRP	Vol Alc

PEGASUS BAY

Pegasus Bay near Christchurch in New Zealand has created an enviable reputation for their wines with a distinct regionality, style and quality.
Winemakers: *Mathew Donaldson & Lynette Hudson*
Open: *Daily 10am–5pm,*
Stockgrove Road, Waipara North Canterbury
Ph: *(64) 3314 6869* *www.pegasusbay.com*

PEGASUS BAY
SAUVIGNON SEMILLON ★★★★

This wine has excellent fruit freshness, complexity, balance and length. Oatmeal, stone fruit and tropical fruits with complexity. In the mouth a complex cascade of flavours awash in tropical zesty acidity with fresh ripe citrus, passionfruit, guava, lemon and pink grapefruits all offering flavours to drive exceptional length and complexity.

2011	90	2016	$37.00	13.5%
2012	92	2017	$37.00	13.5%
2013	94	2020	$37.00	14.5%

PEGASUS BAY
RIESLING ★★★★

A rich off dry style with more than a nod to Germany's off dry rieslings showing a rush of candied limes, pineapple fruits with wax, lanolin and apricot aromas. In the mouth very Germanic sweetness with a rushing fresh acidity and tropical fruit flavours. Very mature as a young wine offering a lot of flavour intensity and excellent value.

2010	89	2016	$38.00	12.5%
2012	92	2016	$32.00	12.5%
2013	90	2017	$32.00	13.0%

PEGASUS BAY
PRIMA DONNA PINOT NOIR ★★★★★

After the oppulent 2011 the 12 is a more detailed wine with a flicker of peppery green herbs, like rocket, running with the red berry fruit. In the mouth the silky texture and strawberry flavours unfold with hall mark complexity. Medium bodied, medium length, medium intensity and well judged oak to match the stemmy fruits.

Vintage	Rank	Drink	RRP	Vol Alc
2010	95	2025	$115.00	14.0%
2011	94	2018	$115.00	13.8%
2012	88	2017	$115.00	14.5%

PEGASUS BAY
MAESTRO ★★★★★

The berry fruit here has a savoury edge which grows more obvious with time and provides a
counter point to the rich fruit. Medium bodied and complex with good use of the four varieties. Ages well to gives a complex wine with a steady maturation curve across the vintages in an appealing house style. The 2008 is full of warm ripe red raspberry, blueberry, cranberry with a slight floral volatile acidity lift to the berries and a mineral briar edge keeping it balanced. The palate has florals, red fruit and savoury edges, is mouth filling, deep and fruity and the tannins keep the finish clean with well judged oak layering the mouth feel and the suggestion that time will help your appreciation of it.

Vintage	Rank	Drink	RRP	Vol Alc
2005	89	2014	$66.00	14.5%
2006	92	2016	$66.00	14.5%
2008	91	2018	$66.00	14.0%

PEGERIC
Pegeric is a small vineyard in the Macedon Ranges region dedicated to handmade pinot noir. Somewhat eccentrically, their wine is aged for at least four years before release, making it a unique style. They also produce a sweet edition.
Winemakers: *Llew Knight, Ian Gunter and Chris Cormack*
Open: *By Appointment Only PO Box 227 Woodend*
Ph: *(03) 9354 4961 www.pegeric.com*

PEGERIC
PINOT NOIR ★★★
Very savoury miso, Chinese plum sauce, cinnamon, dark spices and tea, smoked duck, and dark fruit aromas. A ripe smooth middle palate with medium length finishing in a rustic mix of sweet fruits, black tea, smoked duck, and bitter citrus orange peel. You have to try these to believe the range of secondary aromas and flavours.

Vintage	Rank	Drink	RRP	Vol Alc
2008	87	2013	$50.00	13.5%
2009	90	2019	$55.00	13.5%
2010	90	2018	$55.00	13.5%

PENFOLDS WINES

Penfolds is a great example of ingenuity and dedication to quality within the Australian wine industry. Its distinctive red wines show continual refinement yet are true to their style of intense fruit with considerable texture from concentrated yet supple tannins that can grow in the bottle. Their whites are also very interesting. To offset the recent run of warm vintages and maintain their standards, they have diversified their vineyard resources to include Robe, Wrattonbully and Coonawarra.
Winemaker: *Peter Gago, et al*
Open: *Daily 10am–5pm, 78 Penfold Road, Tanunda*
Ph: *(08) 8301 5537 www.penfolds.com*

PENFOLDS
THOMAS HYLAND SHIRAZ ★★★★
Black fruits with grainy oak aromas of black cherry, cherry jelly and plum. The palate has soft tannins, is medium weight fruit, and more length than plumpness with plum and dark cherry.

Vintage	Rank	Drink	RRP	Vol Alc
2009	88	2013	$23.00	14.50%
2010	88	2014	$23.00	14.50%
2011	85	2014	$23.00	14.00%

| Vintage | Rank | Drink | RRP | Vol Alc |

PENFOLDS
KOONUGA HILL SHIRAZ CABERNET ★★★

Drink now fresh and bright. Blackberry, cola and cooked dark plum fruits with sweet fruit soft tannin length and softness all the way through.

2010	87	2013	$16.00	13.50%
2011	87	2013	$16.00	13.50%
2012	90	2016	$16.00	13.50%

PENFOLDS
KOONUGA HILL SEVENTY SIX SHIRAZ CABERNET ★★★★★

Subtle floral with raspberry and darker fruits aromas. The berry spice and liquorice elements swing in the wine and in 2013 floral pretty fruits with a full bodied depth and youthful finish.

2010	90	2015	$25.00	14.50%
2011	Not made			
2012	91	2019	$25.00	14.00%
2013	90	2019	$25.00	14.00%

PENFOLDS
BIN 51 RIESLING ★★★★★

Very pure riesling with lemon rind and lemon grass and hints of the classic spice aromas. In the mouth, the tension from chalky lime acidity delineates the elegant long structure giving a platform for the lemon pink grapefruit flavours to flow into talc and pith which linger for 30 seconds on the finish. Like a frisbee this wine cuts and glides through your mouth offering poised style before landing neatly.

2013	89	2019	$30.00	11.00%
2014	93	2025	$30.00	12.50%
2015	94	2020	$30.00	11.50%

PENFOLDS
BIN 311 CHARDONNAY ★★★★

White nut and bready lees complexity with short bread biscuit aromas in a low key complex nearly honeyed style. The palate is medium bodied, freshly poised with fine acidity and complex flavours in the middle palate. Lemon curd, honey dew, and a long tapered finish. A wine with very little oak and using carefully balanced fruit and grape tannins, add a pithy edge to the white stone fruit finish.

2012	88	2016	$35.00	12.50%
2013	94	2019	$38.00	13.00%
2014	92	2018	$38.00	12.50%

PENFOLDS
RESERVE BIN A CHARDONNAY ★★★★★

The style is very much about enhancing the fruit without oak. Minerally, flint like, savoury lift with deliberate low key grapefruit-like primary fruits gives this a European edge. The palate is pure Adelaide Hills fruited white nectarine and peach, cool, complete and concise with the savoury flavours running the tastes while the fruit provides the core and mouthfeel. The finish is subtle, youthful, and complex.

2010	90	2017	$90.00	13.30%
2011	Not made			
2012	93	2019	$90.00	12.50%
2014	93	2020	$100.00	12.50%

PENFOLDS
YATTARNA CHARDONNAY ★★★★★

Also known as Bin 144, the 144 refers to 144 trials before the first release. Sophisticated international style, very restrained, very white burgundy minerality, white flowers, honeycomb looking Chassagne, Montrachet and in for the long haul. The tight elegant long refined palate is fresh and focused, driven by an elegant pairing of concentrated fruit and fine acids and concentration with fresh acid layers in almond, cashews and subtle oak edge and a flick of toast to flare the finish.

2010	96	2022	$130.00	13.00%
2011	95	2020	$130.00	13.00%
2013	96	2016	$130.00	13.00%

PENFOLDS
CELLAR RESERVE GEWURZTRAMINER ★★★★

Classic varietal lychee and rose aromas. The palate is fresh and vital with good acidity and a taut South Australian view of controlling the oily lushness of this variety with a long fresh acid structure, helped by artful and subliminal to most, residual

Vintage	Rank	Drink	RRP	Vol Alc

sugar produces classic turkish delight and citrus flavours that linger.

2009	Not made			
2010	90	2013	$30.00	13.50%
2011	Not made			
2012	88	2016	$30.00	13.00%

PENFOLDS
CELLAR RESERVE PINOT NOIR ★★★★★

Very pretty complexity of raspberry and strawberry varietal fruit backed by choice quality oak. The palate is layered, complex and refined, with plush silky strawberry and raspberry, generous with complexity and has the capacity to age giving structure, density, polish and refined length.

2010	88	2018	$49.00	14.50%
2011	89	2014	$49.00	14.00%
2013	95	2027	$49.00	14.00%

PENFOLDS
CELLAR RESERVE SANGIOVESE ★★★★★

Cork finished ripe red cherry fruits weave into oregano and liquorice dark chocolatey oak. The palate starts silky tannins red fruits that build slowly along the mid weight palate finishing in the house firm finishing style. Up front it starts ripe tannins sweet fruited graphite red cherry and finishes youthfully detailed slightly drying youthful tannin and acid balance.

2011	90	2018	$45.00	14.00%
2012	92	2020	$45.00	14.00%
2013	93	2029	$85.00	13.50%

PENFOLDS
BIN 2 SHIRAZ MOURVEDRE ★★★★★

Appealing dark blackberry and stern iron stone earthy mataro mineral in the aromas. The palate is fleshy with upfront fruit. A complex, perfumed middle palate and with a crisp zip, the flavours are ready to drink now and it has a distinctive firming tannin finish.

2008	86	2012	$19.00	13.50%
2012	90	2017	$44.00	14.50%
2013	88	2016	$44.00	14.50%

PENFOLDS
BIN 23 PINOT NOIR ★★★★★

The red fruit lifts into red rose ripeness that is fresher, and more subdued with less dark fruit opulence this year. In its place is a beetroot, red cherry wine, with earthy just picked root vegetable aromas. The palate is acid edged, too young to drink on release, with a middle palate full of raspberry, almost cranberry, root vegetable earthy elements. In the middle mouth it finishes raspberry and raspberry leaf fruits.

2012	90	2018	$40.00	14.00%
2013	90	2018	$38.00	14.00%
2014	94	2022	$38.00	14.00%

PENFOLDS
BIN 28 KALIMNA SHIRAZ ★★★★

A show case of warm climate shiraz flavours; blackberry, anise, and fruit pudding with spice. The mouth is ripe sweet fruits leading to a long tannic palate with good middle palate McLaren Vale youthful ripe blackberry fruit structure. A classic cellaring wine with plenty of black and blue fruits, persistent tannin structure, and mineral flavours to finish. Drink after 2017.

2011	88	2018	$42.00	14.50%
2012	89	2022	$42.00	14.50%
2013	92	2029	$42.00	14.50%

PENFOLDS
BIN 128 ★★★★

The classic Coonawarra aromas of berry, raspberry and blackberry with a lick of dark olive. Lovely silky tannins and excellent length in a lovely shiraz. This has a varietal middle palate and a youthful fresh acid finish with a good structure. Needs a few years. Elegance in the fine tannins. Drink after 2017.

2011	90	2019	$38.00	13.50%
2012	90	2022	$42.00	14.50%
2013	91	2025	$42.00	14.50%

PENFOLDS
BIN 138 SHIRAZ GRENACHE MOURVEDRE ★★★★

Fragrant with red cherry, blueberry and blackberry bouquet garni in a rich generous nose. In the mouth, plum, full bodied complex fruit richness, lovey soft grenache influenced tannins, playing in a lighter year style with fruit ripeness adding sweeter liquored cherry fruit length.

Vintage	Rank	Drink	RRP	Vol Alc
2011	89	2020	$38.00	14.50%
2012	91	2025	$42.00	14.50%
2013	91	2022	$40.00	14.50%

PENFOLDS
BIN 150 SHIRAZ ★★★★★

Like walking past a coffee shop. Cloaked in warm vanilla and cappuccino oak, there is sage and almost a gherkin like aroma as well as a shopping basket of dark fruits, salad vegetables, and a prickle of acidity greeting the nose. The palate is long. Even long chalky fine tannins clipped the finish with a firm tannic back drop.

Vintage	Rank	Drink	RRP	Vol Alc
2011	90	2018	$75.00	14.50%
2012	92	2019	$75.00	14.50%
2013	90	2017	$75.00	14.40%

PENFOLDS
BIN 389 CABERNET SAUVIGNON SHIRAZ ★★★★

A lavish aroma, chocolate panaforte from Thomas Dux with red cherry dark chocolate biscuity dark spices, clove, vanilla and cinnamon. The palate comes on fresh blackberry into black currant, long intense fruit. The fruit flavour is very fresh clear and refined and the tannins take some time to assert themselves. As a young wine it is easily drinkable, seemingly tender, it is deceptive as it has a solid firm oak tannin brake on the finish.

Vintage	Rank	Drink	RRP	Vol Alc
2011	89	2022	$83.00	14.50%
2012	94	2032	$83.00	14.50%
2013	94	2028	$83.00	14.50%

| Vintage | Rank | Drink | RRP | Vol Alc |

PENFOLDS
BIN 407 CABERNET SAUVIGNON ★★★★
A well-knit complex youthful wine with tight oak, cappuccino and roast meat, black fruits, berry and currant aromas. The palate is well crafted and long, leaps into varietal flavours of black currant. A fresh middle palate, well-honed with oak, and medium long in flavour at this time with fruit and oak tannins defining the finish.

2011	90	2020	$75.00	14.30%
2012	89	2020	$75.00	14.50%
2013	93	2025	$75.00	14.50%

PENFOLDS
ST HENRI SHIRAZ CABERNET SAUVIGNON ★★★★★
A focused and polished wine with outstanding balanced fruit aromas. Very stylish and polished, raspberry blossom, red shiraz fruits, red liquorice, and complex raspberry, red cherry, subtle nutmeg, and sweet rhubarb perfumes. The palate is a finely woven, long, classic shiraz middle palate, and picks up the red fruits length again remaining even. Refined texture, red fruit and red liquorice flavours are seamless with pliant fine tannins that carry the flavours long after swallowing. This is the wine that many rightfully see as great value.

2010	92	2025	$95.00	14.50%
2011	95	2030	$95.00	14.50%
2012	96	2040	$95.00	14.50%

PENFOLDS
MAGILL ESTATE SHIRAZ ★★★★★
Now this is the Penfolds of history; intense ripe dark fruit with spice, blackberry, maraschino, soya sauce, date, marjoram and oregano in quality oak and a generous balanced opulence to the perfumes. The palate is youthful, less jammy and fat than in the past, with graceful silkiness of youthful tannins, a deep and long mouthful of ripe berries, round middle palate density and fine grained red fruit tannins in vanilla pie crust oak woven on the long finish into subtle grace.

2011	92	2025	$130.00	13.60%
2012	95	2030	$130.00	14.50%
2013	96	2028	$130.00	14.40%

Vintage	Rank	Drink	RRP	Vol Alc

PENFOLDS
RWT SHIRAZ ★★★★★

An ocean of deep dark solid impenetrable colour in youth. The terroir and house are evident with warming roasted Christmas pudding, and fresher lifted dark berry fruits, and Asian spiced minerals woven into a warm date mocha oak. The palate has texture, youthful fruit concentration and power and rumbles. Intensely balanced, supported by glossy refined long bridging silky tannins and a firm fullness of closed meaty black flavours. Needs 5 years to break out of the youthful quality clutch of the winemaker's careful style and in the excitement zone up to 15 years.

2011	93	2030	$175.00	14.50%
2012	95	2030	$175.00	14.50%
2013	94	2030	$175.00	14.50%

PENFOLDS
BIN 707 CABERNET SAUVIGNON ★★★★★

A very youthful wine. VA lift to the tight black olive, currant and gentle citrusy fruit elements with polished oak and tight age-worthy aromas. The palate is sumptuous, ripe and so far from Bordeaux with deep ripe fruits. A long mouth filling, mouth coating wine that takes the air from the room as your process the fruit and tannins carnivorous appetite working your mouth's, every taste bud, every saliva gland and every cell, brought into play to engage with the concentration on the finish. This is a modern Penfolds wine with length and balance rather than a varietal wine to me.

2010	96	2035	$350.00	14.50%
2011	Not made			
2012	96	2040	$350.00	14.50%
2013	96	2036	$350.00	14.50%

PENFOLDS
BIN 95 GRANGE SHIRAZ ★★★★★

This vintage is magnificently complex; defined and dense with brulee vanilla elements of the oak and the mineral fresh blackberry, black and red plum fruit. The fresh long deep palate has fruit clarity, magnificent complexity, silky tannins and

middle palate fruit density. It's seamless subtle acid integration structure is Herculean with the capacity to age. Still owns it South Australian plum fruit aromas and flavours, but the sweep of the intensity and the length give it grandeur.

Vintage	Rank	Drink	RRP	Vol Alc
2008	94	2040	$685.00	14.50%
2009	94	2032	$685.00	14.50%
2010	95	2046	$685.00	14.50%

PENFOLDS
50 YEAR OLD RARE TAWNY SHIRAZ GRENACHE ★★★★★

Just 330 bottles can be released each year to maintain the high standards of this blend which incorporates wines from over 98 years with an average age of 50 years. The style is surprisingly fresh and vibrant, clean with walnut brulee and moccha, caramel patisserie aromas. In the mouth, a marvel of the blenders art with balanced silkiness, long luscious texture, rich candied fruit and home made baked fruit cake length and a candied stone fruit lingers enticingly and carries its age effortlessly to the silky finish. A triumph and not to be aged but drunk on purchase.

Vintage	Rank	Drink	RRP	Vol Alc
NV	96	2015	$3,550	19.70%

PENFOLDS
GRANDFATHER TAWNY ★★★★★

An average age greater than 20 is revealed by the khaki then walnut brown rim with layers of subtle maple syrup browns. Aged rancio fruit with spirity brandy notes showing dried spices, raisins, coffee, prune and chocolate. In the mouth sweetness then lusciousness with mocha, dried fruits, crème brûlée, toffee crust balanced by tannins with savoury rancio aged finish which lasts 30 seconds before the fruit stops coating your mouth then the flavour lasts minutes more.

Vintage	Rank	Drink	RRP	Vol Alc
NV	94	2014	$95.00	19.50%

PETER LEHMANN
FUTURES SHIRAZ ★★★★★

Solid drink now style with mature on release dark spices, clove and ripe dark plum fruits in mid weight. In the mouth mocha plum fruits driven by oak tannin that will age till 2017.

Vintage	Rank	Drink	RRP	Vol Alc
2011	89	2017	$26.00	14.5%
2012	88	2017	$26.00	13.5%
2013	85	2017	$26.00	14.5%

PETER LEHMANN
EIGHT SONGS SHIRAZ ★★★★★

The overall impression is balance. Fresh and cooked red plum, blackberry and backing mocha oak. The palate is ready to go as are the 2013's Barossa generous middle palate with vanilla oak that really dominates the finish.

Vintage	Rank	Drink	RRP	Vol Alc
2011	92	2016	$45.00	14.5%
2012	94	2024	$42.00	14.4%
2013	89	2018	$42.00	14.5%

PETER LEHMANN
STONEWELL SHIRAZ ★★★★★

This in the expensive Barossa style for lovers of full bodied reds. Big and built for decisive cellaring with quality oak intensity, mocha, dark chocolate, plum and dark cherry fruits. Enjoyable vigour in the mouth, with ripe fruits, considerable fruit sweetness, middle palate depth and a cascade of tree fruits following the black berry into dark cherry with red plum. It is offering a lot as a young wine and has medium term cellaring potential.

Vintage	Rank	Drink	RRP	Vol Alc
2009	91	2018	$100.00	14.5%
2010	89	2020	$100.00	14.0%
2011	92	2021	$100.00	14.5%

PETER LEHMANN
BOTRYTIS SEMILLON (375ML) ★★★★

Lanolin, beeswax, honey and dark toffee. Lovely complexity. Very fresh lemony acids. A hint of lanolin on the palate. Quite a dry finish.

Vintage	Rank	Drink	RRP	Vol Alc
2008	89	2018	$24.00	11.5%
2009	88	2015	$24.00	11.5%
2010	87	2013	$24.00	11.0%
2011	90	2018	$24.00	10.0%

PETER LEHMANN
MARGARET SEMILLON ★★★★★

Bench mark example. Classic bottle age semillon complexity of lanolin, hay, bees wax and frangipani top notes. Palate is really well judged mature lemon curd, long and creamy, mature roundness with fleshy length and the finish has definite grip to close. Oysters or fish and chips.

Vintage	Rank	Drink	RRP	Vol Alc
2007	87	2015	$32.00	11.5%
2008	94	2017	$32.00	11.5%
2009	94	2020	$35.00	10.5%

PETER LEHMANN
PORTRAIT CABERNET SAUVIGNON ★★★★

Bay leaf, plum and gum leafy fruits in straight forward drying young style. In the mouth black currants, stalks and pips up front and into the middle of your tongue a flicker of charry toasty oak.

Vintage	Rank	Drink	RRP	Vol Alc
2012	88	2016	$18.00	14.5%
2013	86	2016	$18.00	14.5%
2014	86	2017	$18.00	14.0%

PETER LEHMANN
MENTOR CABERNET ★★★★

Green olive, green grass seed elements in balanced oak aromas. The moderate intensity palate is ripe tannins medium bodied sweet fruited with dark olive leafy elements that hold long in the mouth with an abrupt finish.

Vintage	Rank	Drink	RRP	Vol Alc
2011	89	2018	$42.00	14.5%
2012	88	2020	$45.00	14.5%
2013	91	2018	$45.00	14.5%

PETER LEHMANN
PORTRAIT SHIRAZ ★★★

Fresh looking dark chocolate and raspberry aromas. In the mouth up front raspberry and simple flavours with mocha oak flavours to finish. Drinkability from the get go.

Vintage	Rank	Drink	RRP	Vol Alc
2012	86	2016	$18.00	14.5%
2013	86	2016	$18.00	14.5%
2014	85	2017	$18.00	14.0%

www.robgeddesmw.com

Vintage	Rank	Drink	RRP	Vol Alc

PETALUMA
COONAWARRA EVANS VINEYARD ★★★★★
Youthful yet powerful old school style with vanilla shortbread oak and raspberry jam tart fruit aromas. The oak is bourbon scented intensity awash amongst silky fruit tannins with pretty red and black fruits. An oak finish, like an over coat, wraps the fruit requiring time.

2008	88	2015	$55.00	14.5%
2010	91	2019	$60.00	14.5%
2012	92	2025	$60.00	14.5%

PETER LEHMANN WINES
Peter Lehmann Wines is a greatly respected Barossa winemaker with a reliable range of pleasantly underpriced fine wines.
Winemaker: Ian Hongell
Open: Weekdays 9.30am–5pm Weekends and Pub Hols 10.30am–4.30pm
Para Road, Tanunda
Ph: *(08) 8563 2500 www.peterlehmannwines.com*

PETER LEHMANN
PORTRAIT EDEN VALLEY DRY RIESLING ★★★★
Ready and roaring to go. Floral lift of lemon, elderflower and subtle sweet spices while the pineapple lime palate is fresh bright and really well balanced. Fantastic value.

2012	86	2015	$18.00	11.0%
2013	89	2018	$18.00	11.0%
2014	89	2016	$18.00	11.0%

PETER LEHMANN
WIGAN RIESLING ★★★★★
A great wine from a tough year for whites and reds. Smelling of brown lime, honey comb, creamed honey and toast. The palate has developed honey, orange peel, brown lime and toast flavours and the texture sits nicely acidic with a good middle palate depth and racy acid.

2009	86	2026	$32.00	11.5%
2010	95	2028	$32.00	12.0%
2011	93	2018	$32.00	11.0%

| Vintage | Rank | Drink | RRP | Vol Alc |

PETALUMA
Petaluma offers some of Australia's finest wines due to carefully selected and managed company vineyards, with the best sites in prime locations such as the Clare and Piccadilly Valleys and Coonawarra; all backed up by a stringent focus on quality.
Winemaker: Andrew Hardy
Open: Daily 10am–5pm 254 Pfeiffer Road, Woodside
Ph: (08) 8339 9300 *www.petaluma.com.au*

PETALUMA
HANLIN HILL RIESLING ★★★★★
Ripe and rich, almost tropical fruits with pineapple, lime, talc and rose aromas. In the mouth the full flavoured house style with generous lime fruits in the middle palate and a fresh finish.

2012	90	2022	$30.00	13.0%
2013	95	2020	$30.00	13.0%
2014	89	2019	$28.00	13.0%

PETALUMA
YELLOW LABEL PICCADILLY CHARDONNAY ★★★★★
Aromas are fruit driven by stone fruit and pineapple. A big and generous ripe varietal fruited wine with oak in the back seat and the components needing to time to mesh with crunchy acids. Hold for two years to get a fresh but creamy textured wine.

2011	89	2016	$40.00	12.5%
2012	91	2017	$40.00	14.0%
2013	90	2019	$40.00	14.0%

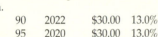

PETALUMA
WHITE LABEL ADELAIDE HILLS SHIRAZ ★★★★★
Ripe and inviting black fruits, liquorice, cola and modest oak aromas. Plenty of soft tannin luxury and easy to drink young. Balanced, ripe blackberry fruits and dark spice with an up front fruit intensity.

2010	90	2022	$26.00	14.0%
2012	88	2018	$26.00	14.5%
2013	88	2018	$26.00	14.5%

PEPPER TREE
CALCARE SINGLE VINEYARD RESERVE CABERNET SAUVIGNON ★★★★★

Appealing cabernet elements of red currant fruit, green olive, mint and eucalypt side aromas. In the mouth upfront red fruit purity with bright raspberry, touch of leafy herbs, dried herbs, medium long well balanced acid/ tannin for medium term aging with even flavour length and a youthful firm finish.

Vintage	Rank	Drink	RRP	Vol Alc
2010	94	2035	$42.00	14.3%
2012	93	2040	$42.00	14.0%
2013	92	2020	$42.00	14.2%

PEPPER TREE
COQUUN SINGLE VINEYARD RESERVE SHIRAZ ★★★★★

Carefully chosen oak adds a balanced gentle vanilla ginger toast to the sappy raspberry bush and cane red fruit aromas. The flavour is intriguing, dives right into your mouth with a deep red berry fruitiness that does not let up on the middle palate and comes gracefully to close with oak tannin dryness and lingering red berry fruits on the extended finish.

Vintage	Rank	Drink	RRP	Vol Alc
2010	93	2027	$60.00	14.5%
2011	94	2040	$60.00	14.0%
2013	96	2028	$60.00	14.5%

PEPPER TREE
ELDERSLEE ROAD SINGLE VINEYARD CABERNET SAUVIGNON ★★★★★

The aromas here are cool cabernet spearmint, black current, dark chocolate and green olive. In the mouth ripe berry fruits with a juicy bright flavoured, medium body with vivid black currant high intensity middle palate flavours and ripe smooth tannins carrying the long berry, blackcurrant leaf, mineral, and olive flavours.

Vintage	Rank	Drink	RRP	Vol Alc
2010	94	2043	$42.00	14.5%
2012	94	2041	$42.00	14.0%
2013	94	2023	$42.00	14.2%

Vintage	Rank	Drink	RRP	Vol Alc

PENFOLDS
GREAT GRANDFATHER TAWNY ★★★★★

Orange rim to extremely khaki before maple syrup brown at the centre from over 40 years average in casks. Old port wood cellars with intricate aromas of caramel fig, toffee, roasted chestnuts and braised nuts on a fire with caramel wood smoke. The palate is luscious, starts out silky sweet, caramel and walnut raisin and milk chocolate, complexities with a magnificent intensity that is almost painful in its acid, oak and alcohol intensity and concentration.

| NV | 95 | 2014 | $335.00 | 19.00% |

PENNY'S HILL
Penny's Hill is a close-planted vineyard in McLaren Vale taking the regional shiraz style to greater heights. Good cabernet as well.
Winemaker: Alexia Roberts

Open: *Daily 10am–5pm, 281 Main Road, McLaren Vale*
Ph: *(08) 8557 0800 www.pennyshill.com.au*

PENNY'S HILL
CRACKING BLACK McLAREN VALE SHIRAZ ★★★★

Aromas are juicy, ripe, dark berry and liquorice. In the mouth silky smooth regional tannins with the fruit forward juicy plush fruits of the 2013's and soft integrated medium long middle palate flavours and tannins of the vintage.

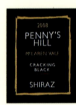

2011	89	2017	$22.00	14.5%
2012	89	2017	$22.00	14.5%
2013	90	2017	$22.00	14.5%

PEPPER TREE
A consistent quiet achiever where the term value for money means exceptional quality. Their cellar door in the Hunter Valley offers wines from choice vineyards in Orange, Wrattonbully Coonawarra and the Hunter Valley. Recent quality has been exceptional across all regions. Their Cellar Door precinct is also home to a coffee roaster.

Winemaker: *Gwyn Olsen*
Open: *Weekdays 9 to 5pm Weekends 9.30am–5pm*
86 Halls Road, Pokolbin
Ph: *(02) 4909 7100 www.peppertreewines.com.au*

PEWSEY VALE

Pewsey Vale is an extremely reliable 50-hectare mature vineyard in the cooler heights (480 metres) of the Eden Valley, owned and operated as a single vineyard estate by the Hill Smith family.

Winemaker: Louisa Rose
Open: Daily at Yalumba 10am–5pm, Eden Valley Road, Angaston
Ph: (08) 8561 3200 *www.pewseyvale.com*

PEWSEY VALE
SINGLE VINEYARD ESTATE RIESLING ★★★★★

The Pewsey style of bold flavour is immediately approachable with musk stick dominating as a young wine. The fleshy palate is full flavoured juicy stone fruited and compelling up front with stone fruits and the classic quality fingerprint of dark spice with acidity clicking its heels to attention on the finish. Big, bold, rich and well balanced.

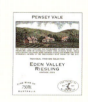

Vintage	Rank	Drink	RRP	Vol Alc
2013	94	2020	$23.00	12.5%
2014	92	2017	$25.00	12.5%
2015	92	2019	$25.00	12.0%

PEWSEY VALE
EDEN VALLEY PRIMA RIESLING ★★★★★

The best yet. Evolving lime classic riesling aromas with plenty of floral and musk intensity, then rose, pineapple, lime, juicy fruit chewing gum and extra quality intensity of gingery brown spices on the aromas. The palate wraps off with dry sweetness and sweet lime-toward nectarine like. Gains momentum with middle palate rose and juicy stone fruit fullness and subtle acidity. A great introduction to riesling.

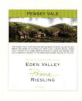

Vintage	Rank	Drink	RRP	Vol Alc
2013	88	2018	$27.00	9.5%
2014	89	2018	$27.00	9.5%
2015	94	2018	$26.00	9.5%

PEWSEY VALE
CONTOURS MUSEUM RELEASE RIESLING ★★★★★

The mature rielsing aromas are part citrus lime rind and lemon pulp and part honey. Apricot and subtle earthy fruits are lean but long with a thin middle palate and dry short finish. A tough year and brave call with the winemakers doing a great job.

Vintage	Rank	Drink	RRP	Vol Alc
2008	92	2018	$30.00	12.5%
2009	95	2017	$34.00	12.5%
2011	89	2017	$31.00	11.0%

PFEIFFER WINES

Pfeiffer Wines is a north-east Victorian maker showing a reliably well-produced range of wines with a characteristic understated delicacy, all the more remarkable because of their reputation as an excellent fortified wine specialist.

Winemaker: *Jen Pfeiffer*
Open: *Mon to Sat 9am–5pm Sun 10am–5pm,*
167 Distillery Road, Wahgunyah
Ph: *(02) 6033 2805 www.pfeifferwinesrutherglen.com.au*

PFEIFFER
MARSANNE ★★★★

Ginger powder leads, apple, pear main stream fruit aromas with honeysuckle starting to show. This is a light medium bodied fresh balanced long wine with subtle acids holding the gingered pear fresh fruit in a tidy line.

Vintage	Rank	Drink	RRP	Vol Alc
2008	86	2014	$17.00	13.5%
2011	87	2014	$19.90	13.5%
2013	89	2018	$19.90	13.8%

PFEIFFER
PINOT NOIR ★★★

Mustard greens, raspberry, liquorice and eucalypt, leads to tomato herbal fruit, bright acid with short palate.

Vintage	Rank	Drink	RRP	Vol Alc
2010	86	2013	$22.50	13.5%
2011	87	2016	$24.00	13.5%
2012	84	2014	$24.00	13.5%

PFEIFFER

CARLYLE CABERNET SAUVIGNON MERLOT ★★★

Dusty black currant, date, dark chocolate oak, and rustic edged aromas. In the mouth ripe black currant, violets, and red wine gums with good length, firm tannins and oak spice flavours of nutmeg, cinnamon toast. Bring on the BBQ steak.

Vintage	Rank	Drink	RRP	Vol Alc
2011	86	2014	$18.50	14.0%
2012	88	2018	$18.50	14.0%
2013	89	2017	$18.50	14.0%

PFEIFFER

CABERNET SAUVIGNON ★★★★

Big aromas here with jammy black currant, liquorice and meat stock fruit. In the mouth, bright ripe fruits and fresh moderate tannin. High intensity black currant flavours in the middle plate and a firm finish.

Vintage	Rank	Drink	RRP	Vol Alc
2010	88	2015	$22.50	14.5%
2011	89	2017	$24.00	14.0%
2012	88	2016	$18.50	14.0%

PFEIFFER

LATE HARVEST MUSCADELLE (375ML) ★★★★

Honey and wattle blossom aromas. The palate is sweet, fresh cut pears in syrup and low in acid so it is fresh. Fresh fruit salad would suit this wine.

Vintage	Rank	Drink	RRP	Vol Alc
2008	87	2013	$16.00	9.0%
2012	88	2015	$19.50	9.0%
2013	88	2016	$19.50	9.0%

PFEIFFER

CHRISTOPHER'S VP ★★★★★

Brandy spirit lifts fresh pretty blackberry, black fruit, flowers and rose petals leading to soft sweet bright fresh long and silky ripe fruits.

Vintage	Rank	Drink	RRP	Vol Alc
2006	94	2030	$25.00	18.0%
2008	95	2034	$25.00	18.0%
2012	94	2014	$29.90	19.0%

| Vintage | Rank | Drink | RRP | Vol Alc |

PHILIP SHAW

Philip Shaw, formerly chief winemaker for Rosemount, has vast experience and a mature vineyard in the high altitude Orange region. He waited 18 years for the vineyard to reach its full potential before releasing his first wines. Current releases are exciting.

Winemakers: *Philip Shaw*
Open: *Daily 11am till 5pm, 100 Shiralee Road, Orange*
Ph: *(02) 6365 3422 www.philipshaw.com.au*

PHILIP SHAW
No 19 SAUVIGNON BLANC ★★★★★

An adult sauvignon blanc. Grassy, green peas into honeysuckle sauvignon, oak spices and subtle contribution of winemaking to wed complexity to the grassy horsepower of sauvignon. The wine is a driven balances richness of fruit, kiwi fruit freshness and subtle spice flavour in a weighty style perfectly wed to crispness with a persistent fruit finish.

2013	89	2016	$25.00	13.0%
2014	94	2017	$25.00	11.5%
2015	94	2020	$25.00	12.0%

PHILIP SHAW
No 11 CHARDONNAY ★★★★★

Pretty, positive aromas of classically framed chardonnay, fresh and clean white fruit with fine oak adding complexity. The silky palate just a pup in 2016, the finish is classical high-quality chardonnay with a gentle complexity and barrel ferment of butter scotch and warm oak spices. Balance and intensity with great respect for the fruit and delicate oak.

2013	94	2020	$35.00	13.0%
2014	92	2025	$35.00	11.5%
2015	94	2020	$35.00	12.5%

PHILIP SHAW
THE IDIOT SHIRAZ ★★★★

Rich ripe and youthful with an idiosyncratic edge thanks to the balance of winemaker verses vineyard. Ripe fruit notes, liquorice, cola and smoked meats with sweet oak notes. The red fruits are tip of tongue, rich ripe medium bodied with well

Vintage	Rank	Drink	RRP	Vol Alc

woven mulberry raspberry fruits with youth vibrant flavours and spices to the finish.

2012	89	2017	$20.00	12.5%
2013	91	2018	$20.00	13.7%
2015	90	2019	$22.00	13.5%

PHILIP SHAW
No 8 PINOT NOIR ★★★★

Bright strawberry, brown spice, light soya sauce savoury, the palate is a lively gig of bright red fruits and savoury umami miso sauce like flickers. The tannins carry the flavour and cashew white butter. Lovely use of quality oak to frame. Drink after 2017.

2011	90	2015	$40.00	13.0%
2013	88	2018	$40.00	13.0%
2015	91	2020	$40.00	12.5%

PHILIP SHAW
No 89 SHIRAZ VIOGNIER ★★★★★

The aromas are the complete cool climate shiraz of violets, smoked meats, red berry, sandalwood and peppery spice. The fine grained tannins are medium full bodied with even length and rich, yet refined, flavours of dark berry, bitter chocolate and apricot with concentration and great length thanks to the complex tannin profile. Finishes sandalwood dark chocolate and youthful.

2011	94	2021	$50.00	13.5%
2012	94	2020	$50.00	14.0%
2013	94	2026	$50.00	13.8%

PHILIP SHAW
No 17 MERLOT CABERNET FRANC SAUVIGNON ★★★★

The aromas are detailed and nuanced red and black fruit with leafy cabernet franc and fine spice. The palate is ripe berry and mulberry with savoury elements to the fruit showing cabernet family linear density in the length of flavours rather than rich mouth filling fruit sweetness while the tannins have line and subtle oak.

2011	88	2017	$25.00	13.5%
2012	88	2018	$25.00	13.0%
2013	91	2019	$25.00	13.8%

PHILIP SHAW
No 5 CABERNET SAUVIGNON MERLOT ★★★★

This is slow to unfold and very much in the savoury spectrum of Australia cabernet. It is a detailed portrait with Bordeaux cedar fruit, oak and artistry as the black currant, earthy, blue berry fruits meet cabernet rhubarb and ginger spicy oak. In the mouth it jumps into sweet fruited moderate tannins with ripe blackcurrant length and builds into a full middle with appealing fruit sweetness and tidy acid fruit oak tannins.

Vintage	Rank	Drink	RRP	Vol Alc
2009	90	2017	$75.00	13.5%
2010	91	2025	$75.00	13.5%
2012	91	2020	$75.00	13.5%

PIERRO VINEYARDS
Pierro Vineyards is a Margaret River maker with a sense of style and class and an innate understanding of the natural bounty of the regions climate and blending. With 10 hectares of vines, their excellent range includes a distinctive chardonnay and a refined cabernet merlot. A very reliable producer across all styles.
Winemaker: *Dr Michael Peterkin*
Open: *Daily 10am–5pm Caves Road, Busselton*
Ph: *(08) 9755 6220 www.pierro.com.au*

PIERRO
LTC SEMILLON SAUVIGNON BLANC ★★★★★

Aromas are delicate, detailed and focused with passionfruit, banana, and honey, gentle green and dried herbs. In the mouth initially fresh and zesty acid, yielding to a light bodied yet full flavoured explosion of fresh passionfruit and lemon flavours in the middle palate. Intensity with lightness, a success.

Vintage	Rank	Drink	RRP	Vol Alc
2012	90	2016	$27.00	13.5%
2013	88	2015	$33.50	14.0%
2014	94	2019	$33.50	13.5%

PIERRO
CHARDONNAY ★★★★★

Quality fruit and oak with a traditional ripe balanced frame with less oatmeal than early editions. The whole fruits are textured, silky and deep in the middle palate, well framed by classy quality oak and lingering peanut brittle into toast complexity.

Vintage	Rank	Drink	RRP	Vol Alc
2012	94	2020	$82.00	13.5%
2013	93	2017	$82.00	14.0%
2014	92	2019	$82.00	14.0%

PIERRO
CABERNET MERLOT LTCF ★★★★★

Aromas offer the delicacy, unique style and depth of this label. Fresh black fruits with a pretty oregano lift of spices on the back. The medium bodied palate has long fine fruit weaving raspberry, red currant and black olive with fine grained acidity underpinning the elegant regional tannins. 20 seconds worth of lingering subtle raspberry fruit in a classic house style from Margaret River.

Vintage	Rank	Drink	RRP	Vol Alc
2010	89	2016	$33.00	14.0%
2011	88	2019	$40.00	14.0%
2012	94	2018	$40.00	14.5%

PIERRO
RESERVE CABERNET MERLOT ★★★★★

Very stylish in the Pierro manner raspberry, cassis, cedar, smoked meats in vanilla creme brulee oak aromas. The fruit is complex, fresh raspberry, flowers and canes building into integrated chocolaty flavours within the medium bodied, very long, supple, silky complex, an understated wine made stylish by extended post ferment skin contact.

Vintage	Rank	Drink	RRP	Vol Alc
2009	94	2036	$64.00	13.5%
2010	92	2022	$64.00	13.5%
2011	94	2022	$64.00	13.5%

PIKE AND JOYCE

One of the most amazing views from any cellar door with the folds and valleys of the Adelaide Hills spread like a table cloth at your feet. There is a restaurant and well worth the scenic drive to the highest cellar door in South Australia. Part of the Pike family which includes a brewery and cellar door in the Polish Hill River sub region of the Clare Valley.

Winemaker: *Neil Pike*
Open: *Thurs to Mon 11am–5pm, 730 Mawson Road, Lenswood*
Ph: *www.pikeandjoyce.com.au*

PIKE AND JOYCE
DESCENTE SAUVIGNON BLANC ★★★★

Positive and fresh aromas of pear drop, herbal, nettle into green capsicum with a nashi pear top note. The palate is light, lithe and refined. Energetic acidity in this fresh, drink young style with crisp dryness to the palate of snow peas and green herbs. Authentic to the height and location of the vineyard.

Vintage	Rank	Drink	RRP	Vol Alc
2015	92	2016	$24.00	13.0%

PIKE & JOYCE
ADELAIDE HILLS

PIKES WINES

Pikes Wines is in Polish Hill River, Clare's coolest sub-region which is adding an increasing array of interesting wines to its already reliable offering of very fine wines, including sangiovese and pinot grigio.

Winemaker: *Neil Pike*
Open: *Daily 10am–4pm, Polish Hill River Road, Sevenhill Via Clare*
Ph: *(08) 8843 4370   www.pikeswines.com.au*

PIKES
TRADITIONALE RIESLING ★★★★

The pine lime juicy fruit aromas of great riesling with immediate pleasing flavour fullness. In the mouth, structure and a superior style to many 2015 with a full palate and fine acidity. Most of this is drunk in seafood restaurants and it will sing for your seafood with the fullness that Pikes have delivers reliably for years.

Vintage	Rank	Drink	RRP	Vol Alc
2013	88	2015	$23.00	11.5%
2014	90	2015	$26.00	11.0%
2015	94	2019	$27.00	12.0%

Vintage	Rank	Drink	RRP	Vol Alc

PIKES
'THE MERLE' RIESLING ★★★★★

The swirling intensity of flowery lemon rind and pulp, sweet pink pickled ginger aroma elements only hint at the complexity in this wine. The palate has weight, length, evenness and plenty of personality with ripe "sweet lime" and great length.

2012	94	2022	$38.00	12.0%
2013	93	2022	$45.00	12.0%
2014	95	2033	$42.00	12.0%

PIKES
EASTSIDE CLARE VALLEY SHIRAZ ★★★★

The red fruits here are balanced with quality oak. In the mouth, red and black raspberry into black berry with freshness and medium length.

2012	93	2019	$30.00	14.5%
2013	88	2016	$30.00	14.0%
2014	87	2018	$28.00	14.0%

PIKES
EWP RESERVE SHIRAZ ★★★★★

Deep expression here with complex mocha chocolate oak and dark blackberry, meaty aromas. In the mouth the high intensity fruit starts red cherry with fine acidity highlighting the redder cherry fruits moving to blackberry in a complex web of unfolding red fruit flavours and finally mocha choco oak flavours. The finish is fresh acid, firm tannins, youthful and needs time to find its full expression.

2009	91	2024	$70.00	14.5%
2010	91	2033	$70.00	14.5%
2012	96	2039	$70.00	13.5%

PINDARIE WINES

Pindarie may be a new name but the faces are extremely well known around the Barossa, thanks to owner Wendy Allen's role as a grower liaison officer for Penfolds for 12 years. They have planted shiraz, sangiovese and tempranillo.

Winemaker: *Mark Jamieson*
Open: *Weekdays 11am–4pm, Weekends and Pub Hols 11am–5pm*
Gomersale & Rosedale Road, Tanunda
Ph: *(08) 8524 9019 www.pindarie.com.au*

PINDARIE

TSS TEMPRANILLO SANGIOVESE SHIRAZ ★★★★

Red wine gums, red geranium, red liquorice and some whole berry raspberry ferment in the aromas. In the mouth, bold seamless intense flavours of fresh raspberry and raspberry syrup flow into the middle palate and finish with liquorice and spice flavours.

2011	87	2016	$23.00	13.5%
2012	89	2018	$21.00	13.5%
2014	94	2018	$44.00	13.5%

PINDARIE

BAROSSA WESTERN RIDGE SHIRAZ ★★★★

This is in the zone for flavour and structure and over delivers on quality and price.
Compact powerful red with sweet fruit and a lick of dense tannins to decorate the dark olive, liquorice, plum, date and mineral flavours.

2008	88	2017	$23.00	14.5%
2010	88	2020	$23.00	14.5%
2012	89	2020	$25.00	14.5%

PIPERS BROOK VINEYARD

Pipers Brook is a pioneer of wine growing and one of the largest near Launceston with 200 hectares under vine. A long history, old vines, and high standards produce wines that have the typical freshness and delicacy of Tasmanian wine at the top end.
Winemaker: *Rene Bezemer*
Open: *Daily from 10am–5pm, 1216 Pipers Brook Road, Pipers Brook*
Ph: *(03) 6382 7527   www.kreglingerwineestates.com*

PIPERS BROOK

ESTATE PINOT GRIS ★★★★★

Pungent power house varietal aroma with intense white fruits, cinnamon, nutmeg and spiced pears. The acids are lime juice like and the palate is silky initially, subtle oak spiced and medium long.

2011	85	2013	$34.00	13.5%
2012	85	2017	$34.00	13.5%
2013	89	2022	$34.00	13.5%

PIPERS BROOK
VINEYARD RIESLING ★★★★★

Ripe fruits, pineapple crush, hints of rose with varietal spice leads to a full long ripe riesling palate. In the mouth a creamy element with floral and rose again then stone fruit flavours and a lemon acidity to finish. No worries as a drink young restaurant style where it will deliver honestly.

Vintage	Rank	Drink	RRP	Vol Alc
2012	94	2017	$28.00	13.0%
2013	90	2018	$28.00	13.0%
2014	86	2018	$34.00	13.0%

PIPERS BROOK
GEWÜRZTRAMINER ★★★★

Blossoms with lychee, fresh rose, spring garden and white fruits with poise and delicacy in the aromas. The palate pulls into gear with a good length. Rose, apple, green spices, fennel, lemon peel citrus in the chalky texture of the variety in youth. Interesting now and great in the future if you like the lychee rose water luxury that this variety brings with age.

Vintage	Rank	Drink	RRP	Vol Alc
2012	89	2016	$28.00	13.5%
2013	89	2018	$28.00	13.5%
2014	95	2029	$28.00	13.0%

PIPERS BROOK
ESTATE CHARDONNAY ★★★★★

Nectarine, subtle stone fruit aromas with the balance on fruit complexity and oak balance. The palate has good length and builds weight with fresh stone fruit front rolling with food friendly acidity into the firm structured finish. Honest cool climate chardonnay style.

Vintage	Rank	Drink	RRP	Vol Alc
2008	87	2013	$34.00	13.0%
2009	89	2015	$34.00	13.5%
2013	88	2018	$34.00	13.0%

Vintage	Rank	Drink	RRP	Vol Alc

POONAWATTA WINES

Poonawatta Wines come from an old vineyard in the Eden Valley where the region exhibits a steely grip on the local shiraz and riesling, making the wines distinctive and of high quality

Winemaker: Christa Dean, Reid Boward, Andrew Holt
Open: By Appointment Only
1227 Eden Valley Road, Flaxman Valley
Ph: 0448 031 880 *www.poonawatta.com*

POONAWATTA
THE EDEN RIESLING ★★★★★

Fresh cut pineapple, citrus into musk floral aromas with riesling racy acidity giving chalky texture with florals, bath salts, musk and good length. In youth the palate is a good regional varietal example of the flavours and textures.

Vintage	Rank	Drink	RRP	Vol Alc
2013	86	2017	$26.00	11.5%
2014	90	2019	$26.00	12.0%
2015	90	2026	$26.00	12.0%

POONAWATTA
FOUR CORNERS SHIRAZ ★★★★

Aromas are shy, blackberry, dark olive, smoked meat and peppery spices. In the mouth a surprise as the initially savoury smoked meats and shy fruits unfold into long ripe red cherry, red currant fruit flavours with fine tannins and fresh acidity. The best wine under this label I have seen.

Vintage	Rank	Drink	RRP	Vol Alc
2010	85	2016	$35.00	14.8%
2011	88	2018	$35.00	13.7%
2012	95	2020	$35.00	14.7%

POONAWATTA
THE CUTTINGS SHIRAZ ★★★★

Classy year, 2012 wears its cool season coat of pepper spice and smoked meats notes a plenty here. The core is ripe red fruits, twangs off into clove and smoked meats. The fruits bright fresh and long with the Eden valley elegance red current red cherry middle palate and finesse as the spice notes detail and decorate the finish.

Vintage	Rank	Drink	RRP	Vol Alc
2010	85	2020	$49.00	14.8%
2011	90	2018	$49.00	13.6%
2012	93	2022	$49.00	14.6%

POONAWATTA
THE 1880 SHIRAZ ★★★★

The local shiraz is picked four to six weeks after the Barossa giving more nuance and personality with regional raspberry, sage and spice flavours. Lovely expressions of different years can be found here with a common thread of succulent richness within the riper spectrum of regional flavours. Dates and prunes, black cherry aromas lead to an intense experience with deep set full bodied generous silky ripe tannins that coat the mouth with black fruit and black liquorice that linger long, full bodied and soft finishing.

Vintage	Rank	Drink	RRP	Vol Alc
2008	92	2022	$80.00	15.0%
2009	89	2024	$80.00	14.9%
2010	90	2022	$85.00	14.7%

PORT PHILLIP ESTATE

Port Phillip Estate in the Mornington Peninsula is one of the landmark cellar doors with a restaurant. It is also home to Kooyong QV. They are powering on with wines that revel in their varietal personality under the current winemaker.
Winemaker: *Sandro Mosele*
Open: *Daily 11am–5pm, 263 Red Hill Road, Red Hill South*
Ph: *(03) 5989 4444 www.portphillipestate.com.au*

PORT PHILLIP ESTATE
RED HILL CHARDONNAY ★★★★

Always interesting and complete, these wines have their subtle chardonnay fruits with the volume turned up, linked into oat meal, vanilla white butter and flint. Generous and full, this is enough for most chardonnay drinkers. Appealing tension and complexity between ripeness and savoury with a generous, full and commanding middle palate and a firm well defined finish. Loves a feed.

Vintage	Rank	Drink	RRP	Vol Alc
2012	93	2020	$35.00	13.5%
2013	94	2020	$35.00	13.5%
2015	90	2018	$34.00	13.0%

| Vintage | Rank | Drink | RRP | Vol Alc |

PORT PHILLIP ESTATE
RED HILL PINOT NOIR ★★★★
A strong colour leads to appealing concentrated fruit and spices with raspberry, strawberry, brown spices and mocha oak all working in harmony. The palate has fabulous strawberry fruit length and evenness with very well judged winemaking adding support and not dominance to the overall coherence with persistence of red fruit on the long even finish.

2012	88	2016	$38.00	13.5%
2013	90	2022	$40.00	14.0%
2014	94	2026	$38.00	13.0%

PORT PHILLIP ESTATE
SHIRAZ ★★★★
Cold fried onion like reduction, hence the need for a decant to open the wine up. The palate is well constructed, silky medium bodied tannins and medium long with roasted meats dark savoury flavours.

2008	89	2013	$30.00	14.0%
2009	88	2013	$38.00	13.0%
2013	85	2017	$38.00	13.5%

PRESSING MATTERS
Pressing Matters is a 2002 planting of 2.9ha of Riesling and 3.7 ha of Pinot Noir with very low yields and home to some of Australia's most delicious sweet wines. Displaying purity of riesling varietal fruit, lusciousness and wonderful balance. The dry rieslings are generous and elegant and show the greatness to come from the Coal River in the future.
Winemaker: Paul Smart
Open: By Appointment Only, 665 Middle Tea Tree Road, Tea Tree
Ph: 03 6268 1947 *www.pressingmatters.com.au*

PRESSING MATTERS
R9 RIESLING ★★★★★
Full of floral fruit, pretty white nectarine with appealing lychee floral top notes and a classic edge of cinnamon spice, much like the classic German wines. The palate is full, integrated, seamless and long, with rich fruited lychee lemon zest that gives ripe flavour intensity. The sugar carries the flavours

Vintage	Rank	Drink	RRP	Vol Alc

and the white stone fruits sit at the finish with mouth-watering acidity. Fabulous balance and interest with lingering flavours.

2014	94	2020	$33.00	10.9%
2014	94	2020	$33.00	10.9%
2015	96	2029	$33.00	11.9%

PRESSING MATTERS
R69 RIESLING ★★★★★

This is a remarkable balancing act showing intensity with delicacy. Aromas are very intense focused riesling aromas with a tropical top note, white peach intensity and a creamy ripe smooth sweet palate. This has a nectar quality-sweet not syrupy luscious ripe stone fruits very long in the mouth with deep powerful flavour and a lemon sherbet clean finish.

2011	94	2020	$33.00	10.0%
2013	90	2022	$33.00	10.4%
2015	94	2025	$33.00	10.4%

PRESSING MATTERS
R139 RIESLING 375 ML ★★★★★

Stylish balance showing intensity without heaviness; fresh and dried apricot into lemon citrus. The palate is honeyed texture luscious texture bright lemon citrus fruits up front, pineapple, ripe white peach with length. Purity, freshness and concentration and pretty much unique to the vineyard.

2009	95	2027	$30.00	9.5%
2010	93	2030	$30.00	9.2%
2015	96	2024	$30.00	10.1%

PRIMO ESTATE VINEYARDS

Primo Estate is a family-owned producer with flair and some brilliant and different styles. Its landmark cellar door in McLaren Vale is home to stylish and original wines from a former dux of the Roseworthy winemaking course showing that good taste and talent do run together.

Winemaker: *Joe Grilli*
Open: *Daily 11am–4pm, McMurtrie Road, McLaren Vale*
Ph: *(08) 8323 6800* *www.primoestate.com.au*

PRIMO ESTATE
LA BIONDINA ★★★★

Big punchy pineapple lime fruits with plenty of personality. The tropical flavours are juicy, ripe middle palate, full flavoured with zippy acidity. A fabulous flavourful casual glass of wine with friends.

2014	88	2016	$16.00	12.0%
2015	89	2017	$16.00	12.0%
2016	88	2017	$17.00	12.0%

PRIMO ESTATE
JOSEPH D'ELENA PINOT GRIGIO ★★★★

This is exuberant, balanced citrus and spice riesling-like into lush pear and perfume lifted aromas. The palate is grigio with more flavour weight than many; juicy fruited, silky textured, mid-weight and friendly roundness with medium length.

2014	95	2017	$30.00	13.0%
2015	89	2017	$30.00	13.0%
2016	89	2018	$30.00	12.0%

PRIMO ESTATE
IL BRICCONE SHIRAZ SANGIOVESE ★★★★

As always a very approachable complex style ready to drink on release. Liquorice, dark fruits, stewed plums and cedar with a slightly elevated glycerol ripe soft palate that floods the front. Grainy tannins and rancio from the oak add to the secondary spectrum flavours.

2012	90	2019	$25.00	14.5%
2013	86	2019	$25.00	14.5%
2014	87	2017	$25.00	14.5%

PRIMO ESTATE
JOSEPH NEBBIOLO ★★★★★

Aromas are brooding black fruits and balsamic hoi sin, dark tobacco with a subtle cedar caramel oak leading to a ripe fruited varietal more Barabaresco style than Barolo palate. Starts medium bodied, stays even, long finely tannic, very much at the plush end of this

Vintage	Rank	Drink	RRP	Vol Alc

variety. Fleshy fruit start showing youth with rich balsamic fruit flavours into red cherry and longer savoury oregano dried dark spices, framed with driving acidity with very even palate weight. Drinks well on release.

2013	91	2062	$80.00	14.5%
2014	92	2023	$90.00	13.5%

PRIMO ESTATE
JOSEPH MODA CABERNET MERLOT ★★★★★

Complex aromas of rose, floral evolving into cedar, anise, black currant and dried cranberry, crushed dried herbs into meat stock. The palate is full bodied, elegant and long run by concentrated fruits and velvety tannins, billowing through the middle palate with finely wrought black fruits woven long holding with oak spice dried herbs to the finish.

2012	90	2020	$75.00	15.0%
2013	96	2028	$80.00	15.0%
2014	94	2025	$90.00	14.5%

PRIMO ESTATE
JOSEPH LA MAGIA BOTRYTIS RIESLING TRAMINER ★★★★

Ginger orange dried flower aromatics and lively appeal. In the mouth intense, fresh richly fruity balanced bright acids luscious and fresh, bright and long.

2008	90	2013	$25.00	11.0%
2009	89	2013	$25.00	11.0%
2013	92	2019	$30.00	11.0%

PRINCE ALBERT VINEYARD
Prince Albert is a two-hectare Geelong-area vineyard with excellent soils planted solely to pinot noir, and certified organic by the Organic Vineyards Association of Australia, producing appealing wines.
Winemaker: *David Yates*
Open: *By Appointment Only,*
90–100 Lemins Road, Waurn Ponds
Ph: *(03) 5241 8091*

PRINCE ALBERT
PINOT NOIR ★★★★

A solid fruit oak intensity greets the nose. Wild Greek oregano oak meets ripe red Australian pinot cherry fruits. The plush palate shows well grown varietal sweet fruit and up front silky fruit tannins with intense oak tannin length. The oak is dominating the ripe berry fruits in youth. Drink after 2017.

Vintage	Rank	Drink	RRP	Vol Alc
2011	87	2019	$32.00	13.5%
2012	90	2022	$42.00	14.5%
2013	88	2023	$56.99	14.3%

PRINTHIE WINES

Printhie is the largest family-owned winery in Orange. They produce delicious medium-bodied wines with the region's fresh fruit flavours and gentle tannin texture. Their new winemaker has made a positive impact.
Winemaker: *Drew Tuckwell*
Open: *Mon to Sat 10am–4pm, 489 Yuranigh Road, Molong*
Ph: *(02) 6366 8422* *www.printhiewines.com.au*

PRINTHIE
MCC CHARDONNAY ★★★★★

Aromas are complex and diverse showing a weave of winemaking lees, fruity white nectarine, complex oak spice and Belgian white butter aromas. The youthful 'still to come together' palate has medium weight fruit, piquant acidity with vanilla oatmeal complex with bergamot and herbal tea.

Vintage	Rank	Drink	RRP	Vol Alc
2012	91	2018	$35.00	13.5%
2013	93	2018	$35.00	13.0%
2014	88	2018	$35.00	12.5%

PRINTHIE
MCC SHIRAZ ★★★★★

Mocha choc chino oak spice, blue berry and black fruits with a high level of complexity. A blanket of oak flavours over a mattress of soft tannins with the black fruits providing silky sheets on the medium length fruit.

Vintage	Rank	Drink	RRP	Vol Alc
2012	92	2022	$35.00	13.5%
2013	92	2022	$35.00	14.5%
2014	89	2018	$35.00	13.5%

Vintage	Rank	Drink	RRP	Vol Alc

QUEALY
Quealy and Balnarring Vineyard is Kathleen Quealy, an original thinker who, with husband Kevin McCarthy, drive T'Gallant. This reincarnation offers a delightfully different take on the future of our white wines.

Winemaker: Kathleen Quealy
Open: Daily 10am–5pm at Merricks General Wine Store, 62 Bitten Dromana Road, Balnarring
Ph: 03 5983 2483 *www.quealy.com.au*

QUEALY
POBBLEBONK ★★★★★

A boost in colour and complexity, along with the term "field blend" on the label, are notable changes in 2012. Youthful closed aromas, with apple, pear and apricot muscat that are more lactic savoury than fruity in 2013. The palate is crisp, tight and youthful, with very zesty acidity and apple pear citrus fruit. An appealing middle palate texture hints at the development to come, with very fresh crisp acidity to finish.

2010	91	2015	$25.00	12.5%
2011	87	2014	$25.00	12.3%
2012	93	2017	$25.00	13.2%

QUEALY
MUSK CREEK PINOT GRIS ★★★★

Winemaker Kath Quealy could be called the queen of pinot gris with this bargain priced wine showing the regal perfume and refinement in acid balance giving clear precision and fullness of flavour. Could be a big almost bronze colour with complex aromas, but that is just the start, struck flint note leads and lift these often anonymous aromas. Funky winemaking hits a beat here with savoury wild ferment top notes. The palate has fleshy apricot, saffron, and almond weight sits and stays in the middle mouth. Round creamy texture complete lingering ripe pears. Shows that the empress has plenty of clothes, to rephrase a popular wine quote.

2012	90	2017	$35.00	13.7%
2014	92	2018	$32.00	14.3%
2015	94	2018	$25.00	14.5%

QUEALY
MUSK CREEK PINOT NOIR ★★★★

A lovely aroma with fresh raspberry fruit citrus rinds and incense spices from oak, like a negroni in a nice way. Svelte elegance sweeps into your mouth; silky tannins smooth their way across your mouth, gentle strawberry fresh fruits and oak spices weave in without intruding to add length from oak spices and tannins.

Vintage	Rank	Drink	RRP	Vol Alc
2010	88	2016	$45.00	13.3%
2012	94	2023	$35.00	13.5%
2015	91	2019	$40.00	13.9%

QUEALY
SEVENTEEN ROWS PINOT NOIR ★★★★★

Sightly sinister Pinot aromas, like Sympathy for the Devil by the Rolling Stones with dark stalk aromas, smoked meats and dark chocolate backing up to varietal strawberry, subtle musk fruit with whole bunch web of brown spice in support. The palate is tight, silky savoury, focused seamless ripe tannins, toned berry fruits in the middle with a herbal tea edge from oak before the red fruits return. Just a pup.

Vintage	Rank	Drink	RRP	Vol Alc
2010	89	2020	$50.00	13.0%
2011	84	2017	$50.00	12.5%
2013	90	2020	$70.00	13.5%

QUEALY
TURBUL FRIULANO ★★★★

Funkster colour indicates wine with modernist leanings yet fresh and fruitful. This smells exotic- in a positive way- blossom, ripe lemon, barley sugar confectionary, feijoa and rain forest honey. The palate is sleek, creamy and energetic with myriad exotic subtle confectionary fruits, purple, yellow and red with lemon rind.

Vintage	Rank	Drink	RRP	Vol Alc
2012	90	2016	$25.00	12.7%
2013	90	2018	$35.00	12.5%
2014	92	2018	$35.00	12.5%

| Vintage | Rank | Drink | RRP | Vol Alc |

RAVENSWORTH

Ravensworth is a quietly emerging Canberra region vineyard and winery based in Murrumbateman. Bryan's experience with food and beverage and wine retail shows in his wine styles. Someone to watch as the quality steadily increases.
Winemaker: *Bryan Martin*
Open: *No Cellar Door, 312 Patemans Lane, Murrumbateman*
Ph: *(04) 1702 8335 www.ravensworthwines.com.au*

RAVENSWORTH
SANGIOVESE ★★★★★

A mix of forest floor and briar, with shy cherry fruits and peppery brown spices adding to the tapestry. Medium-bodied, ripe red cherry fruits with delicacy, medium long varietal cherry flavours and Italian-like tannins in youth to finish. Needs a decant as a young wine.

2010	90	2016	$21.00	14.0%
2011	86	2016	$23.00	13.0%
2012	88	2018	$23.00	13.0%

RAVENSWORTH
THE GRAINERY MARSANNE ★★★★

This is one of the hidden secrets of NSW wine value. With its fragrant blossom and honey suckle and a hint of white pepper. Medium bodied and brightly citrusy in the middle, with honeysuckle and candied fruit, firm and long fresh flavours and lingering deliciously.

2009	88	2013	$22.00	13.0%
2010	90	2013	$21.00	14.0%
2011	90	2016	$20.00	12.0%

RAVENSWORTH
MURRUMATMAN SHIRAZ VIOGNIER ★★★★

Excellent colour, with a bright ruby rim. Blackberry, floral, apricot and spice notes, with a peppery savoury edge. The palate has good construction of just-ripe fruit flavours, with a viognier lift. The tannins are firm in the middle palate and need a little time to soften and unlock the blackberry fruit. Drink after 2015.

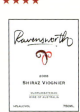

Vintage	Rank	Drink	RRP	Vol Alc
2009	93	2020	$30.00	14.0%
2010	91	2017	$30.00	14.0%
2012	90	2022	$30.00	13.5%

REDMAN
Redman has been true to its name for over 100 years, producing Coonawarra red wines of note. Recent quality has been exciting and wines have maintained their ability to age without swinging too far towards the modern fashions of high alcohol and oak.
Winemakers: Bruce, Malcolm and Daniel Redman
Open: Weekdays 9am–5pm, Weekends and Pub Hols 11am–4pm
Riddoch Hwy, Coonawarra
Ph: (08) 8736 3331 www.redman.com.au

REDMAN
SHIRAZ ★★★★
The traditional Redman shiraz was light in colour and texture and moderately tannic while modern Redman shiraz is peppery and spicy, with a dense raspberry, requiring time to develop.

2008	89	2017	$23.00	14.8%
2009	89	2020	$23.00	14.8%
2010	87	2018	$23.00	14.2%

REDMAN
CABERNET SAUVIGNON ★★★★★
No doubt about the varietal here, with black currant, black currant flowers and subtle leafy fruits. In the mouth, fresh fruit length and youthful flavours and long, with old-school austere Bonox meaty tannins and hidden fruit. Time is the answer. Drink in 2019.

2010	86	2020	$34.00	14.4%
2011	85	2018	$34.00	12.5%
2012	90	2029	$34.00	13.7%

REDMAN
CABERNET SAUVIGNON MERLOT ★★★★
A traditional style of Coonawarra oak, cabernet herbs and leaf. Subtle berry fruit leads to a high acid, short, hot evolved palate with meat stock soya flavours.

Vintage	Rank	Drink	RRP	Vol Alc
2008	85	2013	$36.00	15.0%
2009	91	2019	$36.00	14.5%
2010	79	2016	$35.00	14.5%

REDMAN
THE REDMAN ★★★★★
Created to celebrate the Redman centenary, this is a six-year-old wine on release from cabernet shiraz merlot, with subtlety and a lot of good quality tannins and richness.

Vintage	Rank	Drink	RRP	Vol Alc
2003	90	2018	$70.00	14.0%
2004	92	2019	$70.00	14.0%
2005	91	2020	$70.00	14.0%

RICHARD HAMILTON
Richard Hamilton draws on some extremely old vines within its 50 hectares of mature McLaren Vale vineyard. Shared winemaking with Leconfield brings the talented Paul Gordon into play. An old name playing a new game and focusing on keeping alcohol down.
Winemakers: *Paul Gordon and Tim Bailey*
Open: *Daily 11am–5pm*
Cnr Main and Johnston Roads, McLaren Vale
Ph: *(08) 8323 8830* *www.leconfieldwines.com*

RICHARD HAMILTON
'CENTURION' OLD VINE SHIRAZ ★★★★★
This wine has won 7 gold medals and looks worthy of more. The fruit does the talking here and the cool sea breezes of McLaren Vale really help this vineyard. Fresh blackberry and olive tapenade aromas. The palate is alive, waltzing across the tongue. The tannins are smooth, slick and really long, refined and focused. Totally in unison with the blackberry and dark plum fruit. Lively and energetic, this wine has a great presence and easy to drink now.

Vintage	Rank	Drink	RRP	Vol Alc
2012	89	2028	$75.00	14.0%
2013	95	2014	$75.00	14.5%
2014	96	2024	$75.00	14.5%

| Vintage | Rank | Drink | RRP | Vol Alc |

RICHMOND GROVE

Richmond Grove has a well-earned reputation for being a solid producer across a wide range of varieties, often capable of ageing up to five years. Reliable and safe, they continue to deliver outstanding value and contemporary quality.
Winemaker: *Steve Clarkson*
Open: *Daily 10.30am–4.30pm, Para Road, Tanunda*
Ph: *(08) 8563 7303* *www.richmondgrovewines.com*

RICHMOND GROVE
LIMITED RELEASE WATERVALE RIESLING ★★★★

Fine aromas, with subtle stone fruit leading to a ripe, long mouthful of Riesling. Lime lemon sherbet flavours with evenness and appeal. Will age well.

2011	94	2024	$23.00	11.6%
2012	90	2022	$23.00	12.2%
2013	90	2023	$23.00	12.0%

RICHMOND GROVE
LIMITED RELEASE ADELAIDE HILLS CHARDONNAY ★★★★

Appealing, mid-weight Adelaide Hills fruit, with an oak balance. Apple and stone fruit aromas lead to a medium full palate, with richness up front and a layer of oak texture contributing subtle honey caramel background. The finish is medium long.

2008	89	2011	$22.00	14.0%
2011	87	2014	$23.00	12.5%
2012	88	2016	$23.00	13.0%

RICHMOND GROVE
BAROSSA SHIRAZ ★★★

A very tidy regional wine for mid-week drinking but not excessive. Dusty, earthy spiced plum fruit aromas herald a faithful rendition of regional rich fruit, with soft tannins and chewy dark chocolate oak to finish.

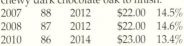

2007	88	2012	$22.00	14.5%
2008	87	2012	$22.00	14.6%
2010	86	2014	$23.00	13.4%

| Vintage | Rank | Drink | RRP | Vol Alc |

RINGBOLT
Ringbolt is a Margaret River vineyard recently acquired by Yalumba. They have invested in developing the style and the results are showing a steady improvement, from leafy cabernet to riper fruit flavours.
Winemaker: *Peter Gambetta*
Open: *No Cellar Door* **www.ringbolt.com**

RINGBOLT
CABERNET SAUVIGNON ★★★★★
The aromas are in the Margaret River with a savoury leafy Bournville cocoa and cedar, oregano element that says cabernet and MR. The palate is very correct regional varietal style with appealing dark fruit flavours, a youthful balance of firm fine tannins, very long, even and quite elegant with lingering dark berry fruits and a floral finish.

2010	90	2013	$25.00	13.5%
2011	93	2012	$25.00	14.0%
2012	92	2020	$27.95	14.0%
2013	92	2020	$28.00	13.5%

RINGBOLT
21 BARRIQUES CABERNET SAUVIGNON ★★★★★
The aromas are framed by a quality balance with delicacy. Dark berry, mulberry, black currant and mint. The palate is youthful with tannins that are trim and slightly drying today. Very full in the middle palate, no donuts here. Complex black fruit and a very refined length. Black currant wine gums on the finish that makes this very good value for money. A very popular choice in Canada.

| 2010 | 96 | 2020 | $37.95 | 13.1% |
| 2012 | 95 | 2028 | $38.00 | 14.0% |

ROBERT CHANNON

Robert Channon is an urbane winery in the Granite Belt with high standards that will challenge southerner's perception of white wines from Queensland. Good pinot gris as well.

Winemaker: Paola Cabezas
Open: Monday, Tuesday, and Friday 11am–4pm and Weekends 10am-5pm, 32 Bradley Lane, Stanthorpe
Ph: (07) 4683 3260 www.robertchannonwines.com

ROBERT CHANNON
VERDELHO ★★★★★

In need of a decant to blow the funk way. Custard apple, caramel pie crust varietal marzipan meringue note. The palate has oily weight, creamy well-knit full flavours and texture with the custard apple through to pineapple top notes. A very enjoyable ripe glass of wine with power. Tropical fruit salad with a glace cherry on top.

Vintage	Rank	Drink	RRP	Vol Alc
2012	87	2015	$27.50	12.5%
2013	83	2015	$27.50	13.0%
2015	94	2019	$28.00	13.5%

ROBERT CHANNON
RESERVE CHARDONNAY ★★★★★

The toffee like lees notes of honeyed yellow peach aromas with savoury dried herbs and an oak like edge are a feature of the complex chardonnay fruit style of this property. The mid-weight middle palate fruit is peaches, honey and a fresh acidity that holds the palate and medium long flavours.

Vintage	Rank	Drink	RRP	Vol Alc
2007	92	2011	$35.00	13.5%
2009	90	2012	$35.00	13.5%
2015	86	2017	$25.00	12.0%

| Vintage | Rank | Drink | RRP | Vol Alc |

ROBERT STEIN WINES
Robert Stein Wines is part of the resurgence of Mudgee wineries based on old vines (these were planted in 1976) and new ways of thinking. Vintage motorcycle collection and a covered BBQ space.
Winemaker: *Jacob Stein*
Open: *Daily 10am–4.30pm, Pipeclay Lane, Mudgee*
Ph: *(02) 6373 3991 www.robertstein.com.au*

ROBERT STEIN
MUDGEE RESERVE RIESLING ★★★★

Grapefruit mineral and lemon aromas; this is indeed a "reserved" wine. The palate is a classic understated style, with long, lean, age-worthy, apple, citrus and tight flavours that need time to unlock.

2011	89	2013	$30.00	11.0%
2012	86	2015	$30.00	11.0%
2013	88	2018	$30.00	11.0%

ROCHFORD WINERY
The Rochford Winery in the Yarra Valley has a showcase property with a restaurant and vineyards in the valley and the Macedon Ranges.
Winemaker: *Marc Lunt*
Open: *Daily 9am–5pm,*
Cnr Hill Road and Maroondah Highway, Coldstream
Ph: *03 5962 2119 www.rochfordwines.com.au*

ROCHFORD
MACEDON RANGES
CHARDONNAY ★★★★★

Bright, lemon-boiled fruit and tight, light medium-bodied texture, with lots of oak nuances. The 2010 is a little gem.

2009	86	2013	$22.00	13.0%
2010	90	2014	$22.00	13.5%
2011	88	2015	$29.00	12.5%

ROLF BINDER
Rolf Binder was established in 1955, with 250 acres of vines in the Barossa. One of the most interesting winemakers who can be found one Saturday a month behind the cellar door bar and who still enjoys it. Producer of full-bodied rich red wines with a growing reputation.
Winemakers: *Christa Deans and Rolf Binder*
Open: *Mon to Sat 10am–4.30pm and Sundays of long weekends*
185 Stelzer Road, Tanunda
Ph: *(08) 8562 3300 www.rolfbinder.com*

ROLF BINDER
HEINRICH SHIRAZ ★★★★★

This is a little bottler with sweet rose, leather and dark plum aromas, wrapped in appealing chocolaty oak. The palate has a lovely texture driven by grenache lyricism. It's silky, long generous and soft, not excessively full bodied. Has berry flavours, yet is rich, satisfying and long, with more iodine earthy flavours on the finish.

| 2009 | 92 | 2016 | $35.00 | 13.5% |
| 2010 | 92 | 2020 | $35.00 | 13.5% |

ROSEMOUNT
With a team of experienced winemakers and drawing on McLaren Vale vineyards, Rosemount has revived its reputation with a string of excellent wines in recent years. The wines have become more refined. Many vintages from the 1990s are still drinking well, particularly Balmoral, Mountain Blue and Show Reserve Shiraz. The love hate relationship with the new owners continues with them closing the McLaren vale cellar door in June 2016.
Winemaker: *Matt Koch*
Open: *No Cellar Door*
Ph: *(08) 8323 6220 www.rosemountestate.com*

ROSEMOUNT ESTATE
BALMORAL SYRAH ★★★★★

Classic McLaren Vale liquorice and olive tapenade make their mark on this wine, along with some black cherries and deeply spiced oak. The oak finish on this wine needs some time to soften on this vintage.

Vintage	Rank	Drink	RRP	Vol Alc
2012	95	2035	$74.99	14.0%
2013	95	2038	$74.99	14.0%
2014	92	2027	$74.99	14.0%

ROSEMOUNT
GSM ★★★★

This wine has a great presence and intensity, but is not heavy. Liquored with raspberry, cranberry and white pepper spice. Full bodied rich red and medium tannin intensity with long lingering red fruits and a tidy fresh finesse to the finish.

Vintage	Rank	Drink	RRP	Vol Alc
2012	95	2027	$39.99	14.0%
2013	96	2028	$39.99	14.0%
2014	94	2023	$39.99	14.0%

ROSNAY ORGANIC

Rosnay has a 20-hectare vineyard and olive grove near Cowra. They were the first organic and biodynamic vineyard in the area. Their wines are unfined with minimal filtration and low sulphur. Recent releases have been more focused and vibrant.

Winemaker: *Sam Statham*
Open: *By appointment only. Rivers Road, Canowindra*
Ph: *(13) 0076 7629* *www.rosnay.com.au*

ROSNAY ORGANIC
GRAND-PERE SHIRAZ MATARO ★★★★

A very complete medium full bodied wine with youthful freshness that is virtually irresistible as a young wine. Starts out red fruit aromas with a top note of lush red fruit ripeness and underlying umami savoury meaty dried rosemary offering both ripeness and fresh balance. The palate has a dive right in quality with front palate silky red fruits rush the palate with a more subtle longer slower mineral quality showing in the drying medium intense tannins

Vintage	Rank	Drink	RRP	Vol Alc
2013	92	2019	$30.00	14.0%
2014	91	2026	$30.00	13.0%
2015	94	2023	$30.00	14.0%

ROSS HILL

Ross Hill Vineyard is a family run and sustainable operation established in 1994 by Peter and Terri Robson, with son James and his wife Chrissy now taking over the reins. The mature vineyard is planted at a high altitude that carries through into the wines including Chardonnay, Pinot Gris and Sauvignon Blanc, Pinot Noir, Shiraz, Cabernet Franc and Cabernet Sauvignon. Winemaker since 2008 Phil Kearney is doing a fabulous job.

Wine maker: Phil Kearney
Open: *Daily 10.30am–5pm, 134 Wallace Lane, Orange*
Ph: *(04) 0014 2005 www.rosshillwines.com.au*

ROSS HILL
PINNACLE SERIES CABERNET SAUVIGNON ★★★★★

Extraordinary fragrance that you can wait years to find in a wine with the classic floral cabernet sauvignon top aroma notes of violets, blue berry, and red currant. Often these aromas do not follow through; here the playful energy is excellently executed. Tip of tongue silky tannins, gliding silky satin mouth feel, blue berry cool fruits cranberry into boysenberries splashed in rose water. Effortlessly fine tannins. Drink young to catch the magic.

Vintage	Rank	Drink	RRP	Vol Alc
2012	90	2020	$40.00	13.9%
2013	91	2018	$40.00	14.5%
2014	96	2018	$40.00	13.6%

ROSS HILL
ORANGE NSW

ROSS HILL
PINNACLE SERIES CABERNET FRANC ★★★★★

Intense, brooding fruit notes blue berry, mints and oak spice aromas. Very fine tannins, a savoury line wed to blue fruits, middle palate fullness and width of flavour with an appealing complexity between berry fruit and smoked meats savoury and finishes firm with oak adding length.

Vintage	Rank	Drink	RRP	Vol Alc
2013	90	2016	$40.00	14.5%
2014	92	2019	$40.00	13.9%

ROSS HILL
ORANGE NSW

Vintage	Rank	Drink	RRP	Vol Alc

ROSS HILL
PINNACLE SERIES SAUVIGNON BLANC ★★★★★
An interesting take on the variety with a spring blossom floral like quality to the aromas, flavours thanks to the delicate hands off style. Floral into honeydew melon, fresh quince subtleties and finesse. The palate is clean, long and lightly woven fruit and acidity with flavours that will make you think of the first sniff of orchards blooming in spring.

2013	90	2016	$30.00	12.9%
2014	90	2016	$30.00	12.6%
2015	91	2018	$30.00	12.3%

ROSS HILL
ORANGE NSW

ROSS HILL
PINNACLE SERIES SHIRAZ ★★★★★
Ripe shiraz, blackberry, camphor with dark spices of nutmeg and black pepper tell you it's cool climate shiraz. The fruits are very ripe and juicy giving a lot of fruit sweetness initially. Wed to oak, medium long.

2012	94	2022	$40.00	14.5%
2013	93	2024	$40.00	14.5%
2014	92	2022	$40.00	14.1%

ROSS HILL
ORANGE NSW

RYMILL COONAWARRA
Rymill Coonawarra is a family winery producing a distinctive style made exclusively from grapes grown on their own Coonawarra terra rossa vineyards. These have improved, now the former assistant winemaker has taken over. French trained, she has a flair which shows in the increased freshness, subtlety and refinement in their wines.
Winemakers: *Sandrine Gimon and Federico Zaina*
Open: *Daily 10am–5pm, Riddoch Highway, Coonawarra*
Ph: *(08) 8736 5001 www.rymill.com.au*

RYMILL
'MC2' MERLOT CABERNET FRANC CABERNET SAUVIGNON ★★★★
Dark berry and leafy, with vanilla butterscotch and smoky oak notes on the nose. In the mouth, this has a bright fruit note up front, a very elegant touch to the fruit and oak, with a good line of persistent ripe red fruit. Medium bodied and fresh to finish.

2010	90	2016	$19.95	14.0%
2012	92	2017	$21.50	14.0%
2013	89	2018	$21.50	14.0%

RYMILL COONAWARRA
SHIRAZ ★★★★

Complexity, with intensity of blackberry primary fruit and savoury aromas with cardamom, white pepper, thyme and butterscotch. The palate is a well-knitted ripe blackberry, toasty dark chocolate oak, and subtle fresh herbs on the finish, in a big, middle-palate intense wine.

Vintage	Rank	Drink	RRP	Vol Alc
2010	90	2022	$30.00	14.5%
2012	94	2035	$30.00	14.5%
2013	91	2018	$30.00	14.5%

RYMILL
CABERNET SAUVIGNON ★★★★

Well composed aromas and balance of olive and black currant fruit, with tight complexity. The elegant palate has very fine-grained tannins and an appealing middle palate texture and flavour intensity.

Vintage	Rank	Drink	RRP	Vol Alc
2010	94	2027	$33.50	14.5%
2012	94	2034	$33.50	14.0%
2013	91	2021	$33.50	14.5%

RYMILL
THE SURVEYOR CABERNET SAUVIGNON ★★★★★

For full bodied red lovers comes this fresh, modern tight, showing Coonawarra dark fruits, violets, leafy olive cabernet fruits amidst oak spice, cedar and warm white butter. The ripe fruit flavour length and structure comes with restraint supported by fine grained tannins that bridge front to back of the mouth. The oak provides a whisper of a support sitting in the back of the finish.

Vintage	Rank	Drink	RRP	Vol Alc
2010	93	2030	$80.00	14.5%
2011	Not made			
2012	Not made			
2013	94	2035	$90.00	14.5%

Vintage	Rank	Drink	RRP	Vol Alc

S.C.PANNELL
S.C. Pannell is Steve and his wife, Fiona. A former chief winemaker for Hardys, Steve has struck out on his own, with a string of high-quality wines. A dream win in the Melbourne Wine Show in 2015, as he opened his new cellar door, is just one more success for this hard-working great palate.
Winemaker: *Steve Pannell*
Open: *Daily 11am–5pm, 60 Olivers Road, McLaren Vale*
Ph: *(08) 8323 8000 www.pannell.com.au*

S.C. PANNELL
NEBBIOLO ★★★★★
The varietal's orange rim is typical. Sweet, flowery chicken stock and liquorice tar aromas, while the palate is new age, with good fruit length and ripe red and flowery fruit flavours. The tannins gain their puckering force towards the finish, which is umami rich, with layers of different cooked and smoked meats.

Vintage	Rank	Drink	RRP	Vol Alc
2007	92	2022	$55.00	14.0%
2009	89	2019	$55.00	14.0%
2010	94	2019	$55.00	14.0%

S.C. PANNELL
SYRAH ★★★★★
Black cherry and blackberry ripe fruit richness in salami and smoked oak aromas. A lovely, artisanal palate of silky tannins to start and a bit of whole-bunch fresh red cherry front palate, with vibrant acidity and a fresh blue berry fruited middle palate, with floral top notes and appealing stemmy tannin tension that holds the boldness of the middle palate fruit in check. A very dramatic transition from silky front palate tannins to chalky back palate. Drink after 2017.

Vintage	Rank	Drink	RRP	Vol Alc
2010	92	2020	$33.00	14.0%
2012	93	2026	$33.00	14.0%
2013	96	2026	$33.00	14.0%

SALTRAM ESTATE

Saltram Estate wines are showing ripe, rich flavours with freshness in several different varietal styles and price points that offer interest and personality. The key is shiraz, grenache and cabernet, with newer varieties such as fiano and tempranillo that create a worthwhile distraction. The cellar door is well worth a visit, with a very professional team–show their wines.
Winemaker: Shavaughn Wells
Open: Daily 10am–5pm, Murray Street, Angaston
Ph: (08) 8561 0200 *www.saltramwines.com.au*

SALTRAM ESTATE
MAMRE BROOK CABERNET SAUVIGNON ★★★★
A big balanced wine with dark oak notes containing bay leaf, dark olive, mulberry, ripe rhubarb and date black fruit. In the mouth, this is a wine needing bottle age to soothe the tight fine tannins which support very good fruit length with a firm silky texture. Finishes cranberry cassis.

2011	86	2016	$37.99	13.5%
2012	90	2020	$37.99	14.0%
2013	90	2022	$37.99	14.5%

SALTRAM ESTATE
THE JOURNAL SHIRAZ ★★★★★
The Barossa has a unique take on shiraz and this wine has it in spades, with its cola, tar, dark-cooked plums, malt and dark spice. Generous and soft in the mouth, with classic line and length of ripe tannins and ripe flavours. Cola, dark chocolate similar to Lindt, blueberry and long, minerally tannins to finish. In time, this wine will show a decisive mineral finish ideal for roast meats.

2006	88	2016	$174.95	14.5%
2009	90	2019	$174.95	14.5%
2010	92	2020	174.95	14.5%

Vintage	Rank	Drink	RRP	Vol Alc

SALTRAM ESTATE
No. 1 SHIRAZ ★★★★★

Complex coconut, chocolate oak with marachino cherry, cinnamon, mint and black plum unfurl to blackberry, graphite and spice on the palate. No. 1 has the abundance of full, rich and smooth personality of a wine that is assured of its place. The mocha finish does not overwhelm, attesting to some smart large format oak work. The tannins are shapely and will help keep this wine fresh for the years to come.

Vintage	Rank	Drink	RRP	Vol Alc
2009	94	2027	$99.99	14.5%
2010	95	2035	$99.99	14.5%
2012	95	2030	$99.99	14.5%

SANDALFORD

Sandalford is one of the Margaret River's more significant producers. They have recently undergone a complete reorganisation based on their old vineyards under the Estate Reserve. A tidy range of wines flow from its long-serving highly experienced winemaker with bright fruit in a modern style.

Winemaker: Hope Metcalf
Open: Daily 10am–5pm, 3210 West Swan Road, Caversham
Ph: (08) 9374 9374 *www.sandalford.com*

SANDALFORD
PRENDIVILLE RESERVE CABERNET SAUVIGNON ★★★★★

Black currant cassis and cedar aromas with a savoury mineral marmite edge. In the mouth, pure back currants, fine grained tannins and good middle palate length of ripe almost black currant and black plum fruits with medium intensity fine grape tannins and moderate oak.

Vintage	Rank	Drink	RRP	Vol Alc
2009	90	2017	$90.00	14.3%
2013	91	2018	$90.00	14.5%
2014	88	2022	$90.00	14.5%

SANDALFORD
ESTATE RESERVE CHARDONNAY ★★★★
A little bit of everything here, fresh cut white pear and granny smith apples oak and a fleshy up front pear fruits palate with near universal affordable appeal.

2013	86	2015	$35.00	13.5%
2014	93	2018	$35.00	13.5%
2015	92	2018	$35.00	12.5%

SANDALFORD
ESTATE RESERVE SHIRAZ ★★★★★
The focus on the fruit here also shows youthful restraint, needing time to fill out. Black berry, black plum and raspberry fruit aromas with spicy sausage, smoked meats and gentle low key oak. This is a mouth filling medium-full bodied bright and fresh fruited ripe red and black berry fruited flavours with a savoury finish and toned tannins to tidy and dry the finish.

2012	88	2017	$35.00	14.5%
2013	92	2023	$35.00	14.0%
2014	92	2024	$35.00	14.5%

SANDALFORD
ESTATE RESERVE CABERNET SAUVIGNON ★★★★
Very consistent; blackcurrant and some stalky and olive notes. Full-bodied cellaring style, with deep-set fruit, low oak and a solid core of fine tannins to finish. In 2010, lots of black currant/mint/cassis with a lick of mocha coffee oak. Needs time to build complexity.

2008	90	2015	$35.00	14.5%
2009	88	2016	$35.00	14.5%
2010	92	2010	$35.00	14.5%

Vintage	Rank	Drink	RRP	Vol Alc

SAVATERRE WINES

Savaterre wine is born in the vineyard and Keppell Smith near Beechworth has done a great job as parent with his 1997 close planted (7,500 vines per ha) pinot noir and chardonnay at a cool 440 metres. As mid wife, each year he ensures the birth of high quality wines thanks to low crops and early picking dates. Currently a self-described "baby sitter" he raises exceptional pinot noir, chardonnay and shiraz to great effect.
Winemaker: Keppell Smith
Open: No Cellar Door PO Box 337 Beechworth
Ph: (03) 5727 0551 www.savaterre.com

SAVATERRE
CHARDONNAY ★★★★★

The first vintage under screw cap and showing an uplift in finesse, brightness and refinement that will take longer to come around. This wine has generosity, style and the wonderful balance of ripeness and freshness for chardonnay. The palate is classic lees aided richness, with a lovely creamy texture, and layers of flavour with pear and apple and fine acidity. Nougat like flavours will show more in time.

Vintage	Rank	Drink	RRP	Vol Alc
2008	91	2013	$75.00	13.5%
2009	94	2015	$70.00	13.5%
2010	92	2014	$70.00	13.5%

SAVATERRE
PINOT NOIR ★★★★★

Fleshy in style with lushness in the aroma and texture, starts out blueberry, strawberry, 5 spice, almost soya aromas. The cherry strawberry raspberry palate is ripe with lots of dense almost thick soft tannins with lowish acidity making it generous and full while the finish is dry and food friendly.

Vintage	Rank	Drink	RRP	Vol Alc
2008	86	2013	$75.00	13.5%
2009	86	2014	$70.00	13.5%
2010	93	2016	$70.00	13.5%

SCARBOROUGH

Scarborough is a Hunter Valley-based, family owned winery with a deep understanding of the area and its history, including owning the old Lindemans Sunshine vineyard site. A diverse range of coloured label chardonnay and semillons based on different soils, including the remarkable Blue Label Chardonnay are offered. Their excellent hill-top cellar door is the ideal showcase for them.
Winemakers: *Ian Scarborough and Jerome Scarborough*
Open: *Daily 9am–5pm, 179 Gillards Road, Pokolbin*
Ph: *(13) 0088 8545 www.scarboroughwine.com.au*

SCARBOROUGH
YELLOW LABEL HUNTER VALLEY CHARDONNAY ★★★★

By releasing with bottle age this is a harmonious style with good colour and mellow aromas of lees, yellow and citrus fruit and back ground oak- all with balance. The palate is tightly woven complex creamy flicks, the oak switch settles back into creamy white fruits with plenty of glycerol keeping the texture flowing and the oak purrs away in the background.

2011	88	2016	$23.00	13.5%
2012	90	2017	$23.00	13.5%
2013	88	2017	$28.00	13.5%

SCHILD ESTATE

Schild has extensive vineyards in the southern Barossa, around Lyndoch and are proving themselves across a range of price points. The winery's Moorooroo is liquid Barossa history, having been planted by Jacob Gramps, brother of -- you guessed it -- Jacobs Creek.
Winemaker: *Scott Hazeldine*
Open: *Daily 10am–5pm, 1 Lyndoch Valley Road, Lyndoch*
Ph: *(08) 8524 5560 www.schildestate.com.au*

Vintage	Rank	Drink	RRP	Vol Alc

SCHILD ESTATE
MOOROOROO SHIRAZ ★★★★★

It's a beast of a wine. Dark fruits, roasted red peppers, dark chocolate roasted coffee oak and some wild herbs with oregano and the smell of bushy shrubs takes you on a journey with the first sniff. The palate is silky smooth and long, with earthy elements, silky textured tannins and savoury cooked plum fruit. For big red lovers. Harmonious, with power as part of the personality.

Vintage	Rank	Drink	RRP	Vol Alc
2008	94	2018	$90.00	14.5%
2010	93	2019	$90.00	14.5%

SCHILD ESTATE
BEN SCHILD RESERVE SHIRAZ ★★★★★

From Roland Flat in the southern end of the Barossa where red fruits and finer tannin intensity prevails. Polished aromas with complexity from classy oak integration with red cherry, fruitcake with spices, dried raspberry, black plum, date with an appealing tobacco oak. The polish extends to the palate with fruit ripeness keeping it fresh raspberry and dried raspberry on a feather doona of tannins floating through your mouth very full and deep in the middle palate with the Southern Barossa red fruit flavours never straying and lasting many seconds after. Drinks fabulously on release. You can see why Jacob Gramps chose this spot for his winery.

Vintage	Rank	Drink	RRP	Vol Alc
2009	90	2017	$35.00	14.5%
2011	90	2016	$35.00	14.5%
2012	96	2022	$40.00	14.8%

SCORPO WINES

In a very short space of time Scorpo has built a reputation for making good wine from their Mornington Peninsula vineyard located halfway between Port Phillip Bay and Westernport.
Their close planted vineyard has pinot noir, chardonnay, pinot gris and shiraz many of which are released with bottle age as deliberate part of the style.
Winemaker: *Paul Scorpo*
Open: *By Appointment Only,*
23 Old Bittern Dromana Road, Merricks
Ph: *(03) 5989 7697* ***www.scorpowines.com.au***

| Vintage | Rank | Drink | RRP | Vol Alc |

SCORPO
ESTATE GROWN PINOT GRIS ★★★★★

Funky savoury wild ferment, flint, white fruits, older oak spice notes and oatmeal with the house style. Subtle building fullness in the middle palate medium bodied style spiced white fruit, nashi pear and minerals and a warm finish.

2011	93	2014	$35.00	13.5%
2014	93	2018	$35.00	13.5%
2015	90	2019	$35.00	14.0%

SCORPO
ESTATE GROWN CHARDONNAY ★★★★★

Hold back this chardonnay for 3–4 years, except the Aubaine to allow for its development. This wine is well worth seeking out. From a vineyard at 100m altitude on the warmer end of the region. The aroma is savoury and subtle oak, lees and wild yeast. The weave of fruits and acids allows the plump fruits to hold with a long acidity building and holding creamy yoghurt white butter with a long line of acid to finish.

| 2010 | 96 | 2020 | $42.00 | 13.5% |

SCORPO
AUBAINE CHARDONNAY ★★★★★

Drink young style with savoury and pretty fruits, fresh food friendly acidity and no new oak creates a laid back subtle savoury style with fresh white nectarine middle palate flavours, medium weight and long. Inner city restaurant style.

| 2014 | 90 | 2017 | $35.00 | 13.0% |

SEPPELT

Seppelt is the Victorian arm of Treasury Wine Estates, with the mature Drumborg vineyard in Henty. Add in a tapestry of old shiraz vineyards around Great Western and talented winemakers for 15 years and you have an essential cellar dweller in shiraz, riesling, chardonnay and sparkling shiraz.
Winemakers: *Adam Carnaby and Melanie Chester*
Open: *Daily 10am–5pm, 36 Cemetery Road, Great Western*
Ph: *(03) 5361 2239 www.seppelt.com.au*

Vintage	Rank	Drink	RRP	Vol Alc

SEPPELT
ST PETERS SHIRAZ ★★★★★

The fresh cherry fruit here is rather beguiling, being topped with black pepper and some delicate dried herbs. Curvy, long and polished. You don't have to have food to enjoy this wine, nor do you have to cellar it. Although, it does make a great cellar candidate.

Vintage	Rank	Drink	RRP	Vol Alc
2012	95	2052	$65.00	14.5%
2013	95	2030	$80.00	13.5%
2014	93	2027	$79.99	14.0%

SEPPELT
JALUKA CHARDONNAY ★★★★★

Everything you want in a modern Australian Chardonnay; more fruity than previous years with fresh citrus and youthful vitality creating balance and harmony. In the mouth, fresh, fine, medium bodied middle palate flavours of grapefruit into subtle white butter oak. Seems to be no malo and will take some time to come round.

Vintage	Rank	Drink	RRP	Vol Alc
2012	91	2018	$26.90	12.5%
2013	95	2020	$26.90	13.5%
2015	92	2020	$26.99	12.5%

SEPPELT
DRUMBORG RIESLING ★★★★★

One truly spectacular Australian Riesling with rose, sherbet and lime bath salts. Lovely finesse ripe fruited palate, exceptionally complex layers of citrus, lemon blossom and feijoa flavours with a fine mineral lime edge to the zingy zesty crisp acidity and chalky finish. A subtle, really unique regional style with a pristine tight structure making for great aging ability yet early drinking pleasure as it has residual sugar rather than sweetness that allows you to drink it young. 40% is from a 50 year old planting, 25% is whole bunch press and solids giving deft balance of fruit and acid.

Vintage	Rank	Drink	RRP	Vol Alc
2015	95	2035	$39.99	12.5%

SEPPELT
DRUMBORG CHARDONNAY ★★★★★
A contemplative wine style with a distinctive toasty oak dimension. Aromas include creamy lees with finesse to the nectarine fruit. The savoury oak and acid edges hem the lovely cool length and subtle flavours. Exceptional mid palate weight and length of fruit in a silky envelope that glides long and flicks into oak flavours.

| 2012 | 94 | 2022 | $40.00 | 13.0% |
| 2013 | 95 | 2020 | $40.00 | 13.0% |

SEPPELT
ORIGINAL SPARKLING SHIRAZ ★★★★★
Appealing aromas of black berry raspberry and Chinese five spice into cinnamon spice. The plate is fresh up front ripe berries with length and very youthful balance and structure of fruit and acid. These wines keep well.

| 2012 | 92 | 2019 | $28.99 | 13.0% |
| 2013 | 94 | 2022 | $26.99 | 13.0% |

SEPPELTSFIELD
Seppeltsfield is a sight to behold, visit, taste and marvel. Once one of the mightiest wineries in the world, it is now in the hands of a dedicated team, with industry quiet achiever, Warren Randall. The source of the only commercial release, 100-year-old wine in the world, as well as an increasingly complex and stylish group of table wines.

Winemaker: *Warren Randall*
Open: *Daily 10am–5pm, Seppeltsfield Road, Seppeltsfield Barossa*
Ph: *(08) 8568 6217 www.seppeltsfield.com.au*

SEPPELTSFIELD
CENTENNIAL COLLECTION PARA TAWNY ★★★★★
Price quoted is for 100ml, also available as 375ml for $1500.00. Stirring Christmas pudding after the fruits have been steeped; raisin, brandy to start then timeless intensity, panaforte, dates, burnt toffee, espresso coffee and dark spices form the swirling amalgam of aromas in the glass. A sip reveals a ball of intense front to middle palate flavours, cinnamon spice flows into clove in the mouth and lingers with

Vintage	Rank	Drink	RRP	Vol Alc

feisty intensity lingering with dark chocolate espresso coffee bitterness and burnt dark toffee.

1909	99		$500.00	21.3%
1914	100		$500.00	21.3%
1915	99		$500.00	21.3%

SERAFINO
Serafino Wines in McLaren Vale brings together a group of talented and experienced wine people and 300 acres of vine to offer excellent shiraz, while the Bellisimo releases are well crafted examples that highlight new-to-Australia varietals such as sangiovese and lagrein.
Winemaker: *Charles Whish*
Open: *Daily 10am–4.30pm, Kangarilla Road, McLaren Vale*
Ph: *(08) 8323 0157 www.serafinowines.com.au*

SERAFINO
McLAREN VALE SHIRAZ ★★★★★

Classic, ripe, intense regional dark fruits, with a sophisticated balance. The palate balances ripeness with richness, to hold onto the middle palate fruit fullness. Very good length of fresh flavours, running red cherry to blackberry, with a tapenade savoury element on the finish.

2010	90	2017	$25.00	14.5%
2012	91	2022	$25.00	14.0%
2013	92	2017	$25.00	14.0%

SERAFINO
BELLISSIMO LAGREIN ★★★★

Dark chocolate, blueberry and fresh plum aromas lead a palate that is silky with a long full bodied sweep of fine grained tannins. Intense blueberry, blackberry, dark chocolate flavours in the middle palate and a refreshing sweep of acidity to close the flavours and texture.

2010	90	2018	$18.00	14.0%
2012	90	2018	$18.00	14.0%
2013	92	2018	$18.00	13.0%

SERAFINO
BDX CABERNET MERLOT ★★★★
BDX is Bordeaux in short hand and the dark cocoa, cherry berry fruit with a leafy edge is in the zone for the name. In the mouth, it is fruit not oak that drives it, with fresh red and dark berry length. The fluidity holds its flavours and drives straight down the tongue with even red and black fruit and nimble freshness on the finish.

Vintage	Rank	Drink	RRP	Vol Alc
2011	90	2018	$26.00	14.5%
2012	92	2024	$26.00	14.0%
2013	90	2018	$26.00	14.0%

SEVENHILL CELLARS
Sevenhill Cellars is a significant historic property and tranquil Jesuit winery established in the Clare Valley in 1851. They have lifted the quality and diversity of their wines in recent times.

Winemakers: *Brother John May and Liz Heidenreich*
Open: *Weekdays 9am–5pm, Weekends and Pub Hols 10am–5pm, College Road, Sevenhill*
Ph: *(08) 8843 4222 www.sevenhillcellars.com.au*

SEVENHILL
INIGO RIESLING ★★★★
A good call on the winemaking side by picking early in what was a fast ripening year. Rose, talc, floral bouquet, subtle baked apple and cinnamon spice, perfumed in the classic riesling. Powerful nose for such a subtle palate. Finesse, ripe medium length, soft acidity, gentle apple spice and cinnamon middle palate.

Vintage	Rank	Drink	RRP	Vol Alc
2013	86	2016	$20.00	11.5%
2014	93	2019	$20.00	12.0%
2016	90	2022	$22.00	10.5%

SEVENHILL
ALOYSIUS RIESLING ★★★
Maturing aroma with a sweet lime edge, rather than brown lime. In the mouth, exotic white fruits, juicy balanced, sweet fruited, long fine acids and lovely, even flavours from tip to back. Complex white fruits and citrus on the finish. A step up on previous vintages.

Vintage	Rank	Drink	RRP	Vol Alc
2008	7	2014	$29.00	12.5%
2009	90	2014	$35.00	11.5%
2010	94	2025	$35.00	11.5%

SEVENHILL
INIGO SHIRAZ ★★★★

Shiraz likes chocolaty oak and the marriage gives a fleshy presence to the aroma. The fruits are ripe cherry, fruit sweetness and chocolaty oak make the sum more than the individual components plush round tannins silky mid palate morello and cherry weight with dried spices to close.

Vintage	Rank	Drink	RRP	Vol Alc
2013	84	2017	$25.00	15.2%
2013	84	2017	$25.00	15.2%
2014	90	2020	$28.00	14.5%

SEVENHILL
INIGO CABERNET SAUVIGNON ★★★★

Really bright and fresh, quite different, vivid red fruits appealing leafy cabernet with a rosemary like edge. The herbal leafy note is picked up on the palate which has lovely cabernet structure running long and fine, not fat, with appealing cranberry minty black current fruits. A real step up.

Vintage	Rank	Drink	RRP	Vol Alc
2012	88	2018	$25.00	15.5%
2013	92	2018	$22.00	14.0%
2014	93	2022	$28.00	13.5%

SEVENHILL
ST IGNATIUS CABERNETS ★★★★★

These wines are stepping up in freshness and quality. Very well made complex layers of cabernet black fruits with violets, black currant shades of mulberry, cooked raspberry and date on the edge. The fruit is long; tannins from soft to grainy, linear flavours gather momentum, black currant in the middle palate mulberry, malbec juicy and a savoury lift at the end.

Vintage	Rank	Drink	RRP	Vol Alc
2010	91	2020	$40.00	14.2%
2012	88	2019	$40.00	15.0%
2013	93	2019	$40.00	14.5%

SEVENHILL
INIGO MERLOT ★★★★
Spot on harvesting captures the upfront charm of the variety really well with the classic perfume and structure. Aromas lead with a floral top note, ripe blue berry fruits and plum conserve fruit aromas with dark spice. The palate captures the silky fine tannin floral middle palate mouth filling qualities of merlot. The flavours are juicy and generous with layers of fruit violets into blue berry and plum and very fine tannins.

Vintage	Rank	Drink	RRP	Vol Alc
2013	90	2016	$25.00	14.5%
2014	92	2019	$28.00	14.5%

SEVILLE ESTATE
Seville Estate is a small Yarra Valley vineyard which has been revitalised in recent years, making the most of its old vine assets. Difficult to find, but worth the effort.

Winemaker: Dylan McMahon
Open: Daily 10am–5pm, 65 Linwood Road, Seville
Ph: (03) 5964 2622 *www.sevilleestate.com.au*

SEVILLE ESTATE
CHARDONNAY ★★★★★
Appealing charm, generosity without heaviness, ripe white nectarine fruited and well backed with oak. The palate is creamy and very long, sinuous, sophisticated balance with good harmony and length, balanced long. Bright and great drinking from the get go.

Vintage	Rank	Drink	RRP	Vol Alc
2013	90	2016	$36.00	13.0%
2014	91	2018	$36.00	13.0%
2015	90	2020	$36.00	13.5%

SEVILLE ESTATE
RESERVE CHARDONNAY ★★★★★
Graceful complexity so seamless unpicking fruit from winemaking is redundant, the effect is citrus savoury oat meal layers with a lovely length and balance. The palate is so fine it is almost understated with flickers of citrus fruits, white fruit and well-judged oak spice that adds a cinnamon spice to the finish,

Vintage	Rank	Drink	RRP	Vol Alc

long and layered to the lingering finish. The classic power with elegance of chardonnay.

2013	94	2023	$70.00	13.0%
2014	94	2022	$70.00	13.0%
2015	95	2024	$70.00	13.0%

SEVILLE ESTATE
OLD VINE RESERVE PINOT NOIR ★★★★★

The weave of aromas here is strawberry, French crème de fraise liqueur, cedar oregano delicate oak notes. The fruits are detailed, flavours and texture, delicate sustained with silky tannins and ethereal balance, not trying to hard the fruits have strawberry length and finesse and fine tannins to close.

2013	90	2020	$70.00	13.5%
2014	Not made			
2015	95	2025	$70.00	13.5%

SEVILLE ESTATE
OLD VINE RESERVE SHIRAZ ★★★★★

Bright colour leads to aromas with fine white pepper spice, truffles, dark and red fruits. The palate has gravitas, intensity, incredible tightness, acidity adds length and youth it lands wide and stays medium bodied to run long with fine tannin s savoury smoked spice Drink after 2018.

2012	93	2026	$60.00	13.0%
2013	94	2023	$70.00	13.5%
2014	94	2028	$70.00	13.0%

SHAW & SMITH

Shaw & Smith is a stylish and perfectionist winemaking partnership between Martin Shaw and Michael Hill Smith, MW. The renown of the releases goes well beyond Australia.

Winemakers: *Martin Shaw and Darryl Catlin*
Open: *Daily 11am–5pm, 136 Jones Road, Balhannah*
Ph: *(08) 8398 0500* ***www.shawandsmith.com***

SHAW & SMITH
SAUVIGNON BLANC ★★★★★

Meticulous vineyard management and hand picking helps retain the perfume of this variety although it nearly doubles the cost of wine making. It also explains this wine's continuing charm. Low cropping is another aspect that helps lower the ripeness at harvest offering subtlety, ripe restraint and purity of punchy pear drops, white fruits with the house style complexity. In the mouth ripe and round, not a NZ herb in sight, white fruits juicy ripe pears and apples in the middle palate and a food friendly finish.

Vintage	Rank	Drink	RRP	Vol Alc
2014	91	2016	$25.00	12.0%
2015	87	2017	$26.00	12.5%
2016	93	2019	$26.00	12.0%

SHAW & SMITH
M3 CHARDONNAY ★★★★★

Ripe and rich power with elegance showing white nectarine fruits, very subtle contributions of winemaker complexity lees, oak and wild ferment. The overall density and fruit concentration of the palate has length running textures along the tongue. The flavours start with creamy white fruits up front, middle palate citrus and firming on the finish layering vanilla oak and white fruits. Savoury wine making extending the finish.

Vintage	Rank	Drink	RRP	Vol Alc
2012	95	2016	$40.00	13.0%
2013	90	2018	$45.00	12.5%
2014	95	2019	$44.00	12.5%

SHAW & SMITH
SHIRAZ ★★★★★

This is another success from this company; sophisticated stylish fruit understated oak, lingering finish. The aromas are red fruits, distinctive thyme like green herb adds a grace note to the aromas, and there is mocha oak as well. In the mouth complex compact, subtle red fruits herbs and spice. The red fruits are red currant through to crunchy red cherry and the tannins remain fine-grained and even the full length of the palate with subtle back pepper spice notes to close.

Vintage	Rank	Drink	RRP	Vol Alc
2012	94	2019	$44.00	13.5%
2013	93	2023	$45.00	14.0%
2014	95	2024	$44.00	14.0%

Vintage	Rank	Drink	RRP	Vol Alc

SHAW & SMITH
PINOT NOIR ★★★★★

Gravitas, solid appealing strawberry into sweet rhubarb varietal red fruits and a stemmy note. The palate has an even length and fresh red fruit flavours on the silky middle palate. This has the varietal grace, medium weight and good length.

2012	92	2018	$45.00	12.5%
2013	94	2022	$45.00	12.5%
2014	90	2018	$45.00	13.0%

SHAW VINEYARD ESTATE

Shaw Vineyard Estate is at Murrumbateman, 30 minutes from Canberra and features a restaurant open Wednesday evenings to Sunday as well as quality wines drawn from their 33-hectare planting.

Winemaker: *Tony Steffania and Graham Shaw*
Open: *Wed to Sun 10am–5pm, 34 Isabel Drive Murrumbateman*
Ph: *(02) 6227 5827   www.shawvineyards.com.au*

SHAW VINEYARD ESTATE
ISABELLA RIESLING ★★★★

Good line and length of flavour. An off dry 16gms of residual, boiled lemon sweets and brown lime- typical of the region, with a long ripe palate and sweet lime fruits with a clean acidity on the finish.

2014	90	2018	$30.00	11.5%

SHINGLEBACK

Since 1998 the Davy family aim is to produce affordable, quality wines that express the rich ripe middle palate softness and generous flavours of McLaren Vale. They have been successful under the affordable "Red Knot" and more senior "The Gate"brand. Their focus is predominantly shiraz, with some cabernet, chardonnay and semillon.

Winemaker: *John Davey*
Open: *daily 10am–5pm, 3 Stump Hill Road, McLaren Vale*
Ph: *(08) 8323 9919   www.shingleback.com.au*

SHINGLEBACK
UNEDITED SHIRAZ ★★★★★
Ripe chocolatey black cherry and black berry pie fruits in the regional style without the appealing herbal elements of the 2012. The tannins are luscious, silky and very fine with enormous volume revealing middle palate liqueur and black berry flavours that firm showing interesting sage flavours and dry on the finish.

| 2012 | 92 | 2027 | $79.95 | 14.5% |
| 2013 | 94 | 2021 | $79.95 | 14.5% |

SHINGLEBACK
D BLOCK RESERVE CABERNET SAUVIGNON ★★★★★
Relatively closed aromas that will fill out in time with pretty red currant and black currant fruits with plenty of fresh life. Black tea, black olive and menthol aromas at the back. The fruit is ripe and tannins are slightly pithy with a dry drawing mouth feel that sets the fresh dark berry fruits off advantageously. The tannins will soften in time and the fruits will prosper. Drink after 2017.

| 2012 | 94 | 2022 | $55.00 | 14.5% |

SINGLEFILE
Singlefile were founded in 2007 by Phil and Viv Snowden, at Denmark in the Scotsdale Valley within the Great Southern region of Western Australia. The winery includes a diverse collection of mature vineyards in the Porongurup's, Mt Barker, Pemberton, Denmark and Franklin River. Their wines offer consistent quality as well as great value for the price.
Winemaker: Coby Ladwig and Larry Cherubino
Open: Daily 11am–5pm, 90 Walter Road, Denmark
Ph: (08) 9840 9749 www.singlefilewines.com

| Vintage | Rank | Drink | RRP | Vol Alc |

SINGLEFILE
SINGLE VINEYARD RIESLING ★★★★★

Elegant, lemony towards citrus and a touch of spice-almost ginger in the background. In the mouth the fruit flows with freshness, flavour and length, while the acidity takes a back seat.

2013	93	2020	$25.00	12.0%
2014	94	2028	$25.00	11.3%
2015	90	2020	$25.00	12.2%

SINGLEFILE
FUME BLANC SAUVIGNON BLANC ★★★★★

Exotic, lively, vigorous aromas with lychee and honey suckle musk leading to a clear, fresh palate with a clean honeysuckle line of flavours that linger delicately.

| 2014 | 94 | 2016 | $30.00 | 13.7% |
| 2015 | 90 | 2018 | $30.00 | 13.1% |

SMITH & HOOPER

Smith & Hooper is a vineyard in the Wrattonbully region, with similar red soil to that of Coonawarra. Part of the Hill Smith Family vineyards.
Winemaker: *Peter Gambetta*

Open: *Daily at Yalumba, 10am–5pm, Mt Pleasant-Angaston Road, Angaston*
Ph: *(08) 8561 3200 www.smithandhooper.com*

SMITH & HOOPER
CABERNET MERLOT ★★★★

Great value wine, with Coonawarra-esque quality. The ripe berry fruits are red currant and leafy; oak is a hushed whisper. In the mouth, well made, Sunday-lunch soft tannins and ripe fruit, weight with good length, supported by chocolaty oak. Well made, well integrated and complex with supple tannins and fresh, ripe fruit length.

2008	87	2014	$18.00	14.0%
2009	88	2014	$22.00	13.5%
2012	91	2017	$22.00	13.7%

SMITH & HOOPER
MERLOT ★★★
Mulberry and raspberry fruit aromas, with freshness and life. In the mouth, crunchy bright red fruits with good length of silky tannins, unfolding red cherry, red plum, rhubarb and raspberry. Middle palate intensity, warm on the finish with lingering fresh raspberry. Good food wine, like a Loire red, with low complexity and high intensity fruit.

2010	89	2015	$22.00	14.0%
2012	90	2017	$22.00	13.5%
2013	91	2018	$22.00	13.5%

SMITH & HOOPER
RESERVE MERLOT ★★★★★
Clean and fresh punnet of purple and blue berries, mulberry, fresh red plum and toast aromas. A palate that will please most with silky fine tannins, in an elegant medium bodied wine. Quite French in tannin style and flavour ripeness with rose, blackberry, vanilla, and plum fruits in the middle palate. An overall fresh ripe flavour profile and fine tannin length and black tea tannins. Very varietal in flavour, texture and shape. Carefully oaked to keep freshness. Value.

2012	90	2017	$27.00	13.5%
2013	95	2022	$27.00	14.0%

SONS OF EDEN
Sons of Eden draw on Eden and Barossa Valley fruit to produce wine-ripe fruit, supple generous flavours and richness.
Winemakers: *Simon Cowham and Corey Ryan*
Open: *By appointment only, Penrice Road, Angaston*
Ph: *(08) 8564 2363* *www.sonsofeden.com*

SONS OF EDEN
FREYA EDEN VALLEY RIESLING ★★★★
Fresh lemon riesling veering into pear and ripe grapefruit aromas. A well composed palate with fruit generosity delivering a good line of lemon pith and curd flavours into the middle palate. A touch of pear drop on the finish with overall substance and lingering lemony fresh fruit weight.

2012	92	2022	$22.00	12.0%
2013	90	2022	$25.00	12.0%
2014	91	2027	$25.00	12.0%

SONS OF EDEN
ZEPHYRUS BAROSSA SHIRAZ ★★★★★
Pretty fragrant, tarry, dark chocolate, dried herbs and liquorice leads to a ripe, silky, very lifted mix of petals and berry wrapped in silky dark fruited powdery tannins adding a silky freshness to the finish.

Vintage	Rank	Drink	RRP	Vol Alc
2010	87	2017	$35.00	14.5%
2012	90	2017	$35.00	14.5%
2013	89	2018	$35.00	14.5%

SONS OF EDEN
KENNEDY GRENACHE SHIRAZ MOUVEDRE ★★★★★
Mocha, sweet raspberry and darker spices with berry fruit are the back story in the nose. The palate unites well judged mocha oak and moderate tannins with ripe berry fruits so that it lands ripe raspberry and slips across the tongue. The finish springs up with a striking chord of raspberry chocolate liquorice flavours and tidy acid. Artfully picked and well made.

Vintage	Rank	Drink	RRP	Vol Alc
2011	91	2015	$22.00	14.0%
2012	90	2017	$25.00	14.5%
2013	92	2021	$25.00	14.5%

SONS OF EDEN
ROMULUS BAROSSA SHIRAZ ★★★★★
Fresh red plum and cherry fruits in the thyme edged, dark chocolate fruit aromas. The palate is open, fresh and long, more a ripe sweet fruited style with medium length and moderate tannins.

Vintage	Rank	Drink	RRP	Vol Alc
2010	90	2018	$60.00	14.5%
2012	90	2018	$70.00	14.5%
2013	89	2018	$70.00	14.5%

SONS OF EDEN
REMUS EDEN VALLEY SHIRAZ ★★★★★
Fascinating aromas spread across red cherry and herbal including curry leaf, cardamom herbs amidst brooding deep dark liquorice berry fruits with a viscous dark clinging colour appearance. The

tannins are soft and the fruits ripe. Generous red cherry and blackberry middle palate with a ripe generosity that runs long, mouth filling, ripe and subtly spicy.

2010	89	2019	$60.00	14.5%
2012	95	2018	$70.00	14.5%
2013	92	2018	$70.00	14.5%

SOUMAH
Soumah is a fast-rising Yarra Valley star, with Trattoria on site and a swag of great wines themed on Eastern France and Northern Italy. Good prices and quality across the range. One to watch closely, as their values align with the best thinking on many areas of wine.
Winemaker: *Scott McCarthy*
Open: *Weekdays 10am–5pm, Weekends 10am–6pm*
16 Hexham Road, Gruyere
Ph: *(03) 5962 4716 www.soumah.com.au*

SOUMAH
SINGLE VINEYARD CHARDONNAY ★★★★★
The honey vanilla classy oak and wed to ripe fruits that quickly turned savoury smoky wild yeast ferment flavours wed to white pear fruits up front grapefruits with taunt acid definition.

2011	90	2019	$38.00	12.0%
2013	94	2020	$38.00	12.7%
2014	91	2016	$38.00	13.1%
2015	90	2017	$38.00	13.0%

SOUMAH
SINGLE VINEYARD PINOT NOIR ★★★★
Vibrant aromas of cherry pie with vanilla pie crust oak. Drinking well on release with cranberry into strawberry red fruits and some citrusy elements on the medium length palate with a fresh acidity.

2013	94	2018	$33.00	13.3%
2014	90	2019	$33.00	12.4%
2015	90	2017	$38.00	13.0%

SOUMAH
SINGLE VINEYARD SAVARRO ★★★★★

The house style of white pear fruits with purity and graceful aromas. In the mouth a fleshy texture and white fruits then nougat middle palate which is quite creamy texture like very good pinot gris in texture until the finish when the nutty white fruits and spices clean the finish.

Vintage	Rank	Drink	RRP	Vol Alc
2014	90	2017	$28.00	12.5%
2015	91	2018	$28.00	13.3%

SPRING VALE
Spring Vale is a reliable, if tiny, vineyard whose wines are often found on quality wine lists. Their wines have clear varietal fruit with intensity and delicacy. They have a policy of re-releasing back vintages when they are mature.
Winemaker: *David Cush*
Open: *Daily 11am–4pm, 130 Spring Vale Road, Cranbrook*
Ph: *(03) 6257 8208 www.springvalewines.com*

SPRING VALE
PINOT GRIS ★★★

Generous, all-over style with wine gums and yellow fruits on the nose, fleshy upfront fruit weight, middle palate ripe pear, lemon zest and quite warm on the finish, with sweet pear fruit.

Vintage	Rank	Drink	RRP	Vol Alc
2012	88	2015	$28.00	13.4%
2013	91	2016	$28.00	13.4%
2014	90	2016	$28.00	13.8%

SPRING VALE
CHARDONNAY ★★★★

The fruit is the thing; fresh and lifted gentle orchard blossom and pear chardonnay aromas. The palate is gentle, smooth, creamy fresh white nectarine mid-palate, medium long and very regional in style.

Vintage	Rank	Drink	RRP	Vol Alc
2013	89	2017	$22.00	12.4%
2014	89	2016	$22.00	12.4%
2015	88	2014	$28.00	13.0%

Vintage	Rank	Drink	RRP	Vol Alc

SPRING VALE
RESERVE CHARDONNAY ★★★★

Layers of fruit with the hallmark subtle oak. Creamy yoghurt lees in a ripe deep palate, with creamy ripe white peach fruits in the middle. Good varietal intensity, aligned to silky texture and even length, thanks to subtle oak and food-friendly oak tannins to close the performance.

Vintage	Rank	Drink	RRP	Vol Alc
2011	92	2017	$40.00	13.4%
2012	91	2018	$40.00	13.4%
2013	92	2019	$40.00	12.7%

SPRING VALE
GEWURZTRAMINER ★★★★

Rose water, floral, very varietal with appealing purity and a lively lift. The palate has the texture of gris and the explosive middle palate floral punch with roses, lychee kept clean by fresh acidity.

Vintage	Rank	Drink	RRP	Vol Alc
2013	90	2017	$35.00	13.6%
2014	88	2017	$35.00	13.5%
2015	91	2020	$30.00	13.5%

SPRING VALE
PINOT NOIR ★★★★★

Strawberry, into cranberry fresh fruits, tobacco edged, ripe and intense and as generous as an old friends hug. The palate is tight, fresh, suggesting whole bunch and bright fresh strawberry into strawberry conserve middle palate and needs a year or two to get the tannins to soften and release more fruit. A chalky finish, delicate brown spice tidies the finale. Drink 2017 onwards.

Vintage	Rank	Drink	RRP	Vol Alc
2013	85	2016	$40.00	13.0%
2014	93	2023	$40.00	13.8%
2015	93	2020	$45.00	13.7%

SPRING VALE
MELROSE PINOT NOIR ★★★★★

Aromas are developed for a young wine, with cooked, fresh and candied cherry aromas and a dark spice element. In the mouth, up front lively fresh berry, whole bunch raspberry and red cherry middle palate, ripe intensity and medium long. Red wine drinker's pinot.

Vintage	Rank	Drink	RRP	Vol Alc
2012	88	2015	$22.00	13.4%
2013	85	2015	$22.00	13.4%
2014	88	2017	$22.00	13.5%

Vintage	Rank	Drink	RRP	Vol Alc

ST HALLETT
St Hallett is a well-established Barossa Valley maker, sourcing grapes from both valleys to produce stylish wines with more elegance and freshness than many in the region.
Winemakers: Stuart Blackwell and Toby Barlow
Open: Daily 10am–5pm, St Hallett Road, Tanunda
Ph: (08) 8563 7000 www.sthallett.com.au

ST HALLETT
EDEN VALLEY RIESLING ★★★★★

Getting toasty as a one year old this shows the honey and early maturity aromas quite quickly. The palate has great flavours of brown lime, a touch of chalky acid holds it long and it is quite full in the middle. Drink young and on the road to full maturity quite quickly.

Vintage	Rank	Drink	RRP	Vol Alc
2013	88	2019	$19.00	11.0%
2014	90	2024	$19.00	12.0%
2015	88	2018	$19.00	11.5%

ST HALLETT
OLD BLOCK BAROSSA SHIRAZ ★★★★★

Surprisingly aromatic wine. Red fruited into dark wine gums, red liquorice and menthol edged aromas. The plush tannins frame a medium full bodied intensity with length of fruits; raspberry, red cherry and black berry up front with middle plate fullness and fine grained tannins holding the length. A really good wine for the 2013, partly due to the increased Eden valley component and less overt oak.

Vintage	Rank	Drink	RRP	Vol Alc
2010	94	2033	$100.00	14.2%
2011	Not made			
2012	88	2022	$100.00	13.7%
2013	94	2025	$100.00	13.9%

ST HALLETT
BLACKWELL SHIRAZ ★★★★

For lovers of full bodied reds. Complex meaty edged, liquorice, dark berry fruits with oak spice. The palate is generous, soft, even, mid-weight full flavoured, flowing silky tannins with fresh red fruits and well-judged

Vintage	Rank	Drink	RRP	Vol Alc

oak contributing oak spice and dried herb. Best drunk to enjoy the youthful balance.

2012	95	2029	$38.00	14.5%
2013	89	2019	$38.00	14.5%
2014	93	2019	$38.00	14.5%

ST HUGO
After distinguished service under the wing of Orlando and then Jacobs Creek, St Hugo has evolved into its own stand-alone brand, with a Grenache Shiraz, a shiraz cabernet and the Coonawarra Cabernet Sauvignon. The standards are very high with new oak playing a role in supporting the fruit.
Winemaker: *Dan Swincer* ***Open:*** *Tasting available at Jacobs Creek Visitor Centre, Barossa Valley Way Rowland Flat*
Ph: *(08) 8521 3000* ***www.sthugo.com***

ST HUGO
CABERNET SAUVIGNON ★★★★★

Peppermint patty mint aromas come from the dawn of cabernet in Australia and it still appears heralding the complexity of Coonawarra. With side notes of spearmint, bay leaf and ripe aromas of blackcurrant, bramble and mulberry. The palate is so soft as to be huggable and so drinkable. Up front, soft tannins rim a lipid pool of dark berry fruits adding a subtle savoury and drying edge to the mocha, black currant and dark olive flavours.

2010	94	2030	$50.00	14.1%
2011	Not made			
2012	93	2035	$50.00	14.0%
2013	91	2025	$52.00	14.1%

ST JOHN'S ROAD
St John's Road is an affable, affordable, full bodied red drinker's winery. These wines are part of the middle ground of the Barossa where regionality, ripe flavours and value intersect. Full of interest their recently released single vineyard wines have been interesting and impressive across all styles.
Winemaker: *Phil Lehman*
Open: *No Cellar Door, Lot 100 Kapunda Truro Road, St Kitts*
Ph: *(08) 8232 8622* ***www.stjohnsroad.com***

Vintage	Rank	Drink	RRP	Vol Alc

ST JOHN'S ROAD
BLOCK 3 EBENEZER SHIRAZ ★★★★★

The fleshy blueberry, boysenberry, fruits, into an edge of white coffee are more welcoming than the equally intense Block 8, with the addition of a frame of smoked meats. The palate has concentrated fruit sweetness, high toned red fruits are almost luscious silky tannins, red fruits and a flicker of tapenade milk coffee oak. The chalky fine grape tannins add a contrast and set the high toned fruits.

| 2014 | 97 | 2027 | $38.00 | 14.5% |
| 2015 | 94 | 2035 | $38.00 | 14.5% |

ST JOHN'S ROAD
BLOCK 8 EBENEZER SHIRAZ ★★★★★

Vivid colour with a big, expansive aroma with a steep incline of intensity that layers liquorice and berry fruit from clean red cherry fruits into black berry with raspberry fruits offering the peak. The palate has form and depth. Firm earthy tannins and dark fruit flavours are the outer rings and concentric circles of the flavours. Fresh acidity and silky tannins create a safety net of tension to keep the flavour long and focused with lingering red fruits. The fruit richness mid-weight tannin balance is superb. Not over ripe or over made. Hands off winemaking in the right places.

| 2014 | 96 | 2026 | $38.00 | 12.7% |
| 2015 | 94 | 2034 | $38.00 | 13.4% |

ST JOHN'S ROAD
PEACE OF EDEN RIESLING ★★★★★

Very correct and fresh, citrus, lemon into floral overall bright nimble aromas. In the mouth, flavour, finesse, balance, appealing fruit and acidity with fine long ripe talc lemon fruit flavours and the lingers gentle ripe lemon fruits.

| 2014 | 92 | 2024 | $22.00 | 12.0% |
| 2015 | 93 | 2023 | $22.00 | 12.5% |

| Vintage | Rank | Drink | RRP | Vol Alc |

STANTON AND KILLEEN
Stanton and Killeen are sixth generation winemakers, making full-bodied Rutherglen wines with powerful, regional, dense ripe fruit and fleshiness, as well as one of our best vintage fortifieds from Portuguese varieties. Their shiraz durif blend is a bargain.
Winemaker: *Andrew Drum*
Open: *Mon to Sat 9am–5pm, Sun and Pub Holidays 10am–5pm*
440 Jack's Road, Murray Valley Highway, Rutherglen
Ph: (02) 6032 9457 *www.stantonandkilleenwines.com.au*

STANTON AND KILLEEN
DURIF ★★★★★

Black in colour, Christmas pudding, shortbread into rum and raisin with some aldehyde development to the aromas. Rich, dark, dried fruits are very up front with soft tannins and a ripe glace cherry core of flavours that finish savoury.

2009	90	2017	$33.00	15.0%
2010	Not made			
2011	82	2015	$35.00	12.5%
2015	85	2017	$35.00	14.8%

STANTON AND KILLEEN
THE PRINCE RESERVA TOURIGA NACIONAL TINTO CAO TINTA RORIZ ★★★★

Warm ripe notes, butter scotch and warm ripe black berry. The palate is different to most; ripe not over ripe with meaty linear tannins, fruit cake, dark cherry and marmite savoury with fine grained chalky tannins and a subtle deceptive structure that allows the dark fruits to linger. A great experience as it will change accents over the course of dinner.

| 2015 | 92 | 2020 | $45.00 | 13.8% |

STANTON AND KILLEEN
VINTAGE FORTIFIED ★★★★★

Brandy spirit lift, maturing to dark savoury fruits. Plum and blackberry jam leads to long, sweet oak-edged taut and savoury cola plum fruit. A leathery dry finish.

2005	93	2027	$30.00	18.5%
2006	92	2031	$30.00	18.2%
2007	88	2017	$35.00	18.0%

STARGAZER

Samantha is a Nomadic Kiwi. Based in the Hunter, she is a wine show chairman and passionate about wine quality. Formerly holding down a demanding position as the field officer for the Australian Wine Research Institute she ran seminars for winemakers to aid them improving wine quality. H9er stints at Tower Estate, and Wirra Wirra in South Australia, have been associated with increases in quality. In her "spare" time she produces riesling and pinot from Tasmania.
Winemaker: *Samantha Connew*
Open: *No cellar door, 1616 Broke Road, Pokolbin*
Ph: *(04) 0817 3335 www.stargazerwine.com.au*

STARGAZER
RIESLING ★★★★

Discretion and sophistication are the hallmark. Varietal without shouting with rose florals through quince into mineral and the dark spice of quality rielsing. In the mouth, medium body, ripe fruit and germanic balance, the acidity is laid back, elegant fine fruit with unravelling floral, attractive fruit balance and a gentle lemon pithy finish. For the technical minded it has the German dry wine balance where the sugar is lower than the sum of the total acidity.

2013	93	2018	$30.00	12.5%
2014	94	2024	$30.00	12.5%
2015	92	2019	$30.00	12.5%

STARGAZER
PINOT NOIR ★★★★

From a year with half the normal crop and tiny berry size comes this flavourful pinot. Fresh varietal strawberry; cooked and preserved, and dark spiced oak in the background from the larger oak. The flavours are ripe strawberry and taut raspberry with impeccable balance and deceptive concentration. Chalky finish.

2012	94	2020	$50.00	12.5%
2013	93	2024	$50.00	13.5%
2014	95	2024	$50.00	13.5%

| Vintage | Rank | Drink | RRP | Vol Alc |

STELLA BELLA WINES
Stella Bella Wines is a small vineyard in Margaret River, producing a range of very consistent quality wines. Stylishly packaged, they are as interesting to enjoy as their names – Stella Bella, Suckfizzle and Skuttlebutt – indicate.
Winemaker: Luke Jolliffe
Open: Daily 10am–5pm, 205 Rosa Brook Road, Margaret River
Ph: (08) 9758 8611 *www.stellabella.com.au*

STELLA BELLA
CHARDONNAY ★★★★★
Tight and youthful, the aromas are honey, caramel, barrel ferment and wild ferment. Fresh fruited rich Margaret river fruit flavours, winemaking has added a creamy core of barrel ferment, lees influence creamy texture and fruit complexity wrapped with the regional acidity. Very honest it shows the matrix of regionality in the acidity, varietal fruit favours with winemaking artful complexity.

2011	91	2019	$32.00	13.0%
2012	88	2015	$32.00	13.0%
2014	90	2017	$32.00	13.0%

STELLA BELLA SUCKFIZZLE
SAUVIGNON BLANC SEMILLON ★★★★★
Complex and funky wild ferment notes, tropical and passion fruit aromas. The palate is easy drinking with length and smoothness with the passion fruit flavours extending the finish.

2013	89	2016	$21.00	13.5%
2014	86	2016	$21.00	13.5%
2015	88	2017	$24.00	13.5%

STELLA BELLA
MARGARET RIVER SHIRAZ ★★★★★
Dark berry, earthy, salami and dark chocolate aromas mark this wine. In the mouth, ripe berry fruits, blackberry and dark chocolate oak against acid warmth in the mid palate and berry fruit that fades fast.

2009	90	2020	$27.00	14.5%
2010	92	2016	$27.00	14.5%
2011	84	2015	$27.00	14.0%

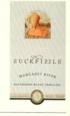

Vintage	Rank	Drink	RRP	Vol Alc

STELLA BELLA
CABERNET SAUVIGNON MERLOT ★★★★

Fruit bomb spicy appealing with ripe cabernet blackcurrant wed to cocoa oak creating a jammy intensity. The palate lands sweet fruit, fine grained tannins, pretty up front flavours and meaty.

2009	87	2014	$32.00	14.0%
2012	84	2015	$24.00	13.5%
2014	85	2016	$24.00	13.5%

STELLA BELLA
SUCKFIZZLE CABERNET SAUVIGNON ★★★★

Pure, complex, fresh and vibrant youthful aromas with the cabernet cool climate black olive tapenade and dark fruit with well-balanced oak seamlessly styling the aromas. Delivers up front with cabernet dark backcurrant leafy fruits, however, no drive to the fruit flavours and the tannins are very soft.

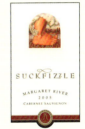

2008	89	2016	$55.00	14.5%
2009	93	2020	$55.00	14.0%
2012	90	2019	$55.00	13.5%

STONEY RISE

Stoney Rise on the Tamar River is the brainchild of Joe Holyman and was started in 2000 to produce wines that are food-friendly, complex and without too much oak, or over-ripe fruit characters. He also produces the smaller made Holyman qv range.

Winemaker: *Joe Holyman*
Open: *Thursday to Monday 11am–5pm,*
96 Hendersons Lane, Gravelly Beach
Ph: *(03) 6394 3678* ***www.stoneyrise.com***

STONEY RISE
TAMAR VALLEY PINOT NOIR ★★★★

Ripe, punchy primary berry and some beaujolias-like cherry shortbread oak. In the mouth, the fruit is ripe and sits well on the palate with bright strawberry. The tannins are a bit firm with citrus acidity and the wine needs food. More about the fruit than the variety. An interesting take on making wine with an Australian fruit profile.

Vintage	Rank	Drink	RRP	Vol Alc
2012	91	2017	$29.00	13.0%
2013	90	2026	$29.00	13.5%
2014	90	2019	$29.00	13.0%

STONEY VINEYARD
Stoney Vineyard is the other label of Peter Althaus, the perfectionist owner of Domaine A.
Winemaker: Peter Althaus
Open: Mon to Fri 10am–4pm, 105 Tea Tree Road, Campania
Ph: (03) 6260 4174 www.domaine-a.com.au

STONEY VINEYARD
SAUVIGNON BLANC ★★★★★

Discernible varietal and traditional style, with herbal, white apple varietal fruits. The freshness and fruit are cool, richly covering the long palate with subtle lychee, rose, spiced pear and stone fruit, plus fruit salad flavours with great weight. The finish is cut short. Drink fresh.

2011	87	2015	$35.00	13.5%
2013	91	2019	$35.00	13.5%
2014	90	2018	$35.00	15.0%

STONIER
Stonier winery in the Mornington Peninsula has significant vineyard holdings and has become perhaps the exemplar of the area's promise in pinot and chardonnay. Delicacy and understatement are part of the style. In recent vintages, the wines have gained in harmony and complexity at every price point; a remarkable performance. Excellent winemaking approach and use of regional fruit.
Winemaker: Mike Symons
Open: Daily 11am–5pm, 2 Thompsons Lane Merricks
Ph: (03) 5989 8300 www.stoniers.com.au

STONIER
SPARKLING CHARDONNAY PINOT NOIR ★★★★
Creamy white fruits with a polished seamless complexity in the aroma. The palate is very citrusy chardonnay; white fruits up front, good structure, a yoghurt ball of lees in the middle palate and a crisp finish. Not a bad drink and could be aged 18 months to soften the edges.

Vintage	Rank	Drink	RRP	Vol Alc
2009	90	2015	$30.00	11.5%
2010	92	2016	$30.00	13.5%
2011	94	2018	$30.00	12.5%

STONIER
CUVEE ★★★★★
Lovely exotic fresh and preserved strawberry aromas with complexity and subtle truffle, brioche and honey toast. The palate is silky and full with strawberry fruit mid palate and a very fine acidity to finish with a lingering strawberry fruit. It is fully mature and broadening.

Vintage	Rank	Drink	RRP	Vol Alc
2003	90	2010	$45.00	12.0%
2007	91	2013	$46.00	12.5%

STONIER
MORNINGTON PENINSULA CHARDONNAY ★★★★
Fresh cut ripe pear lift and surprisingly varietal purity with a lick of flint-like yeast complexity. Fresh fruit, medium bodied with pear and subtle oak to add a chewy dimension and firm acid to finish.

Vintage	Rank	Drink	RRP	Vol Alc
2012	88	2016	$25.00	13.5%
2013	90	2016	$25.00	13.5%
2014	93	2018	$25.00	13.0%

STONIER
RESERVE MORNINGTON PENINSULA CHARDONNAY ★★★★★
1400 dozen made from vineyards facing the cooler Bass Straight side of Mornington. Complex with fine French oak and winemaking inputs adding a creamy yoghurt layer which follows through on the palate with silky richness and complexity. Flavours of stonefruit and layered, creamy vanilla toast, peanut brittle and nutty fine fresh oak. A tidy clip of grip on the finish. Drink in 2015.

Vintage	Rank	Drink	RRP	Vol Alc
2010	92	2017	$45.00	14.5%
2011	92	2017	$45.00	13.0%
2012	94	2018	$45.00	13.5%

STONIER
KBS CHARDONNAY ★★★★★
Focus and concentration; a seamless web of honeyed almond, oatmeal and oak spice aromas. The palate is luxurious, concentrated and focused running excellent length and flawless texture holding the fruits complex and lingering honeyed flavours. If you like the richness then keep this a long time, otherwise drink in 5 years to catch the vibrancy.

2011	90	2016	$55.00	13.5%
2012	95	2017	$75.00	13.5%
2013	94	2024	$55.00	14.0%

STONIER
MORNINGTON PENINSULA PINOT NOIR ★★★★
Tight red fruits and subtle tobacco into sassafras aromas. The palate treads fresh and balanced with finesse, red fruit top notes, closed flavours, youthful unsweetened cherry conserve and lingering strawberry fruits. Finesse and better in 2018.

2012	91	2017	$28.00	13.0%
2013	88	2018	$28.00	13.5%
2015	88	2018	$28.00	13.5%

STONIER
RESERVE PINOT NOIR ★★★★★
Tiny crops in 2014 meant no single vineyard pinot noir could be produced and this is the result with the old vine Windmill and KBS sites going into this wine. Intensity of red fruits not heaviness, perfumed pinot strawberry and spice. Silky palate, a flicker of acidity, very fine tannins, very good length and drive. Finishes fresh raspberry almost rhubarb and strawberry.

2012	92	2017	$60.00	13.0%
2013	89	2018	$55.00	13.5%
2014	93	2024	$55.00	13.0%

STONIER
WINDMILL VINEYARD PINOT NOIR ★★★★★
Quite big and intense. Rhubarb, strawberry, ripe berry, earthy fruits with oak showing in the background. The palate has silky generosity, ripe middle palate and medium length firming finish.

Vintage	Rank	Drink	RRP	Vol Alc
2010	94	2021	$65.00	14.0%
2012	92	2026	$65.00	13.5%
2013	89	2019	$65.00	13.5%

STONIER
KBS PINOT NOIR ★★★★★
Cellar door only. Subtle sweet fruited ripe strawberry and cooked strawberry notes. The palate is creamy tannin textures supporting ripe strawberry fruits with good length and a really nice drinking wine. Moreish.

Vintage	Rank	Drink	RRP	Vol Alc
2011	93	2021	$75.00	13.0%
2012	94	2028	$75.00	13.5%
2013	91	2019	$75.00	14.0%

SWINGING BRIDGE

Swinging Bridge based at Canowindra has had a dream start, picking up NSW Red Wine of the Year with its 2007 Estate Shiraz and six weeks later its 2007 Estate Chardonnay, which collected the trophy for the Best Single Vineyard Wine at the Royal Melbourne Show.
Winemakers: Chris Derrez and Tom Ward
Open: By Appointment, 1052 Fish Fossil Drive, Canowindra
Ph: 0409 246 609 *www.swingingbridge.com.au*

SWINGING BRIDGE
MRS PAYTEN CHARDONNAY ★★★★
Named after Tom's grandmother, this is the classic youthful Orange chardonnay style. Cool and restrained white nectarine that will become more harmonious in 2015. Fine in the mouth, delicate with more flesh than the Yarra and less than Margaret River. Creamy white fresh pear, fleshy fruit that turns textural with an interesting length.

Vintage	Rank	Drink	RRP	Vol Alc
2012	90	2016	$32.00	13.0%
2013	92	2017	$32.00	12.9%

SWINGING BRIDGE
CANOWINDRA CENTRAL RANGES SHIRAZ ★★★

Mulberry, dark spices and toffee oak in an appealing way. In the mouth, fresh blackberry fruit and medium-bodied generous flavour, modest tannins and highly quaffable. Style is balanced and fresh.

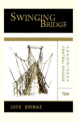

Vintage	Rank	Drink	RRP	Vol Alc
2009	87	2013	$17.50	14.5%
2010	87	2014	$17.50	13.4%
2012	90	2016	$23.00	13.5%

SYMPHONY HILL

Symphony Hill are an important part of the exciting new wines being made in the Granite Belt region. With an altitude of 1000 metres, these wines will surprise with their elegance.

Winemaker: Mike Hayes
Open: Daily 10am–4pm, 2017 Eukey Road, Ballandean
Ph: (07) 4684 1388 *www.symphonyhill.com.au*

SYMPHONY HILL
RESERVE VERDELHO ★★★★★

Sweet, ripe, pungent fruit aromas with pineapple, custard apple, icy pole and leafy edges to temper the intensity. The full-bodied palate is creamy, with ripe pineapples building lychee and exotic, round and intense and densely structured concentrated flavours with gravitas and grunt.

Vintage	Rank	Drink	RRP	Vol Alc
2012	90	2016	$25.00	13.3%
2013	91	2017	$25.00	13.3%
2014	95	2018	$25.00	13.3%

SYMPHONY HILL
PINOT GRIS ★★★★

White pears, subtle oak, butyric, pear drop aromas with a solid, complex, young and unyielding flavour and texture. There seems to be a lees note, a high acid balance and firm structure.

Vintage	Rank	Drink	RRP	Vol Alc
2013	90	2016	$30.00	12.6%
2014	94	2018	$30.00	12.6%
2015	85	2017	$30.00	13.5%

SYMPHONY HILL
WILD YEAST VIOGNIER ★★★★

Opulent, dense and powerful; possibly Australia's most pungent varietal example. Jasmine, peach and musk, a very silky lush textured palate. Balanced firm acidity holds the intense varietal fruit in check on the finish.

Vintage	Rank	Drink	RRP	Vol Alc
2008	88	2011	$25.00	13.6%
2009	86	2012	$25.00	14.1%
2010	90	2013	$30.00	13.3%

SYMPHONY HILL
RESERVE LAGRIEN ★★★★★

Great colour, quite closed dark berry pip and pulp aromas with low key oak. The palate is a nod to malbec in the personality of the flavours sharing a sappy edge and beetroot, dark red fruits into pomegranate rhubarb flavours. Bridging tannins and fresh bright red fruits. Medium weight with chalky tannins

Vintage	Rank	Drink	RRP	Vol Alc
2013	90	2019	$95.00	12.5%
2014	94	2020	$95.00	14.0%

SYMPHONY HILL
RESERVE SHIRAZ ★★★★

A fabulous shiraz made with great understanding, poise and balance. The dark plum cola fruits are wed to warm butter and caramel oak with white pepper. Long, dynamic and elegant black fruit in the mouth with minerality from the balance of grainy tannins and acids that suits the wine. Finishing with savoury roast meats and oregano.

Vintage	Rank	Drink	RRP	Vol Alc
2012	93	2020	$65.00	14.5%
2013	96	2022	$65.00	14.5%
2014	93	2022	$30.00	14.0%

SYMPHONY HILL
RESERVE CABERNET ★★★★
Sweet black fruit ripeness, roast bloody beef, meaty, liquorice and mint. In the mouth, sweet fruit, a medium bodied and long wine with black currant length. Charming tannins and varietal fruit weight, well handled elegance and length.

Vintage	Rank	Drink	RRP	Vol Alc
2008	87	2014	$45.00	14.0%
2009	90	2016	$45.00	14.3%
2012	90	2016	$45.00	14.3%

T'GALLANT
T'Gallant in the Mornington Peninsula pioneered Australian pinot gris, setting standards for the variety and producing a wide range of styles that represent the diversity and the region are capable of.
Winemaker: *Kevin McCarthy*
Open: *Daily 10am–5pm*
1385 Mornington Flinders Road, Main Ridge
Ph: (03) 5931 1300 www.tgallant.com.au

T'GALLANT
IMOGEN PINOT GRIS ★★★★
Complex rather than fruity with marzipan, pear aromas. In the mouth creamy nougat and sweet fruited up front caramel nougat like complexity and drink soon.

Vintage	Rank	Drink	RRP	Vol Alc
2008	88	2012	$26.00	14.5%
2012	94	2015	$26.00	13.5%
2013	86	2016	$26.00	14.5%

T'GALLANT
GRACE PINOT GRIGIO ★★★★
Bright floral notes sit side by side with juicy pear and nuts in classic Pinot Grigio style and continue long into the palate. Grace shows plenty of elegance with silken curves that round out the palate. A consistently good example of Pinot Grigio by the label, who are seen as pioneers of this variety.

Vintage	Rank	Drink	RRP	Vol Alc
2013	88	2016	$24.00	12.5%
2014	90	2017	$25.00	12.5%
2015	89	2019	$24.99	12.5%

| Vintage | Rank | Drink | RRP | Vol Alc |

T'GALLANT
TRIBUTE PINOT GRIS ★★★★★

Creamy honey and pear that dallies with tropical ripeness and a varietal nuttiness. The full bodied, sweet, fleshy even fruit has a spicy finish and a soft acid line that saunters down the long length. A wine that will continue to deliver its food friendly charm over the longer term.

2012	93	2016	$39.00	15.0%
2013	91	2016	$39.00	14.5%
2014	90	2022	$33.99	14.5%

TAGAI
Small batch wines from Langhorne Creek – Can't wait to learn more about them!
Ph: *(04) 1171 8886*
www.tagai.com.au

TAGAI
SCAR TREE SHIRAZ ★★★★★

Good table manners, versatile food pairing here as well as fresh medium weight with blue and spicy red fruits for drinking with good food and friends. Blue fruits and coffee oak are juicy and medium bodied. Drink this wine young for fresh bright spicy fruit complexity with medium tannin intensity, pleasantly lingering blue berry and black cherry. Good restaurant wine.

2012	90	2011	$40.00	14.0%
2013	92	2021	$40.00	14.0%
2014	91	2019	$40.00	14.0%

TAHBILK
Tahbilk has been producing wine in the Goulburn Valley since the middle of the 19th century and counts shiraz and marsanne plantings, from 1860 and 1927 respectively, amongst its legacy. The historic vineyard and beautiful winery are still family owned and operated and the wines have an elegance and seniority proportional to this legacy. There has been a significant jump in quality with the 2013 red vintage which has been maintained providing compelling quality for the price for the estate varietals
Winemaker: *Alister Purbrick*
Open: *Weekdays 9am–5pm, Weekends 10am–5pm, 254 O'Neils Road, Nagambie*
Ph: *(03) 5794 2555 www.tahbilk.com.au*

TAHBILK
MARSANNE ★★★★

Terse flowery quince, more floral and less waxy than most of the marsanne in Australia. The palate is round easy drinking finishing vibrant marsanne flavours with lingering honeysuckle on the close. Don't serve too cold.

Vintage	Rank	Drink	RRP	Vol Alc
2013	90	2019	$18.00	12.5%
2014	88	2017	$18.00	12.9%
2015	88	2015	$19.50	12.5%

TAHBILK
1927 VINES MARSANNE ★★★★★

complex lemon, quince and honey suckle varietal aromas. The palate has effortless quality; light on its feet, the medium bodied lemony honeysuckle flavours are subtle with great length and delicacy with drive to the finish. Has intensity without heaviness putting it into the spectrum of great Australian wine.

Vintage	Rank	Drink	RRP	Vol Alc
2004	94	2024	$46.50	11.0%
2006	96	2021	$48.00	10.5%
2007	95	2025	$46.30	10.5%

TAHBILK
OLD VINES CABERNET SHIRAZ ★★★★★

Great colour, a youthful vibrant red excellent rim. The aromas are cellaring style reserved but muscular dark berry and a top note of red fruits background oak, very good balance and harmony. The palate is ripe, even, acid balance is ideal for food, long mulberry blueberry and spice flavours with fine tannin closing it down. Very long flavours.

Vintage	Rank	Drink	RRP	Vol Alc
2010	94	2035	$46.00	13.5%
2013	95	2030	$46.00	14.2%

TAHBILK
ESP SHIRAZ ★★★★★

Distinctive regionality in the aromas, blueberry, smoked meats, bay leaf and earthy. The berry fruit has length, freshness, drive with great composure along the medium full bodied palate with powdery soft fine tannins and a delicious freshness on the finish.

Vintage	Rank	Drink	RRP	Vol Alc
2007	92	2022	$69.00	14.4%
2008	94	2024	$69.50	14.5%
2009	94	2023	$69.50	13.5%

TAHBILK
ESP CABERNET SAUVIGNON ★★★★★

Always mature on release this smells youthful, bay leaf, black olive add interest to the currant, black currant and sweet oak which adds subtle coffee and dark chocolate in a complex and classy format. The palate is intense old style value, medium bodied, dark plum with plenty of acid, fine even tannins run long and firm turning savoury with smoked and roast meats on the firm finish.

Vintage	Rank	Drink	RRP	Vol Alc
2007	90	2020	$65.00	13.6%
2008	90	2020	$69.50	14.5%
2009	94	2033	$69.50	13.5%

TAHBILK
1860 VINES SHIRAZ ★★★★★

Pale colour leads to an exotic array of youthful primary aromas with understated berry fruit, considerable savoury spectrum of earthy, bay leaf, sage, eucalypt and roast meat. The flavour intensity is amazing, fine tannins frame the firm structure and the red cherry, cherry liqueur fruits run long. It's light to medium bodied with quality tannins, graceful eloquence and a refined firm finish. A wine to contemplate, rather than consume.

Vintage	Rank	Drink	RRP	Vol Alc
2007	95	2035	$207.00	14.0%
2008	96	2032	$260.00	13.5%
2009	95	2045	$260.00	12.5%

TALTARNI WINES

Taltarni has a distinctive style with the firm framed Pyrenees to their wines which has had the attention of drinkers for 30 years. The company sources from diverse vineyards including Tasmania and Heathcote.

Winemaker: *Robert Heywood*
Open: *Daily 10am–5pm 339 Taltarni Road, Moonambel*
Ph: *(03) 5459 7900 www.taltarni.com.au*

TALTARNI
PYRENEES CABERNET SAUVIGNON ★★★★★
Age worthy complex cabernet spectrum aromas with power and complexity cassis threading into subtle tomato leaf and on to meat stock. The wine has a silky entry, ripe but shy dark fruit flavoured middle palate with a big tannin structure. Fine acid keeps the line of flavour energetic and makes for savoury chalky tannins that are held close to the line of fruit finishing young and unresolved.

Vintage	Rank	Drink	RRP	Vol Alc
2009	91	2030	$40.00	14.0%
2010	91	2023	$40.00	14.0%
2012	92	2022	$40.00	14.5%

TALTARNI
RESERVE PYRENEES SHIRAZ CABERNET SAUVIGNON ★★★★★
Dark coloured power house of fresh red fruit, liquorice, eucalypt and dark cherry aromas. In the mouth this has density with vibrant fresh dark berry, dark cherry and cherry syrup flavours with bright acidity and a large quantity of ripe soft tannins supporting the long sweep of ripe black fruits.

Vintage	Rank	Drink	RRP	Vol Alc
2004	95	2029	$65.00	14.0%
2005	91	2020	$65.00	14.0%
2008	93	2018	$65.00	14.5%

TAPANAPPA
Tapanappa is the older, wiser and more experienced Brian Croser of Petaluma fame back with a vengeance with a selection of thoughtfully located and managed South Australian vineyards making the best wines of his life.
Winemaker: *Brian Croser*
Open: *No Cellar Door PO Box 174 Crafers*
Ph: *(04) 1984 3751* *www.tapanappawines.com.au*

TAPANAPPA
PICCADILLY VALLEY TIERS VINEYARD CHARDONNAY ★★★★★

One of our greatest vineyards. Less oak in the '08; from 60% in 2007 to 38% new oak in 08 has created rich fruit wines with amazing balance of melon and grapefruit. The '10 has even more ripe fruit richness.

Vintage	Rank	Drink	RRP	Vol Alc
2007	88	2015	$75.00	13.5%
2008	94	2016	$75.00	13.5%
2010	94	2015	$75.00	12.5%

TAPANAPPA
FOGGY HILL FLEURIEU PENINSULA PINOT NOIR ★★★★★

Aromas of strawberry and fresh raspberry lead to initial raspberry fruit in the mouth, refined and elegant, silky fresh fruits with good middle palate depth and freshness and then complex on the finish with dark spices to close.

Vintage	Rank	Drink	RRP	Vol Alc
2010	92	2021	$55.00	12.9%
2012	92	2025	$55.00	14.1%
2013	92	2020	$45.00	13.9%

TAPANAPPA
WHALEBONE VINEYARD ★★★★★

A very compelling wine that shows superb mastery and interpretation of merlot. The aromas show exquisite balance and oak judgement weaving blueberry, violets, red cherry, raspberry fruit, vanilla and cedar oak with a delicious complexity on the nose. The palate is elegant. Velvet soft tannins with ripe bright berry fruits, getting wider from the tongue tip to the back of mouth with briar, mulberry, and dark fruits in the middle. A red carpet experience through to the finish and a masterpiece example of these varieties.

Vintage	Rank	Drink	RRP	Vol Alc
2009	90	2022	$75.00	13.8%
2012	96	2025	$79.00	14.1%

Vintage	Rank	Drink	RRP	Vol Alc

TAR & ROSES

Founded in 2004 by very experienced winemakers Don Lewis and Narelle King, the term Tar & Roses reflects common descriptors for Nebbiolo although their Tempranillo is the current star in my eyes. Tempranillo is an early ripener Heathcote although prone to over cropping and requires very detailed viticuture to get the best each year.
Winemaker: *Don Lewis, Narelle King*
Open: *No Cellar Door, 61 Vickers Lane Nagambie*
Ph: *03 5794 1811 www.tarandroses.com.au*

TAR & ROSES
SANGIOVESE ★★★★

Very generous, positive varietal aromas with lifted ripe red berry, cola and meat stock. In the mouth, a young juicy finely tannic red berry fruit up front and into the middle turning very tannic and chalky on the finish with savoury mouth watering appeal. Medium bodied firm finishing style that needs food.

2007	86	2015	$24.00	14.0%
2012	90	2018	$24.00	13.7%
2013	90	2022	$24.00	14.6%

TAR & ROSES
TEMPRANILLO ★★★

You won't make enemies serving up this medium bodied savoury red and blue berry fruited wine. Initially red fruit complexity with savoury graphite and meat stock aromas. Ripe berry front fruits leads to a long smoothly textured palate. For early consumption with food friendly chalky tannins to finish.

2011	90	2017	$24.00	13.0%
2012	95	2019	$24.00	14.2%
2013	90	2018	$24.00	14.5%

Vintage	Rank	Drink	RRP	Vol Alc

TARRAWARRA ESTATE
TarraWarra Estate in the Yarra Valley is adjacent to the TarraWarra Museum of Art, combining an art gallery with winery and restaurant for a world class experience . The estate's reserve style combines ripeness and fragrance with finesse giving an individual style to their pinot noir and chardonnay.
Winemaker: *Clare Halloran*
Open: *Daily 11am–5pm,*
311 Healesville-Yarra Glen Road, Yarra Glen
Ph: *(03) 5962 3311 www.tarrawarra.com.au*

TARRAWARRA ESTATE
CHARDONNAY ★★★★
Straight up complex with a refined oak rich pear, nougat and toasty aromas. The fruits meld into nectarine in the middle palate with a creamy varietal style.

2012	90	2014	$25.00	13.0%
2013	92	2018	$25.00	13.0%
2014	88	2018	$28.00	12.5%

TARRAWARRA ESTATE
RESERVE CHARDONNAY ★★★★★
A stylish wine with a complex aroma balancing wine making with early picked fruit. Savoury notes of oak, oat meal, nougat, flint and cool citrus fruits. The palate has creamy weight and textural length, crisp Chablis like acidity and lingering pears and fine grained tannins to close. A keeper.

2012	95	2025	$50.00	12.8%
2013	94	2024	$50.00	12.8%
2014	93	2020	$50.00	12.5%

TARRAWARRA ESTATE
RESERVE PINOT NOIR ★★★★★
The depth and complexity of subtle aroma here marks it as senior – not a punnet of berries to be seen, wild strawberry dusted with dark chocolate. The palate is elegant; walks with a tight rope of red cherry fruit flavours, even soft and generous. Oak tannins add length and it is pitched toward cellaring by its acid tannin balance.

2012	88	2029	$60.00	13.5%
2013	95	2025	$70.00	13.5%
2014	93	2024	$70.00	13.0%

| Vintage | Rank | Drink | RRP | Vol Alc |

TAYLORS
Taylors have had more than 40 years of success in Clare, producing reliable wines under the family name, with a wide range of styles and different labels. St Andrews is from higher quality fruit with deliberate bottle maturation, while Jaraman is an exercise in matching different regions to varieties. They continue to be a major force in retail sales with reliable varietal wines under $20.00 that show remarkable consistency.
Winemakers: *Mitchell Taylor, Adam Eggins and Chad Bowman*
Open: *Weekdays 9am–5pm, Saturdays and Pub Hols 10am–5pm, Sun 10am to 4pm, Taylors Road, Auburn*
Ph: *(02) 8849 1118 www.taylorswines.com.au*

TAYLORS
JARAMAN RIESLING ★★★★★
Pretty stone fruit and lime zest aromas lead to a juicy bright long palate with sweet lime fruit, richness, elegant with good length.

2011	89	2016	$24.50	12.0%
2012	88	2016	$24.50	12.0%
2013	93	2024	$24.00	12.0%

TAYLORS
ST ANDREWS RIESLING ★★★★★
A very intense wine with varietal perfumed lime and a stone fruit edge to the aromas. In the mouth, ripe and balanced, rich long middle palate, balanced structure, intense lime and citrus with an exotic ginger spiced edge to the fruit flavours.

2013	90	2023	$35.00	11.5%
2014	90	2018	$35.00	11.5%
2015	90	2022	$35.00	12.5%

TAYLORS
JARAMAN CHARDONNAY ★★★★
Rich fruited solid intensity black currant earth, conserve, dried herb oak spice- very cabernet. The robust palate delivers texture, fruit intensity with complexity, black fruits with oak spice, classic Australian softness and in the

zone. well-judged tannin hold that extends the fruit complexity. The oak tannins add length and contribute to the coffee chocolate edge to the finish.

Vintage	Rank	Drink	RRP	Vol Alc
2012	88	2016	$24.00	13.0%
2013	90	2017	$25.00	13.0%
2014	93	2020	$24.00	14.5%

TAYLORS
ST ANDREWS SINGLE VINEYARD CHARDONNAY ★★★★★

Released as a two year old wine to bring all the elements together. The vineyard has been replanted, better clones, and mid slope fruit sourcing, whole bunch press and better oak has created a complex and characterful, smoky, peanut brittle, vanilla, cashew, savoury and nutty oak. In the mouth acid and fruit harmony with white nectarine fruit delicacy and cashew oak balance with finesse and length. Drink young for finesse or 3-5 if you prefer richness.

Vintage	Rank	Drink	RRP	Vol Alc
2012	90	2017	$35.00	12.5%
2013	86	2016	$35.00	13.0%
2014	94	2019	$35.00	13.0%

TAYLORS
JARAMAN CABERNET SAUVIGNON ★★★★

Initially this has minty, bay leaf, eucalypt and black currant aromas. Very varietal, fresh and well weighted with fruit carrying appealing almost luscious black currant flavours long and even and well-judged fine web of tannin. Well managed wine.

Vintage	Rank	Drink	RRP	Vol Alc
2010	90	2018	$30.00	14.5%
2012	90	2019	$30.00	14.5%
2013	90	2019	$29.00	14.5%

TAYLORS
ST ANDREWS CABERNET SAUVIGNON ★★★★★

Seven gold medals, the aromas are very varietal black currant, cassis, and blueberry with savoury black olive notes. The soft tannin texture is full bodied, smooth, middle palate full, briary fruit, black currant and blue berry with fine-tuned oak tannins with middle palate plumpness.

Vintage	Rank	Drink	RRP	Vol Alc
2010	86	2018	$60.00	14.4%
2011	Not made			
2013	90	2023	$60.00	14.5%

TAYLORS
JARAMAN SHIRAZ ★★★★★

Dark chocolate oak and fresh ripe berry fruit aromas in a big and bold format. The fruit is rich, structured and well made in a classic generous full bodied rich red style. A big block buster. Plenty of drink now joy.

Vintage	Rank	Drink	RRP	Vol Alc
2009	92	2019	$30.00	14.5%
2010	90	2018	$30.00	14.5%
2011	Not made			
2012	90	2016	$30.00	14.5%

TAYLORS
ST ANDREWS SHIRAZ ★★★★★

The winemaker's hands are all over this with lavish oak, oregano oak spice vanilla, this is a full frontal approach to complexity. The fruit has punch and holds its own against a tide of oak and dark berry with fresh plum, vibrant front middle palate flavours and a balanced finish.

Vintage	Rank	Drink	RRP	Vol Alc
2010	88	2016	$60.00	14.5%
2011	Note made			
2012	89	2018	$60.00	14.0%

TAYLORS
THE VISIONARY ★★★★★

Complex aromas showing developed ready to drink mint, black currant, and dark berry fruits with a savoury leafy, seaside back note. Not a heavy wine. The restrained tannins are sophisticated; neither fine and chalky, or dry and grippy, and add to the charm by flowing long and holding the dark berry fruits in an embrace that helps the fruit linger. A Grand reserve style with approximately two years in oak, two more of bottle age before release.

Vintage	Rank	Drink	RRP	Vol Alc
2010	91	2024	$150.00	13.8%
2011	Not made			
2012	93	2019	$200.00	14.0%

TAYLORS
THE PIONEER ★★★★★

Bold and built with toasty oak and ripe, rich plum fruit cake spectrum aromas. In the mouth, a generous middle palate with medium bodied ripe fruits and quality caramel nutty oak woven into the palates textures and flavours to create a fresh bold long wine. Drinkability, food friendly and stylish.

2011 Not made
2012 92 2019 $200.00 14.0%

TEMPLE BRUER

Temple Bruer is the winery of former oenology lecturer David Bruer. He has a well-established 26 Ha certified organic vineyard in Langhorne Creek using a number of unique innovative approaches far ahead of his time. He has added 21 ha in Eden Valley and 6 ha in Loxton where he experiments with varieties suited to their respective climates to create an increasingly diverse range of wines. His very well considered analysis of the environmental impact of wine growing based on sound scientific principles has led him to farm organically to produce carbon neutral, vegan friendly, preservative free wines.

Winemaker: *David Bruer*
Open: *Weekdays 8.30am–4.30pm for sales only Strathalbyn – Milang Road, Strathalbyn*
Ph: *(08) 8537 0203 www.templebruer.com.au*

TEMPLE BRUER
PRESERVATIVE FREE CABERNET MERLOT ★★★★★

A preservative free red. Fresh black currant, saline minerals, evolving into an edge of spices. In the mouth very soft tannins, medium bodied, characteristic elegant structure of cabernet sauvignon with energetic black currant fruits, a silky glide of fruit and tannin into the middle mouth with a high degree of sophistication and a saline mineral quality part of the finish.

2015 90 2018 $20.00 12.0%
2016 90 2018 $20.00 12.0%

TERRE A TERRE

Husband and wife team Xavier Bizot and Lucy Croser, started Terre a Terre, a French expression meaning "Down to Earth." In 2008, they planted a vineyard next to Brian Croser's celebrated Whalebone vineyard in Wrattonbully. They chose a close spacing of 4,444 vines per hectare to Sauvignon Blanc, Cabernet Sauvignon, Shiraz and Cabernet Franc. The results are a significantly different style with elegance and finer tannins than the norm for the region. With two additional vineyards at Piccadilly and Summertown in the Adelaide Hills, they have diverse wines from sparkling through to single varietals. The new release wines are called Crayeres from 2016.
Winemaker: *Xavier Bizot*
Open: *Thurs–Mon 11am–4pm,*
15 Spring Gully Road, Piccadilly
Ph: *(04) 0070 0447 www.terreaterre.com.au*

TERRE A TERRE
CRAYERES CABERNET SAUVIGNON
This is a wine with many layers and different people will take different things from it, initially, intense fruit aromas of black and red currant with leafy rosemary. The palate is glossy silky slick long tannins that carry the red cherry front and middle palate fruit on a wave of structure that grows firmer on the finish. More about terroir than variety.

Vintage	Rank	Drink	RRP	Vol Alc
2013	92	2017	$40.00	14.4%
2014	94	2024	$55.00	14.5%

TERRE A TERRE
CRAYERES SAUVIGNON BLANC
Age worthy balance of tilting sweet oak, warm butter, caramel notes and honeysuckle fruits. The palate is complex with the oak adding a creamy texture that wraps the fruits in a warm embrace with the strength of the middle palate fruits. Followed then by bright sauvignon acidity and passion fruit to close. The level of complexity and balance means a year or two would deliver honeysuckle intensity with appeal.

Vintage	Rank	Drink	RRP	Vol Alc
2015	90	2020	$32.00	13.9%

Vintage	Rank	Drink	RRP	Vol Alc

TERTINI WINES

Tertini Wines is located near Berrima in the cool climate Southern Highlands region in New South Wales, at the relatively high altitude of 715 metres. Quality has been very high under their current winemaking team with pinot noir emerging as the star. This is a winery that does not judge itself by return on investment but on wine quality alone placing it amongst small elite of wineries globally.

Winemaker: Jonathan Holgate and Nick Bullied MW
Open: Thurs to Mon 11am–5pm or by appointment, Kells Creek Road (off Wombeyan Caves Road) Mittagong
Ph: (02) 4878 5213 www.tertiniwines.com.au

TERTINI WINES
SOUTHERN HIGHLANDS RIESLING ★★★★★

Riesling with the full range of floral aromatics showing talc, rose and gentle citrus zones. The drink now acidity gives a satiny sheen to the medium long apple and flowery spring blossom mid palate fruits with a clean finish.

2013	90	2020	$30.00	11.2%
2014	93	2022	$30.00	11.2%
2015	89	2020	$30.00	11.2%

TERTINI WINES
SOUTHERN HIGHLANDS ARNEIS ★★★★

At first subtle with exotic white stone fruits there is a lift perfumed ripe apricot and talc. The palate is silkier creamy – think of velvet- chardonnay barrel ferment helps meld silky white fruits flowing seamlessly with apricot lift in the middle palate right through to the long finish.

2011	91	2013	$38.00	12.9%
2013	92	2017	$38.00	13.1%
2015	94	2018	$38.00	12.8%

TERTINI WINES
SOUTHERN HIGHLANDS PINOT GRIS ★★★★★

Generous all over style with wine gums and yellow fruits on the nose. Silky texture allows for the fleshy upfront fruit to glide into middle palate ripe pear, fuji apple and lemon zest, finishing with ripe pear and spice fruit.

| 2011 | 93 | 2016 | $26.00 | 13.5% |
| 2014 | 90 | 2017 | $26.00 | 13.0% |

TERTINI WINES
SOUTHERN HIGHLANDS PINOT NOIR ★★★★★

Subtle sweet ripe strawberry aromas with delicate round silky tannins with blue berry and milk chocolate flavours. Difficult year and the wine was well made with balance and thorough execution.

Vintage	Rank	Drink	RRP	Vol Alc
2010	96	2018	$38.00	13.0%
2012	95	2022	$38.00	13.8%
2013	86	2018	$45.00	13.6%

TERTINI WINES
SOUTHERN HIGHLANDS RESERVE PINOT NOIR ★★★★★

Seriously complex and detailed vigorous aromas with an edge of savoury spice. Silky texture with classy tannins and long fine flavours that last long. Has the fine wine contradiction with intensity of flavour and delicacy of body and texture.

Vintage	Rank	Drink	RRP	Vol Alc
2008	88	2016	$45.00	14.0%
2009	96	2020	$58.00	14.0%

THE LANE VINEYARD

The Lane Vineyard in the Adelaide Hills is success story on many levels. They have an excellent vineyard, intelligent winemaking, a first-class restaurant at cellar door serving appealing wines that can be found in many restaurants thanks to their food friendly style.
Winemaker: *John Edwards and Michael Shreurs*
Open: *Daily 10am–4pm Ravenswood Lane Hahndorf*
Ph: *(08) 8388 1250   www.thelane.com.au*

THE LANE
GATHERING SAUVIGNON BLANC SEMILLON ★★★★★

Rich mouth feel balanced with mouth watering acidity here. A lot of vibrant fruit expression in the aromas, fruit sweetness, detailed and complex fruit salad notes with barrel ferment complexity. The palate takes you for a ride, citrus front orange and mandarin, fresh pineapple and lime sorbet middle plate fine grained acidy frames the length adding a vibrant twang while the barrel ferment notes frame the finish building complexity.

Vintage	Rank	Drink	RRP	Vol Alc
2010	91	2014	$35.00	12.5%
2013	90	2017	$35.00	13.0%
2014	94	2020	$35.00	13.0%

THE LANE
BLOCK 14 BASKET PRESS SHIRAZ ★★★★★
Just on the edge of mint before the spicy blackberry aromas. Complex with hot cross bun oak spices, medium bodied, very food friendly style with black and red fruit fine soft tannins with a refined structure.

Vintage	Rank	Drink	RRP	Vol Alc
2012	96	2022	$39.00	13.5%
2013	90	2025	$39.00	13.5%

THE LANE
SINGLE VINEYARD BEGINNING CHARDONNAY ★★★★★
Very contemporary modern style with freshness, floral edged, compact fruit white nectarine with focus, aromas show winemaking savoury into oatmeal lees and quality french oak giving a gingery edge to the oak spices. The palate has medium bodied fresh fruit, lovely varietal silkiness, freshness with length and delicacy, flavours from pear into white nectarine to orange blossom top notes, fresh acidity, tight tender fruits, finely judged subliminal oak with the acid to draw the flavours and keeps it fresh and pirouetting on the finish gentle oak spice, oatmeal white fruit freshness.

Vintage	Rank	Drink	RRP	Vol Alc
2012	87	2016	$39.00	13.0%
2013	90	2020	$39.00	13.0%
2015	94	2020	$39.00	13.0%

THE LANE
SINGLE VINEYARD REUNION SHIRAZ ★★★★★
A charming style with fruit and spice details. Aromas are black fruits and spices with Chinese five spice black pepper notes. Medium bodied ripe shiraz and soft tannins, appealing medium bodied wine that doesn't try too hard and finishes with silky tannins oak spices and dark shiraz spices with raspberry at the finale.

Vintage	Rank	Drink	RRP	Vol Alc
2010	91	2024	$65.00	14.0%
2011	Not made			
2012	93	2018	$65.00	13.5%
2013	92	2020	$65.00	14.0%

THE STANDISH WINE COMPANY

The Standish Wine Company is the creation of Dan Standish, a sixth-generation Barossa Valley vigneron. Brought up in the ways of the valley, pruning vines at six, he has enormous passion for shiraz and the wines of the Rhône Valley.

Winemaker: *Dan Standish*
Open: *By Appointment Only 100 Barritt Road, Lyndoch*
Ph: *0407 366 673 www.standishwineco.com*

THE STANDISH
SHIRAZ ★★★★★

Fabulous colour leads to blue and blackberry fruit aromas with star anise, five spice, tapenade and dark olive to offset the luxurious berries. The palate is long and complex starting silky, soft, vibrant fresh fruit with a penetrating lift of cherry blossom floral fruits and red cherry flowing into the deep full flavoured majestic middle palate with a spread of dark plum, berries and spices spiked with white pepper, plum and date completes the finish.

2008	93	2022	$95.00	14.5%
2009	96	2026	$95.00	14.5%
2012	95	2034	$95.00	14.5%

THICK AS THIEVES

Syd has always liked growing plants. Trained in Rutherglen and Yarra with a number of key producers from 2003 to 2009 before branching out on his own as a King Valley and Yarra specialist. His focus on alternative varieties and styles means the Thick As Thieves label, is always interesting and finds a place on many restaurant wine lists.

Winemaker: *Syd Bradford*
Open: *By Appointment Only*
355 Healesville-Kooweerup Road, Badger Creek
Ph: *(04) 1718 4690 www.tatwines.com.au*

THICK AS THIEVES
THE ALOOF ALPACA ARNEIS ★★★★
Pear and citrus aromas alongside cheese, marmite savoury wild ferment, skin contact and old oak complexity. The palate is white fruited lychee and pear fruit salad, middle weight and length with enough weight to partner canapés.

Vintage	Rank	Drink	RRP	Vol Alc
2013	90	2015	$30.00	13.2%
2014	91	2016	$25.00	13.5%
2015	86	2016	$25.00	14.1%

THICK AS THIEVES
PLUMP PINOT NOIR ★★★★★
Plump is as it says starting floral, stemmy juicy strawberry with varietal spice and a mouthful of up front fruits, good palate weight with strawberry flowing into red cherry on the finish.

Vintage	Rank	Drink	RRP	Vol Alc
2012	92	2016	$35.00	13.2%
2013	93	2020	$35.00	13.0%
2015	89	2017	$35.00	12.6%

THOMAS WINES
Thomas Wines, named after former Tyrrells winemaker Andrew Thomas, produces exciting wines, animated by his talent and extensive experience in the Hunter Valley. Only 500 cases of shiraz and semillon are made with a feature being the re-release of each semillon as cellar reserve maturation releases.
Winemaker: *Andrew Thomas*
Open: *Daily 10am–5pm,*
Corner Hermitage Road & Mistletoe Lane Pokolbin
Ph: *(02) 6574 7371 www.thomaswines.com.au*

THOMAS
BRAEMORE INDIVIDUAL VINEYARD SEMILLON ★★★★★
Passion fruits and blossom are hallmarks of young Hunters in 2015. The palate is long, very fine in flavour and texture, tight evenness and as usual among the best of the year. Flavours are a spectrum of green banana with lingering lemony length.

Vintage	Rank	Drink	RRP	Vol Alc
2013	94	2023	$30.00	10.8%
2014	94	2033	$30.00	10.8%
2015	94	2029	$30.00	10.3%

THOMAS
BRAEMORE SEMILLON CELLAR RESERVE ★★★★★
Bright aromas with toast, lanolin, baby blanket wool in the regional varietal expression of the hunter on the nose. The palate is very well composed with early mature texture, power and weight, round front and middle tongue gaining intensity and finishing with lovely lemon curd precision tangling the finish and a whisper of toasted bread like a new oak barrel, which of course it has never seen.

Vintage	Rank	Drink	RRP	Vol Alc
2007	93	2018	$45.00	10.5%
2008	92	2029	$50.00	10.0%
2009	94	2017	$50.00	11.2%

THOMAS
INDIVIDUAL VINEYARD KISS SHIRAZ ★★★★★
Low yielding vineyards planted in 1969 give up their fruit for the Kiss. In this kiss you will find pepper and nutmeg sitting alongside with chocolate, lavender, plump black cherry and berry fruit. It has an irresistible quality and one that has you coming back for more. Good thing that it lasts well in the cellar.

Vintage	Rank	Drink	RRP	Vol Alc
2011	94	2026	$60.00	13.5%
2013	93	2028	$60.00	13.6%
2014	95	2028	$75.00	14.2%

THOMAS
INDIVIDUAL VINEYARD SWEETWATER SHIRAZ ★★★★★
The Sweetwater Shiraz comes off a vineyard in the Belford area of the Hunter. There is an earthy note to the ripe blueberry and floral fruit that resonates deeply. It is fuller in body and peppery on the finish. A wine to enjoy now or to keep for mid to long term.

Vintage	Rank	Drink	RRP	Vol Alc
2012	94	2020	$35.00	14.0%
2013	92	2025	$35.00	14.0%
2014	94	2028	$35.00	14.0%

THORN-CLARKE WINES

Thorn-Clarke is comprised of extensive family owned Barossa and Eden Valley vineyards with a quality winemaker at the helm. This young brand is a good value producer under the Shotfire label. Under the William Randall range starting to win some heavy weight awards under the experienced eye of Helen McCarthy.

Winemaker: Susie Mickan
Open: Mon to Fri 9 to 5pm & Sat 11am–4pm
266 Gawler Park Road, Angaston
Ph: (08) 8564 3036   www.thornclarkewines.com.au

THORN-CLARKE
SHOTFIRE QUARTAGE ★★★★★

Stern with leafy garden herbs and looking elegant for the price. The palate is the opposite of shiraz in every way known; long, lean, meaty savouriness, well balanced, poised and very long with increasing dark graphite mineral flavours in the finish. Great understanding.

2012	90	2017	$25.00	14.5%
2013	91	2018	$25.00	14.5%
2014	94	2018	$25.00	14.5%

THORN-CLARKE
RON THORN SHIRAZ ★★★★★

Ripe fruited with balanced oak, raspberry, dark cherry and vanilla aromas. In the mouth a ripe full bodied sweep of flavour starting sweet vanilla chocolate oak front palate and raspberry fruited in the middle mouth with a long vanilla mocha choco chino oak length to close. For full bodied red lovers.

2010	93	2022	$95.00	14.8%
2012	93	2020	$95.00	14.8%

Vintage	Rank	Drink	RRP	Vol Alc

THORN-CLARKE
WILLIAM RANDALL SHIRAZ ★★★★★

2014 has a bounce in its step after the hot 2013 vintage; the colours are fresher as are the aromas; solid and bright with rose, ripe black berry, blue berries and green spiced fruits leading to a seamless long palate. Very engaging flavours showing minerality, fine tannins rather than bulging with heavy tannins helps the fruits of the forest flavours with their redder flavours showing appealing thyme herbal spice adds complexity contributing to the appealing dark plum finish. Good now, it will really shine in 2017 onwards.

2010	94	2024	$60.00	14.5%
2012	93	2023	$60.00	14.5%
2014	94	2026	$60.00	14.5%

THORN-CLARKE
WILLIAM RANDALL CABERNET SAUVIGNON ★★★★★

The nose is complex red currant, sweet rhubarb, scrubby bush, dark liquorice with sweet spices from oak knitting it all together. A great wine with lovely balance and texture. The tannins are well knit, this has length and smoothness with the velvety tannins carrying the blue and red fruits long in the mouth to a savoury finish.

2010	93	2020	$60.00	14.0%
2012	92	2029	$60.00	14.5%
2014	94	2026	$60.00	14.5%

TIDSWELL WINES
Tidswell Wines are located near Naracoorte in the Limestone coast region of South Australia. Established in 1994, they are a major regional vineyard with 115 hectares planted on limestone covered terra rossa soils.
Winemaker: *Ben Tidswell and Jo Irvine*
Open: *10am–4pm, 14 Sydenham Road, Norwood*
Ph: *(08) 8363 5800   www.tidswellwines.com.au*

TIDSWELL WINES
JENNIFER CABERNET SAUVIGNON ★★★★★ RED
A good year for cabernet in the region has lifted this wine. Very solid oak supporting blueberry, black currant and dark olive tapenade like fruit aromas. The palate is black fruits with vanilla that support youthful firm tangled tightness, dense, tannic, rancio- in need of a decant.

Vintage	Rank	Drink	RRP	Vol Alc
2010	88	2019	$45.00	14.5%
2012	95	2026	$65.00	14.5%
2013	88	2020	$65.00	14.5%

TIM ADAMS
Tim Adams in Clare has established and held a reputation for making quality wines that have the power of Clare fruit and the presence of mind not to be excessive in any way. An excellent range of wines, all underpinned by Tim's careful winemaking, make the cellar door a must visit.
Winemaker: *Tim Adams*
Open: *Weekdays 10.30am–5pm, Weekends 11am–5pm*
Warenda Road, Clare
Ph: *(08) 8842 2429 www.timadamswines.com.au*

TIM ADAMS
CLARE VALLEY RIESLING ★★★★★
Always true to style and personality this dry crisp wine is full of aroma; rich red apple, rose, lime and ready to drink. The hallmark green apple acidity has the classic orthodox riesling balance to the acidity. Well handled in a tough year for riesling.

Vintage	Rank	Drink	RRP	Vol Alc
2013	95	2023	$22.00	11.5%
2014	90	2025	$22.00	11.5%
2015	88	2019	$20.00	11.5%

TIM ADAMS
CLARE VALLEY RESERVE RIESLING ★★★★★
Very subtle and fine aromas with riesling rose florals and minerals like wet stones. In the mouth, bright fresh floral over lime, lemon, pink grapefruit with refined long even texture and flavours and lingering mineral acids that says keep me for decades. Classic Clare style.

2008	93	2025	$29.00	10.0%
2010	94	2030	$29.00	11.0%
2011	95	2032	$22.00	10.5%

TIM ADAMS
THE FERGUS ★★★★★
Fine-tuned oak and fruit balance with a freshness showing a cool edge and minty herbal subtlety over ripe red berry. Ripe, lovely medium weight, complex and long; ideal for our climate as it is plush fruits up front, dusty tannins and dried herbs. Lovely older oak flavours and fine fruit tannins add structure that create a savoury length and tone the finish. Runs fruit past the slight herbal to finish alongside raspberry grenache.

2010	90	2018	$22.00	14.5%
2012	93	2022	$25.00	14.5%
2013	93	2020	$24.00	14.0%

TIM ADAMS
THE ABERFELDY SHIRAZ ★★★★★
A very elegant wine. The seamless aromas show mocha, dark berry fruits, blackberry, and dark chocolate with polish and poise. The palate has the requisite fruit sweetness, dark fruit flavours and oak complexity, balance and fine tannins. The style is earnest and understated- less dependent on ripe swagger than many in the neighbourhood. The innate understanding shows in the refinement across aromas, palate, finish and age-ability. Better after 2018.

2009	95	2017	$44.00	14.5%
2010	94	2032	$44.00	14.5%
2011	Not made			
2012	95	2039	$65.00	14.5%

| Vintage | Rank | Drink | RRP | Vol Alc |

TIM ADAMS
CABERNET MALBEC

Aromas are classic cabernet berry and herbs with mulberry leaf and subtle ripe malbec notes. The palate is medium bodied with tannins, dark fruit flavours, slightly positive mint and then mulberry fruits with an oak spice note. The palate has complexity, length and harmony with the firmer tannins of cabernet softening with maturity driving the finish.

Vintage	Rank	Drink	RRP	Vol Alc
2008	90	2019	$24.00	14.0%
2010	94	2028	$26.00	14.5%
2012	90	2018	$26.00	14.5%

TINKLERS

Tinklers are long term Hunter Valley grape growers with holdings in some of the choicest sites in Pokolbin. Under the management of young Usher, they have made excellent wines and run a friendly hospitable cellar door that features museum releases and home grown, hand sorted local fresh produce according to season.

Winemaker: *Usher Tinkler*
Open: *Daily 10am–5pm, Pokolbin Mountains Road, Pokolbin*
Ph: *02 4998 7435 www.tinklers.com.au*

TINKLERS
SCHOOL BLOCK SEMILLON ★★★★★

Very fine varietal lemon, lemon pith aromas with plenty of freshness and poise. The palate is perfection in the style with lemon fruit rimmed by long elegant racy acidity and very clean juicy finish. The acid quality is such that the wine is almost sherberty with length and persistence. Exceptional wine.

Vintage	Rank	Drink	RRP	Vol Alc
2010	91	2023	$22.00	11.9%
2011	90	2015	$22.00	12.0%
2013	95	2033	$22.00	10.7%

TINKLERS
U & I SHIRAZ ★★★★★
Fresh black fruits, liquorice and sweet lavender with brown spices. In the mouth, very intense, youthful and great balance with medium bodied depth and fine tannins. Full middle palate, dark berry flavours with freshness and youth on the finish with cola and pyrethrum peppery spice.

Vintage	Rank	Drink	RRP	Vol Alc
2010	91	2021	$35.00	14.5%
2011	94	2038	$35.00	13.5%
2013	93	2029	$35.00	13.5%

TOLPUDDLE VINEYARD
One of the most informed vineyard plantings near Hobart. The climate is the most wine friendly for table wines, the vineyard layout immaculate and the precision of the management team world class. Tolpuddle is set to become one of the stars of the next generation of pinot noir and chardonnay in Australia.
Winemaker: *Adam Wadewitz*
Open: *No Cellar Door, Tastings available at Shaw + Smith*
www.tolpuddlevineyard.com

TOLPUDDLE
CHARDONNAY ★★★★★
The art of wine personified, with a finely wrought layered wine with elegant walnut, yeast subtleties, citrus, vanilla oak notes and a palate that glides in freshness and finesse. A creamy, structured, inconspicuous complexity, a fleshy line of flavours with the ability to age in the more spare middle palate and finish. An excellent thread of acidity, citrus fruits and a fine tannin thread to close the long palate texture with a fresh flush of saliva. A nod to burgundy but not a copy.

Vintage	Rank	Drink	RRP	Vol Alc
2012	94	2023	$65.00	13.0%
2013	95	2022	$65.00	12.5%
2014	95	2021	$65.00	13.0%

TOLPUDDLE
PINOT NOIR ★★★★★

Serious wine potential, interesting, detailed red cherry, strawberry touches of whole berry ferment stems, and toasty black pepper. In the mouth the red fruit length and power is buoyed by supporting oak. The flavours run through the red berry fruits and there is just a hint of stem savoury spice note adding an extra defining line to the taut palate with acid freshness.

Vintage	Rank	Drink	RRP	Vol Alc
2012	94	2025	$65.00	13.0%
2013	95	2023	$65.00	12.5%
2014	94	2019	$75.00	12.5%

TOPPER'S MOUNTAIN

Topper's Mountain in the New England tableland region of Northern NSW near Armidale is planted on a cap of red basalt soil at an elevation of 870 metres. The cool elevated site and the mix of varieties make the wines well worth seeking out. Tiny amounts of high quality shiraz, tannat, viognier and tempranillo are offered with gewürztraminer the star.

Winemaker: *Mike Hayes*
Open: *By Appointment Only 5km Guyra Road, Tingha*
Ph: *(04) 1188 0580* *www.toppers.com.au*

TOPPER'S MOUNTAIN
GEWURZTRAMINER ★★★★★

The winning team of Mark Kirkby and Mike Hayes continue to show just what Australia's New England region is capable of. Pure rose petal and Turkish delight are layered with grape and lychee fruit. Where Gewurz can have alcohol warmth, this vintage is evenly balanced with the moderate alcohol giving a fragrant lift. I would drink it now to the short-term to enjoy that generously given pure fruit.

Vintage	Rank	Drink	RRP	Vol Alc
2013	93	2018	$35.00	12.8%
2014	92	2018	$35.00	12.6%
2015	93	2019	$35.00	13.9%

TOPPER'S MOUNTAIN
WILD FERMENT NEBBIOLO ★★★★
Raspberry and citrus spear mint aromas savoury minerals in the background low oak and looking like it should. Good line of flavour and texture in the mouth this light bodied wine has very good fruit length with great energy from front to back. The tannins are the fine, grainy and the savoury expression worth a try catches the varietal texture and structure.

Vintage	Rank	Drink	RRP	Vol Alc
2011	94	2019	$38.00	12.8%
2012	93	2020	$38.00	13.9%
2013	90	2019	$38.00	12.1%

TORBRECK
Torbreck is associated with the generous flavoured soft Barossa shiraz style so popular in America; however, within the portfolio lies special wines with complexity and vivid fruit. There are also very affordable priced wines featuring full flavoured easy drinking wines.
Winemaker: *Craig Isbel*
Open: *Daily 10am–5pm Lot 51, Roennfeldt Road, Tanunda*
Ph: *(08) 8562 4155* **www.torbreck.com**

TORBRECK
THE STRUIE SHIRAZ ★★★★★
The Eden valley contribution gives freshness, brighter fruits and acidity that makes them highly compatible. Aromas here are cascaded red into sweet rhubarb and bass notes of oak. The Eden valley freshness of red fruits starts the journey and is a classic example of very good line linking fruit and tannins together with length all the way down the palate. Barossa fills the middle palate and adds length of oak spiced pepper on the finish. Great balance and drive.

Vintage	Rank	Drink	RRP	Vol Alc
2011	91	2019	$50.00	15.0%
2012	93	2022	$50.00	15.0%
2014	94	2024	$48.50	15.0%

Vintage	Rank	Drink	RRP	Vol Alc

TORBRECK
DESCENDANT ★★★★★

This is deep coloured, brooding blue berry black fruits, gentle floral, cedar, chocolate and coffee quality oak that adds background dimension. Generous in the mouth, ripe fruits, blueberry, beetroot, mineral earthy into mocha mouth filling full bodied covers the tongue like a blanket on a bed, firm finishing with even middle palate length and appealing balanced cedar "summer rain on asphalt" complexity. Not a long term keeper like the 2012.

2010	94	2025	$125.00	15.0%
2012	94	2032	$125.00	15.5%
2013	89	2021	$125.00	15.5%

TORBRECK
THE PICT MATARO ★★★★★

The aroma is an essay in balanced oak spice and monastrell/mataro dark plum, cooked dark fruit cake, plum fruits with marjoram, oregano, rosemary and dusty outback roads. The palate is thick and full bodied; a long, even platform of stewed plums with cloves curving and very varietal with a mouth full of thick fruits angostura like dark with intense chewy soft tannins.

| 2012 | 93 | 2027 | $125.00 | 15.5% |
| 2013 | 94 | 2019 | $125.00 | 15.0% |

TORBRECK
THE FACTOR SHIRAZ ★★★★★

Aromas are fresh for the vintage; roasted black fruit, earthy mineral and oak spice with the dusty 2013. The palate has focus, good length, dark Christmas cake fruits, silky tannins and an even long palate with a fresh fruit quality and a well-crafted tannin balance.

2010	89	2018	$125.00	15.5%
2012	95	2034	$125.00	15.5%
2013	92	2022	$125.00	15.5%

TORBRECK
RUNRIG SHIRAZ ★★★★★

Has Barossa written all over it with dusty dark plums, blueberry and subtle morels, cherry fruits backed by the seamlessly integrated weight of coffee, vanilla, roasted brown spices and honey oak. Sip away into an engaging and confident wine integrated with dark fruit, Christmas cake, blueberry muffin edged flavours supported by the finest tannins of the Torbreck 2013 vintage release reds. This dodges heaviness, the oak stays light on its feet contributing oregano, cedar, and saffron flavours to sustain and frame the fruit length. Fifty percent new French oak for two and half years. Average vine age is (according to the company) over 100 years old 800 dozen produced.

Vintage	Rank	Drink	RRP	Vol Alc
2010	92	2025	$225.00	16.0%
2011	Not made			
2012	96	2030	$225.00	15.5%
2013	93	2022	$250.00	15.5%

TORBRECK
THE LAIRD SHIRAZ ★★★★★

From a single vineyard and matured three years in oak and two in bottle prior to release and still smells very intense, complex, super concentrated, almost criminal to open in youth. Layers of quality French oak, vanilla, mineral, mulberry, dark plum, date and liquorice aromas. The dark chocolaty fruit has tightly held dark flavours with silky tannins creating big shoulders that flow warmly, solidly down the palate with a rich dark plum, blackberry and black plum. The extended flavours are salty plum, savoury dark spices, five spice and liquorice and blood plum. The Barossa have a word for these wines- "stompf" meaning strength.

Vintage	Rank	Drink	RRP	Vol Alc
2006	96	2021	$700.00	14.8%
2008	96	2038	$900.00	15.5%
2010	96	2030	$750.00	15.5%

TRINITY HILL

Trinity Hill owner John Hancock trained at Roseworthy College before returning to New Zealand where he has been a leading figure for three decades. His Hawkes Bay chardonnay and Gimblett Gravels syrah (shiraz) are world class wines under the watchful and talented eye of Warren Gibson.

Winemaker: Warren Gibson
Open: Summer (October through Easter) 10am–5pm 2396 State Highway 50 Hastings
Ph: (64) 6879 7778 www.trinityhill.com

TRINITY HILL
HAWKES BAY CHARDONNAY ★★★★★

Developed colour with winemaker complexity, struck flint, bacon bone, oatmeal and oak create aromatic fullness. The palate is balanced and complex with ripe fruit, even length and even structure showing middle palate stone fruits and white nectarine with fine chablis like acidity pulling the reins of the oak and ripe fruit into a food friendly finish for food.

Vintage	Rank	Drink	RRP	Vol Alc
2011	92	2016	$25.00	13.0%
2012	92	2015	$25.00	12.5%
2013	93	2017	$25.00	13.0%

TRINITY HILL
GIMBLETT GRAVELS SYRAH ★★★★★

The senior edition syrah of the Trinity Hill stable is exotic and engaging. This has considerable concentration evident from the first sniff, with a balanced berry fruit, liquorice and black pepper spice savoury elements. The palate is finely structured red fruited and the tannins are powdery fine and very elegant, with a layered spicy black fruit finish.

Vintage	Rank	Drink	RRP	Vol Alc
2008	89	2015	$45.00	13.5%
2010	96	2016	$45.00	14.5%
2011	93	2022	$45.00	13.0%

TSCHARKE

Damien Tscharke is a well thought out professional. Like many young winemakers he has a manifesto, believing wines need to be varietal, fresh, and restrained, with more transparency than intense fruit and oak. He understands that having a delicate style allows tasters to experience the detail of wine with a sense of deliciousness that encourages another glass.
Winemaker: *Damien Tscharke*
Open: *Thurs to Mon 10am–5pm, 376 Seppeltsfield Road, Marananga*
Ph: *(08) 8562 4922* *www.tscharke.com.au*

TSCHARKE
GIRLS TALK SAVAGNIN ★★★★
A highly individual and successful style thanks to the gentle weave of oak adding extra intensity without losing balance. Marzipan, pears, and subtle oak adds white butter vanilla background aromas. In the mouth, soft and creamy on entry, gaining structure and seeming sweet from oak which makes for a creamy middle palate with buttered banana on vanilla toast flavours. The finish is soft and the wine is exotic in flavour and texture.

Vintage	Rank	Drink	RRP	Vol Alc
2011	90	2016	$20.00	12.5%
2012	90	2018	$20.00	12.5%
2014	92	2017	$20.00	12.5%

TSCHARKE
MATCHING SOX TOURIGA NACIONAL ★★★★
Ripe and fresh bright fruit, violets, black berry, jammy intensity turned savoury inky liquorice elements with low oak. In the mouth, soft tannins, a fresh acidity that starts ripe black cherry, bramble and blackberry with a medium full body, generous flavour, fruit complex, silky tannins and dark prune fruits to finish. Fresh style with fruit complexity in an easy drinking format.

Vintage	Rank	Drink	RRP	Vol Alc
2012	89	2018	$22.00	14.0%
2013	91	2017	$22.00	12.5%
2014	91	2018	$22.00	13.5%

| Vintage | Rank | Drink | RRP | Vol Alc |

TULLOCH

Tulloch is a famous maker in the Hunter Valley, established in 1895 and recently reinvigorated to great effect by the family after a period when it was out of their control. Very careful winemaking ensures excellent quality and value across all their offerings. Great to see a famous name rapidly exceeding its old form.
Winemaker: *J.Y. Tulloch*
Open: *Daily 10am–5pm, 638 DeBeyers Road, Pokolbin*
Ph: *(02) 4998 7580* *www.tulloch.com.au*

TULLOCH
VERDELHO ★★★

Custard apple and fresh pineapple tropical fruits with lime and kaffir lime aromatics all wrapped up within. It is a classic varietal weighted and fruited wine with a lovely rich front and middle. Fresh as a daisy cocktail party drinking wine that is food friendly and versatile.

2011	88	2013	$18.00	13.0%
2013	84	2016	$16.00	13.2%
2014	91	2016	$18.00	14.0%

TULLOCH
JULIA SEMILLON ★★★★★

Lemon juice and skin aromas with a smoked meat background. Excellent mouth covering fruit structure and flavour with lively fine acidity and fresh lemon fruits running long in the mouth and lingering afterwards. It drinks well now and will age as well.

2011	90	2028	$28.00	11.5%
2013	90	2025	$30.00	11.0%
2014	94	2026	$30.00	11.0%

TULLOCH
POKOLBIN DRY RED SHIRAZ ★★★

Fresh, modern, modest red fruits, on the edge of savoury elements in the fruit aromas. The mouth feel is tender, sweet middle palate with raspberry and white pepper spice, youthful, medium bodied, bright and then chalky on the finish.

2010	87	2015	$25.00	13.2%
2011	88	2017	$25.00	13.0%
2013	90	2018	$25.00	12.3%

TULLOCH
PRIVATE BIN POKOLBIN DRY RED SHIRAZ ★★★★

Traditional style that respects the need for lower oak to balance the regional fruit. Deep fruit aromas with blackberry, blueberry and the beginnings of liquorice. The palate is ripe up front and middle, with plenty of raspberry and a zingy acidity, cedar oak spice, and chalky finish.

Vintage	Rank	Drink	RRP	Vol Alc
2010	90	2022	$40.00	12.9%
2011	90	2028	$50.00	13.5%
2013	89	2019	$50.00	12.5%

TULLOCH
HECTOR OF GLEN ELGIN DRY RED ★★★★★

Beautiful vanilla oak dominates the cooked plum, salty plum on release, but the fruit has tenacity and will spring back in a decade. The palate is initially sweet fruited, silky tannins and dark fruit run seamlessly on the palate and the oak integrates beautifully.

Vintage	Rank	Drink	RRP	Vol Alc
2006	93	2016	$60.00	14.0%
2007	91	2022	$60.00	14.5%
2009	93	2030	$70.00	14.0%

TYRRELL'S

Tyrrell's is a Hunter Valley-based family-owned and run company with a dedicated following. A regional specialist, increasingly some of Australia's finest wines appear under their varied labels with greater focus on single mature vineyards with unique terriors and winemaking that preserves these differences. Quality, while always high, is on the move up.
Winemaker: *Andrew Spinaze, Mark Richardson, Chris Tyrrell*
Open: *Mon to Sat 9am–5pm Sun 10am–4pm,*
1838 Broke Road, Pokolbin
Ph: *(02) 4993 7000 www.tyrrells.com.au*

TYRRELL'S
STEVENS SINGLE VINEYARD SEMILLON ★★★★★

Lemon to red apple, subtle white nectarine fruit poised and slightly riper than the Vat 1 style. The palate is correspondingly softer, plumper and the acid is less linear and intense with

Vintage	Rank	Drink	RRP	Vol Alc

appealing red apple to nectarine fruit on the finish. Pair with Japanese foods on release and will age.

Vintage	Rank	Drink	RRP	Vol Alc
2010	88	2016	$30.00	11.0%
2011	90	2022	$30.00	11.0%
2012	88	2020	$30.00	10.5%

TYRRELL'S
BELFORD SEMILLON ★★★★★

Got to hand it to the family for handling this varietal with integrity; lemon, lanolin minerally aromas and in the mouth, concentration and a steady even lemony palate with green apple, grapefruit edges with plenty of drink now fruit intensity and layers on the finish.

Vintage	Rank	Drink	RRP	Vol Alc
2007	91	2015	$36.00	13.1%
2009	91	2017	$35.00	11.0%
2013	91	2024	$35.00	11.5%

TYRRELL'S
HVD SEMILLON ★★★★★

Very fine lemon juice aromas and not a flicker of the 5 years age showing. In the mouth this has depth. Starts out ripe fruit texture with juicy evolving lemon flavours and great length, the middle palate is lemon curd and the finish fresh lemon and lemon pie.

Vintage	Rank	Drink	RRP	Vol Alc
2007	93	2017	$33.00	11.0%
2009	93	2019	$35.00	11.0%
2010	95	2030	$35.00	11.0%

TYRRELL'S
HUNTER SEMILLON VAT 1 ★★★★★

Judging high quality young semillon is an Australian speciality. Subtle fruit with strength, citrus, lemon, sunlight soap backed by a stony minerality. The fruit structure is there but it is a youthful shy flavour appearing with a lemon finish late after the long fruit platform. It has the texture, length, acid texture and structure and it will take its time to shine.

Vintage	Rank	Drink	RRP	Vol Alc
2010	90	2022	$68.00	12.0%
2011	94	2022	$73.00	11.5%
2012	96	2039	$68.00	10.5%

TYRRELL'S
CHARDONNAY VAT 47 ★★★★★

Savoury more minerally flint driven aromas with the nectarine fruit in the background as a young wine. The palate has delicacy and poise with savoury and ripe fruit elements linked sinuously along the palate to the bright fresh finish.

Vintage	Rank	Drink	RRP	Vol Alc
2010	92	2018	$68.00	13.5%
2011	92	2022	$68.00	13.5%
2012	96	2020	$68.00	12.5%

TYRRELL'S
BELFORD CHARDONNAY ★★★★

Smokey solids, ferment, oak and oatmeal fresh citrus fruits aroma. In the mouth, substantial structure, bright lemon citrus, creamy oatmeal middle palate flavours, even youthful structure, light white butter finish. Very fresh aromas and complexity with lingering popcorn vanilla flavours.

Vintage	Rank	Drink	RRP	Vol Alc
2009	90	2015	$34.00	13.8%
2010	89	2014	$34.00	12.5%
2012	93	2017	$34.00	13.0%

TYRRELL'S
BROKENBACK SHIRAZ ★★★★

Raspberry fruits with black tea backing into dried herbs aromas. The palate is tight, needs time, firm acidity, a touch of lemon, shy black fruits, good middle palate fullness, structure and length of the medium bodied shy shiraz. Black fruit finishing savoury and green pepper corn. A delicate flavoured dainty tannic red.

Vintage	Rank	Drink	RRP	Vol Alc
2010	87	2017	$21.00	12.9%
2011	84	2016	$20.00	13.0%
2013	89	2020	$20.00	13.0%

TYRRELL'S
LUNATIQ SHIRAZ ★★★★★

Fragrant ripe red cherry and fruits with a lick of leather in the back ground. In the mouth medium bodied fresh blood plum, long with fresh energy and length of supple flavours with fine tannins.

Vintage	Rank	Drink	RRP	Vol Alc
2010	93	2022	$29.00	14.0%
2012	92	2018	$38.00	13.5%

Vintage	Rank	Drink	RRP	Vol Alc

TYRRELL'S
STEVENS SHIRAZ ★★★★

Tyrrell's are not in favour of lavish new oak which is a plus as the wines have a clear authentic character such as this. Bright colour, red cherry, subtle savoury dried Mediterranean herbs, minerals and oak a back ground murmur. The palate has medium bodied tannin length and fruit structure with evenness, fresh fruits and youthful restraint in the red fruits and fine tannins.

Vintage	Rank	Drink	RRP	Vol Alc
2010	89	2018	$40.00	13.0%
2011	90	2021	$38.00	13.0%
2013	92	2034	$38.00	13.0%

TYRRELL'S
OLD PATCH SHIRAZ ★★★★★

From the Stevens vineyards oldest vines a 1.5-acre, old, patch planted in 1867. Matured in a single large 2,500 litre barrel, oak is not part of the recipe. Has solid aromas and richness with savoury tapenade edges. The palate has a medium body sweet fruit and fine tannins with a youth firm tannin acid edge at release. These wines have a delicious mid palate supple richness.

Vintage	Rank	Drink	RRP	Vol Alc
2007	95	2030	$46.00	13.5%
2009	95	2029	$70.00	13.5%
2010	92	2025	$70.00	13.4%

TYRRELL'S
4 ACRES SHIRAZ ★★★★★

Planted by great-great-grandfather Tyrrell in 1879, situated on the drive into the winery, this is living history. The year '06 shows rich berry fruit with raspberry, liquorice and very drying fine tannins with a very long red fruit finish lasting over 45 seconds. The '09 is refined with delicacy, freshness and aromas of crystallised red-berry fruit. Only just medium body with finesse in the very fine tannins and great delicacy of berry fruits, acidity and length of flavour.

Vintage	Rank	Drink	RRP	Vol Alc
2007	93	2030	$46.00	13.5%
2008	Not made			
2009	93	2022	$70.00	13.0%

TYRRELL'S
VAT 8 SHIRAZ CABERNET ★★★★
Aromas from dark fruits into savoury territory with smoked meats to mocha spectrum oak, dark berry and chocolate. A fresh vibrant style, the palate is linear with imposing middle palate red berry fruit length, white pepper spices, grainy tannins, lingering shiraz flavours to finish. The acids a touch prominent in youth and will settle with food or age.

Vintage	Rank	Drink	RRP	Vol Alc
2010	94	2028	$85.00	13.5%
2011	90	2023	$85.00	13.8%
2013	95	2037	$85.00	13.5%

TYRRELL'S
HUNTER VALLEY VAT 9 SHIRAZ ★★★★★
This is enticing with a crescendo of pink aromas, camellia, flower floral aromas adding to the red cherry, dried Mediterranean herbs and cedar. The palate is an essay in age worthy balance, firm and long with refined medium bodied structure of red flavours, tannin texture bridging front to back with a clip of acid and fine tannins on the finish. Just a pup.

Vintage	Rank	Drink	RRP	Vol Alc
2010	92	2020	$85.00	13.0%
2011	91	2018	$85.00	12.9%
2013	94	2036	$85.00	13.0%

VASSE FELIX
Vasse Felix is a very fine Margaret River winemaker, located within the Wilyabrup sub region, offering a range of elegant wines including a sumptuous chardonnay, delicious cabernet merlot and shiraz. All the wines exhibit great style and finesse.
Winemaker: Virginia Willcock
Open: Daily 10am–5pm, Cnr Caves Road & Harmans Road, South Cowaramup
Ph: (08) 9756 5055 www.vassefelix.com.au

VASSE FELIX
FILIUS CHARDONNAY ★★★★
Eight years in the creation and meaning "son of" in Latin. This is the old green capsule chardonnay with a more detailed name and upgraded fruit. Ripe and tropical in the Margaret River sense, yet reserved rather than austere in youth. Shy and looking durable for the next 4 years, pear and just ripe pineapple, lees, creamy yoghurt and a solid

oatmeal complexity with a flowing fruit richness, elegant acidity and medium bodied refined middle palate with acid finesse.

| 2013 | 90 | 2018 | $29.00 | 13.0% |
| 2014 | 90 | 2016 | $29.00 | 15.5% |

VASSE FELIX
CHARDONNAY ★★★★

Polished, seamless, subtle and gentle perfumes. In the mouth, a classy weave of oak, stone fruit in a great structure of discrete flavours with a mineral note on the finish.

2012	89	2017	$29.00	12.5%
2013	92	2022	$37.00	13.0%
2014	92	2017	$37.00	13.0%

VASSE FELIX
HEYTESBURY CHARDONNAY ★★★★★

Exquisite balance, wine maker funky savoury elements, grapefruit and white fruits, tight refined oak. The freshness on the palate is immediate with a lighter body than previous editions. Lovely seamless drive of complex flavours and textures with gentle pink grapefruit and beautifully balanced tight grained French oak adding to the drive. A mouth-watering youthful layered finish.

2012	93	2017	$65.00	13.0%
2013	96	2026	$70.00	13.5%
2014	95	2022	$90.00	13.0%

VASSE FELIX
CABERNET SAUVIGNON ★★★★★

Finesse is a byword here with the company of the best wines of its history. Blue berry mint fruits in a fine expose of the Margaret River cabernet style. The tannins are fine red fruits on the tip of the tongue showing maturity and a drink up style with red and black currant and acid to close. Needs Italian.

2011	92	2017	$40.00	14.0%
2012	89	2017	$40.00	14.5%
2013	90	2017	$40.00	14.5%

VASSE FELIX
HEYTESBURY CABERNET SAUVIGNON MALBEC ★★★★★

Appealing, stylish wine from the chardonnay wonder kid of her generation. Tobacco black currant with tightly wound aromas. Picked to perfection, fresh cabernet aromas and flavours. The palate is an indulgence with refined silky tannins, fresh and vibrant red fruit flavours, extraordinary balance and a fine-grained tannin perfectly integrated with the flavours. Acidity underpins flavour and tannin, creating an energetic palate with evenness of texture, structure and flavour and lingering fruit.

2009	93	2029	$90.00	14.5%
2010	96	2034	$90.00	14.5%
2012	96	2036	$90.00	14.5%

VICKERY WINES

Clare valley winery well known for its signature riesling. John Vickery has helped shape the face of Australian riesling, and these classic wines tell you what it is all about.

Winemaker: Phil Lehmann
Open: No Cellar Door, PO Box 184 Tanunda
Ph: (02) 4773 4161 *www.vickerywines.com.au*

VICKERY
WATERVALE RIESLING ★★★★★

A ripe clean fresh drink showing florals, pine lime/kaffir lime and the spice of a great riesling. The palate is vibrant, plush and generous with ripe lively length. Very good weight of fruits, modern and stylish. Drink young or age.

2014	95	2034	$24.00	11.5%
2015	93	2025	$23.00	13.0%
2016	92	2022	$23.00	12.5%

VICKERY
EDEN VALLEY RIESLING ★★★★★

Regional varietal finesse of white floral and lemon zest aromas. The palate is streamlined, long lemon intensity, relatively tighter, more vitality and less plush than Watervale with white flower flavours and an integrated acidity on the finish.

2015	91	2022	$23.00	12.5%
2016	94	2026	$23.00	12.5%

VOYAGER ESTATE

A picturesque Margaret River winery which is a must to visit. Voyager's intense focus on quality – latterly on chardonnay and cabernet blends – places it among the region's leading estates. The team's energy and drive suggests there is more excitement to come as their project wines program develops.

Winemakers: *Steve James and Travis Lemm*
Open: *Daily 10am–5pm, Stevens Road, Margaret River*
Ph: *(08) 9757 6354* ***www.voyagerestate.com.au***

VOYAGER
PROJECT 95 CHARDONNAY ★★★★★

Single vineyard and single clone #95 and 120 dozen made. Flowery citrus sweet fruit and oak in a refined chardonnay style with gentle elegance through the fennel into white mushrooms. The palate has width and length, very middle palate rich with guava and kiwi fruit flavours into feijoa. Not big in weight, but silky and flowing. Drink 2017 onwards.

2010	95	2019	$58.00	12.5%
2011	89	2017	$58.00	12.8%
2012	95	2023	$55.00	12.4%

VOYAGER
CHARDONNAY ★★★★★

Perfumed white peach, citrus, savoury and complex with plenty of charm and minerality. The buoyant palate has creamy glycerol, lees and fleshy fruit upfront and the middle palate is ripe and silky. The firm youthful finish is refined, lemon pith before the ripe stone fruits emerge.

2011	92	2019	$45.00	13.3%
2012	93	2020	$45.00	13.0%

| Vintage | Rank | Drink | RRP | Vol Alc |

VOYAGER
ESTATE CABERNET SAUVIGNON ★★★★★
Delicate fruit in the finer boysenberry aroma elements and just ripe fruits of the forest. Almost jammy upfront and very drinkable now with the juicy fleshy silky palate winter green edge. A rich ripe year, with ripe tannin elegance, showing a juicy cassis opulence to the middle palate. Powdery fine tannins with graphite, briar, and black currant layered flavours on the finish.

2009	94	2024	$70.00	13.6%
2010	94	2020	$70.00	13.6%
2011	95	2027	$70.00	14.0%

VOYAGER
PROJECT U12 NORTH BLOCK CABERNET SAUVIGNON ★★★★★
The Wallcliffe fruit provides a very appealing personality to the very fine aromas of cooking fruits, compote of dark berry, black currant, butterscotch and vanilla oak. Plenty of sweet ripe fruits, cocoa powder and almost Pauillac in structure. Dark cassis fruits, butterscotch, vanilla oak and fine grained tannins add a seamless complexity to the finish.

2009	94	2018	$90.00	14.2%
2010	95	2026	$90.00	13.9%
2011	96	2033	$90.00	14.0%

WANGOLINA
Wangolina was planted in 2001 on limestone terra rossa soils, situated between the coastal towns of Kingston & Robe in the Mt Benson region, part of the broader Limestone Coast Wine region in South Australia. Winemaker Anita Goode has extensive experience in Australia and the USA and with Kim Milne MW consulting the settings look very bright for this young company.
Winemaker: *Anita Goode*
Open: *Weekdays 10am–5pm, Weekends 11am–4pm, 8 Limestone Coast Road, Wangolina*
Ph: *(08) 8768 6187 www.wangolina.com.au*

WANGOLINA
SPECTRUM SYRAH ★★★★★

Thoughtfully made and justifying the price. Aromatic oak and fresh black fruits with a delicious oak and fruit balance. The palate has intensity, balance and good length with briary bramble, blackberry black fruits and tobacco leather side notes adding complexity. Good concentration and weight with puckering tannins and plenty of pedigree from the balance and structure. Drink 2017.

Vintage	Rank	Drink	RRP	Vol Alc
2012	92	2018	$50.00	14.0%
2013	94	2025	$50.00	14.5%

WANGOLINA
MT BENSON SEMILLON ★★★★

Subtle, spicy edged, white stone fruit aromas. Oak is part of the complexion, but just whispers its presence. The palate is precise. It runs buttered oak and white stone fruit with fine balance, just enough. It turns intense with French oak, white butter biscuit caramel flavours that linger. Very good value for short term cellaring and for the joy of watching it change.

Vintage	Rank	Drink	RRP	Vol Alc
2015	93	2020	$20.00	12.5%

WARRABILLA

Warrabilla, in the Rutherglen area, is producing some of the biggest full-bodied reds in the country, from this painstakingly nurtured vineyard. Arguably the leading exponent of high-alcohol red wine making in Australia. If power, richness and concentration are your interest, look no further.
Winemaker: *Andrew Smith*
Open: *Daily 10am–5pm, 6152 Murray Valley Highway, Rutherglen*
Ph: *(02) 6035 7242* *www.warrabillawines.com.au*

WARRABILLA
RESERVE SHIRAZ ★★★★

Liquorice, graphite, savoury and very ripe fruits aromas. The palate is a ginger snap biscuit with butterscotch toffee oak and incredible warming alcohol sweetness and oak length.

Vintage	Rank	Drink	RRP	Vol Alc
2008	90	2017	$24.00	17.0%
2009	88	2018	$24.00	17.0%
2013	88	2018	$25.00	16.5%

WARRABILLA
RESERVE DURIF ★★★★
Cola jammy black cherry fruit, mineral spice, and subtle date dried fruits. The middle palate is silky cola and date fruited, with Christmas pudding dried fruit cakes and ginger cinnamon pepper spices adding to the black cherry jam finish.

2008	90	2015	$24.00	16.5%
2009	89	2018	$24.00	16.5%
2013	90	2019	$27.00	16.5%

WARRABILLA
RESERVE CABERNET ★★★★
Light soya/tamari sauce with blackberry. In the mouth, sweet blackberry fruit and firm, fine tannins, with a core of silky tannins and mouth-filling intensity and generosity, finishing dark wine gum and fruit jubes.

2007	90	2018	$24.00	15.6%
2009	90	2018	$24.00	16.0%
2013	90	2019	$27.00	15.5%

WARRABILLA
LIMITED RELEASE PAROLA'S DURIF ★★★
For full bodied red lovers. Liquorice, raisins, blackberry cola fruit, peppery alcohol and oak spice with fruit lift. The silky tannins slide the ripe dark berry and slightly minty fruit long into the mouth and the finish punches regional warmth, which is the hallmark lingering jammy berry fruit of this style. Clean, ripe and immensely powerful, these are in a class of their own.

2006	89	2040	$32.00	18.0%
2009	90	2025	$32.00	18.0%
2013	92	2023	$37.00	17.5%

WARRABILLA
LIMITED RELEASE PAROLA'S CABERNET SAUVIGNON ★★★★
For full-bodied red lovers; a very rich and oaky style, with dusty date and prune aromas. In the mouth, sweet fruits with chocolate preserved cherry, morello cherry, liqueured cherry fruits, fine tannins and a distinctive American oak bourbon finish.

Vintage	Rank	Drink	RRP	Vol Alc
2005	90	2030	$32.00	16.0%
2006	90	2025	$32.00	15.0%
2013	88	2018	$37.00	15.5%

WARRABILLA
PAROLA'S RESERVE SHIRAZ ★★★★

Leaps out of the glass with Christmas cake, raisin, dark soya and plum fruit aromas, while in the mouth it is balanced and incredibly alcoholic, with dark berry and cola fruits that unfold with a succession of flavours. The finish sees fine-grained oak tannins and fruit that linger for nearly a minute.

2007	90	2017	$32.00	17.0%
2008	91	2017	$32.00	17.0%
2013	92	2030	$35.00	17.0%

WARRABILLA
RESERVE VINTAGE PORT ★★★★

Captures the intense, ripe cherry fruit and massive tannins needed for the long haul.

2001	92	2020	$18.00	19.5%
2004	90	2022	$22.00	19.5%
2005	89	2022	$22.00	19.5%
2006	91	2025	$22.00	19.5%

WARRAMATE

Warramate is an old, low-key and small unirrigated Yarra Valley vineyard between Yarra Yering and Coldstream Hills, offering value and quality hand-crafted wines.

Winemaker: Sarah Crowe
Open: No Cellar Door, 27 Madden's Lane, Gruyere
Ph: (03) 5964 9219   www.warramatewines.com.au

WARRAMATE
CABERNET ★★★★

Stylish, soft powdery tannins and medium-bodied restraint, with a firm finish in youth. This wine is one of the fullest of the "old guard" Yarra vineyards. It always has a measure of ripeness and restraint and the nose hints at richness and warm black fruits, while the palate has soft silky tannins with ripe black plum and black currant, although the regional claret-like style fruit weight and tannins are there.

2007	86	2014	$35.00	13.5%
2008	88	2016	$35.00	13.5%
2009	Not made			
2010	90	2019	$35.00	13.5%

WARRAMATE
WHITE LABEL SHIRAZ ★★★★★
Fabulous tannins, medium bodied with low-key oak like the old-fashioned clarets that made the valley famous. Red plum and pepper with a savoury edge.

2008	88	2016	$45.00	13.5%
2009	Not made			
2010	88	2018	$45.00	13.5%
2012	89	2022	$45.00	13.0%

WARRENMANG
Warrenmang is a 10-hectare vineyard in the Moonambel district. Mature vines and long term management means the wines are consistently styled with abundant ripe middle palate fruit and, for the region, subtle tannins.
Winemakers: *Luigi Bazzani and Greg Foster*
Open: *Daily 10am–5pm, Mountain Creek Road, Moonambel*
Ph: *(03) 5467 2233 www.warrenmang.com.au*

WARRENMANG
GRAND PYRENEES ★★★★★
Almost rum and raisin with a black pepper spice. In the mouth a liqueur like wash of ripe fruits and caramel oak with dried plum and clove fruits to close. The persistent dark spices, clove and cinnamon unbalances the finish.

2008	88	2016	$35.00	13.5%
2009	90	2021	$35.00	14.0%
2010	83	2017	$35.00	13.7%

| Vintage | Rank | Drink | RRP | Vol Alc |

WARRENMANG
ESTATE SHIRAZ ★★★★

Aromas are regional central Victoria with older oak, pepper plum dried herbs, bay leaf earthy angostura bitters. In the mouth tertiary flavours, silky tannins, vanilla date and prune. Full bodied and quite dry at the finish.

Vintage	Rank	Drink	RRP	Vol Alc
2008	88	2018	$60.00	14.0%
2009	87	2017	$60.00	15.0%
2010	84	2016	$60.00	15.5%

WARRENMANG
BLACK PUMA SHIRAZ ★★★★

For full bodied red lovers. This is an authentic regional varietal style with Victorian dark pepper, bay leaf, clove spice, liquorice and sausage meat style. In the mouth, super fine tannins, lively flickering flavours, dark plum, cedar and liquorice- the intensity is enough to make you think there is a whole butchers smoke house on the finish. Very on the money.

Vintage	Rank	Drink	RRP	Vol Alc
2008	90	2015	$80.00	14.5%
2009	88	2019	$80.00	14.5%
2012	93	2022	$80.00	14.5%

WARRENMANG
BAZZANI SHIRAZ CABERNET ★★★★

A big red lover's wine with fruit richness. Regional pepper and pot-roast shiraz aromas lead to a bright ripe juicy fruit-driven, initially spicy wine. Turning black fruits with firm oak tannins and length. Plenty of fruit weight and stylish flavours.

Vintage	Rank	Drink	RRP	Vol Alc
2009	90	2021	$15.00	15.0%
2010	88	2013	$15.00	13.5%
2011	90	2017	$15.00	14.0%

| Vintage | Rank | Drink | RRP | Vol Alc |

WATER WHEEL
Water Wheel Vineyards of Bridgewater on Loddon in the Bendigo region produces admirable wines entirely from grapes grown on its own vineyards. The style is full bodied and ripe.
Winemaker: *Peter Cumming*
Open: *Weekdays 9am–5pm, Weekends and Pub Hols 12pm–4pm Raywood Road, Bridgewater-on-Loddon*
Ph: *(03) 5437 3060 www.waterwheelwine.com*

WATER WHEEL
BARINGUP SHIRAZ ★★★
The freshness is the key element here, wed to ripe red fruits. Eucalypt-like camphor elements, red berry, raspberry and red cherry aroma, with an edge of espresso coffee. The palate is refined silky tannins, supple in the middle palate, with generous ripe red fruits in a silky tannin spectrum.

2011	90	2014	$18.00	14.5%
2012	88	2018	$20.00	14.0%
2013	91	2021	$20.00	15.5%

WATER WHEEL
BENDIGO CABERNET SAUVIGNON ★★★
Full bodied, with a hearty generous personality full of ripe fruit with black currant jam, Ribena and lots of fruity sweetness.

2007	85	2012	$19.00	14.0%
2008	85	2012	$19.00	15.0%
2009	Not made			
2010	86	2013	$18.00	13.5%

WENDOUREE
Of the thousands of wineries in Australia, there are only a few vineyards as great as Wendouree. The wines are only available from the mailing list, which has been closed since 1995. The blends are more approachable than the single varietals when young and all possess elegance, supple fruit and extraordinarily fine tannin.
Winemaker: *Tony Brady*
Open: *Mailing List Only, Wendouree Road, East Clare*
Ph: *(08) 8842 2896*

WENDOUREE
CABERNET MALBEC ★★★★★
The aromas are solid and relatively shy with mineral, dark spices, cardamom and vanilla oak in woodsy red fruit. The tannins glide onto the tongue with refined softness and the red fruits follow. The finish is firm layers of oak and red fruit – the classic iron fist in the velvet glove. Beautiful fruit detail and soft tannin depth, while the flavours and textures leave the mouth fresh. The estate's standards are so consistent that this is a safe name every year.

| 1994 | 93 | 2020 | $90.00 |
| 2012 | 95 | 2040 | $90.00 |

WENDOUREE
SHIRAZ MALBEC ★★★★★
Dark spectrum bramble, blueberry and blackberry, date, graphite and dusty mineral aromas. The palate is medium full bodied, with a fine tannin line and deceptive medium-bodied fruit flavours, tannins and textures. The middle palate fruits are tantalising raspberry, blueberry and red currant, with a floral top note.

| 2008 | 94 | 2035 | $50.00 | 14.0% |
| 2012 | 95 | 2035 | $50.00 | 13.4% |

WIGNALLS WINES
Wignalls was established on the outskirts of Albany in 1982 by Dr Bill Wignall. The vineyard is arguably Western Australia's most southerly vineyard and the cool Great Southern Ocean significantly influences their wine styles. Recent releases have been exciting.
Winemaker: *Mick Perkins & Rob Wignall*
Open: *Daily 11am–4pm, 448 Chester Pass Road, Albany*
Ph: *(08) 9841 2848 www.wignallswines.com.au*

WIGNALLS WINES
PREMIUM SINGLE VINEYARD CHARDONNAY ★★★★

Cracking old school style, well made and well-balanced. A ripe cool style with popcorn vanilla oak aromas and maritime citrus oyster shell. In the mouth it carries medium bodied weight in an appealing middle palate. Pear fruits, gentle oak and a mix of pear vanilla honey oak adding balanced length to close.

| 2013 | 94 | 2018 | $32.00 | 13.5% |

WIGNALLS WINES
SINGLE VINEYARD SAUVIGNON BLANC ★★★★

Fresh passionfruit and black currant leaf, think ribena and parsley aromas, leads to a dry lively balanced middle palate set of pineapple passion fruit flavours. Vibrant and fresh with lingering tropical flavours.

| 2014 | 89 | 2017 | $20.00 | 13.4% |
| 2015 | 90 | 2018 | $20.00 | 13.4% |

WIGNALLS WINES
SHIRAZ ★★★★★

Value plus here. A well awarded wine with a great cool climate shiraz spectrum of aromas. Very black pepper spicy with red and blue berry and the top quality note of charcuterie similar sausage meat. The palate has cool climate acid line, fruits are red and last long wearing a black pepper t-shirt with the very fine tannins and fruit has balance and good length. Fresh medium bodied.

| 2013 | 94 | 2023 | $24.00 | 13.8% |
| 2014 | 92 | 2020 | $29.00 | 14.5% |

WILLOW CREEK

Willow Creek on the Mornington Peninsula is a consistent producer, with an interesting spread of quality across its flights of chardonnay and pinot noir.

Winemaker: Geraldine McFaul
Open: Daily 11am–5pm, 166 Balnarring Road, Merricks North
Ph: (03) 5989 7448 www.willow-creek.com.au

| Vintage | Rank | Drink | RRP | Vol Alc |

WILLOW CREEK
CHARDONNAY ★★★★★

This has power and complexity with good grace, oat meal, straw, white butter and butter scotch. The winemaker judged the fruit well and balanced the style. Creamy textured, gentle vanilla within sophisticated subtle white fruit flavours. Good length and structure with a tightness that will age short term.

Vintage	Rank	Drink	RRP	Vol Alc
2012	88	2016	$40.00	13.0%
2013	86	2017	$40.00	13.5%
2014	92	2019	$40.00	13.0%

WILLOW CREEK
PINOT NOIR ★★★★

Ripe red fruits running gentle strawberry, bulging into raspberry keeping to itself with oak in the background. The palate is delicate seamless fine tannins and pleasant strawberry fruits with a subtle guiding hand from oak and building complexity in the middle mouth with the fruit bowing to the oak on the finish.

Vintage	Rank	Drink	RRP	Vol Alc
2012	91	2025	$40.00	13.0%
2013	89	2019	$40.00	13.8%
2014	90	2019	$40.00	13.2%

WILSON VINEYARD

The Wilson Vineyard in the cool elevated Polish Hill River region near Clare are now reliable producers of some of the region's highest quality rieslings and exciting shirazs.

Winemaker: *Daniel Wilson*
Open: *Weekends 10am–4pm and by appointment, Polish Hill River Road, Sevenhill*
Ph: *(08) 8843 4310* *www.wilsonvineyard.com.au*

WILSON VINEYARD
WATERVALE RIESLING ★★★★

This is a well balanced, regional varietal. Classic riesling florals with white flowers, and honeysuckle. The palate is textbook fresh fruit, with red apple, pine lime generosity, and good middle palate weight. A great early drinking style.

Vintage	Rank	Drink	RRP	Vol Alc
2013	90	2020	$19.00	12.0%
2014	92	2019	$19.00	12.0%
2015	93	2018	$19.00	12.5%

WILSON VINEYARD
DJW CLARE VALLEY RIESLING ★★★★★
Bruised apple, and lime youthful aromas lead to a very good palate with detail and delicacy.
Tasting it unfolds across the tongue from citrus into florals,

2013	95	2035	$24.00	12.0%
2014	89	2018	$24.00	12.0%
2015	90	2018	$24.00	12.5%

WILSON VINEYARD
POLISH HILL RIESLING ★★★★★
Fragrant and distinctive. Lime and lemon, wet stone mineral aromas on a rainy day, leads to a palate with typical Polish Hill regional flavours. Excellent concentration and fruit weight and a tangy acidity freshening the palate. Complexity, drive and regional style.

2012	90	2017	$28.00	12.5%
2013	92	2028	$29.00	12.0%
2014	92	2019	$29.00	12.0%

WITCHES FALLS
Witches Falls' cellar door is at Mount Tamborine but its wines are from the Granite Belt. A solid range of wines as good as the views from this spectacular area. The chardonnay is a real star. Noteworthy marsanne, fiano and cabernet also.
Winemaker: *Jon Heslop*
Open: *Weekdays 10am–4pm, Weekends 10am–5pm*
79 Main Western Road, North Tamborine
Ph: (07) 5545 2609 www.witchesfalls.com.au

WITCHES FALLS
WILD FERMENT CHARDONNAY ★★★★★
Peaking between 2 and 4 years they come complex, big and bold with maturity. Aromas are creamed honey, violet crumble, and toasty oak and rich expressive yellow fruits. The silky palate verges on syrup but the toasty vanilla oak and acidity keep it tame.

2012	89	2016	$22.00	13.0%
2013	86	2017	$32.00	13.4%
2014	87	2018	$32.00	13.4%

WOLF BLASS

Wolf Blass has been a powerhouse brand in Australia since the 1970s. The state of the art winery in the Barossa Valley today produces significant ranges of South Australian derived wines under different coloured labels representing value and volume, as well as the limited production wines featured here. A riesling specialist, this brand is best known for its ability to blend different regions to produce complex, ripe, full-flavoured and full-bodied reds.

Chief Winemaker: *Stephen Frost, Marie Clay, Matt O'Leary*
Open: *Weekdays 9.15am–5pm, Weekends 10am–5pm*
97 Sturt Highway, Nooriupta
Ph: (08) 8568 7311 *www.wolfblass.com*

WOLF BLASS
GOLD LABEL PINOT NOIR CHARDONNAY ★★★★★

Almost vegemite toasty aged sparkling aromas, with smoked meats giving a savoury edge. The palate has easy drinking sweetness, good for toasts and birthday cakes, with stone fruits up front and subtle toast on the finish.

Vintage	Rank	Drink	RRP	Vol Alc
2007	88	2013	$18.00	12.0%
2008	87	2013	$18.00	12.0%
2011	87	2016	$27.99	11.5%

WOLF BLASS
GOLD LABEL CHARDONNAY ★★★★★

The focus is on fruit, riper this year than most by a degree, almost tropical, with generous barrel ferment vanilla almost brulee oak. The palate is rich, white fruit complex and long pears and apple, great structure, density and bright acidity defining the length while the finish is subtle, clean and complex. Offers balance and yet again a reliable 'go to' style for Adelaide Hills chardonnay.

Vintage	Rank	Drink	RRP	Vol Alc
2012	91	2017	$25.00	13.0%
2013	91	2017	$28.00	13.0%
2015	93	2018	$27.99	13.5%

WOLF BLASS
GOLD LABEL SYRAH ★★★★

Aromas are ripe and fleshy black berry with a floral and a white pepper lift. In the mouth, initially fleshy ripeness, silky tannins and juicy black berry fruit up front with a welcoming flavour and texture. Medium long.

2010	89	2018	$22.50	14.5%
2012	88	2017	$27.99	14.5%
2013	90	2019	$27.99	14.5%

WOLF BLASS
GOLD LABEL CABERNET SAUVIGNON ★★★★

The varietal fruit surges here, with minty-edged intense black currant pastille and maraschino cherry top notes, wrapped in dark oak toast and spice. The fresh, ripe, sweet fruited, medium-bodied palate is very varietal. Elegant and medium long flavours, offering ripe black currant fruits to a medium long finish.

2010	90	2014	$23.00	14.0%
2012	88	2018	$27.99	14.0%
2013	89	2019	$27.99	14.5%

WOLF BLASS
GREY LABEL CABERNET SHIRAZ ★★★★★

Rich buttered toast, coconut and chocolate give the peppery, plum and cherry fruit in this grey label some added complexity. There is a solid block of fruit and spice that moves all the way from the front to the back of the palate. It is a powerful peppery red that show cases the prettiness of Langhorne Creek without leaving you feeling overwhelmed.

2013	91	2021	$45.00	14.5%
2014	92	2025	$45.00	14.5%

Vintage	Rank	Drink	RRP	Vol Alc

WOLF BLASS
PLATINUM LABEL SHIRAZ ★★★★★

Very Blass style intensity for lovers of full-bodied reds. So dark as to be impenetrable with vanilla, coffee, cola, mocha oak, blue berry and black berry in a seamless lift of aromatic complexity. The palate has shiraz sweet tannins, ripe roundness with liqueur and very well balanced oak driving and enticing the fruit finish. Notes of nutmeg and brown spice with fresh nimble tannins drying the mouth to close in what is a heroic mouthful of wine.

2010	91	2022	$199.99	14.5%
2012	94	2025	$199.99	14.5%
2014	94	2028	$199.00	14.5%

WOLF BLASS
BLACK LABEL CABERNET SAUVIGNON SHIRAZ ★★★★★

Concentrated and subdued dark olive cabernet bay leaf and dark berry shiraz. This is seriously age worthy having very complex fruit, quality mocha and chocolate oak aromas. The palate is superb with stunning length and complexity, very complete with tightly wound fruit tannin and gentle oak balance, massive fruit drive and energy-looking like a 20 years plus cellaring.

2011	93	2026	$130.00	14.0%
2012	93	2027	$130.00	14.7%
2013	95	2039	$129.99	15.0%

WOODSTOCK

Woodstock has extensive vineyards in McLaren Flat, dating back to 1900 and a very strong offering of quality and value wines that are flavoursome and reliable. The Woodstock Coterie Restaurant is on the property, open daily 12pm–3pm for lunch.
Winemakers: *Ben Glaetzer and Scott Collett*
Open: *Cellar Door open daily 10am–5pm, 215 Douglas Gully Road, McLaren Vale*
Ph: *(08) 8383 0156 www.woodstockwine.com.au*

WOODSTOCK
SEMILLON SAUVIGNON BLANC ★★★

Freshness and interest, with ripe passionfruit and orange citrus aromas leading to the style's hallmark of lowish alcohol. Light-bodied, delicate crisp style with fresh length of passionfruit, lemon verbena and citrus fruit. The moderate alcohol gives a fresh, easy drinking style; dry but with an engaging structure and flavour.

Vintage	Rank	Drink	RRP	Vol Alc
2012	88	2014	$19.00	11.0%
2013	89	2016	$19.00	12.0%
2014	90	2016	$19.00	11.5%

WOODSTOCK
PILOT'S VIEW McLAREN VALE SHIRAZ ★★★

Mocha oak and black berry jam shiraz with a good balance of ripeness and a pleasing intensity. The palate is easy to like, generous, full bodied soft tannins chocolaty cocoa oak helps the raspberry fruit and the finish is clean and youthful.

Vintage	Rank	Drink	RRP	Vol Alc
2012	88	2018	$38.00	15.0%
2013	91	2019	$38.00	14.5%

WOODSTOCK
McLAREN VALE SHIRAZ ★★★★★

For lovers of full-bodied reds. Big vanilla oak, creamy and bold, with dark plum, date fruit and a savoury edge of dark olive. The wine lands fruit sweet and fleshy, with an appealing, rich and smooth palate running blackberry and plum with good supporting tannins and plenty of middle-palate generosity. A youthful, layered finish.

Vintage	Rank	Drink	RRP	Vol Alc
2011	86	2014	$25.00	14.0%
2012	86	2017	$25.00	15.0%
2013	91	2019	$25.00	14.8%

WOODSTOCK
McLAREN VALE CABERNET SAUVIGNON ★★★★★

Black olive tapenade and prune aromas. In the mouth, rich fruits full on the front palate with condensed concentrated fruits, massive up-front cola and liquorice middle palate and fresh acid to finish.

Vintage	Rank	Drink	RRP	Vol Alc
2010	88	2018	$25.00	14.5%
2012	86	2016	$25.00	15.0%
2013	87	2028	$25.00	14.8%

WOODSTOCK
'THE STOCKS' SINGLE VINEYARD SHIRAZ ★★★★

Another wine for lovers of full-bodied reds. Big and bold with black fruits, shiraz ripeness, dark cherry and cooked cherry with balanced, dusty dark chocolate coconut and cardamom spice. In the mouth, full-bodied, soft, luscious, ripe and rich juicy shiraz with coconut and tobacco oak, woven into the long, full flavours running to clove dark chocolate and vanilla.

Vintage	Rank	Drink	RRP	Vol Alc
2010	87	2018	$60.00	14.9%
2012	90	2022	$65.00	15.5%
2013	90	2020	$65.00	15.4%

WOODSTOCK
BOTRYTIS SEMILLON (375 ML) ★★★★★

Botrytis has created a rich, tropical-fruited wine, with candied and fresh pineapple with luxurious intensity. In the mouth, sweet candied pineapple, with a bold intense middle palate of buttered pineapple flavours. A firm acid drives the richness down on the finish.

Vintage	Rank	Drink	RRP	Vol Alc
2006	89	2012	$20.00	10.5%
2009	91	2015	$20.00	10.5%
2013	90	2018	$20.00	10.5%

WYNDHAM ESTATE

Wyndham Estate in the Hunter Valley features a widely available and affordable range of wines that are distinctive from its parent Jacobs Creek. Shiraz is the common theme and the style is soft, generous, ripe and flavoursome. Affordable, widely available and reliable.

Winemaker: *Ben Bryant, Tony Hooper, Steve Meyer*
Open: *Daily 9.30am–4.30pm 700 Dalwood Road, Dalwood*
Ph: *(02) 4938 3444 www.wyndhamestate.com*

WYNDHAM ESTATE
GEORGE WYNDAM FOUNDERS RESERVE SHIRAZ ★★★★

Honest, fruit driven, mint eucalypt, bark and berry aromas make this pleasant current drinking, with medium-body fruit and tannins that are in balance, good concentrated middle palate, morish tannins and fruit, finishing with dark plum. Will suit dining.

2009	86	2015	$22.00	14.5%
2010	85	2014	$20.00	14.5%
2012	90	2019	$19.50	14.9%

WYNDHAM ESTATE
GEORGE WYNDAM SHIRAZ CABERNET ★★★★

Since the 2009 vintage, these have been Limestone Coast instead of South Australian, moving from heavier fruit flavours and a large volume of soft tannins, to cooler fresher bright fruit flavours. The 2009 vintage features fresh red berry fruit, very modern in style, medium bodied, fresh long flavours and good length.

2005	88	2014	$21.50	14.1%
2006	87	2015	$21.50	15.0%
2009	88	2015	$21.50	14.5%

WYNDHAM ESTATE
GEORGE WYNDAM SHIRAZ GRENACHE ★★★★

Tapenade, liquorice dark fruits and dark spice in pretty regional varietal aromas. The fruit sweetness of ripe grenache and moderate tannin flavours verge on confectionery "jubey-ness". Drink young to enjoy the freshness.

2007	90	2014	$21.50	15.0%
2008	90	2015	$21.50	14.5%
2012	86	2018	$22.00	14.5%

Vintage	Rank	Drink	RRP	Vol Alc

WYNNS COONAWARRA
Wynns Coonawarra has performed exceedingly well, with Sue Hodder in the cellar and the viticultural team adding considerable kudos to its celebrated history. The cellar door offers a wide selection of older vintages and larger formats.
Winemaker: Sue Hodder
Open: Daily 10am–5pm, 1 Memorial Drive, Coonawarra
Ph: (08) 8736 2225 *www.wynns.com.au*

WYNNS COONAWARRA
SHIRAZ ★★★★
Well-judged intensity and balance with solid raspberry, red cherry and toasty oak cedar spice. Medium body, soft tannins, a cloak of oak at release with very good red cherry fruit length and fine tannin structure, raspberry fruits and a tightly wound finish.

2011	90	2017	$20.00	13.5%
2012	88	2019	$20.00	13.5%
2014	93	2024	$24.99	13.5%

WYNNS COONAWARRA
BLACK LABEL CABERNET SAUVIGNON ★★★★★
The aromas are an essay in youthful modern cabernet. Black currant and dark olive ripeness with a very positive personality thanks to well-judged oak layering in cocoa powder and dark chocolate with a subtle savoury edge. The berry fruits give immediate front palate fruit ripeness and the palate is tight oak tannic with good length of black currant fruit.

2012	90	2032	$44.99	13.5%
2013	90	2028	$44.99	13.5%
2014	92	2030	$44.99	13.5%

WYNNS COONAWARRA
CABERNET SAUVIGNON SHIRAZ MERLOT ★★★★
Appealing sweet oak adds fragrance to the berry fruit, while the palate has ripe fruit length, soft tannins and medium, intense flavour.

2010	87	2013	$18.00	14.0%
2011	87	2017	$19.99	13.5%
2012	86	2016	$20.00	13.5%

WYNNS COONAWARRA
MICHAEL SHIRAZ ★★★★★

Plenty of wine here: concentrated intense dark berry, tobacco, blue berry with quality vanilla oak and the balance of a long lived cellaring style. In the mouth it is supple, long, it's not big or thick with long fine grained tannins and generous complexity to close.

2009	94	2039	$70.00	14.0%
2010	95	2035	$149.99	13.5%
2013	95	2040	$149.99	13.8%

WYNNS COONAWARRA
JOHN RIDDOCH CABERNET SAUVIGNON ★★★★★

Another wine with 30-year future; balance and harmony are key to cellaring styles and the aromas show that here. Aromas are fine-tuned French oak with complex dark berry fruits. In the mouth, dense, plush fruits with long fine-grained tannins and great structure for cellaring and the lingering finish is varietal cabernet. Don't touch this for ten years.

2008	90	2018	$75.00	14.0%
2010	95	2044	$149.99	13.5%
2013	94	2032	$149.99	14.5%

WYNNS COONAWARRA
V & A LANE CABERNET SHIRAZ ★★★★★

The nose starts out with pure and youthful Coonawarra berry fruit, black currant cabernet and blackberry shiraz. The palate is silky and ripe berry fruited. It is complex, harmonious and elegant with a fire fight of black berry and black currant, morello top notes and very classy length. Medium body and very fine with black currant pithy edges.

2012	95	2032	$60.00	13.5%
2013	94	2029	$60.00	13.5%
2014	95	2020	$60.00	13.5%

XANADU
Xanadu in Margaret River continues to evolve and the wines are showing increased focus and drive; oak is backing off and fruit freshness increasing on the latest releases.

Winemaker: *Glenn Goodall*
Open: *Daily 10am–5pm, Boodjidup Road, Margaret River*
Ph: *(08) 9757 2581* ***www.xanaduwines.com***

XANADU
MARGARET RIVER CHARDONNAY ★★★★
Balanced and bold complexity, honey white butter oak toast notes with soft ripe rich fruits. Up front yellow peach into mid palate and medium length fruits framed by acidity. It will age for a few years.

Vintage	Rank	Drink	RRP	Vol Alc
2013	87	2018	$37.00	13.0%
2014	91	2019	$37.00	13.0%

XANADU
MARGARET RIVER CABERNET SAUVIGNON ★★★★
The mocha choc chino oak heralds black currant fruited oregano smoked meats oak quality. The palate is upfront black currant, minty green olive fruits woven into medium long fruit length with oak support.

Vintage	Rank	Drink	RRP	Vol Alc
2012	88	2019	$37.00	14.0%
2013	90	2020	$37.00	14.0%

XANADU
RESERVE MARGARET RIVER CHARDONNAY ★★★★
A change of style showing less high toast oak with more vibrant fruit nectarine and peach and oatmeal with a more subtle winemaking approach lifting the fruit profile. The palate has fruit complexity; notes of fresh orange and peach wed to subtle cedar cinnamon oak spices and vanilla to close.

Vintage	Rank	Drink	RRP	Vol Alc
2012	89	2019	$85.00	13.0%
2013	92	2020	$85.00	13.0%

XANADU
RESERVE MARGARET RIVER CABERNET SAUVIGNON ★★★★★
Focused varietal regional fruit complexity with blue berry, violets and black currant fruit aromas. The fruit sweet front palate flows into a soft middle palate framed by grape tannins which firm and dry on the medium long finish.

Vintage	Rank	Drink	RRP	Vol Alc
2012	91	2026	$85.00	14.5%
2013	90	2022	$85.00	14.0%

YABBY LAKE
Yabby Lake, based in the Mornington Peninsula, has 40 hectares under vine, planted in 1998. Initially managed by two immensely talented and experienced winemakers, Tod Dexter and Larry McKenna, they continue accelerating with Tom Carson's foot on the pedal.
Winemaker: Tom Carson
Open: Daily 10am–5pm, 86–112 Tuerong Road, Tuerong
Ph: (03) 5974 3729 *www.yabbylake.com*

YABBY LAKE
SINGLE VINEYARD CHARDONNAY ★★★★
Ethereal understated style with gentle white pear and apple fruits, subliminal oak and oatmeal elements. The palate is soft, it covers all of your palate with a silky texture, fresh pear fruit and subtle oak.

Vintage	Rank	Drink	RRP	Vol Alc
2012	90	2016	$45.00	12.5%
2013	94	2020	$55.00	12.5%
2015	87	2019	$45.00	12.5%

YABBY LAKE
SINGLE VINEYARD PINOT NOIR ★★★★★
This is focused, tight strawberry fruit, spices and subtle fine oak. There is a superior refinement in the aromas, poised like a ballerina about to enter the limelight. The palate is sensitive, silky, understated sleek tannins, strawberry fruit and oak spice that helps to hold the middle palate length. Finishes with layers from whole bunch spice and fruit tannins.

Vintage	Rank	Drink	RRP	Vol Alc
2010	93	2010	$60.00	14.0%
2013	94	2022	$55.00	13.5%
2015	90	2018	$60.00	13.5%

Vintage	Rank	Drink	RRP	Vol Alc

YALUMBA

Yalumba is the best known name in the Samuel Smith and Sons group. The tried and tested team is ever active in researching and creating wines that continually improve – from honest, reliable everyday drinking to carefully crafted regional classics. Their development of viognier since 1980 makes them the world leader in this variety. Their reds have a continual increase in quality in recent times to assume a leadership role in the path towards fresher fruit and finer grape tannins at all price points.
Winemaker: *Kevin Glastonbury*
Open: *Daily 10am–5pm, Eden Valley Road, Angaston*
Ph: *(08) 8561 3200* *www.yalumba.com*

YALUMBA
EDEN VALLEY VIOGNIER ★★★★

A youthful, tight, complex wine with savoury elements holding bold stone fruit, apricot and peach kernel in a winemaker hug of funky aromas. In the mouth, a deceptive balance. It seems light but builds with creamy length, middle palate intensity of apricot, peach nectar top notes and a dignified fresh finish with grainy tannins that suit food and ensures it won't get too heavy in the short term.

2011	90	2015	$25.00	12.5%
2012	90	2015	$25.00	14.0%
2013	92	2017	$25.00	13.0%

YALUMBA
EDEN VALLEY ROUSSANNE ★★★★

A hard to get right variety – you don't see much good roussanne, so this is a gem. Wild ferment builds a complexity without detracting from the fruit on the nose or palate. This sings like a hit single, fresh pear varietal, refined pears, pear tart, and black tea. The fresh pear fruits are immaculate, long and silky in texture, showing an evenness of length and a nougat flinch of flavour in the finish.

| 2014 | 91 | 2017 | $25.00 | 12.5% |
| 2015 | 95 | 2018 | $25.00 | 12.6% |

Vintage	Rank	Drink	RRP	Vol Alc

YALUMBA
THE VIRGILIUS VIOGNIER ★★★★★

In 2015 this is a complete wine with toned back varietal flavours and inbuilt layers of texture which, because of the nature of the variety is a great success. As a youngster, it plays it cards close to its chest. Very complex gentle peach, citrus and pith notes with restrained oak, wild ferment tones down the exuberant fruit. In the mouth, very complex length of apricot flavour and a savoury smoked meats edge with bounding energy filling the mouth and each layer building on the other.

2010	94	2016	$50.00	13.5%
2013	94	2018	$50.00	13.5%
2015	95	2021	$45.00	14.0%

YALUMBA
OLD BUSH VINE GRENACHE ★★★★

Classic regional varietal raspberry, red geranium, and white pepper aromas. In the mouth it is fresh. Ripe raspberry, cooked red cherry in the weave of fresh fruits, modest tannins, medium body and high alcohol that marks grenache. A good varietal.

2011	92	2014	$22.00	14.0%
2012	88	2016	$21.95	13.5%
2014	92	2020	$21.95	13.5%

YALUMBA
THE SCRIBBLER ★★★★

Very good complexity for the price, with red and black fruit, a leafy cabernet edge and looking fresher and brighter than earlier vintages. Aromas are red berry, black shiraz and a bloody meat complexity. The fruits have better than the price ripeness and complexity. Intense black currant, blackberry middle palate fruits with a firm tannin finish. Food friendly style.

2009	89	2013	$20.00	13.5%
2010	89	2016	$20.00	13.5%
2012	91	2017	$24.00	13.5%

| Vintage | Rank | Drink | RRP | Vol Alc |

YALUMBA
PATCHWORK BAROSSA SHIRAZ ★★★

Dark colour, with oak making a spicy appearance in the blackberry, dark plum and liquorice aromas. In the mouth, it lands ripe berry fruited, with a hint of thyme against the bold flavours, soft tannins and medium intensity, subtle oak finish.

2008	87	2013	$20.00	13.5%
2010	89	2014	$21.95	13.5%
2013	88	2017	$22.00	13.5%

YALUMBA
HAND PICKED SHIRAZ VIOGNIER ★★★★

Complex savoury shiraz aromas with blackberry, dark pepper, bacon bone and resinous, smoked meat and spice aromas. In the mouth, a lot of action. An opulent, full-bodied silky tannin ripe-fruited complex shiraz style with middle palate white pepper smoked meats building aromatic intensity into raspberry and red plum aligned with silky tannins and a fruit- filled long finish.

2007	87	2009	$30.00	14.5%
2010	89	2014	$34.00	13.5%
2012	93	2020	$34.00	13.5%

YALUMBA
FDR1A CABERNET SHIRAZ ★★★★★

You have to work your way through the layers of complexity; dark plum, cassis cranberry and fresh berry initially, then savoury black olive, fragrant dark spice with subtle eucalypt and dark chocolate in the back ground. In the mouth, berry fruits, good weight for food or good friends, with ripe raspberry black currant and solid silty tannins and lingering berry fruits.
Makes any meal a feast.

2006	90	2016	$37.00	13.5%
2008	94	2019	$39.00	13.5%
2010	92	2017	$37.00	13.5%

YALUMBA
THE MENZIES COONAWARRA CABERNET SAUVIGNON ★★★★★

Aromas of leafy dark cocoa powder and Coonawarra mint, in the focused varietal modern style. The palate is even and long, leafy cabernet black currant, well-structured evenness of fruit and mouthfeel with a dry finely tannin and lingering black currant.

2010	92	2022	$53.00	14.0%
2012	88	2019	$53.00	14.0%
2013	94	2030	$60.00	14.0%

YALUMBA
'THE SIGNATURE' CABERNET SAUVIGNON SHIRAZ ★★★★★

This is a deep, complex brooding wine with myriad of aromas with blueberry, blackberries and currants fruits, edges of dates and dark spices in the black fruits. Ripe fruit tannins with solid oak tannin support. The overall appealing weight of fruit freshness with cabernet cranberry fruits carrying the wine to the back where there are age worthy tannins.

2010	94	2022	$53.00	13.5%
2012	94	2026	$60.00	13.5%
2013	94	2026	$60.00	14.0%

YALUMBA
'THE OCTAVIUS' OLD VINE SHIRAZ ★★★★★

Deep, brooding, super complex plum pudding spice and fruit cake aromas with plenty of fruit power and more subtlety than many Barossa "big boys." The palate has excellent fruit structure with length, fine-grained tannins and long black fruits and dark spice. Fresh and respectful oak to fruit weight.

2008	95	2030	$100.00	14.5%
2009	94	2028	$112.00	13.5%
2012	95	2030	$100.00	14.0%

YALUMBA
THE RESERVE CABERNET SHIRAZ ★★★★★

On the Yalumba stairway to heaven this one has the most seamless fruit, with power and concentration from Barossa cabernet and shiraz. Released as a seven-year-old wine, they like it at 10 years but this one will age for 20-plus years.

Vintage	Rank	Drink	RRP	Vol Alc
2001	94	2012	$110.00	14.5%
2002	93	2012	$110.00	14.0%
2004	94	2015	$150.00	13.5%

YANGARRA

Californian premium wine producer, Kendall Jackson's Australian outpost, Yangarra, is based on the belief that "McLaren Vale has the best Mediterranean climate on earth". Trust the Americans to point out a home truth. Yangarra's 170-hectare vineyard is in transition to organic principles and located close to the foothills on sandy soils. This area produces spicy wines that have more elegance than vineyards closer to the coast.
Winemaker: *Peter Fraser*
Open: *Daily 10am–5pm, Kangarilla Road, Clarendon*
Ph: *(08) 8383 7459 www.yangarra.com*

YANGARRA
McLAREN VALE ROUSSANNE ★★★★

Aromas are complex, subtle spring flowers, fresh pear and baked white peach aromas. The palate is creamy ripe fruited concentrate and full in the middle palate with complex Moroccan preserved honey pears, white peach, orange zest, herbal tea oak spice and a long firming finish.

Vintage	Rank	Drink	RRP	Vol Alc
2011	89	2014	$25.00	12.0%
2014	93	2017	$32.00	13.5%
2015	90	2019	$32.00	13.5%

YANGARRA
McLAREN VALE OLD VINE GRENACHE ★★★★★

Lifted fruit raspberry, stewed strawberry Christmas cake with sweet spices- a side trip to India. The palate builds firmer tannins; earthy and grippy, with a white pepper spice and a subtle earthiness that

Vintage	Rank	Drink	RRP	Vol Alc

runs a length of palate offsetting the riper red fruits. Roast lamb wine.

2011	92	2018	$28.00	13.5%
2013	92	2025	$32.00	14.5%
2014	93	2022	$32.00	14.5%

YANGARRA
McLAREN VALE SMALL POT WHOLE BUNCH SHIRAZ ★★★★★

Burlesque shiraz, a peek here of spice and a tease there of oak within a complex chorus of wine structure and fruits. Aromas start intense, seductive perfumed red cherry fruits, unfurling spices into caramelised red tipped fruits. The palate is softer than many whole bunch wines. Here the tannin shape is very silky, large grained, prominent in size, round tannins complimenting the middle palate, layers of red flavours and oak.

2012	94	2020	$45.00	14.5%
2013	94	2029	$45.00	14.0%
2014	95	2029	$45.00	14.5%

YARRA YERING

Yarra Yering founder, Dr Bailey Carrodus, planted 12 hectares in 1969 and re-established wine growing in the Yarra Valley. Since he passed away in 2008, there has been a smooth transition to the new (although not new to the Yarra) owners. Both are loyal to Yarra Yering traditions and its medium-bodied red style. The style is softer and more middle palate centric in recent releases.

Winemaker: Sarah Crowe
Open: Daily 10am–5pm, 4 Briarty Road, Gruyere
Ph: (03) 5962 9239 *www.yarrayering.com*

YARRA YERING
PINOT NOIR ★★★★★

Refined aromas with a matrix of perfumed red fruits, subtle spice and stemmy notes all adding to the finesse. The palate has the varietal form with old vines fine tannins and fruits flavours, subtlety and grace, red cherry, cooked and fresh strawberry middle palate with less oak

Vintage	Rank	Drink	RRP	Vol Alc

than the ripe 2013 and more length with subtle layers on the subtle stemmy finish.

2012	91	2022	$92.00	13.5%
2013	90	2025	$92.00	13.5%
2014	93	2023	$92.00	13.0%

YARRA YERING
DRY RED NO 1 ★★★★★

Fruit focused with the left bank Bordeaux red fruits with leafy notes of cocoa powder into chocolate edged aromas. The palate is fine with even red fruited mineral cabernet length and precision and acidity framing the even long tannins. The middle palate peaks with a juicy bright fresh fruit note. Great line of fresh, complex flavour without the strength of finish of the house.

2012	95	2037	$92.00	13.5%
2013	93	2025	$92.00	13.5%
2014	93	2029	$92.00	13.5%

YARRA YERING
DRY RED NO 2 ★★★★★

Very pretty wines with soft tannins and immediate drinkability. Very exotic fruit notes with the intensity of lavender, liquorice, galangal from the white grapes with darker cherry fruits and a subtle peppery note in the background. The palate is focused red fruits with refined silky tannins and a compact long middle palate that leaps and bounds with ripe flavours and soft lingering tannins.

2012	93	2028	$92.00	13.0%
2013	92	2029	$92.00	13.5%
2014	93	2022	$92.00	13.0%

YARRA YERING
UNDERHILL SHIRAZ ★★★★★

Immediately positive fruit and oak perfume, dark berry into subtle peppery spices silky smooth medium bodied runs long into the mouth red fruits flavours of mineral cut terracotta tiles sawn rich brick in an acid tannin tenseness supporting the fruit, oak in moderation overall a long

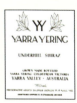

elegant perfumed focused fruit complexity and fine tannins.

Vintage	Rank	Drink	RRP	Vol Alc
2012	94	2025	$92.00	13.0%
2013	89	2019	$92.00	13.5%
2014	93	2022	$92.00	13.0%

YARRABANK

Yarrabank Devaux and Yering Station Cuvee use the traditional method and, while we are no longer allowed to label Australian sparkling as champagne, there is no difference in the method employed and very little difference in the character of the wines.
Winemaker: *William Lunn*
Open: *Daily 10am–5pm, 38 Melba Highway, Yarraglen*
Ph: *(03) 9730 0100 www.yering.com*

YARRABANK
LATE DISGORGED ★★★★★

Hints of age but quite restrained and impressive. Disgorged after eight years on lees, the aromas are complex; yeasty, vanilla-like brioche and pastry over-subtle caramelised apple and glace fruit. The palate is very long and elegant, dry and fine, with vibrant creamy yeast flavours and textures, giving great length to the persistent complex preserved lemon fruit flavours. It is "sauvage" in style, meaning it has a very low dosage.

Vintage	Rank	Drink	RRP	Vol Alc
2002	93	2016	$55.00	13.0%
2004	90	2014	$55.00	12.5%

YARRABANK
CUVEE ★★★★★

This is one of the secrets of Australian sparkling wine, with impeccable credentials. It is surprising that it isn't better known. Upper Yarra fruit aged for four years on lees prior to sale, to temper the fresh acidity, creates a wine of balance and subtle complexity. The aromas are elegant, fine-cut lemon citrus to stone fruit, with honeyed pinot filling out into almond bread yeast and subtle nougat in the background. The wine lands dry, turns complex with good texture on the palate and runs with crisp acid into a layered creamy finish. Flavours of lactic and yeast origin,

green apple and stone fruit before
turning cleanly crisp and fresh.

Vintage	Rank	Drink	RRP	Vol Alc
2007	93	2015	$38.00	13.0%
2008	93	2014	$38.00	13.0%
2009	94	2015	$38.00	13.0%

YARRABANK
CRÈME DE CUVEE ★★★★★

Marshmallow-like aromas entwine strawberry and pear, with almond yeastiness. The palate balances creamy sweetness with acid cut and a melody of stone fruit, citrus and pastry characters, finishing with excellent length.

Vintage	Rank	Drink	RRP	Vol Alc
NV	90	Now	$32.00	13.0%

YERING STATION

Yering Station is the model of a modern Yarra Valley winery producing distinctive, vibrant fresh wines amidst extraordinary visitor facilities. Delicious wines across the range, including their Yarrabank NV cuvees.

Winemaker: *William Lunn*
Open: *Daily 10am–5pm, PO BOX 390, Yarra Glen*
Ph: *(03) 9730 0100* **www.yering.com**

YERING STATION
CHARDONNAY ★★★★★

The harmony of fruit and oak has always been an important part of the style here, always seeming to capture a ripe deliciousness of chardonnay and oak spice. The palate steps up with very varietal creamy fruits building from white fruits like a subtle apple pie into spices and brown pie crusty oak notes at the back.

Vintage	Rank	Drink	RRP	Vol Alc
2012	90	2018	$25.00	12.5%
2013	92	2019	$40.00	12.5%

YERING STATION
RESERVE CHARDONNAY ★★★★★
White butter, wheatmeal, finesse, tobacco elements with overall subtle complexity. In the mouth it is gorgeous. Depth and fullness with white fruits flowing into flavour intensity with gentle texture, middle palate richness and a fine grained oak layer on the finish. Very young and pure, made with great sophistication.

Vintage	Rank	Drink	RRP	Vol Alc
2010	95	2018	$75.00	13.0%
2012	95	2018	$75.00	12.5%

YERING STATION
PINOT NOIR ★★★★
The step from Village is noticeable; fruit intensity of red cherry and strawberry with the lovely sweet spice cedar oak back drop building complexity. The palate has the silky rope pinot tannins starting flavours of ripe strawberry and the oak spice a nano-step behind the fruits adds charm by deepening the confit of strawberry with lingering fruit oak spice.

Vintage	Rank	Drink	RRP	Vol Alc
2011	90	2017	$38.00	11.5%
2012	87	2018	$38.00	13.0%
2013	91	2018	$25.00	13.5%

YERING STATION
SHIRAZ VIOGNIER ★★★★★
More restrained aromas than the usual basket of dark ripe fruits showing interesting mineral notes. The palate is the usual exciting swathe of ripe silky tannins plush in middle palate structure these wines are seductive mineral red fruits in the middle palate and the soft tannins hold to the end with gentle brown spices to close. A very satisfying drink with generous texture and subtle flavours, making this a great fireside red.

Vintage	Rank	Drink	RRP	Vol Alc
2011	94	2019	$38.00	14.0%
2012	91	2020	$40.00	13.8%
2013	91	2021	$40.00	13.8%

YERING STATION
RESERVE PINOT NOIR ★★★★★

Fresh and cooked strawberries, and vanilla oak while the whole bunch stalk backs up the aromas to make this complete and complex. In the mouth, medium body and weight, with unfolding fruit, complexity through red fruits – raspberry, red cherry and blueberry lingering long on the finish. Fast maturing style.

Vintage	Rank	Drink	RRP	Vol Alc
2010	92	2018	$75.00	13.8%
2012	91	2019	$75.00	13.8%

YERING STATION
RESERVE SHIRAZ VIOGNIER ★★★★★

Youthful, elegant, floral complexity with elderflower, then iris preceding the black fruit and black pepper aromas. In the mouth, velvety tannins, flowing ripe berry fruits, medium bodied with a high intensity violet and red fruit lift in the middle palate. A long spicy evolving finish with layers of black peppery nutmeg, cloves cinnamon and black fruit.

Vintage	Rank	Drink	RRP	Vol Alc
2010	93	2024	$75.00	14.5%
2012	96	2029	$90.00	13.5%

YERING STATION
CABERNET SAUVIGNON ★★★★

Oregano, dried herbs, subtle minty cabernet fruits and black currant aromas. The palate is the thing- soft tannins in the style of the winery, a really well-crafted complexity, black currant, graphite, black cherry and the most subtle weave of mocha-choc chino oak building the length.

Vintage	Rank	Drink	RRP	Vol Alc
2010	89	2016	$38.00	14.0%
2012	92	2026	$38.00	14.0%
2013	93	2020	$40.00	14.3%

YERINGBERG

Yeringberg has some of the oldest vines in the Yarra Valley. The family-owned, two-hectare hillside vineyard annually produces 1200 cases of graceful handmade wines, characterised by understated elegant fruit with minimum winemaker input that creates fresh, stylish wines.
Winemakers: *Guill and Sandra de Pury*
Open: *By appointment only, Yeringberg Coldstream*
Ph: *(03) 9739 0240* *www.yeringberg.com*

YERINGBERG
CHARDONNAY ★★★★★

The fruit aromas are gentle citrus into grapefruit and a youthful balance with vanilla white butter oak qualities. Very polished and fine, medium bodied with elegance and length. A certain understatement in the style and lovely subtle white butter barrel ferment flavours.

Vintage	Rank	Drink	RRP	Vol Alc
2013	93	2020	$50.00	13.0%
2014	94	2020	$55.00	12.5%
2015	92	2022	$65.00	13.0%

YERINGBERG
MARSANNE ROUSSANNE ★★★★★

Refined, complex and elegant with white flowers and stone fruit roussanne aromas and dried herb marsanne. The cool climate delicacy makes for a light-bodied palate with a fresh long line of acid. Complex, gently ripe, even textured middle palate flavours of white stone fruit, with persistent length. The balance is age worthy. Middle Eastern food style.

Vintage	Rank	Drink	RRP	Vol Alc
2013	94	2025	$50.00	13.0%
2014	94	2022	$55.00	13.0%
2015	94	2022	$65.00	13.5%

YERINGBERG
SHIRAZ ★★★★★

Medium ruby red sets up the style expectation; raspberry with a blackberry core, moderate oak adding spice and dried herbs. Medium weight, medium bodied ripe tannin elegance, spare youthful flavours and fine tannins to close.

Vintage	Rank	Drink	RRP	Vol Alc
2012	91	2020	$60.00	12.5%
2013	94	2029	$65.00	13.5%
2014	88	2022	$65.00	13.5%

Vintage	Rank	Drink	RRP	Vol Alc

YERINGBERG
PINOT NOIR ★★★★
Aromas are red fruits and strawberry with strength and depth without sacrificing the varietal delicacy. A silky yet solid core of red fruits, flavoursome tannins and a youthful reserve with a capacity for tannins to soften and open. Delicious medium bodied elegance.

2012	88	2018	$75.00	13.5%
2013	90	2020	$80.00	13.5%
2014	93	2028	$80.00	13.5%

YERINGBERG
CABERNETS ★★★★★
Briar into black currant and blue berry with fine oak spice. In the mouth a seamless ripe tannin profile, very good length with the complexity, elegance and linearity of mouth feel typical of a Bordeaux blend. The fine tannins are well handled.

2012	94	2040	$75.00	13.5%
2013	94	2025	$75.00	13.5%
2014	94	2029	$98.00	13.5%

YERINGBERG
VIOGNIER ★★★★★
Effortlessly aromatic, very pretty fresh fruits, ripe apricot and yellow peach aromas. This has ripe fruits up front with a savoury edge, medium bodied texture, appealing medium weight, good length, concentrated yellow fruits and creamy white flowers to finish.

2013	95	2019	$35.00	14.0%
2014	93	2018	$35.00	13.5%
2015	93	2021	$36.00	14.0%

ZEMA ESTATE
Zema Estate is a painstakingly purist red wine vineyard in Coonawarra. The wines are very even in style across all varieties, with a seductive luscious fruit, very soft powdery tannins and ripe varietal flavours.
Winemaker: *Greg Clayfield*
Open: *Weekdays: 9am–5pm, Weekends and Pub Hols: 10am–4pm*
Riddoch Highway, Coonawarra
Ph: *(08) 8736 3219 www.zema.com.au*

ZEMA ESTATE
CLUNY CABERNET MERLOT MALBEC CABERNET FRANC ★★★★

Black currant, mint and mulberry fruit aromas with a smooth easy drinking palate that is ready to go on release. Neat and dry.

Vintage	Rank	Drink	RRP	Vol Alc
2010	87	2016	$25.00	13.5%
2011	Not made			
2012	88	2016	$25.00	14.0%
2013	87	2017	$25.00	14.0%

ZEMA ESTATE
SHIRAZ ★★★

Ripe fruited with an appealing green herb edge in place of the usual peppery spices. Red cherry and sage aromas, balanced subtle oak and a focus on fruit power, as is the wineries style. The palate is unified ripe fruits silky tannins medium-bodied middle palate filled with red fruits and fine soft tannins.

Vintage	Rank	Drink	RRP	Vol Alc
2010	85	2015	$25.00	14.0%
2011	Not made			
2012	87	2018	$25.00	14.5%
2013	89	2019	$25.00	14.5%

ZEMA ESTATE
CABERNET SAUVIGNON ★★★★

The ripeness and generosity is there from the first sniff; cocoa powder, black currant, mint, and bay leaf aromas. Middle palate is plump and ripe with drink now qualities such as generous flavours, fine tannins with savoury that holds the spine together and it has mouth filling black berry black cherry fruit.

Vintage	Rank	Drink	RRP	Vol Alc
2010	88	2018	$29.00	14.0%
2011	Not made			
2012	86	2018	$29.00	14.0%
2013	92	2023	$29.00	14.5%

ZEMA ESTATE
FAMILY SELECTION SHIRAZ ★★★★

Fruit cake, spice, cedar and chocolate notes. Oak leads to a ripe palate; appealing supple soft tannins, low key spice, red fruit, caramel and vanilla. Well integrated oak tannins add length to the fruit.

2008	90	2028	$46.00	14.5%
2010	86	2017	$46.00	14.5%
2011	Not made			
2012	93	2021	$46.00	14.0%

ZEMA ESTATE
FAMILY SELECTION CABERNET SAUVIGNON ★★★★★

Classic, classy aroma with cabernet varietal cassis into black olive and currant fruit aromas. The palate is on song with a mouthful of long black currant, herbal bay leaf flavours and a hint of mature savoury cigar box on the finish. Lovely balance. A generous bear hug of a Coonawarra cabernet.

2008	92	2016	$46.00	14.5%
2010	84	2018	$46.00	14.0%
2011	Not made			
2012	93	2019	$46.00	14.0%

ZONTE'S FOOTSTEP

Zonte's Footstep draws on grapes grown in the Langhorne Creek and McLaren Vale/Fleurieu regions of South Australia. All the wines have personality derived from very ripe fruit and some have a touch of residual sugar, to increase their appeal. The reds are in the big ripe soft tannin South Australian mould. The Langhorne Creek malbec, McLaren Vale shiraz petite syrah and Langhorne Creek sangiovese barbera make for interesting drinking. All are reliable, affordable and easy drinking.
Winemaker: *Ben Riggs*
Open: *No Cellar Door, Lot 281 Main Road, McLaren Vale*
Ph: *(08) 8383 2083 www.zontesfootstep.com.au*

Vintage	Rank	Drink	RRP	Vol Alc

ZONTE'S FOOTSTEP
SCARLET LADYBIRD ROSÉ ★★★★★

Very aromatic grenache leads with layers of pink fruits, watermelon, rose petal, raspberry and red leafy notes. In the mouth it has depth of fruit flavour that starts out raspberry grenache and deepens into watermelon and red currant. Verges into light dry red flavours, so for those that like rose with strong flavours this is ideal. Serve well chilled.

2013	94	2016	$18.00	13.0%
2014	92	2016	$18.00	13.5%
2015	90	2017	$18.00	13.5%

ZONTE'S FOOTSTEP
CANTO DI LAGO SANGIOVESE BARBERA ★★★★

Exotic light soya sauce, bay leaf and black fruit aromas. The palate is medium dense and medium long with a pretty dark fruit middle palate. Length of earthy ripe fruits with plum, bay leaf and dark berry flavours and a food friendly juicy acid to finish.

2011	87	2016	$22.00	14.5%
2012	93	2017	$25.00	14.5%
2013	88	2018	$25.00	14.5%

ZONTE'S FOOTSTEP
VIOLET BEAUREGARD MALBEC ★★★★★

When you have some of the best Malbec on the market being made in Langhorne Creek, you don't really need to look to Argentina. The use of 'Violet' in the name is very evocative when you are looking deep into the purple hued depths of this wine. It has floral overtones within its ripe berry and vanilla spice profile. Violet Beauregard – just pour and let it win your heart! It is just as good the next day too.

2012	89	2019	$25.00	14.0%
2013	96	2021	$25.00	14.5%
2014	92	2019	$25.00	14.1%

Vintage	Rank	Drink	RRP	Vol Alc

ZONTE'S FOOTSTEP
Z FORCE SHIRAZ PETITE SIRAH ★★★★★

A McLaren Vale blend of 85% Shiraz and 15% Durif that holds great appeal for lovers of voluptuous inky reds. The plentiful pepper all spice brightens up the red plum and rum raisin dark chocolate notes that move seamlessly from nose to palate. The tannins muscle their way along the length with its warming finish. Lots on offer in this wine- particularly for those wishing to cellar it.

Vintage	Rank	Drink	RRP	Vol Alc
2012	90	2018	$49.95	14.5%
2014	92	2025	$49.95	14.5%

Z-FORCE
by
ZONTE'S FOOTSTEP

Australian Wine Vintages
is now an app!

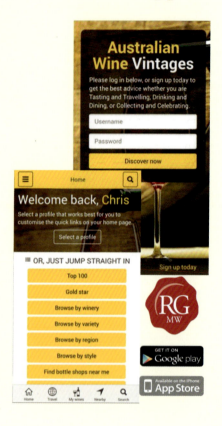

17,000+ Tasting notes

The best of Australian wine at your finger tips.

Add wines to your virtual cellar then hunt them down.

Know when to drink a wine and what to pair it with.

Available at www.robgeddesmw.com

TASTING TERMS

Describing taste, from the bottle to the brain and onto paper, is a complex task. The taster's background, culture and experience will all affect their perceptions.

While the language of tasting is inherently inside us all, it is the knowledge of traditions and a bit of science, tempered with experience that creates a taster's skill.

Most activities have their own language and a lot of wine language is about provenance. The following list of terms could help explain the smells, flavours, textures and sense of place that I encounter as a taster:

Alcohol in line with current thoughts, I describe low alcohol as less than 12%, medium alcohol refers to 12–14% and high alcohol above 14%.

Aldehyde. Usually a negative description except when used as acetaldehyde in a description of the positive smell of flor sherry. Used negatively in table wines aldehyde indicates premature, oxidised browning apple over aged aromas from the oxidation of alcohol indicative of a winemaking failure. The chain of evolution is aldehyde-like smells which left unchecked assume ethyl acetate or nail polish remover and the beginnings of vinegar like sharpness. A little deliberately elevated in high alcohol long matured reds can be a good thing to enhance fruit aromas.

Animale in whites literally a lactic (ripe yoghurt), lanolin (woollen baby blanket) smell, similar to the smell of the fleece of a lactating ewe. In shiraz, it is a savoury, dried dark spice combined with an earthy aroma that was first described to me as smelling like following a truck laden with sheep on a summer's day and of entering a wool shed or sheep yards when the dirt is dry.

American Oak grown in the USA, where the warmer climates produce larger pore size and richer flavours compared to the species grown in France. This type of oak often has a louder intensity of aromas and flavours that mark wines matured in it as richer, dark chocolate like and fuller in tannin structure.

Balance primary balance is between acid, fruit and alcohol, with oak contributing tannins across the tongue. Balance is also harmonious flavour, without any one flavour dominating. It is about evenness of structure, texture and flavour, and issues are often found on the finish where imbalances will linger. A well balanced wine may have a layered finish.

Bath powder smells of feminine floral talc.

Beurre bosc as in the pears, is a term used to describe the smell of pinot gris or grigio.

Botrytis a fungal infection of ripe grapes contributing positive tropical aromas and very sweet wines.

Brettanomyces "Bretty" A negative term, although, some people enjoy it in small quantities describing aromas from refermentation of small amounts of sugar in red wines by a family of yeast called Brettanomyces. This varies between resembling horse yards and smoke-like or Elastoplasts band aid smells. In extreme amounts such wines have short flavours and finish with a metallic hard dryness. Tasters vary in their susceptibility to it.

Complexity in wines refers to possessing aromas and flavour beyond the simple fruit or oak combination and therefore offering a wider range of characters than just the basic elements. Winemakers working with wines can often induce aromas and flavour at the threshold level, so as to be a nuance rather than a dominant theme in a wine. Exceptional growers, regions and seasons can all contribute to the evolution of elements that develop with repeated smelling and tasting and which make complexity rewarding.

Concentration is a desirable flavour element of wine, as long as the wine also possesses freshness of fruit and flavour to match the concentration. Alas, it often comes with huge alcohol, tannins and oak, so it's a term viewed carefully from a number of perspectives. Fashionable in some circles to produce extremely concentrated shiraz wines, it may also refer to the intensity of flavour, sugar, tannin or oak. One of our most concentrated wines would be Seppeltsfield's 100-year old tawny.

Dark Chocolate derived from oak and smelling like high quality dark chocolate.

Dense can mean dumb flavours and a thick texture but most likely to mean the wine has a feeling of density or thickness from concentration.

Australian Wine Vintages 2017 – Tasting terms

Developed looking or smelling and tasting older than it should.

Development a stage in wines aging when it is moving from primary to secondary fruit aromas and flavours.

Eucalypt can range from mint-like forest floor, to the smell of a crushed gum leaf in reds.

Elegant contains all the elements of flavour and structure that are discretely flavoured, rather than powerful or heavy. The opposite of heavy or rich.

Fining – many winemakers will add an animal or mineral protein as a processing aid, to manage the clarity and texture of white wines in different climatic conditions and prevent an unsightly protein haze forming after bottling. This process assists a more pleasant, silky structure to the wine and may be referenced on the back label.

Finish both a term to comment on the content of the wines fruit, tannin and oak and its ability to contribute to the end of the wines palate structure and how it leaves the mouth. In terms of structure, one hopes for length, i.e. a long finish and then a clean finish which is long and structured and can be said to be either soft or firm finishing.

In terms of tasting you hope for a clean finish, so as to be ready for the next mouthful and a good many white wines are clean from acidity and reds from tannin which can be soft, sandy or gritty. One hopes not to find wines with a hot finish, which refers to alcoholic heat and its ability to distress the mouth.

Floral belongs to the most flowery aromas of rose, jasmine and frangipani.

French Oak refers to the forest of origin. Generally delivers more refined vanilla, fresh-cut tobacco, liquorice with finer tannins and length of structure creating a subtle complexity that builds great chardonnay or pinot noir.

Fresh refers to both the condition of the contents of the bottle, i.e. fruit in good condition and the style of wine, i.e. crisp dry riesling which has a fresh acid finish.

Freshness the aim of many wines is to bring the fruit to the bottle and the consumer in its most pure, youthful state. The wines that seem to contain more of the intrinsic nature of the grape are referred to as fresh, as in fresh and youthful. Some styles are intrinsically fresher than others, such as riesling versus chardonnay. The vintage quality of a year will in part be judged by how long the wines keep their freshness and avoid tiring, so in a sense it could be said to measure the energy of the fruit.

Fruit sweet versus sugar sweet a wine can have sweet fruit, meaning fruit ripeness without sugar. This is a mix of ripe flavours helped by alcohol. To me, its high praise, although sometimes it comes from a lack of acidity and can seem sweet up front with a short length of flavour. Mostly, its a mark of deliciousness. Sugar starts to be tasted by trained winemakers at around 3 grams and by most of the public at 5 to 8 grams per litre, i.e. 0.5 to 0.8 %. However, it's the wines that finish with a sweetness from sugar that earn my ire. The finish of a wine should be about its flavour, not the artefacts used to make it more palatable.

Full bodied a mouth full of flavour and structure from acid, fruit oak and tannin.

Funky is a character of largely yeast-derived aromas and flavours that contribute aromas outside fruit. It includes matchstick smells, flint and sometimes just the aromas left from a wild yeast ferment which can be malt and marzipan, depending on the yeast.

Gentle a term describing how both the aroma, flavour and mouth feel are smooth and subtle but not weak and how that combines in the mouth with a smooth flowing structure. Wines such as pinot noirs have this facility.

Geosmin describes the earthy smell of freshly dug up beets, or rain on warm asphalt.

Herbal refers to green herbs or chillies, not positive, or as part of a wines varietal personality such as sauvignon blanc. The aroma and taste intensity is due to varied amounts of thiols and especially pyrazines, (a compound that has green vegetable-like smells).

Juicy Fruit as an aroma, a smell of banana and pineapple. As a texture, a large volume of ripe fruit that has freshness and integrated acidity.

Mocha an oak aroma from toasting the barrel, smelling and tasting like an espresso coffee with chocolate added.

Australian Wine Vintages 2017 – Tasting terms

Mocha choco chino invented, I believe, by Andrew Caillard MW to describe a complex oak aroma and flavour.

Lees refers to yeast once it has stopped fermenting, or any sediment collected at the bottom of a tank.

Lemon verbena indicates subtle floral lemon zest like aromas.

Length or **Long** positive high praise, as the flavour lasts a long time.

Lush the fruit is soft and richly flavoured with a thick texture.

Malolactic Malic acid is one of the major acids of grapes the other is tartaric. Malic has more intensity and greener edge like eating a green apple. It can be converted by bacteria, so called malolactic fermentation in a controlled winemaking environment to lactic acid (the acid of dairy produce), softening the acid intensity of wine. It is almost obligatory to undertake this in reds and is a winemaker choice in Chardonnay to affect the style of wine produced.

Mint refers to an aroma or flavour compound which may be positive or negative, depending on the extent of its appearance. Mint is associated with cabernet in cool climates where its a part of the methoxypyrazine green flavour that is lost in hotter climates. Too much spoils a wine but there is a 1961 Coonawarra Peppermint Patty which kept the character as a positive part of its flavour for 40 years. It appears with eucalypt in Central Victoria as part of the regional personality. It can also be positive, contributing to the complexity of wines

Mirepoix a French stock comprised of 50% onion, 25% celery, 25% carrots and a significant amount of fine herbs cooked in butter. It gives a complex part herbal/ part vegetable aroma that is very reminiscent of cool-region cabernet sauvignon.

Oatmeal refers to wines aged 'sur lie' (on lees). The smell derived from white wines that have been fresh yeast lees from their fermentation stirred in barrel regularly to enhance texture leaving a distinctive smell somewhere between that of fresh bread or opening a packet of rolled oats and cooked porridge. This 'yeasty' aroma when well balanced adds an elderflower or acacia-like floweriness.

www.robgeddesmw.com

Australian Wine Vintages 2017 – Tasting terms

Palate the front palate is where most tasters first experience flavour and body; its closely linked to the amount of alcohol or sweetness in the wine. The middle palate is the part of the tongue where fruit is most intensely felt and tasted. It is located from just behind the tip of the tongue to near the point of the gag reflex. Australian wine should give flavour here in spades because it is characterised by ripeness. The back palate is where the finish of the wine becomes apparent. For example, a wine would be described as "medium long" if most flavour was experienced in the front and middle of the palate. Conversely, it would be characterised as 'long' if it lingers on the back palate. Length of flavour is a key arbiter of quality. The longer, the better.

Peppery can have two meanings; the positive is the level of spice (white, black pepper, cinnamon, nutmeg and clove), which can be found in shiraz and sometimes grenache. Or else the green pepper, green chilli of unripe green fruit and not liked.

Power refers to wines with more ripe strength to their fruit and often alcohol. Ripe fruit power can be balanced by oak to create richness. At the extreme end, these full-bodied wines can struggle for freshness. The opposite of power is gentle.

Purity in varietal whites is high praise for the aromas and flavours being absolutely typical of the varietal and not in the least boring.

Puncheon Term used to describe an oak barrel of approximately 300 litres, as versed to a barrique which is generally 225 litres. Larger oak imparts less aroma and flavours to wine which, still providing a vessel for subtle changes related to controlled oxidation and resulting polymerisation of tannins which creates wines with more harmony and complexity.

Pyrethrum herbal, vegetal smell, similar to squeezing a tomato stalk on vine ripened tomato or smelling crushed plant leaves. Mortein and Flytox fly spays smelt of it until around 2000.

Quality is a vague term probably meaning 'fit for purpose'. In our case, it refers to the complexity of aroma, length and texture of flavour that combine to be enjoyable and significantly better than many other wines. Quality can also refer to delicacy with interesting flavour complexity, yet without great heaviness or weight in the mouth.

Rancio character derived from maturity, nutty or savoury. Think walnuts and an almond, candied-fruit character, signifying great age. It is generally a term to describe the development of tawny fortified wines into a walnut, old oak spectrum of aromas. It does not mean rancid but a caramel towards angostura bitters aromas spectrum and a long dry finish.

Rich a wine well endowed with ripe fruit and tannin, while the texture is that of a thick structure.

Rhythm a wine that is said to have good rhythm has all its components in balance. It can also be said to have the energy in its fruit, acid or tannins, to enable it to last in the taster's mouth. There is also a certain harmony of balance within them.

Round the wine feels round to the tongue, with richness and body. It implies ripe fruit generosity and not acidity and firmness.

Sauvage is a French term meaning 'wild' or 'natural'. There are three things it might refer to. First, when appearing in a tasting note, it might mean earthy or forest floor flavours. Second, it might reference a wine that was fermented with wild or indigenous yeasts with a struck flint aroma. Thirdly in sparkling wines it indicates that no dosage (sweet syrup added just before bottling), has been added, making it very dry- even drier than a brut sparkling wine. These wines do not age well.

Savoury a positive term meaning an additional detail to the taste and smell of a wine beyond the fruit, occurring in whites, reds and fortifieds. The sense of things smelling and tasting savoury is perhaps less well understood than sweet or acid, or even feeling hot in terms of tasting. Savoury is an expression to define the taste of umami, which is the Japanese term for a meaty flavour and aroma.

In whites, it can come from the fermentation of cloudy juice using wild yeast for fermentation and adds a mineral note to the aromas or it can come from yeast-derived compounds, via ageing on lees. It is a way of balancing the exuberance of some varieties to help create complexity.

Savoury in red wines is often a fruit flavour, ranging from the black pepper in shiraz to something wilder, like

Australian Wine Vintages 2017 – Tasting terms

a smoked meat, gravy, soya sauce or meat stock. It can be created by whole-bunch fermentation in pinot and shiraz.

It is also a term to describe the spice character that appears in wine, especially shiraz or pinot, grown in a cool climate maritime such as Mornington, Yarra, Gippsland and Great Southern. The smells are often resinous or smoked meats.

In fortified wines, it's a hessian-like edge in cask-aged fortifieds that a previous generation called baggy (smells like a bag that has held superphosphate), invoking the idea that the wine spent too long in oak without refreshing or sulphuring.

Seamless refers to the flow of the wine and indicates that the texture moves smoothly from the front of the tongue to the back of the mouth with fruit flavour, acid and tannin or fruit texture running unified along the tongue.

Scented the most appealing form of fruit aromas with a flowery scent.

Short the flavour and texture do not last long in the mouth. Such wines are short of lingering flavour but fat and wide to start and can be too alcoholic.

Silky the highest praise for a wines texture and mouth feel; one of the expressions of greatness. When a wine has a silky texture, the fruit is slippery and the tannins, in reds, are extremely fine.

Soft refers to the quantity of acid in whites and the quality of the tannins in reds or the finish of the wine; the truism here is that a soft wine can struggle to have a long flavour. It takes a very talented viticulturalist and winemaker to induce soft fruit to run long on the tongue. Soft tannins are positive in reds and can be related to silky texture. A soft finish is the opposite of a firm finish and is both a style and an indication that a red wine is ready to drink.

Solids fermenting cloudy juice assists the creation of savoury aromas and flavours that can be a real asset in chardonnay, in particular an earthy aroma and flavour.

Spice can range from a fruit character showing sandalwood, cinnamon, clove, nutmeg, black and white pepper in reds to a clove-like edge in riesling. Oak can also contribute spice.

Australian Wine Vintages 2017 – Tasting terms

Stalks rather than removing the stalks from bunches when fermenting juice, skins and seeds, some winemakers are increasingly using a percentage of stalks, often called 'whole bunch' in their fermentations to add a pyrethrum-like aroma and flavour which can also be called savoury. Works a treat in pinot noir and shiraz from cool climates.

Tannins is a collective term for a wide variety of complex compounds in grapes that affect taste, mouth feel, texture and age worthiness in wine. Tannins are located in skins, seeds, stalks and oak barrels. The feeling of astringency in wine is produced when tannins grab the proteins from your saliva, lessening the lubrication in the mouth and making tissue scratch against tissue. Different grape varieties contribute different volumes of tannin due to varietal DNA, skin thickness and structure creating differences in mouth feel.

Differing levels of acid also interact with tannin; higher acids make them taste bitter, while lower acids create a silky mouth feel. Tannins from green grapes are more astringent, while ripe tannins can create widely differing mouth feel from powdery, silky and velvety, to sandy and hard. Ideally, tannins should bridge with the fruit in the mouth to create a long seamless palate in reds. In aromatic whites, most producers aim to minimise tannins. In chardonnay, oak is used to contribute tannin texture, particularly to the front palate, as well as the finish.

Tapenade dark olive aromas such as opening a jar of olives in brine or the mix with anchovy, caper and olives.

Taut when a youthful wine is tasted, the overall freshness, acidity and youthful fruit will not be soft and silky and, as such, is said to be taut.

Texture the way a wine covers the tongue. Its related to alcohol, with more texture coming from more alcohol. In whites, the quality of the texture is related to grape variety and fruit ripeness, while tannins from grapes and oak contribute to the texture in reds.

Thiol(s) are sulphur compounds associated with sauvignon blanc but present in may varieties where they are muted by the concentration of other compounds. They can smell and taste like grapefruit pith and passion fruit, but in higher doses will start to smell sweaty, as in sweaty running shirt smell and in higher mounts dirty, sour or smoky.

www.robgeddesmw.com

Australian Wine Vintages 2017 – Tasting terms

Tight the flavours are closed and the structure seems acidic, with a low flavour to the taster. It implies good texture and structure but the wine is not offering a lot of this when tasted. This term usually refers to young wines.

Toast the smell of burning wheat bread toast, often associated with, or cross referenced to, kerosene. Such aromas indicate a wine is too old and starting to lose its fruit to tertiary characters. Evident in whites, especially riesling and semillon.

Umami A brothy aroma similar to miso soup and a category of taste besides sweet, sour, salt, and bitter corresponding to the flavour of mushrooms and imitated in food by using monosodium glutamate.

Varietal. As a tasting term refers to wines capacity to reflect the flavour and structural attributes of its parent grape variety. Varietal winemaking focuses on purity which in comparison to terroir winemaking has different outcomes. Winemakers by reflecting the grape vines environment focuses on the uniqueness of the vines interaction with the environment.

Wide mouth-filling as in grenache and cabernet franc but often not long in flavour.

Yeasty can be negative, as in the wine smells of fermentation and beery or yeast-like aromas. Most often smelt in sparkling wine aged on lees. When positive, refers to aromas or flavours and textures derived from yeast breakdown and aging on lees. Sparkling wines are often described as yeasty, due to extended aging in the presence of yeast lees. This introduces a complex smell, akin to oatmeal, fresh bread or to more developed shortbread biscuit or nougat scents and a creamy texture. Yeasty in a chardonnay tasting note indicates a wine with oatmeal like aromas, which some will see as a yoghurt or creamy complexity.

A QUICK GUIDE TO REGIONAL VARIETAL CLASSICS AND BLENDS & WINE STYLES

Aglianico *Barossa, Heathcote*

Barbera *King Valley, Mudgee, Hunter Valley, Barossa Valley, McLaren Vale*

Botrytis Semillon *Griffith, Leeton*

Cabernet Franc *Barossa, McLaren Vale, Orange*

Cabernet Sauvignon *Coonawarra, Margaret River, Langhorne Creek, Great Southern, Granite Belt*

Cabernet Shiraz *Barossa Valley, Clare Valley, Great Southern, Bendigo, Langhorne Creek, Eden Valley*

Cabernet Merlot *Great Southern, Coonawarra, Margaret River, Yarra Valley, Pyrenees, Coal River Valley, Freycinet*

Chardonnay *Hunter Valley, Orange, Adelaide Hills, Beechworth, Mornington Peninsula, Yarra Valley, Macedon, Geelong, Margaret River, Granite Belt, Great Southern, Southern Fleurieu, Tasmania*

Chambourcin *Shoalhaven, Hastings*

Colombard *Adelaide Plains, Adelaide*

Cinsault *Rutherglen*

Durif *Rutherglen, Griffith*

Fiano *Adelaide Hills, McLaren Vale*

Garganega *King Valley*

Gewurztraminer *Tasmania, Central Otago, Eden Valley*

Graciano *McLaren Vale*

Grenache *McLaren Vale, Barossa Valley, Clare Valley*

Gruner Veltliner *Adelaide Hills, Canberra*

Lagrein *Macedon Ranges, McLaren Vale*

Malbec *Great Southern, Langhorne Creek*

Marsanne *Goulburn Valley, Yarra Valley, Canberra*

Marsanne Roussanne *Yarra Valley*

Mataro *see* **Mourvedre**

Australian Wine Vintages 2017 – A quick quide

Merlot   *Orange, Eden Valley, Adelaide Hills, Coonawarra, Margaret River, Great Southern, Tasmania*

Merlot Cabernet Sauvignon   *Orange, Great Southern, Waipara, Canberra*

Mourvedre   *Barossa Valley, McLaren Vale*

Muscat fortifieds   *Rutherglen, Griffith*

Muscat table wines   *Barossa Valley, Riverland, Adelaide Plains*

Nebbiolo   *Heathcote, Langhorne Creek, King Valley, Pyrenees*

Nero d'Avola   *Adelaide Hills*

Primitivo *see* **Zinfandel**

Pinot Blanc   *Adelaide Hills, Southern Fleurieu*

Pinot Gris/Grigio   *Mornington Peninsula, Southern Highlands, Canberra, Tasmania, Eden Valley*

Pinot Meunier   *Great Western, Tasmania*

Pinot Noir   *Orange, Southern Highlands, Adelaide Hills, Mornington Peninsula, Southern Fleurieu, Yarra Valley, Macedon, Geelong, Tasmania, Pemberton*

Pinotage   *King Valley*

Petit Meslier   *Eden Valley*

Petit Syrah *see* **Durif**

Petit Verdot   *McLaren Vale, Griffith, Riverland, Granite Belt*

Riesling   *Canberra, Barossa Hills and Eden Valley, Clare Valley, Great Southern, Tasmania, King Valley*

Rondinella   *Hilltops*

Roussanne   *Yarra Valley, McLaren Vale*

Sangiovese   *King Valley, Mudgee, Hunter Valley, Barossa Valley, McLaren Vale*

Sauvignon Blanc   *Orange, Adelaide Hills, Marlborough, Nelson, Hawke's Bay, Martinborough/Wairapa, Pemberton, Great Southern, Margaret River, Tasmania, Yarra Valley*

Savagnin   *Eden Valley, Barossa Valley*

Semillon   *Hunter Valley, Clare Valley, Barossa Valley, New England, Shoalhaven Coast*

Australian Wine Vintages 2017 – A quick quide

Semillon Sauvignon Blanc   *Margaret River, Yarra Valley, Waipara*

Shiraz/Syrah   *Hunter Valley, Canberra, Hilltops, Adelaide Hills, McLaren Vale, Barossa Valley, Sunbury, Mudgee, Eden Valley, Langhorne Creek, Clare Valley, Coonawarra, Great Western, Canberra, Bendigo, Ballarat, Pyrenees, Yarra Valley, Heathcote, Great Southern, Granite Belt*

Shiraz Viognier   *Canberra, Yarra Valley, Orange, Great Southern*

Sparkling Wine   *Macedon, Tasmania, Orange, Tumbarumba, Southern Highlands, Yarra Valley*

Tempranillo   *Adelaide Hills, McLaren Vale, Canberra, Clare Valley, Margaret River*

Topaque   *Rutherglen*

Touriga   *Rutherglen, Barossa Valley, Yarra Valley*

Verdelho   *Granite Belt, Hunter Valley, Margaret River*

Vermentino   *Riverland*

Vintage dated fortified   *Rutherglen, McLaren Vale, Barossa Valley*

Viognier   *Adelaide Hills, Eden Valley, Geelong*

Zinfandel   *Margaret River, McLaren Vale, Barossa Valley, Mudgee, Clare Valley*

WINE REGIONS OF AUSTRALIA

WESTERN AUSTRALIA
1 Swan District
2 Perth Hills
3 Peel
4 Geographe
5 Margaret River
6 Blackwood Valley
7 Pemberton
8 Manjimup
9 Great Southern

SOUTH AUSTRALIA
10 Southern Flinders Ranges
11 Clare Valley
12 Barossa Valley
13 Eden Valley
14 Riverland
15 Adelaide Plains
16 Adelaide Hills
17 McLaren Vale
18 Kangaroo Island
19 Southern Fleurieu
20 Currency Creek
21 Langhorne Creek
22 Padthaway
23 Mount Benson
24 Wrattonbully
25 Robe
26 Coonawarra
27 Mount Gambier

QUEENSLAND
28 South Burnett
29 Granite Belt

NEW SOUTH WALES
30 New England Australia
31 Hastings River
32 Hunter
33 Mudgee
34 Orange
35 Cowra
36 Riverina
37 Hilltops
38 Southern Highlands
39 Gundagai
40 Canberra District
41 Shoalhaven Coast
42 Tumbarumba
43 Perricoota

VICTORIA
44 Murray Darling
45 Swan Hill
46 Goulburn Valley
47 Rutherglen
48 Glenrowan
49 Beechworth
50 King Valley
51 Alpine Valleys
52 Strathbogie Ranges
53 Upper Goulburn
54 Heathcote
55 Bendigo
56 Pyrenees
57 Macedon Ranges
58 Sunbury
59 Grampians
60 Henty
61 Geelong
62 Yarra Valley
63 Mornington Peninsula
64 Gippsland*

TASMANIA
65 Tasmania*

*South Eastern Australia and Gippsland are zones, Tasmania is a state.

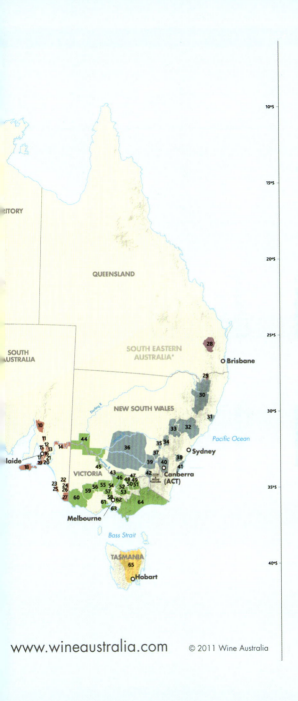

Australian Wine Vintages 2017 – Personal Notes

Australian Wine Vintages 2017 – Personal Notes

Australian Wine Vintages 2017 – Personal Notes

Australian Wine Vintages 2017 – Personal Notes

Australian Wine Vintages 2017 – Personal Notes

Australian Wine Vintages 2017 – Personal Notes

Australian Wine Vintages 2017 – Personal Notes

Australian Wine Vintages 2017 – Personal Notes

Australian Wine Vintages 2017 – Personal Notes

Australian Wine Vintages 2017 – Personal Notes

Australian Wine Vintages 2017 – Personal Notes

Australian Wine Vintages 2017 – Personal Notes

Australian Wine Vintages 2017 – Personal Notes

Australian Wine Vintages 2017 – Personal Notes

Australian Wine Vintages 2017 – Personal Notes